THE CHURCH COMMITTEE REPORT

ALSO BY MATTHEW GUARIGLIA

Police and the Empire City:
Race and the Origins of Modern Policing in New York

The Essential Kerner Commission Report
(with Jelani Cobb)

ALSO BY BRIAN HOCHMAN

The Listeners:
A History of Wiretapping in the United States

Savage Preservation:
The Ethnographic Origins of Modern Media Technology

THE CHURCH COMMITTEE REPORT

REVELATIONS FROM THE BOMBSHELL 1970s INVESTIGATION INTO THE NATIONAL SECURITY STATE

Edited and Introduced by
MATTHEW GUARIGLIA
and **BRIAN HOCHMAN**

Foreword by **BEVERLY GAGE**

Printed in the United States of America
First Edition

For information about permission to reproduce selections from this book, write to Permissions, W. W. Norton & Company, Inc., 500 Fifth Avenue, New York, NY 10110

For information about special discounts for bulk purchases, please contact W. W. Norton Special Sales at specialsales@wwnorton.com or 800-233-4830

Manufacturing by Lakeside Book Company
Book design by Daniel Lagin
Production manager: Gwen Cullen

ISBN 978-1-324-08937-7 (Paperback)

W. W. Norton & Company, Inc.
500 Fifth Avenue, New York, NY 10110
www.wwnorton.com

W. W. Norton & Company Ltd.
15 Carlisle Street, London W1D 3BS

Authorized EU representative: EAS, Mustamäe tee 50, 10621 Tallinn, Estonia

10 9 8 7 6 5 4 3 2 1

CONTENTS

THE CHURCH COMMITTEE REPORT

PART I: INTELLIGENCE ACTIVITIES AND THE RIGHTS OF AMERICANS

PART II:
FOREIGN AND MILITARY INTELLIGENCE

PART III:
RECOMMENDATIONS

FOREWORD

BEVERLY GAGE

"Too many people have been spied upon by too many Government agencies and too much information has been collected." This single, damning sentence sums up the key insight of the Church Committee, which convened to investigate American intelligence agencies fifty years ago. Even now, half a century after its creation, the Church Committee remains the most influential investigation ever undertaken into the work of the country's secretive intelligence bureaucracies. Over months of investigation and testimony, the Committee documented what many Americans had long suspected: that the FBI, the CIA, and the NSA used their national-security mandates to conduct operations that infringed on civil liberties, violated core tenets of American democracy, and, in some cases, broke the law.

Many Americans alive in the 1970s could still recall a time before such agencies existed, when the question of whether a democratic country wanted or needed secret police and intelligence bureaus was still up for debate. The CIA, especially, was a relatively new entity, created in 1947 as part of the national-security expansions of the early Cold War. During just a few key years in the late 1940s, the federal government committed to maintaining a powerful standing army and a position of unparalleled influence around the world. The establishment and empowerment of intelligence agencies was part of the process. But even their champions warned about the potential for abuse. During his 1961 farewell address, President Dwight Eisenhower noted that "the conjunction of an immense military establishment and a large arms industry is new in the American experience." He also worried about "the potential for the disastrous rise of misplaced power" as a result of this development.

Secrecy itself was a major concern for many critics of the growing national-security state. While military and other government bodies often kept secrets in matters of war and diplomacy, the existence of large federal bureaucracies with the ability to classify information and conduct secret operations was itself relatively new in the American experience. During the early decades of the FBI, CIA, and NSA, nobody outside the agencies—including the president and Congress—knew all the details or fully understood what the intelligence agencies were doing. FBI director J. Edgar Hoover, the most powerful federal servant of the twentieth century, fought for decades to prevent anyone beyond the FBI from accessing its files or internal deliberations.

Then came the Church Committee. Hoover died in 1972, three years before the committee began its work. But as the committee's staffers soon learned, his confidence that no outsider would ever see his files meant that those files were remarkably candid about the Bureau's secret methods, illegal practices, and political intentions. A similar dynamic prevailed at other agencies. They wrote down astonishing accounts of indiscriminate surveillance and disruptive political operations, of assassination plots and experiments on unsuspecting subjects. For a few months, the Church Committee penetrated the veil of secrecy that had become the country's default approach to national security. No investigation before or since has yielded quite the same shock effect or level of detail.

The reforms inspired by the Church Committee, including the establishment of congressional intelligence committees, went part of the way toward shining light into the innermost sanctums of the government—and that light has continued to shine over time. But perhaps the most lasting effect of the Church Committee was to affirm the growing public distrust of politics and federal power that has become a hallmark of the twenty-first century. That distrust emerged for a reason: American leaders lied to the public, and conducted outrageous secret operations in their name. Over time, it has eroded Americans' faith that their government, and the public servants who make it work, are indeed serving the greater good.

Fifty years ago, the Church Committee noted the ongoing tension between "liberty" and "security" in a democratic society. This new, edited edition of their work will be an invaluable contribution as Americans struggle to find the right balance for a new generation.

PREFACE

THE YEAR OF INTELLIGENCE AT FIFTY

In January 1975, the United States Senate opened a landmark investigation into the federal government's intelligence agencies. Under the direction of Idaho Senator Frank Church, the Select Committee to Study Governmental Operations with Respect to Intelligence Activities—the Church Committee, as it came to be known—was charged with uncovering evidence of illegal activity at the Federal Bureau of Investigation (FBI), the Central Intelligence Agency (CIA), and the National Security Agency (NSA), among other government entities that had long avoided scrutiny. Over the course of sixteen months, a team of 150 staffers conducted more than 800 interviews, gathered 110,000 pages of classified documents, and convened 21 public hearings. Pundits dubbed the most intense period of investigative action the "Year of Intelligence." In its throes, amid revelations of surveillance abuse and administrative misconduct, the world came to know the underside of American state power: shadowy and arrogant, prying and lawless.

The result of the Church Committee's efforts was a multivolume report that chronicled the worst sins of the nation's spy agencies. Published in April 1976, the findings had already made headlines. At the FBI, there were warrantless wiretaps and undercover informants, illegal break-ins and blackmail. There were attempts to sabotage left-leaning political organizations, intimidate antiwar activists, and criminalize Black nationalist leaders. There was a campaign to pressure Martin Luther King Jr. to abandon his civil rights crusade. An anonymous letter, typewritten by a Bureau official, had even encouraged King to commit suicide.

At the CIA, the picture was just as unflattering: assassination plots against foreign heads of state; experiments with toxic substances and illegal drugs; partnerships in covert action that involved the Mafia. Meanwhile, the NSA—so secretive that its employees referred to the institution as "No Such Agency"—had coerced global telecommunications firms to hand over the private correspondence of American citizens. NSA officials disseminated the ill-begotten information to the FBI and CIA, completing the cycle of wrongdoing.

"No holds were barred," the Church Committee concluded in its account of the spy agencies' accumulated record. In their effort to secure American dominance, the FBI, CIA, and NSA had "exceeded the restraints on the exercise of governmental power . . . imposed by our country's Constitution, laws, and traditions." So, too, had several other arms of the US security state, including the Department of Defense and the National Security Council.

The committee made ninety-six recommendations to curtail the abuses identified in the report. In short order, the White House adopted measures to ban political assassinations and limit covert action. Congress, for its part, went on to establish a new policy framework for regulating intelligence activities, creating permanent oversight committees in the House and Senate and passing the Foreign Intelligence Surveillance Act (1978), which placed controls on the government's ability to conduct surveillance in the field of national security. In theory, the flurry of reforms appeared to chart a new and better course for the workings of American state power—one bound by law, and respectful of the rights and liberties of individuals.

History, we now know, had other plans. Yet five decades later, *The Church Committee Report* remains as explosive as ever. No government document has done more to expose the mechanisms behind America's aspirations of political supremacy in the twentieth century. And with the possible exceptions of the Warren Commission's inquiry into the Kennedy assassination and the Watergate Committee's probe of the Nixon White House, both of which paved the way for the Year of Intelligence, no government investigation has inspired as much paranoid intrigue. Three witnesses who cooperated with the Church Committee were murdered in the months surrounding the publication of the final report. (Although law enforcement agencies failed to establish links between their interviews with Senate investigators and the circumstances surrounding their deaths, the cloud of suspicion has never passed.) Frank Church was himself under FBI *and* NSA surveillance throughout his committee chairmanship. His FBI file, recently declassified, reveals that he also received death threats from critics who accused him of treason. Other members of Church's team suffered similar forms of harassment.

In keeping with the drama of the Senate investigation, the political legacy of *The Church Committee Report* has also remained a fierce point of debate among scholars and policymakers. While some regard the committee's work as a high-water mark for bipartisan congressional action, others have raised doubts about the regime of oversight its recommendations launched. Fifty years on, there seem to be more missed opportunities than successes. The period following the intelligence scandals of the mid-1970s saw the security state return with a vengeance—this time with a veneer of legality, even respectability, ironically created by the Church Committee's own reforms. In the 1980s, federal lawmakers began slackening restrictions on the government's intelligence power. By the turn of the twentieth century, on the eve of the terror attacks of September 11, 2001, the stage was set for a boomerang back toward abuse.

The story that ensued—a story of top-secret programs, mass data-mining platforms, and the creep of digital surveillance into the fabric of American life—mirrored the one that the Church Committee had told about the postwar era. In response, twenty-first-century activists began advocating for a "new Church Committee."[1] As of this writing, amid a movement to re-politicize the federal intelligence bureaucracy and punish the enemies of a new presidential administration, their calls have gone unanswered.

Politics aside, what we can say for certain is that *The Church Committee Report* has endured as a documentary resource of unparalleled reach. In the fifty years since its publication, the report has come to serve as a skeleton key to the American Century, unlocking the hidden corridors in which the nation's Cold War history was made. For Minnesota senator Walter Mondale, who led the Church Committee's investigation of the FBI and went on to serve as vice president, it was this fact, more than anything else, that constituted the report's most durable achievement.

"One of the things that strikes me even today about the work of the Church Committee and the reports that we issued is that . . . they are still

---

[1] Cindy Cohn and Trevor Timm, "In Response to the NSA, We Need a New Church Committee, and We Need It Now," *Electronic Frontier Foundation*, June 7, 2013; Frederick A. O. Schwarz Jr., "We Need a New Church Committee to Fix Our Broken Intelligence System," *The Nation*, March 12, 2014.

cited by scholars, by lawyers, in the literature," Mondale asserted in a 2014 interview. "If you want to study this issue"—the issue of government surveillance and secrecy, the issue of raw political power—"you begin with the findings of the Church Committee."[2]

Mondale's assessment rings true. Generations of scholars and activists have followed the threads of *The Church Committee Report* to uncover the doings of America's intelligence agencies, and to remember the political will it takes to curb their tendency toward excess. The document, as such, contains both a prescription and a warning. Begin with the findings of the Church Committee, then proceed with caution.

***

Most accounts of the Church Committee's origins begin with a front-page article in *The New York Times*.

On December 22, 1974, the Pulitzer Prize-winning journalist Seymour Hersh broke the story of a CIA surveillance program operating on American soil. At the request of the Nixon administration, Hersh reported, a special agency unit had amassed intelligence files on more than 10,000 antiwar protestors, left-wing dissidents, and Black Power activists—a flagrant violation of the CIA's own charter. The product of months of investigative digging, Hersh's article also teased further evidence of "dozens of other illegal activities by members of the CIA inside the United States, including break-ins, wiretapping, and the surreptitious inspection of mail."[3] It was a bombshell story.

In the ensuing days the *Times* ran a series of follow-up articles, all written by Hersh, and all loosely stemming from information detailed in a top-secret report of CIA misconduct known as the "Family Jewels." That report had been commissioned in 1973 by newly appointed CIA Director James Schlesinger to learn about the organization's past abuses. Around the country, press outlets ranging from the *Chicago Tribune* to *The Nation* printed similar stories about CIA excesses, many of which drew on the same set of sources. Within days, calls for answers in Washington prompted President

[2] Katherine Scott, *Select Committee to Study Governmental Operations with Respect to Intelligence Activities (Church Committee) Members and Staff: Oral History Interviews* (Washington, DC: US Senate Historical Office, 2015), 433–34.

[3] Seymour M. Hersh, "Huge CIA Operation Reported in U.S. Against Antiwar Forces, Other Dissidents in Nixon Years," *New York Times*, December 22, 1974, 1.

Gerald Ford to establish a fact-finding commission chaired by Vice President Nelson Rockefeller.

Endorsed by key White House staffers such as Donald Rumsfeld and Dick Cheney—names that would become synonymous with intelligence abuse in the twenty-first century—the formation of the Rockefeller Commission amounted to a transparent act of damage control. The CIA stories appeared to implicate the Office of the President, in addition to casting a harsh light on the workings of the security state. Running the investigation out of the White House was a way to slow the flood of revelations and stave off congressional action.

Lawmakers on Capitol Hill saw through the ploy. One month later, on January 27, 1975, the Senate responded by passing a resolution establishing the Church Committee. The formal charge was to "conduct an investigation and study of governmental operations with respect to intelligence activities and the extent, if any, to which illegal, improper, or unethical activities were engaged in by any agency of the Federal Government"—a directive that exceeded the Rockefeller Commission's limited focus on the CIA.[4] The House launched a parallel investigation shortly thereafter, but its proceedings, chaired by New York Congressman Otis Pike, were soon mired in controversy.

The story of Seymour Hersh's *New York Times* exposé provides a convenient starting point for the Year of Intelligence, especially because its contours fit with a broader story about the power of the press that has dominated historical accounts of US politics in the 1970s. But Hersh's CIA scoops were hardly the only catalyst for the intelligence investigations. In truth, the roots of the Church Committee stretched into more chaotic territory. To follow all of them is to find oneself lost in a convoluted thicket of names and codenames, agencies and authorities, classified designations and public scandals. Tracing their course helps to illuminate the historical foundations on which an intrepid group of politicians, lawyers, and researchers fashioned a report that would be worth reading half a century later.

Certainly the Watergate investigation was the most direct historical precursor to the Church Committee. The connection was so strong that *The New York Times* cast the controversy over the CIA's domestic surveillance

[4] US Congress, Senate, "Resolution to establish a select committee of the Senate to conduct an investigation and study of governmental operations with respect to intelligence activities," S. Res 21, 94th Congress (1975–1976).

operations as the "Son of Watergate," and Hersh himself had hinted at links between the two affairs in his early reporting on the subject.[5] But by the mid-1970s the nation already knew something of the cycle of surveillance scandal and investigative action. A host of developments in the preceding decade had convinced many Americans not just that the government's spy powers were trampling on constitutional rights, but that it was the job of federal lawmakers to provide answers and pass corrective reforms.

In 1964, for example, an article in *Time* magazine titled "Bug Thy Neighbor" claimed that the illegal use of wiretapping and electronic eavesdropping devices was standard practice in almost every corner of the federal bureaucracy, even at agencies that had little to do with the imperatives of crime control and national defense. In response, Missouri senator Edward V. Long opened a wide-ranging inquiry into surveillance abuses at the Internal Revenue Service, the Food and Drug Administration, and the US Department of Health, Education, and Welfare, among other arms of the federal government, eventually substantiating many of *Time*'s allegations. In 1970, a US Army captain named Christopher Pyle blew the whistle on a top-secret army surveillance program that ran parallel to the CIA actions outlined in Hersh's reporting. Pyle's efforts led North Carolina senator Sam Ervin, later a star player in the Watergate drama, to convene a series of public hearings on the army program's threat to constitutional rights.

Hersh, for his part, was a leading voice in a generation of left-leaning journalists, activists, and whistleblowers who had witnessed the escalation of Cold War militarism and fought to expose official wrongdoing. Most of their efforts focused on military atrocities in Southeast Asia, from the massacre at My Lai to the secret bombings of Cambodia and Laos. But the spy agencies didn't escape their attention. The ensuing revelations about paramilitary actions and political cover-ups created an information environment that informed both the Watergate and Church Committee investigations. In the mid-1960s, for example, the editors of *Ramparts* magazine regularly featured stories on the CIA's influence over domestic and international affairs, drawing special attention to the agency's practice of funding "front" organizations that covertly advanced American interests. *Ramparts* was also the first venue to publish the writings of Victor Marchetti, a former CIA officer who went on to author *The CIA and the Cult of Intelligence* (1974),

---

5 "Son of Watergate," *New York Times*, September 18, 1975, 40.

a best-selling account of the CIA's inner workings that provoked a coordinated agency reprisal.

Rumors of the FBI's record of illegal activity, meanwhile, had been swirling since the early 1950s. But the Bureau's ruthless director, J. Edgar Hoover, had managed to suppress the worst episodes of misconduct. That dynamic changed in the early 1970s, after a daring act of civil disobedience provided concrete evidence of abuse during Hoover's tenure. On the night of March 8, 1971, a group of activists broke into the FBI's field office in Media, Pennsylvania, a small town outside of Philadelphia. The Citizens' Commission to Investigate the FBI, as the group styled itself, stole more than a thousand classified documents from the office's filing cabinets. They fed the trove of material to the press, affording the nation its first glimpses of COINTELPRO, a suite of top-secret domestic intelligence programs designed to sabotage the civil rights and antiwar movements, among other forms of organized political activity.

Above all else, the dizzying network of precedents, connections, and disclosures suggests that the Church Committee did not emerge *ex nihilo*. Rather, both Hersh's reporting and the official inquiry that followed were emblematic of a pervasive culture of distrust that had set in over the course of the 1960s and 1970s—what the social scientists Seymour Lipset and William Schneider, in one of the earliest retrospective accounts of the period, would famously diagnose as a national "confidence gap."[6]

The turn of phrase is useful, connecting disillusionment with Cold War conflicts abroad, like Vietnam, with outrage over abuses of power at home, like Watergate. But "confidence gap" lacks the air of paranoia that seems to have seeped into the nation's view of the intelligence establishment, particularly the CIA. By the time the Church Committee began its work, the agency had emerged as an enemy of individual rights and liberties in the minds of many Americans. Popular Hollywood thrillers such as *The Parallax View* (1974) and *Three Days of the Condor* (1975) perhaps captured the nation's unease about the government's spy powers better than social science ever could. Both films cast their heroes as average Joes who find themselves caught up in a byzantine play of intelligence and security forces. Estranged from friends and family, unable to rely on authorities, they are forced to save themselves—and, by extension, the nation—by making sense

[6] Seymour Martin Lipset and William Schneider, *The Confidence Gap: Business, Labor, and Government in the Public Mind* (New York and London: The Free Press, 1983).

of conspiracies beyond their understanding. Both films depict the world of intelligence as ubiquitous and unknowable, with shadowy ties to corporate and political interests. Both films also end on an ironic note. In *The Parallax View*, the hero loses his battle with the security apparatus and becomes the subject of a congressional investigation; in *Three Days of the Condor*, he wins and takes his story to *The New York Times*.

The mood of paranoia and skepticism coincided with a historic changing of the guard in Washington. In May 1972, J. Edgar Hoover died in his sleep, bringing an end to his decades-long reign over American law enforcement and politics. Presidents Harry Truman and Lyndon B. Johnson passed away less than a month apart in the winter that followed. On top of the deaths of John F. Kennedy (November 1963) and Dwight D. Eisenhower (March 1969)—not to mention the demise of Richard Nixon, who resigned from office in 1974—the principal architects of the Cold War security state were gone. No longer could they control the story that the nation told itself about intelligence power.

All of which is to say, the scandal surrounding the CIA's domestic surveillance operation arrived at a rare moment of political opportunity. The Senate seized it first. When the resolution creating the intelligence committee passed in January 1975, majority leader Mike Mansfield approached Michigan Democrat Philip Hart to serve as chair. Hart declined. He was undergoing chemotherapy for the cancer that would eventually take his life. But he opted to join the committee as an ordinary member—the probe of the spy agencies was too important to sit out. Mansfield then turned to Frank Church, a politician who was poised to take the inquiry in a more aggressive direction.

***

By twenty-first-century standards, Frank Church was a political enigma: a pro-gun, pro-labor Democrat from a conservative-leaning state; a military intelligence veteran and a Stanford-educated attorney; and, eventually, an outspoken critic of US militarism, imperialism, and covert government action. Elected to the US Senate from his home state of Idaho in 1956, Church more or less followed the party line as postwar Democrats adopted a platform supporting civil rights at home and communist containment abroad. But as early as 1964, Church broke from his colleagues on the legitimacy of the war in Vietnam.

The contempt that Church's antiwar stance inspired among Democratic

Party leadership, up to and including President Johnson, seemed only to strengthen his resolve in the years that followed. It didn't hurt that Church's opposition to the Vietnam War came with newfound popularity. Left-wing celebrities aligned with the antiwar movement began dropping by Church's home in the DC suburbs for cocktails and late-night discussions. (The Hollywood star Marlon Brando was a regular guest, among other notables.) By 1968, Church was as close to a counter-cultural politician as the US Senate could muster. With his growing reputation came the support of youthful voters, as well as the prospect of higher office.

Church's views on Vietnam were hardly rooted in the calculus of political celebrity. He was a true believer. In lengthy speeches on the Senate floor throughout the late 1960s and early 1970s, he routinely characterized the conflict as one tentacle of a much larger monster: the Cold War security state. This beast, according to Church, was secretive, unaccountable, invasive, and globally implicated. It had transformed US foreign policy into a vehicle for military and corporate interests, normalizing a condition of endless war.

As one Church Committee staffer later recalled, Church's political activities in this period were motivated by a "tremendous righteous indignation" at the hubris of American state power. On the nation's Cold War military entanglements, Church "almost spoke with the sort of force that you would expect from someone who went to divinity school."[7] His opponents took less kindly to his moralizing. Many dismissed him in the press as "Senator Cathedral."

In 1972, Church chaired a Senate foreign relations subcommittee that exposed connections between a major US telecommunications company—International Telephone & Telegraph (ITT)—and a covert CIA operation against the socialist government of Chile. The findings gave credence to Church's criticisms of the runaway security state. More practically, the ITT inquiry also gave him experience in dealing with the most secretive and recalcitrant corners of the federal bureaucracy. When the scandal over the CIA's domestic surveillance operations erupted in the winter of 1974–1975, after the publication of Hersh's series of articles, Church emerged as an obvious choice to lead the Senate's campaign for accountability.

And yet, the myth of Frank Church's intelligence crusade has often obscured the workings of the committee that bore his name. Although

---

[7] Scott, *Select Committee to Study Governmental Operations*, 36.

Church would come to embody the public face of the Year of Intelligence, he could not take full credit for the achievements of the investigation and the final report. On the ground, the Church Committee consisted of a vast organization of staffers, aides, researchers, clerical workers, and attorneys—all packed into the warren of cubicles in the Senate Dirksen Office Building that the Watergate Committee had vacated the previous summer. The committee's leadership was itself composed of heavy-hitting lawmakers from across the political spectrum. Many of them meaningfully shaped the direction of the inquiry. Liberal Minnesotan and future vice president Walter Mondale clashed with Barry Goldwater, the right-wing senator from Arizona who had mounted a failed presidential campaign a decade earlier. There were two Democratic Harts: Gary and Philip (no relation), one a future presidential hopeful and the other the namesake of the building where most sitting US senators now work. John Tower, a Republican from Texas, would later draw on his Church Committee service while leading an inquiry into the Iran-Contra affair, the most sensational intelligence scandal of the 1980s. Even if they were not always aligned on the scope of the investigation, the eleven senators who sat on the Church Committee represented the better part of a century of political ambition, legislative gamesmanship, and bureaucratic know-how. Along with the staffers, the committee was theirs as much as it was Church's.

By all accounts, it was Mondale, not Church, who gave the investigative team its most far-reaching charges. Working closely with the committee's chief counsel, Frederick A. O. Schwarz Jr., Mondale proposed a split in the inquiry's focus. While half of the staffers, working under Church's direction, took on the issue of foreign intelligence abuse abroad, exploring allegations of CIA assassination plots and covert action, the other half followed the trail of illegal intelligence at home. Mondale assumed control of the domestic intelligence task force, steering the investigation toward the FBI's record under J. Edgar Hoover. The two-track approach brought organization to the committee's forays into the murky and chaotic field of intelligence activity. In time, it also gave a shape to the final investigative report.

Both groups, foreign and domestic, commenced their work by filing massive document requests to the spy agencies. Some of the requests were slow-walked or stonewalled. Others ended up bogged down in negotiations over classification status. But off-the-record interviews and inside tips, occasionally from former intelligence officials themselves, would end up breaking the dam of secrecy. A who's who of American intelligence whistleblowing offered up information to the committee throughout the investigation. Victor Marchetti sat for closed-door sessions with members of the foreign intelligence task force. A navy reservist named James Bamford confidentially fed the committee information about top-secret government surveillance installations. (Bamford went on to publish *The Puzzle Palace*, the first-ever book-length study of the NSA, still regarded as a classic.) During the early phases of the inquiry, an active corps of Washington journalists similarly nudged committee staffers in the direction of key stories. "I got a lot of tips from investigative reporters," an attorney on the committee's domestic intelligence task force later recalled. "[T]hey were always feeding me stuff. I never told them anything, but they gave me some leads."[8]

The Senate initially gave the Church Committee one year to issue its findings. The abbreviated timeline—later extended to sixteen months—gave the proceedings a manic feel. Senator Gary Hart compared the experience of moving toward the committee's public phase to "building your boat as you go out to sea."[9] The complexity of the investigative task was extraordinary, and so were the political stakes. At the height of the committee's work, some staffers took to sleeping in the office, with pillows and blankets tucked under their desks.

***

The Church Committee held its opening round of hearings in September 1975. Following a precedent set by the Senate Watergate investigation, the proceedings were televised. The nation would get to watch, in real time, as members of the committee grilled witnesses and aired the spy agencies' dirty laundry. Church embraced the spectacle. As the first session gaveled in on September 16, he posed for the cameras while sitting on the dais. In his left hand, held aloft, was a scoped gun, designed to shoot darts laced with a lethal shellfish toxin. It was an assassin's tool, manufactured in secret by the CIA. The image served as a compelling shorthand for the excesses of American state power.

Despite maintaining a strict policy against news leaks, an approach that bought Senate investigators credibility with their sources in the intelligence community, the Church Committee engineered its public hearings

---

8 Scott, *Select Committee to Study Governmental Operations*, 144–45.

9 Loch K. Johnson, *A Season of Inquiry: The Senate Intelligence Investigation* (Lexington: The University Press of Kentucky, 1985), 79.

to generate media buzz. Throughout the fall of 1975, the proceedings were structured around the most outrageous incidents of abuse uncovered in the inquiry, from unwarranted surveillance operations at the CIA and NSA to the FBI "suicide letter" sent to Martin Luther King Jr. As Schwarz, the committee's chief counsel, explained the strategy, "Unless we bring out shocking facts, we are never going to get support for reform."[10] The witnesses called to testify on the Senate floor were the product of a similar theory of political attention. Well-known directors of federal agencies, past and present, appeared alongside lower-level functionaries who were bound to reveal damning details about the work they carried out in the government's name. The idea was to jolt the nation into action.

Perhaps the most colorful figure to surface in the swirl of news was Johnny Rosselli, an underworld journeyman who had facilitated the CIA's plots to kill Fidel Castro. Dressed in tailored suits and dark glasses, his hair a shock of white, Rosselli became the subject of frenzied media coverage during the summer of 1975—particularly after the most prominent criminal contact involved in the Castro schemes, the Chicago mob boss Sam "Momo" Giancana, was murdered on the eve of a meeting with committee staffers. Giancana was the first casualty surrounding the inquiry, and Rosselli ended up meeting an equally mysterious fate. Four months after Rosselli sat for the last in a series of closed-door interviews in Washington, a fisherman found his body stuffed inside a fifty-five-gallon oil drum floating off the coast of Miami. Both crimes remain unsolved.

The spectacle of the Church Committee hearings raised charges of sensationalism and partiality. At the center of it all was Church himself, a master political showman who was rumored to have designs on the White House. From the perspective of Cold War hawks and intelligence community loyalists, the spy novel-turned-real-life quality of the proceedings amounted to little more than partisan theater. Worse still, the details they revealed, while shocking, seemed to threaten the national security apparatus itself. Conservative columnists had actually expressed pride at the ruthlessness of the spy agencies, praising their commitment to fighting communism and subversion by any means necessary. Now the committee was characterizing seemingly essential intelligence operations as failures, embarrassments, or worse. As one editorial complained, the hearings were doing more damage to the cause of American national security than

---

[10] Scott, *Select Committee to Study Governmental Operations*, 446.

a "hundred KGB agents working overtime for the Kremlin" could ever hope to inflict.[11] Church seemed to be airing state secrets in the service of his own ambition.

Such criticisms proved durable. For decades to come, government officials would blame everything from botched intelligence operations to low agency morale on the effects of the Church Committee hearings. (In 2004, following the publication of the *9/11 Commission Report*, former US Secretary of State Henry Kissinger made the suggestion that the CIA's failure to predict the World Trade Center attacks was a direct product of the Senate investigation's fallout. "Finding themselves in a kind of political wilderness," Kissinger complained in *The Washington Post*, "the intelligence services have been under assault for 30 years, ever since the floodgates were opened in the 1970s.")[12] As the hearings dragged on, and as public interest in the committee's work flagged, the narrative about the dangers of disclosure found an increasingly receptive audience. A Louis Harris poll conducted in December 1975 showed that only 38 percent of respondents approved of the Church Committee's work. And despite the fact that both the FBI and CIA polled just as poorly, a majority of respondents expressed concerns that the investigation was preventing the spy agencies from doing their jobs.[13]

The Ford White House, hostile to the investigation from the outset, seized on the apparent turn in public opinion—and a tragic event would soon set off a coordinated defense of the agencies. On the evening of December 23, 1975, a group of Greek revolutionaries gunned down Richard Welch, the CIA's station chief in Athens, as he returned home from a Christmas party. The incident had nothing to do with the hearings. Months earlier, a Greek intelligence outfit had leaked Welch's name and home address to press outlets in Athens, and the assassins had targeted him to protest US support for Greece's military government. Nevertheless, the coincidental timing of Welch's death seemed to suggest that Church's crusade was causing real-world damage. A week later, the Ford administration worked with the CIA to stage a spectacle of its own. Flying in the face of standard military practice, news cameras were permitted to roll as a helicopter

---

[11] "Why We Need the CIA," *TV Guide*, January 10, 1976. Quoted in Johnson, *A Season of Inquiry*, 168.

[12] Henry Kissinger, "Better Intelligence Reform," *Washington Post*, August 15, 2004. Quoted in James Risen, *The Last Honest Man: The CIA, the FBI, the Mafia, and the Kennedys—and One Senator's Fight to Save Democracy* (New York and Boston: Little, Brown, 2023), 402.

[13] Louis Harris, "CIA, FBI Lose Faith of Public," *Chicago Tribune*, January 22, 1976, A4.

carrying Welch's coffin landed at Andrews Air Force Base: a hero's return, contrived as Church Committee counterprogramming. The message, however misleading, was obvious: This is what happens when you broadcast the nation's secrets.

By the time the *Church Committee Report* finally appeared in April 1976, the backlash narrative had won out. The American public had soured on the committee's efforts. Church had launched his campaign for the White House ("In 1976, vote for the man who saved you from 1984," read one of his mailings), and the most disturbing revelations contained in the report had received extensive treatment in the press.[14] Anyone who bothered to read what was inside, or even skimmed the table of contents, encountered a much more measured and comprehensive account of intelligence abuse than the hearings had advertised. The published findings were even-handed, almost self-recriminating. Countering the persistent charge of partisanship, they cast a harsh light on both Democratic and Republican administrations and offered a condemnation of several decades' worth of lax congressional oversight. To the surprise of *The New York Times*, which summarized the Church Committee's findings for readers, the report functioned as more of a "resource document" for future oversight than a lurid catalog of wrongdoing.[15] Nevertheless, the window of political opportunity had closed. In the spring of 1976, pundits predicted—correctly, it turned out—that the committee's recommendations would prove difficult to implement.

Unrepresented in the debates over the end of the inquiry, needless to say, were the opinions of the individuals who had endured the worst of the spy agencies' abuses. Their experiences motivated committee staffers to stay the course throughout the investigation, and their stories suggest that the significance of the Year of Intelligence ultimately lies between the lines of the final report. For much of the twentieth century, the government's surreptitious effort to undermine protest movements felt more like folk belief than hard fact. The people who marched for civil rights and spoke out against the Vietnam War were aware of the risks: that their phones might be tapped; that their letters might be read; that newcomers to organized forms of political activity might actually be government informants. But it wasn't until the

---

[14] Kathryn S. Olmsted, *Challenging the Secret Government: The Post-Watergate Investigations of the CIA and FBI* (Chapel Hill: University of North Carolina Press, 1996), 55.

[15] Nicholas Horrock, "Senate Intelligence Panel Calls for a Law to Curb Covert Action as Implement of Foreign Policy," *New York Times*, April 27, 1976, 1.

Church Committee published its report that their convictions entered the official record as truth. Over the course of the investigation, staffers worked to identify and interview the targets of clandestine FBI and CIA actions. Time and again, they expressed gratitude for the committee's work. They held out hope that a published report would validate their stories.

Loch Johnson—one of Church's top aides, now a retired political scientist who has written several books on the committee's legacy—recalls one such encounter.[16] In 1975, Johnson traveled to Toronto to interview Anatol Rapoport, a renowned mathematician and outspoken critic of the Vietnam War. Five years earlier, Rapoport had quietly resigned his faculty position at the University of Michigan and moved his family to Canada. The cause of his departure was a series of anonymous mailings that began flooding the offices of university administrators and Michigan state legislators in the late 1960s. Some of the letters accused Rapoport of communist sympathies. Others went a step further, alleging that he maintained active ties with the Soviet Union, the country his refugee parents had fled when he was a young child. The true source of the letters was the FBI. Rapoport had been the target of a COINTELPRO operation.

Johnson remembers handing Rapoport his surveillance file, which committee staffers managed to acquire early in the investigation. As the two men sat together, thumbing through its pages, Rapoport wept. One imagines his tears as an outpouring of anger—outrage at a reputation stained and a life uprooted. Perhaps his tears were also an expression of relief, even vindication. Like many of the victims whose names never appeared in the text of *The Church Committee Report*, Rapoport had known all along what his government was doing.

***

The Church Committee produced six volumes and two supplementary reports. Five of the volumes (Books I–IV and VI) chronicle abuses of power at the FBI, the CIA, and the United States Department of Defense, while an offshoot sixth volume (Book V) explores the intelligence establishment's response to the fatal shooting of John F. Kennedy. A separate interim

---

[16] Loch K. Johnson, interview with authors (January 31, 2024). For accounts of the FBI's surveillance of Rapoport and his interview with the Church Committee, see also Anatol Rapoport, *Certainties and Doubts: A Philosophy of Life* (Montreal: Black Rose Books, 2001), 142, and Loch K. Johnson, *Spy Watching: Intelligence Accountability in the United States* (New York and London: Oxford University Press, 2018), 121.

report, perhaps the most controversial of the set, covers the CIA's plots to assassinate foreign heads of state. An additional staff report outlines the CIA's history of covert action in Chile. In total, the finished document—the product of months of drafts and revisions, feverishly written by staffers whose labor went unattributed in the text—spans more than 3,100 pages. An untold number of interview transcripts, investigative notes, and closed-door hearings remain classified.

This book reproduces several case studies from the original *Church Committee Report* that stand out from the mass of material. Most of the sections included in these pages derive from Books II and III, as well as the interim report on "Alleged Assassination Plots Involving Foreign Leaders." Together they form the backbone of the Church Committee's account of government malfeasance, detailing some of the best-known episodes uncovered in the Year of Intelligence: from the surveillance of Martin Luther King Jr. to the schemes against Patrice Lumumba, Fidel Castro, and Rafael Trujillo; from the FBI's COINTELPRO operations on suspected communists and New Left activists to the CIA's mind-control tests on human subjects. For decades, versions of these case studies have lived independently in unofficial print editions, or in PDF copies circulating online. The book you hold in your hand is the first to bring them together since the original publication of *The Church Committee Report* in April 1976.

In assembling this edition we have imagined ourselves as both stewards and translators of the Church Committee's findings, working to balance the goals of comprehensiveness and readability. We have trimmed portions of each section that describe the investigation's official procedures and detour into purely administrative considerations. We have also omitted the committee's exhaustive footnotes. Although we have standardized formatting and corrected mistakes in spelling, we have chosen to let a few stray errors of fact stand as an unavoidable product of the committee's vast remit. Looking back, it's remarkable to see how much the authors of the report got right, especially considering the pressures of time and politics.

A note of warning: Encountering these episodes for the first time is a harrowing experience. Modern readers are likely to recoil at the vindictiveness, recklessness, and unrepentant racism of individual actors, as well as the broader inclinations toward inertia and self-protection characteristic of almost every institutional bureaucracy. As the Church Committee's chief counsel, Frederick A. O. Schwarz Jr., stressed in a retrospective essay published in 2007, running through the miscellaneous incidents described in the report is a single connective theme: that "in times of crisis, even constitutional democracies are likely to violate their laws and forget their values."[17] But crisis is a feeble explanation, and certainly not an excuse. Cold War intelligence power tended toward excess not because of external historical pressures, but because of overweening authority, lax oversight, and a pervasive culture of fear. Above all else, the report's case studies demonstrate the flawed belief, shared by high-powered officials and low-ranking field agents alike, that the magnitude of the government's intelligence mission exempted their work from rules of law and norms of decency, even from common sense.

Modern readers are also likely to distinguish continuities between past and present. In the domestic surveillance operations pioneered at the CIA and NSA, it's possible to see a blueprint for the digital monitoring programs of the War on Terror and the USA Patriot Act, which offered the US government access to nearly every keystroke made on an internet-connected computer. The FBI's crusade to dismantle antiwar and civil rights groups invites comparisons with more recent political efforts to disrupt Black Lives Matter activists and discredit student protests of the unfolding war in Gaza. Some of the most egregious abuses uncovered in the Church Committee investigation were the products of White House orders, obscured in the fog of plausible denial. In the wake of the Supreme Court's recent ruling on executive immunity, the consequences of the unaccountable actions of five successive administrations, from Truman to Nixon, seem uncomfortably relevant. In the new legal landscape created by *Trump v. United States* (2024), some of the most galling stories detailed in this volume would be protected under an expanded conception of presidential power.

Historical continuities like these should help to illuminate some of the challenges and dangers that ordinary Americans face today. We ask readers of this volume to imagine how J. Edgar Hoover might have used the biometric and geolocation data stored on an iPhone, or how the officials behind CIA Operation CHAOS could have exploited the likes, dislikes, and connections automatically captured by social media algorithms. Intelligence organizations and law enforcement agencies now enjoy relatively easy access to personal digital information—and they operate under regulations

---

[17] Frederick A. O. Schwarz Jr., "Intelligence Oversight: The Church Committee," in *Strategic Intelligence, Volume 5: Intelligence and Accountability—Safeguards Against the Abuse of Secret Power*, ed. Loch K. Johnson (Westport, CT: Praeger Security International, 2007), 19.

devised for the analog age. The vertical expansion of the national security state, abetted by a multi-billion-dollar industry selling surveillance technology to the police, means that your local officer has capabilities that the NSA of 1975 could scarcely have imagined. What would a Frank Church of the twenty-first century have to do to inspire new protections for civil liberties and civil rights? What agencies and tactics would a congressional intelligence investigation need to scrutinize today?

The Church Committee's foes are still with us. Technologies have advanced, state capacities have expanded, but the government's repertoire for disrupting and dismantling social movements has endured almost unchanged. Surveillance, disinformation, infiltration, violence—such strategies have outlived the era of Frank Church, and have time and again been mobilized against individuals challenging the status quo. Five decades after the Year of Intelligence, *The Church Committee Report* remains the best-documented example of the US government's playbook for managing political dissent and maintaining global dominance. While we await another Church Committee, we'd do well to heed its lessons.

Matthew Guariglia
Brian Hochman
January 2025

A NOTE ON THE TEXT

The *Church Committee Report* is a vivid and compelling account of state surveillance and intelligence abuse. But it is also a government document. Hundreds of pages of the original text are devoted to detailing the bureaucratic intricacies of various federal agencies. Even the sections that narrate the most outrageous episodes of wrongdoing contain long digressions into matters of administrative oversight. In accordance with the committee's investigative charges, the organization of the original published product follows a mundane question: Who did what, and under whose authority? The answers sometimes make for tedious reading.

As editors, we have done our best to streamline the original document to showcase its core revelations, trimming sections that stray from the most important story lines. When you encounter the **{ . . . }** symbol in the pages that follow, it represents a portion of the text that we have trimmed for clarity and concision. All other textual marks, including ellipses and bracketed insertions, are the work of the committee and present in the original document.

The abuses of power detailed in the *Church Committee Report* involved several generations of politicians, bureaucrats, appointees, operatives, and collaborators working across multiple government agencies. The inventory of their targets is equally vast. The Church Committee took the extraordinary step to name names over the course of its investigation, but at times the cast of characters is difficult to keep straight. Don't be deterred.

At the beginning of this book, we have included a glossary of acronyms to help you make sense of the alphabet soup of agencies and organizations at the center of the committee's inquiry. We have also included a *dramatis personae* section to offer some context for the names and affiliations of the various players involved. We cannot blame the problems the Church Committee documented on an opaque and monolithic "system." Nor were the people who bore the brunt of intelligence abuse anonymous victims of history. The sprawling list of individuals who appear in the *dramatis personae* is testament to those facts, above all else.

***

We have divided this edition of the *Church Committee Report* into three main parts: "Intelligence Activities of the Rights of Americans," "Foreign and Military Intelligence," and "Recommendations." Each part contains key sections of text that appear in the published volumes. Readers interested in consulting the unabridged versions of these sections can consult the following pages of the original document:

1. Introduction—Book II, pp. 1–20, 137–288
2. COINTELPRO—Book III, pp. 1–78
3. Dr. Martin Luther King, Jr., Case Study—Book III, pp. 79–184
4. Warrantless FBI Electronic Surveillance—Book III, pp. 271–353
5. Warrantless Surreptitious Entries—Book III, pp. 353–72
6. CIA Intelligence Collection About Americans—Book III, pp. 679–732
7. Introduction—Book I, pp. 1–10, 423–72
8. Alleged Assassination Plots Involving Foreign Leaders—*Interim Report on Assassination Plots*, pp. 1–216
9. Testing and Use of Chemical and Biological Agents by the Intelligence Community—Book I, pp. 385–419
10. National Security Agency Surveillance Affecting Americans—Book III, pp. 733–84
11. Committee Recommendations—Book II, pp. 289–342

GLOSSARY OF AGENCIES, PROGRAMS, AND ORGANIZATIONS

BNDD—Bureau of Narcotics and Dangerous Drugs

BPP—Black Panther Party

CIA—Central Intelligence Agency

COINTELPRO—Counterintelligence Program, Federal Bureau of Investigation

COMINFIL—Communist Infiltration Program, Federal Bureau of Investigation

CORE—Congress of Racial Equality

CP—Communist Party

CPUSA—Communist Party USA

DCS—Domestic Contact Service, Central Intelligence Agency

DDP—Deputy Directorate of Plans, Central Intelligence Agency

DIA—Defense Intelligence Agency, United States Department of Defense

FBI—Federal Bureau of Investigation

GODR—Government of the Dominican Republic

HUAC—House Un-American Activities Committee

INR—Bureau of Intelligence and Research, United States Department of State

IRS—Internal Revenue Service

JDL—Jewish Defense League

JOMO—Junta of Militant Organizations

KKK—Ku Klux Klan

NAACP—National Association for the Advancement of Colored People

NOI—Nation of Islam

NSA—National Security Agency

NSC—National Security Council

NSCID—National Security Council Intelligence Directive

NSF—National Science Foundation

OAS—Organization of American States

OSI—Office of Scientific Intelligence, Central Intelligence Agency

PAC—Political Action Committee

RU—Revolutionary Union

SALT—Strategic Arms Limitation Talks

SANE—National Committee for a Sane Nuclear Policy

SCLC—Southern Christian Leadership Conference

SDS—Students for a Democratic Society

SNCC—Student Nonviolent Coordinating Committee

SOD—Special Operations Division, United States Army

SWP—Socialist Workers Party

TSD—Technical Services Division, Central Intelligence Agency

USAINTC—United States Army Intelligence Command

USIA—United States Information Agency

YSA—Young Socialist Alliance

DRAMATIS PERSONAE

Titles and affiliations at the time of the events relevant to the Church Committee inquiry.

THE CHURCH COMMITTEE:

Senator Frank Church (D-ID), Chairman

Senator John Tower (R-TX), Vice Chairman

Senator Howard Baker (R-TN)

Senator Barry Goldwater (R-AZ)

Senator Gary Hart (D-CO)

Senator Philip Hart (D-MI)

Senator Walter Huddleston (D-KY)

Senator Charles Mathias (R-MD)

Senator Walter Mondale (D-MN)

Senator Robert Morgan (D-NC)

Senator Richard Schweiker (R-PA)

Frederick A. O. Schwarz Jr.—Chief Counsel

THE WHITE HOUSE:

Truman Administration (1945–1953)

Harry S. Truman—President of the United States

James V. Forrestal—Secretary of Defense (1947–1949)

Tom C. Clark—Attorney General (1947–1949)

Eisenhower Administration (1953–1961)

Dwight D. Eisenhower—President of the United States

Christian Herter—Secretary of State

Gordon Gray—National Security Advisor

Herbert Brownell Jr.—Attorney General (1953–1957)

William Rogers—Attorney General (1957–1961)

Robert Cutler—Special Assistant to the President

Kennedy Administration (1961–1963)

John F. Kennedy—President of the United States

Dean Rusk—Secretary of State

McGeorge Bundy—National Security Advisor

Robert F. Kennedy—Attorney General (1961–1964)

Byron R. White—Deputy Attorney General (1961–1962)

Burke Marshall—Assistant Attorney General, Civil Rights Division

Herbert J. Miller—Assistant Attorney General, Criminal Division

Edwin Guthman—Press Secretary, Department of Justice

Johnson Administration (1963–1969)

Lyndon B. Johnson—President of the United States

Dean Rusk—Secretary of State

McGeorge Bundy—National Security Advisor

Nicholas Katzenbach—Attorney General (1965–1966)

W. Ramsey Clark—Attorney General (1967–1969)

Warren Christopher—Deputy Attorney General (1967–1969)

Marvin Watson—Special Assistant to the President

Walter Jenkins—Special Assistant to the President

Bill Moyers—White House Press Secretary

Nixon Administration (1969–1974)

Richard M. Nixon—President of the United States

Henry Kissinger—Secretary of State

Melvin Laird—Secretary of Defense

John Mitchell—Attorney General (1969–1972)

Richard Kleindienst—Attorney General (1972–1973)

Elliot Richardson—Attorney General (1973)

William B. Saxbe—Attorney General (1974–1975)

Henry Petersen—Assistant Attorney General, Criminal Division (1972–1974)

H. R. Haldeman—Chief of Staff (1969–1973)

Alexander Haig—Chief of Staff (1973–1974)

John Erlichman—White House Counsel; Domestic Affairs Advisor

David Young—Assistant to Erlichman

Tom Charles Huston—White House Aide

John (Jack) Caulfield—White House "Plumbers" security operative

John Ragan—White House "Plumbers" security operative

Ford Administration (1974–1977)

Gerald R. Ford—President of the United States

Edward H. Levi—Attorney General (1975–1977)

THE FBI:

J. Edgar Hoover—Director

Clyde Tolson—Associate Director

Cartha "Deke" DeLoach—Deputy Associate Director

Alan Belmont—Deputy Associate Director

William C. Sullivan—Assistant Director and Head of COINTELPRO

Courtney Evans—Assistant Director and Liaison to Department of Justice

C.D. Brennan—Assistant Director and Chief of Domestic Intelligence Division

Raymond Wannall—Chief of Nationalities Intelligence Section, Domestic Intelligence Division

George C. Moore—Chief of Racial Intelligence Division

Frederick Baumgardner—Chief of Internal Security Division

THE CIA:

Allen Dulles—Director (1953–1961)

John McCone—Director (1961–1965)

William Raborn Jr.—Director (1965–1966)

Richard Helms—Director (1966–1973)

James Schlesinger—Director (February 1973–July 1973)

William Colby—Director (1973–1976)

Charles P. Cabell—Deputy Director (1953–1962)

Marshall S. Carter—Deputy Director (1962–1965)

Robert E. Cushman—Deputy Director (1969–1971)

Frank Wisner—Deputy Director of Plans (1951–1958)

Richard Bissell—Deputy Director of Plans (1959–1962)

Thomas Karamessines—Deputy Director of Plans (1967–1973)

Tracy Barnes—Assistant Deputy Director of Plans

James Angleton—Chief of Counterintelligence

Richard Ober—Deputy Chief of Counterintelligence, Special Operations Group

Howard Osborn—Director, Office of Security

William Broe—Inspector General

Lawrence Houston—General Counsel

Thomas Parrott—Assistant to Allen Dulles

"Charles Marcules"—Anonymous Case Officer

Congo Operations

Bronson Tweedy—Chief of CIA Africa Division

"Victor Hedgman" (Lawrence Devlin)—CIA Congo Station Officer

"Joseph Scheider" (Sidney Gottlieb)—Director, CIA Technical Services Division

William Harvey—Officer, CIA Directorate of Plans

Michael Mulroney—Officer, CIA Directorate of Plans

WI/ROGUE (David Tzitzichvilli)—foreign agent/assassin supervised by Devlin

QJ/WIN (Jose Marie Andre Mankel)—foreign agent/assassin supervised by Mulroney

Cuba Operations

J. C. King—Chief of Western Hemisphere Division, CIA Directorate of Plans

William Harvey—Officer, CIA Directorate of Plans

Sheffield Edwards—Director, CIA Office of Security

Desmond Fitzgerald—Director, CIA Task Force W

AM/LASH (Rolando Cubela)—Cuban revolutionary recruited to kill Castro

B-1—leader of a Cuban anti-Castro organization

"Case Officer 1"—CIA agent involved with AM/LASH

"Case Officer 2"—CIA agent involved with AM/LASH

Robert Maheu—ex-FBI agent and private investigator, CIA Mafia liaison

John ("Johnny") Rosselli—Mafia fixer

Sam Giancana—Chicago Mafia boss

Joseph Shimon—friend of Rosselli and Giancana

Santos Trafficante—Florida Mafia boss

Edward DuBois—private investigator

Arthur J. Balletti—employee of Edward DuBois

Dominican Republic Operations

Henry Dearborn—Deputy Chief of Mission, Dominican Republic

Joseph Farland—US Ambassador, Dominican Republic

Roy Rubottom—Assistant Secretary of State for Inter-American Affairs

Thomas Mann—Assistant Secretary of State for Inter-American Affairs

Wymberly Coerr—Acting Assistant Secretary for Inter-American Affairs

Richard Goodwin—Deputy Assistant Secretary for Inter-American Affairs

Lester Mallory—Deputy Assistant Secretary of State

Livingston Merchant—Under Secretary of State for Political Affairs

Joseph Scott—Assistant to Merchant

Chester B. Bowles—Under Secretary of State

Adolphe Berle—Chairman, Interagency Task Force on Latin America

Antonio de la Maza—Dominican businessman and political dissident

Drug Testing and Chemical/Biological Agents

Frank Olsen—Scientist, Special Operations Division, US Army Biological Center

Sidney Gottlieb—Director, CIA Technical Services Division

Robert Lashbrook—Deputy, CIA Technical Services Division

Howard Abramson—allergist/immunologist researching LSD for CIA

Vincent Ruwet—Chief of Special Operations Division, US Army Biological Center

John M. Willems—Assistant Chief of Staff for Intelligence, US Army

William Jacobson—Project Officer, US Army Intelligence and Security Command

Charles F. Leonard—Major General, US Army Chief of Staff for Intelligence

Van M. Sim—Researcher, Edgewood Arsenal, US Army Chemical Corps

Ernest R. Clovis—Researcher, Edgewood Arsenal, US Army Chemical Corps

Earl Wheeler—Chief of Staff, US Army

Charles Denholm—Assistant Chief of Staff for Intelligence, US Army

THE NSA:

Marshall Carter—Director (1965–1969)

Noel Gayler—Director (1969–1972)

Samuel C. Phillips—Director (1972–1973)

Lew Allen Jr.—Director (1973–1977)

Louis Tordella—Deputy Director (1958–1974)

Benson Buffham—Deputy Director (1974–1978)

William Yarborough—Assistant Chief of Staff for Intelligence, US Army

John Ingersoll—Director, Bureau of Narcotics and Dangerous Drugs

Donald V. Bennett—Director, Defense Intelligence Agency

THE TARGETS:

Civil Rights Movement

Martin Luther King Jr.—President, Southern Christian Leadership Conference (SCLC)

Coretta Scott King—civil rights activist; wife of King

"Adviser A" (Stanley Levison)—adviser to King; businessman and attorney

"Adviser B" (Jack O'Dell)—adviser to King; SCLC fundraiser

Harry Wachtel—legal adviser to King

Ralph Abernathy—adviser to King; Executive Board Member, SCLC

Andrew Young—assistant to King, civil rights activist

Roy Wilkins—Director, National Association for the Advancement of Colored People

Elijah Muhammad—Leader, Nation of Islam

Malcolm X—civil rights leader

Stokely Carmichael—Student Nonviolent Coordinating Committee/Black Panther Party

H. Rap Brown—Student Nonviolent Coordinating Committee/Black Panther Party

Huey Newton—Black Panther Party

Bobby Seale—Black Panther Party

Eldridge Cleaver—Black Panther Party

Maxwell Stanford—Chairman, Revolutionary Action Movement

Ron Karenga—Chairman, US Organization

New Left/Antiwar Movement/Journalists and Whistleblowers

Bettina Aptheker—civil rights, antiwar, and labor activist

James P. Cannon—National Chairman, Socialist Workers Party

Ralph McGill—editor, *Atlanta Constitution*

Lloyd Norman—reporter, *Newsweek*

Hanson Baldwin—reporter, *New York Times*

Joseph Kraft—syndicated Washington, DC, columnist

Jack Anderson—syndicated Washington, DC, columnist

Morton Halperin—National Security Council, Nixon White House

Charles Radford—US Navy Yeoman, Nixon White House Joint Chiefs of Staff

Foreign Actors and Leaders

Patrice Lumumba—Prime Minister, Republic of the Congo

Joseph Kasavubu—President, Republic of the Congo

Joseph Mobutu—Army Chief of Staff, Republic of the Congo

Antoine Gizenga—Deputy Prime Minister, Republic of the Congo

Pierre Mulele—Minister of Education, Republic of the Congo

Maurice Mpolo—Minister of Youth and Sports, Republic of the Congo

Joseph Okito—Vice President of the Senate, Republic of the Congo

Moïse Tshombe—President, Secessionist State of Katanga (Congo)

Fidel Castro—Prime Minister, Cuba

Raúl Castro—Minister of Revolutionary Armed Forces, Cuba; brother of Fidel Castro

Che Guevara—Minister of Industries, Cuba; political revolutionary

Rafael Trujillo—President of the Dominican Republic

Ramfis Trujillo—son of Rafael Trujillo

Rene Schneider—Commander-in-Chief, Chilean Army

Salvador Allende—President of Chile

Ngo Dinh Diem—President of South Vietnam

Nhu Dinh Diem—State Counsellor of South Vietnam

THE CHURCH COMMITTEE REPORT

PART I

INTELLIGENCE ACTIVITIES AND THE RIGHTS OF AMERICANS

EDITORS' NOTE: *The six chapters in this section are derived from Books II and III of the original Church Committee report. They are arranged to present a streamlined and cohesive view of the illegal and unethical tactics that the FBI and CIA employed against US citizens involved in various forms of social protest throughout the 1950s, 1960s, and 1970s, especially the civil rights and antiwar movements.*

1.
Introduction

PREFACE

In January 1975, the Senate resolved to establish a Committee to:

> Conduct an investigation and study of governmental operations with respect to intelligence activities and the extent, if any, to which illegal, improper, or unethical activities were engaged in by any agency of the Federal Government.

This Committee was organized shortly thereafter and has conducted a year-long investigation into the intelligence activities of the United States Government, the first substantial inquiry into the intelligence community since World War II.

The inquiry arose out of allegations of substantial wrongdoing by intelligence agencies on behalf of the administrations which they served. A deeper concern underlying the investigation was whether this Government's intelligence activities were governed and controlled consistently with the fundamental principles of American constitutional government—that power must be checked and balanced and that the preservation of liberty requires the restraint of laws, and not simply the good intentions of men.

Our investigation has confirmed that properly controlled and lawful intelligence is vital to the nation's interest. A strong and effective intelligence system serves, for example, to monitor potential military threats from the Soviet Union and its allies, to verify compliance with international agreements such as SALT, and to combat espionage and international terrorism. These, and many other necessary and proper functions are performed by dedicated and hard-working employees of the intelligence community.

The Committee's investigation has, however, also confirmed substantial wrongdoing. And it has demonstrated that intelligence activities have not generally been governed and controlled in accord with the fundamental principles of our constitutional system of government.

The task faced by this Committee was to propose effective measures to prevent intelligence excesses, and at the same time to propose sound guidelines and oversight procedures with which to govern and control legitimate activities. { . . . }

Necessarily, the Committee had to be selective. To investigate everything relevant to intelligence—and even everything relevant to the fundamental issues on which we had decided to focus—would take forever. Our job was to discover—and suggest solutions for—the major problems "at the earliest practical date."

Accordingly, the Committee had to choose the particular Governmental entities upon which we would concentrate and then further had to choose particular cases to investigate in depth. Many agencies, departments or bureaus of the Federal Government have an intelligence function. Of these, the Committee spent the overwhelming preponderance of its energies on five:

> The Federal Bureau of Investigation; The Central Intelligence Agency; The National Security Agency; The national intelligence components of the Defense Department (other than NSA); and the National Security Council and its component parts.

The agencies upon which the Committee concentrated are those whose powers are so great and whose practices were so extensive that they must be understood in order fairly to judge whether the intelligence system of the United States needs reform and change.

{ . . . }

INTRODUCTION AND SUMMARY

The resolution creating this Committee placed greatest emphasis on whether intelligence activities threaten the "rights of American citizens."

The critical question before the Committee was to determine how the fundamental liberties of the people can be maintained in the course of the Government's effort to protect their security. The delicate balance between these basic goals of our system of government is often difficult to strike, but it can, and must, be achieved. We reject the view that the traditional American principles of justice and fair play have no place in our struggle against the enemies of freedom. Moreover, our investigation has established that the targets of intelligence activity have ranged far beyond persons who could properly be characterized as enemies of freedom and have extended to a wide array of citizens engaging in lawful activity.

Americans have rightfully been concerned since before World War II about the dangers of hostile foreign agents likely to commit acts of espionage. Similarly, the violent acts of political terrorists can seriously endanger the rights of Americans. Carefully focused intelligence investigations can help prevent such acts.

But too often intelligence has lost this focus and domestic intelligence activities have invaded individual privacy and violated the rights of lawful assembly and political expression. Unless new and tighter controls are established by legislation, domestic intelligence activities threaten to undermine our democratic society and fundamentally alter its nature.

We have examined three types of "intelligence" activities affecting the rights of American citizens. The first is intelligence collection—such as infiltrating groups with informants, wiretapping, or opening letters. The second is dissemination of material which has been collected. The third is covert action designed to disrupt and discredit the activities of groups and individuals deemed a threat to the social order. These three types of "intelligence" activity are closely related in the practical world. Information which is disseminated by the intelligence community or used in disruptive programs has usually been obtained through surveillance. Nevertheless, a division between collection, dissemination and covert action is analytically useful both in understanding why excesses have occurred in the past and in devising remedies to prevent those excesses from recurring.

A. Intelligence Activity: A New Form of Governmental Power to Impair Citizens' Rights

A tension between order and liberty is inevitable in any society. A Government must protect its citizens from those bent on engaging in violence and criminal behavior, or in espionage and other hostile foreign intelligence activity. Many of the intelligence programs reviewed in this report were established for those purposes. Intelligence work has, at times, successfully prevented dangerous and abhorrent acts, such as bombings and foreign spying, and aided in the prosecution of those responsible for such acts.

But, intelligence activity in the past decades has, all too often, exceeded the restraints on the exercise of governmental power which are imposed by our country's Constitution, laws, and traditions.

Excesses in the name of protecting security are not a recent development in our nation's history. In 1798, for example, shortly after the Bill of Rights was added to the Constitution, the Alien and Sedition Acts were passed. These Acts, passed in response to fear of pro-French "subversion," made it a crime to criticize the Government. During the Civil War, President Abraham Lincoln suspended the writ of habeas corpus. Hundreds of American citizens were prosecuted for anti-war statements during World War I, and thousands of "radical" aliens were seized for deportation during the 1920 Palmer Raids. During the Second World War, over the opposition of J. Edgar Hoover and military intelligence, 120,000 Japanese-Americans were apprehended and incarcerated in detention camps.

Those actions, however, were fundamentally different from the intelligence activities examined by this Committee. They were generally executed overtly under the authority of a statute or a public executive order. The victims knew what was being done to them and could challenge the Government in the courts and other forums. Intelligence activity, on the other hand, is generally covert. It is concealed from its victims and is seldom described in statutes or explicit executive orders. The victim may never suspect that his misfortunes are the intended result of activities undertaken by his government, and accordingly may have no opportunity to challenge the actions taken against him.

{ . . . }

B. The Questions

We have directed our investigation toward answering the following questions:

Which governmental agencies have engaged in domestic spying?

How many citizens have been targets of Governmental intelligence activity?

What standards have governed the opening of intelligence investigations and when have intelligence investigations been terminated?

Where have the targets fit on the spectrum between those who commit violent criminal acts and those who seek only to dissent peacefully from Government policy?

To what extent has the information collected included intimate details of the targets' personal lives or their political views, and has such information been disseminated and used to injure individuals?

What actions beyond surveillance have intelligence agencies taken, such as attempting to disrupt, discredit, or destroy persons or groups who have been the targets of surveillance?

Have intelligence agencies been used to serve the political aims of Presidents, other high officials, or the agencies themselves?

How have the agencies responded either to proper orders or to excessive pressures from their superiors? To what extent have intelligence agencies disclosed, or concealed them from, outside bodies charged with overseeing them?

Have intelligence agencies acted outside the law? What has been the attitude of the intelligence community toward the rule of law?

To what extent has the Executive branch and the Congress controlled intelligence agencies and held them accountable?

Generally, how well has the Federal system of checks and balances between the branches worked to control intelligence activity?

C. Summary of the Main Problems

The answer to each of these questions is disturbing. Too many people have been spied upon by too many Government agencies and too much information has been collected. The Government has often undertaken the secret surveillance of citizens on the basis of their political beliefs, even when those beliefs posed no threat of violence or illegal acts on behalf of a hostile foreign power. The Government, operating primarily through secret informants, but also using other intrusive techniques such as wiretaps, microphone "bugs," surreptitious mail opening, and break-ins, has swept in vast amounts of information about the personal lives, views, and associations of American citizens. Investigations of groups deemed potentially dangerous—and even of groups suspected of associating with potentially dangerous organizations—have continued for decades, despite the fact that those groups did not engage in unlawful activity. Groups and individuals have been harassed and disrupted because of their political views and their lifestyles. Investigations have been based upon vague standards whose breadth made excessive collection inevitable. Unsavory and vicious tactics have been employed—including anonymous attempts to break up marriages, disrupt meetings, ostracize persons from their professions, and provoke target groups into rivalries that might result in deaths. Intelligence agencies have served the political and personal objectives of presidents and other high officials. While the agencies often committed excesses in response to pressure from high officials in the Executive branch and Congress, they also occasionally initiated improper activities and then concealed them from officials whom they had a duty to inform.

Governmental officials—including those whose principal duty is to enforce the law—have violated or ignored the law over long periods of time and have advocated and defended their right to break the law.

The Constitutional system of checks and balances has not adequately controlled intelligence activities. Until recently the Executive branch has neither delineated the scope of permissible activities nor established procedures for supervising intelligence agencies. Congress has failed to exercise sufficient oversight, seldom questioning the use to which its appropriations were being put. Most domestic intelligence issues have not reached the courts, and in those cases when they have reached the courts, the judiciary has been reluctant to grapple with them.

{ . . . }

FINDINGS

The Committee makes seven major findings. { . . . } We have sought to analyze in our findings characteristics shared by intelligence programs, practices which involved abuses, and general problems in the system which led to those abuses. { . . . }

Viewed separately, each finding demonstrates a serious problem in the conduct and control of domestic intelligence operations. Taken together, they make a compelling case for the necessity of change. Our recommendations { . . . } flow from this analysis and propose changes which the Committee believes to be appropriate in light of the record.

A. VIOLATING AND IGNORING THE LAW

Major Finding

The Committee finds that the domestic activities of the intelligence community at times violated specific statutory prohibitions and infringed the constitutional rights of American citizens. The legal questions involved in intelligence programs were often not considered.

On other occasions, they were intentionally disregarded in the belief that because the programs served the "national security" the law did not apply. While intelligence officers on occasion failed to disclose to their superiors programs which were illegal or of questionable legality, the Committee finds that the most serious breaches of duty were those of senior officials, who were responsible for controlling intelligence activities and generally failed to assure compliance with the law.

Subfindings

(a) In its attempt to implement instructions to protect the security of the United States, the intelligence community engaged in some activities which violated statutory law and the constitutional rights of American citizens.

(b) Legal issues were often overlooked by many of the intelligence officers who directed these operations. Some held a pragmatic view of intelligence activities that did not regularly attach sufficient significance to questions of legality. The question raised was usually not whether a particular program was legal or ethical, but whether it worked.

(c) On some occasions when agency officials did assume, or were told, that a program was illegal, they still permitted it to continue. They justified their conduct in some cases on the ground that the failure of "the enemy" to play by the rules granted them the right to do likewise, and in other cases on the ground that the "national security" permitted programs that would otherwise be illegal.

(d) Internal recognition of the illegality or the questionable legality of many of these activities frequently led to a tightening of security rather than to their termination. Partly to avoid exposure and a public "flap," knowledge of these programs was tightly held within the agencies, special filing procedures were used, and "cover stories" were devised.

(e) On occasion, intelligence agencies failed to disclose candidly their programs and practices to their own General Counsels, and to Attorneys General, Presidents, and Congress.

(f) The internal inspection mechanisms of the CIA and the FBI did not keep—and, in the case of the FBI, were not designed to keep—the activities of those agencies within legal bounds. Their primary concern was efficiency, not legality or propriety.

(g) When senior administration officials with a duty to control domestic intelligence activities knew, or had basis for suspecting, that questionable activities had occurred, they often responded with silence or approval. In certain cases, they were presented with a partial description of a program but did not ask for details, thereby abdicating their responsibility. In other cases, they were fully aware of the nature of the practice and implicitly or explicitly approved it.

{...}

B. THE OVERBREADTH OF DOMESTIC INTELLIGENCE ACTIVITY

Major Finding

The Committee finds that domestic intelligence activity has been overbroad in that (1) many Americans and domestic groups have been subjected to investigation who were not suspected of criminal activity and (2) the intelligence agencies have regularly collected information about personal and political activities irrelevant to any legitimate governmental interest.

Subfindings

(a) Large numbers of law-abiding Americans and lawful domestic groups have been subjected to extensive intelligence investigation and surveillance.

(b) The absence of precise standards for intelligence investigations of Americans contributed to overbreadth. Congress did not enact statutes precisely delineating the authority of the intelligence agencies or defining the purpose and scope of domestic intelligence activity. The executive branch abandoned the standard set by Attorney General Stone—that the government's concern was not with political opinions but with "such conduct as is forbidden by the laws of the United States." Intelligence agencies' superiors issued over-inclusive directives to investigate "subversion" (a term that was never defined in presidential directives) and "potential" rather than actual or likely criminal conduct, as well as to collect general intelligence on lawful political and social dissent.

(c) The intelligence agencies themselves used imprecise and overinclusive criteria in their conduct of intelligence investigations. Intelligence investigations extended beyond "subversive" or violent targets to additional groups and individuals subject to minimal "subversive influence" or having little or no "potential" for violence.

(d) Intelligence agencies pursued a "vacuum cleaner" approach to intelligence collection—drawing in all available information about groups and individuals, including their lawful political activity and details of their personal lives.

(e) Intelligence investigations in many cases continued for excessively long periods of time, resulting in sustained governmental monitoring of political activity in the absence of any indication of criminal conduct or "subversion."

{ . . . }

C. EXCESSIVE USE OF INTRUSIVE TECHNIQUES

Major Finding

The intelligence community has employed surreptitious collection techniques—mail opening, surreptitious entries, informants, and "traditional" and highly sophisticated forms of electronic surveillance—to achieve its overly broad intelligence targeting and collection objectives. Although there are circumstances where these techniques, if properly controlled, are legal and appropriate, the Committee finds that their very nature makes them a threat to the personal privacy and Constitutionally protected activities of both the targets and of persons who communicate with or associate with the targets. The dangers inherent in the use of these techniques have been compounded by the lack of adequate standards limiting their use and by the absence of review by neutral authorities outside the intelligence agencies. As a consequence, these techniques have collected enormous amounts of personal and political information serving no legitimate governmental interest.

Subfindings

(a) Given the highly intrusive nature of these techniques, the legal standards and procedures regulating their use have been insufficient. There have been no statutory controls on the use of informants; there have been gaps and exceptions in the law of electronic surveillance; and the legal prohibitions against warrantless mail opening and surreptitious entries have been ignored.

(b) In addition to providing the means by which the Government can collect too much information about too many people, certain techniques have their own dangers:

(i) Informants have provoked and participated in violence and other illegal activities in order to maintain their cover, and they have obtained membership lists and private documents.

(ii) Scientific and technological advances have rendered traditional controls on electronic surveillance obsolete and have made it more difficult to limit intrusions. Because of the nature of wiretaps, microphones and other sophisticated electronic techniques, it has not always been possible to restrict the monitoring of communications to the persons being investigated.

(c) The imprecision and manipulation of labels such as "national security," "domestic security," "subversive activities," and "foreign intelligence" have led to unjustified use of these techniques.

{ . . . }

D. USING COVERT ACTION TO DISRUPT AND DISCREDIT DOMESTIC GROUPS

Major Finding

The Committee finds that covert action programs have been used to disrupt the lawful political activities of individual Americans and groups and to discredit them, using dangerous and degrading tactics which are abhorrent in a free and decent society.

Subfindings

(a) Although the claimed purposes of these action programs were to protect the national security and to prevent violence, many of the victims were concededly nonviolent, were not controlled by a foreign power, and posed no threat to the national security.

(b) The acts taken interfered with the First Amendment rights of citizens. They were explicitly intended to deter citizens from joining groups, "neutralize" those who were already members, and prevent or inhibit the expression of ideas.

(c) The tactics used against Americans often risked and sometimes caused serious emotional, economic, or physical damage. Actions were taken which were designed to break up marriages, terminate funding or employment, and encourage gang warfare between violent rival groups. Due process of law forbids the use of such covert tactics, whether the victims are innocent law-abiding citizens or members of groups suspected of involvement in violence.

(d) The sustained use of such tactics by the FBI in an attempt to destroy Dr. Martin Luther King, Jr., violated the law and fundamental human decency.

{ . . . }

E. POLITICAL ABUSE OF INTELLIGENCE INFORMATION

Major Finding

The Committee finds that information has been collected and disseminated in order to serve the purely political interests of an intelligence agency or the administration, and to influence social policy and political action.

Subfindings

(a) White House officials have requested and obtained politically useful information from the FBI, including information on the activities of political opponents or critics.

(b) In some cases, political or personal information was not specifically requested, but was nevertheless collected and disseminated to administration officials as part of investigations they had requested. Neither the FBI nor the recipients differentiated in these cases between national security or law enforcement information and purely political intelligence.

(c) The FBI has also volunteered information to Presidents and their staffs, without having been asked for it, sometimes apparently to curry favor with the current administration. Similarly the FBI has assembled intelligence on its critics and on political figures it believed might influence public attitudes or Congressional support.

(d) The FBI has also used intelligence as a vehicle for covert efforts to influence social policy and political action.

{ . . . }

F. INADEQUATE CONTROLS ON DISSEMINATION AND RETENTION

Major Finding

The Committee finds that the product of intelligence investigations has been disseminated without adequate controls. Reports on lawful political activity and law-abiding citizens have been disseminated to agencies having no proper reason to receive them. Information that should have been discarded, purged, or sealed, including the product of illegal techniques and overbroad investigations, has been retained and is available for future use.

Subfindings

(a) Agencies have volunteered massive amounts of irrelevant information to other officials and agencies and have responded unquestioningly in some instances to requests for data without assuring that the information would be used for a lawful purpose.

(b) Excessive dissemination has sometimes contributed to the inefficiency of the intelligence process itself.

(c) Under the federal employee security program, unnecessary information about the political beliefs and associations of prospective government employees has been disseminated.

(d) The FBI, which has been the "clearinghouse" for all domestic intelligence data, maintains in readily accessible files sensitive and derogatory personal information not relevant to any investigation, as well as information which was improperly or illegally obtained.

{...}

G. DEFICIENCIES IN CONTROL AND ACCOUNTABILITY

Major Finding

The Committee finds that those responsible for overseeing, supervising, and controlling domestic activities of the intelligence community, although often unaware of details of the excesses described in this report, made those excesses possible by delegating broad authority without establishing adequate guidelines and procedural checks; by failing to monitor and coordinate sufficiently the activities of the agencies under their charge; by failing to inquire further after receiving indications that improper activities may have been occurring; by exhibiting a reluctance to know about secret details of programs; and sometimes by requesting intelligence agencies to engage in questionable practices. On numerous occasions, intelligence agencies have, by concealment, misrepresentation, or partial disclosure, hidden improper activities from those to whom they owed a duty of disclosure. But such deceit and the improper practices which it concealed would not have been possible to such a degree if senior officials of the Executive Branch and Congress had clearly allocated responsibility and imposed requirements for reporting and obtaining prior approval for activities, and had insisted on adherence to those requirements.

Subfindings

(a) Presidents have given intelligence agencies firm orders to collect information concerning "subversive activities" of American citizens, but have failed until recently to define the limits of domestic intelligence, to provide safeguards for the rights of American citizens, or to coordinate and control the ever-expanding intelligence efforts by an increasing number of agencies.

(b) Attorneys General have permitted and even encouraged the FBI to engage in domestic intelligence activities and to use a wide range of intrusive techniques—such as wiretaps, microphones, and informants—but have failed until recently to supervise or establish limits on these activities or techniques by issuing adequate safeguards, guidelines, or procedures for review.

(c) Presidents, White House officials, and Attorneys General have requested and received domestic political intelligence, thereby contributing to and profiting from the abuses of domestic intelligence and setting a bad example for their subordinates.

(d) Presidents, Attorneys General, and other Cabinet officers have neglected until recently to make inquiries in the face of clear indications that intelligence agencies were engaging in improper domestic activities.

(e) Congress, which has the authority to place restraints on domestic intelligence activities through legislation, appropriations, and oversight committees, has not effectively asserted its responsibilities until recently. It has failed to define the scope of domestic intelligence activities or intelligence collection techniques, to uncover excesses, or to propose legislative solutions. Some of its members have failed to object to improper activities of which they were aware and have prodded agencies into questionable activities.

(f) Intelligence agencies have often undertaken programs without authorization, with insufficient authorization, or in disregard of express orders.

(g) The weakness of the system of accountability and control can be seen in the fact that many illegal or abusive domestic intelligence operations were terminated only after they had been exposed or threatened with exposure by Congress or the news media.

{ . . . }

CONCLUSIONS

The findings which have emerged from our investigation convince us that the Government's domestic intelligence policies and practices require fundamental reform. We have attempted to set out the basic facts; now it is time for Congress to turn its attention to legislating restraints upon intelligence activities which may endanger the constitutional rights of Americans.

The Committee's fundamental conclusion is that intelligence activities have undermined the constitutional rights of citizens and that they have done so primarily because checks and balances designed by the framers of the Constitution to assure accountability have not been applied.

Before examining that conclusion, we make the following observations.

—While nearly all of our findings focus on excesses and things that went wrong, we do not question the need for lawful domestic intelligence. We recognize that certain intelligence activities serve perfectly proper and clearly necessary ends of government. Surely, catching spies and stopping crime, including acts of terrorism, is essential to insure "domestic tranquility" and to "provide for the common defense." Therefore, the power of government to conduct *proper* domestic intelligence activities under effective restraints and controls must be preserved.

—We are aware that the few earlier efforts to limit domestic intelligence activities have proven ineffectual. This pattern reinforces the need for statutory restraints coupled with much more effective oversight from all branches of the Government.

—The crescendo of improper intelligence activity in the latter part of the 1960s and the early 1970s shows what we must watch out for: In times of crisis, the Government will exercise its power to conduct domestic intelligence activities to the fullest extent. The distinction between legal dissent and criminal conduct is easily forgotten. Our job is to recommend means to help ensure that the distinction will always be observed.

—In an era where the technological capability of Government relentlessly increases, we must be wary about the drift toward "big brother government." The potential for abuse is awesome and requires special attention to fashioning restraints which not only cure past problems but anticipate and prevent the future misuse of technology.

—We cannot dismiss what we have found as isolated acts which were limited in time and confined to a few willful men. The failures to obey the law and, in the words of the oath of office, to "preserve, protect, and defend" the Constitution, have occurred repeatedly throughout administrations of both political parties going back four decades.

—We must acknowledge that the assignment which the Government has given to the intelligence community has, in many ways, been impossible to fulfill. It has been expected to predict or prevent every crisis, respond immediately with information on any question, act to meet all threats, and anticipate the special needs of Presidents. And then it is chastised for its zeal. Certainly, a fair assessment must place a major part of the blame upon the failures of senior executive officials and Congress.

In the final analysis, however, the purpose of this Committee's work is not to allocate blame among individuals. Indeed, to focus on personal culpability may divert attention from the underlying institutional causes and thus may become an excuse for inaction.

Before this investigation, domestic intelligence had never been systematically surveyed. For the first time, the Government's domestic surveillance programs, as they have developed over the past forty years, can be measured against the values which our Constitution seeks to preserve and protect. Based upon our full record, and the findings which we have set forth { . . . } above, the Committee concludes that:

> *Domestic Intelligence Activity Has Threatened and Undermined the Constitutional Rights of Americans to Free Speech, Association and Privacy. It Has Done So Primarily Because the Constitutional System for Checking Abuse of Power Has Not Been Applied.*

2.

COINTELPRO

The FBI's Covert Action Programs Against American Citizens

I. INTRODUCTION AND SUMMARY

COINTELPRO is the FBI acronym for a series of covert action programs directed against domestic groups. In these programs, the Bureau went beyond the collection of intelligence to secret action designed to "disrupt" and "neutralize" target groups and individuals. The techniques were adopted wholesale from wartime counterintelligence, and ranged from the trivial (mailing reprints of *Reader's Digest* articles to college administrators) to the degrading (sending anonymous poison-pen letters intended to break up marriages) and the dangerous (encouraging gang warfare and falsely labeling members of a violent group as police informers).

This report is based on a staff study of more than 20,000 pages of Bureau documents, depositions of many of the Bureau agents involved in the programs, and interviews of several COINTELPRO targets. The examples selected for discussion necessarily represent a small percentage of the more than 2,000 approved COINTELPRO actions. Nevertheless, the cases demonstrate the consequences of a Government agency's decision to take the law into its own hands for the "greater good" of the country.

COINTELPRO began in 1956, in part because of frustration with Supreme Court rulings limiting the Government's power to proceed overtly against dissident groups; it ended in 1971 with the threat of public exposure. In the intervening 15 years, the Bureau conducted a sophisticated vigilante operation aimed squarely at preventing the exercise of First Amendment rights of speech and association, on the theory that preventing the growth of dangerous groups and the propagation of dangerous ideas would protect the national security and deter violence.

Many of the techniques used would be intolerable in a democratic society even if all of the targets had been involved in violent activity, but COINTELPRO went far beyond that. The unexpressed major premise of the programs was that a law enforcement agency has the duty to do whatever is necessary to combat perceived threats to the existing social and political order.

A. "Counterintelligence Program": A Misnomer for Domestic Covert Action

COINTELPRO is an acronym for "counterintelligence program." Counterintelligence is defined as those actions by an intelligence agency intended to protect its own security and to undermine hostile intelligence operations. Under COINTELPRO certain techniques the Bureau had used against hostile foreign agents were adopted for use against perceived domestic threats to the established political and social order. The formal programs which incorporated these techniques were, therefore, also called "counterintelligence."

"Covert action" is, however, a more accurate term for the Bureau's programs directed against American citizens. "Covert action" is the label applied to clandestine activities intended to influence political choices and social values.

B. Who Were the Targets?

1. The Five Targeted Groups

The Bureau's covert action programs were aimed at five perceived threats to domestic tranquility: the "Communist Party, USA" program (1956–71); the "Socialist Workers Party" program (1961–69); the "White Hate Group" program (1964–71); the "Black Nationalist Hate Group" program (1967–71); and the "New Left" program (1968–71).

2. Labels Without Meaning

The Bureau's titles for its programs should not be accepted uncritically. They imply a precision of definition and of targeting which did not exist.

Even the names of the later programs had no clear definition. The Black Nationalist program, according to its supervisor, included "a great number of organizations that you might not today characterize as black nationalist but which were in fact primarily black." Indeed, the nonviolent Southern Christian Leadership Conference was labeled as a Black Nationalist "Hate Group." Nor could anyone at the Bureau even define "New Left," except as "more or less an attitude."

Furthermore, the actual targets were chosen from a far broader group than the names of the programs would imply. The CPUSA program targeted not only Party members but also sponsors of the National Committee to Abolish the House Un-American Activities Committee and civil rights leaders allegedly under Communist influence or simply not "anti-Communist." The Socialist Workers Party program included non-SWP sponsors of antiwar demonstrations which were cosponsored by the SWP or the Young Socialist Alliance, its youth group. The Black Nationalist program targeted a range of organizations from the Panthers to SNCC to the peaceful Southern Christian Leadership Conference, and included most black student groups. New Left targets ranged from the SDS to the Inter-university Committee for Debate on Foreign Policy, from all of Antioch College ("vanguard of the New Left") to the New Mexico Free University and other "alternate" schools, and from underground newspapers to students protesting university censorship of a student publication by carrying signs with four-letter words on them.

C. What Were the Purposes of COINTELPRO?

The breadth of targeting and lack of substantive content in the descriptive titles of the programs reflect the range of motivations for COINTELPRO activity: protecting national security, preventing violence, and maintaining the existing social and political order by "disrupting" and "neutralizing" groups and individuals perceived as threats.

1. Protecting National Security

The first COINTELPRO, against the CPUSA, was instituted to counter what the Bureau believed to be a threat to the national security. As the chief of the COINTELPRO unit explained it:

> We were trying first to develop intelligence so we would know what they were doing [and] second, to contain the threat. . . . To stop the spread of communism, to stop the effectiveness of the Communist Party as a vehicle of Soviet intelligence, propaganda and agitation.

Had the Bureau stopped there, perhaps the term "counterintelligence" would have been an accurate label for the program. The expansion of the CPUSA program to non-Communists, however, and the addition of subsequent programs, make it clear that other purposes were also at work.

2. Preventing Violence

One of these purposes was the prevention of violence. Every Bureau witness deposed stated that the purpose of the particular program or programs with which he was associated was to deter violent acts by the target groups, although the witnesses differed in their assessment of how successful the programs were in achieving that goal. The preventive function was not, however, intended to be a product of specific proposals directed at specific criminal acts. Rather the programs were aimed at groups which the Bureau believed to be violent or to have the potential for violence.

The programs were to prevent violence by deterring membership in the target groups, even if neither the particular member nor the group was violent at the time. As the supervisor of the Black Nationalist COINTELPRO put it, "Obviously you are going to prevent violence or a greater amount of violence if you have smaller groups." The COINTELPRO unit chief agreed: "We also made an effort to deter or counteract the propaganda . . . and to deter recruitment where we could. This was done with the view that if we could curb the organization, we could curb the action or the violence within the organization." In short, the programs were to prevent violence indirectly, rather than directly, by preventing possibly violent citizens from joining or continuing to associate with possibly violent groups.

The prevention of violence is clearly not, in itself, an improper purpose; preventing violence is the ultimate goal of most law enforcement. Prosecution and sentencing are intended to deter future criminal behavior, not only of the subject but also of others who might break the law. In that sense, law enforcement legitimately attempts the indirect prevention of possible violence and, if the methods used are proper, raises no constitutional issues. When the government goes beyond traditional law enforcement methods, however, and attacks group membership and advocacy, it treads on ground forbidden to it by the Constitution. In *Brandenberg* v. *Ohio,* 395 U.S. 444 (1969), the Supreme Court held that the government is not permitted to "forbid or proscribe advocacy of the use of force or law violation except where such advocacy is directed toward inciting or producing imminent lawless action and is likely to incite or produce such action." In the absence of such clear and present danger, the government cannot act against speech nor, presumably, against association.

3. Maintaining the Existing Social and Political Order

Protecting national security and preventing violence are the purposes advanced by the Bureau for COINTELPRO. There is another purpose for COINTELPRO which is not explicit but which offers the only explanation for those actions which had no conceivable rational relationship to either national security or violent activity. The unexpressed major premise of much of COINTELPRO is that the Bureau has a role in maintaining the existing social order, and that its efforts should be aimed toward combating those who threaten that order.

The "New Left" COINTELPRO presents the most striking example of this attitude. As discussed earlier, the Bureau did not define the term "New Left," and the range of targets went far beyond alleged "subversives" or "extremists." Thus, for example, two student participants in a "free speech" demonstration were targeted because they defended the use of the classic four-letter word. Significantly, they were made COINTELPRO subjects even though the demonstration "does not appear to be inspired by the New Left" because it "shows obvious disregard for decency and established morality." In another case, reprints of a newspaper article entitled "Rabbi in Vietnam Says Withdrawal Not the Answer" were mailed to members of the Vietnam Day Committee "to convince [them] of the correctness of the U.S. foreign policy in Vietnam." Still another document inveighs against the "liberal press and the bleeding hearts and the forces on the left" which were "taking advantage of the situation in Chicago surrounding the Democratic National Convention to attack the police and organized law enforcement agencies." Upholding decency and established morality, defending the correctness of U.S. foreign policy, and attacking those who thought the Chicago police used undue force have no apparent connection with the expressed goals of protecting national security and preventing violence. These documents, among others examined, compel the conclusion that Federal law enforcement officers looked upon themselves as guardians of the status quo. The attitude should not be a surprise; the difficulty lies in the choice of weapons.

D. What Techniques Were Used?

1. The Techniques of Wartime

Under the COINTELPRO programs, the arsenal of techniques used against foreign espionage agents was transferred to domestic enemies. As William C. Sullivan, former Assistant to the Director, put it,

> This is a rough, tough, dirty business, and dangerous. It was dangerous at times. No holds were barred. . . . We have used [these techniques] against Soviet agents. They have used [them] against us. . . . [The same methods were] brought home against any organization against which we were targeted. We did not differentiate. This is a rough, tough business.

Mr. Sullivan's description–rough, tough, and dirty–is accurate. In the course of COINTELPRO's fifteen-year history, a number of individual actions may have violated specific criminal statutes; a number of individual actions involved risk of serious bodily injury or death to the targets (at least four assaults were reported as "results"); and a number of actions, while not illegal or dangerous, can only be described as "abhorrent in a free society." On the other hand, many of the actions were more silly than repellent.

The Bureau approved 2,370 separate counterintelligence actions. Their techniques ranged from anonymously mailing reprints of newspaper and magazine articles (sometimes Bureau-authored or planted) to group members or supporters to convince them of the error of their ways, to mailing anonymous letters to a member's spouse accusing the target of infidelity; from using informants to raise controversial issues at meetings in order to cause dissent, to the "snitch jacket" (falsely labeling a group member as an informant), and encouraging street warfare between violent groups; from contacting members of a legitimate group to expose the alleged subversive background of a fellow member, to contacting an employer to get a target fired; from attempting to arrange for reporters to interview targets with planted questions, to trying to stop targets from speaking at all; from notifying state and local authorities of a target's criminal law violations, to using the IRS to audit a professor, not just to collect any taxes owing, but to distract him from his political activities.

2. Techniques Carrying a Serious Risk of Physical, Emotional, or Economic Damage.

The Bureau recognized that some techniques were more likely than others to cause serious physical, emotional, or economic damage to the targets. Any proposed use of those techniques was scrutinized carefully by headquarters supervisory personnel, in an attempt to balance the "greater good" to be achieved by the proposal against the known or risked harm to the target. If the "good" was sufficient, the proposal was approved. For instance, in discussing anonymous letters to spouses, the agent who supervised the New Left COINTELPRO stated:

> [Before recommending approval] I would want to know what you want to get out of this, who are these people. If it's somebody, and say they did split up, what would accrue from it as far as disrupting the New Left is concerned? Say they broke up, what then. . . .
>
> [The question would be] is it worth it?

Similarly, with regard to the "snitch jacket" technique—falsely labeling a group member as a police informant—the chief of the Racial Intelligence Section stated:

> You have to be able to make decisions and I am sure that labeling somebody as an informant, that you'd want to make certain that it served a good purpose before you did it and not do it haphazardly. . . . It is a serious thing. . . . As far as I am aware, in the black extremist area, by using that technique, no one was killed. I am sure of that.

Moore was asked whether the fact that no one was killed was the result of "luck or planning." He answered:

"Oh, it just happened that way, I am sure."

It is thus clear that, as Sullivan said, "No holds were barred," although some holds were weighed more carefully than others. When the willingness to use techniques which were concededly dangerous or harmful to the targets is combined with the range of purposes and criteria by which these targets were chosen, the result is neither "within bounds" nor "justified" in a free society.

E. Legal Restrictions Were Ignored

What happened to turn a law enforcement agency into a law violator? Why do those involved still believe their actions were not only defensible, but right?

The answers to these questions are found in a combination of factors: the availability of information showing the targets' vulnerability gathered through the unrestrained collection of domestic intelligence; the belief both within and without the Bureau that it could handle any problem; and frustration with the apparent inability of traditional law enforcement methods to solve the problems presented.

There is no doubt that Congress and the public looked to the Bureau for protection against domestic and foreign threats. As the COINTELPRO unit chief stated:

> At this time [the mid-1950s] there was a general philosophy too, the general attitude of the public at this time was you did not have to worry about Communism because the FBI would take care of it. Leave it to the FBI.
>
> I hardly know an agent who would ever go to a social affair or something, if he were introduced as FBI, the comment would be, "we feel very good because we know you are handling the threat." We were handling the threat with what directives and statutes were available. There did not seem to be any strong interest of anybody to give us stronger or better defined statutes.

Not only was no one interested in giving the Bureau better statutes (nor, for that matter, did the Bureau request them), but the Supreme Court drastically narrowed the scope of the statutes available. The Bureau personnel involved trace the institution of the first formal counterintelligence program to the Supreme Court reversal of the Smith Act convictions. The unit chief testified:

> The Supreme Court rulings had rendered the Smith Act technically unenforceable. . . . It made it ineffective to prosecute Communist Party members, made it impossible to prosecute Communist Party members at the time.

This belief in the failure of law enforcement produced the subsequent COINTELPROs as well. The unit chief continued:

> The other COINTELPRO programs were opened as the threat arose in areas of extremism and subversion and there were not adequate statutes to proceed against the organization or to prevent their activities.

Every Bureau witness deposed agreed that his particular COINTELPRO was the result of tremendous pressure on the Bureau to do something about a perceived threat, coupled with the inability of law enforcement techniques to cope with the situation, either because there were no pertinent federal statutes, or because local law enforcement efforts were stymied by indifference or the refusal of those in charge to call the police.

Outside pressure and law enforcement frustration do not, of course, fully explain COINTELPRO. Perhaps, after all, the best explanation was proffered by George C. Moore, the Racial Intelligence Section chief:

> The FBI's counterintelligence program came up because there was a point—if you have anything in the FBI, you have an action-oriented group of people who see something happening and want to do something to take its place.

F. Command and Control

1. 1956–71

While that "action-oriented group of people" was proceeding with fifteen years of COINTELPRO activities, where were those responsible for the supervision and control of the Bureau? Part of the answer lies in the definition of "covert action"—*clandestine* activities. No one outside the Bureau was supposed to know that COINTELPRO existed. Even within the Bureau, the programs were handled on a "need-to-know" basis.

Nevertheless, the Bureau has supplied the Committee with documents which support its contention that various Attorneys General, advisors to Presidents, members of the House Appropriations Subcommittee, and, in 1958, the Cabinet were at least put on notice of the existence of the CPUSA and White Hate COINTELPROs. The Bureau cannot support its claim that anyone outside the FBI was informed of the existence of the Socialist Workers Party, Black Nationalist, or New Left COINTELPROs, and even those letters or briefings which referred (usually indirectly) to the CPUSA and White Hate COINTELPROs failed to mention the use of techniques which risked physical, emotional, or economic damage to their targets. In any event, there is no record that any of these officials asked to know more, and none of them appears to have expressed disapproval based on the information they were given.

As the history of the Domestic Intelligence Division shows, the absence of disapproval has been interpreted by the Bureau as sufficient authorization to continue an activity (and occasionally, even express disapproval has not sufficed to stop a practice). Perhaps, however, the crux of the "command and control" problem lies in the testimony by one former Attorney General that he was too busy to know what the Bureau was doing, and by another that, as a matter of political reality, he could not have stopped it anyway.

2. Post-1971

Whether the Attorney General can control the Bureau is still an open question. The Petersen Committee, which was formed within the Justice Department to investigate COINTELPRO at Attorney General {William B.} Saxbe's request, worked only with Bureau-prepared summaries of the COINTELPRO files. Further, the fact that the Department of Justice must work with the Bureau on a day-to-day basis may influence the Department's judgment on Bureau activities.

G. Termination

If COINTELPRO had been a short-lived aberration, the thorny problems of motivation, techniques, and control presented might be safely relegated to history. However, COINTELPRO existed for years on an "ad hoc" basis before the formal programs were instituted, and more significantly,

COINTELPRO-type activities may continue today under the rubric of "investigation."

{...}

II. THE FIVE DOMESTIC PROGRAMS

A. Origins

The origins of COINTELPRO are rooted in the Bureau's jurisdiction to investigate hostile foreign intelligence activities on American soil. Counterintelligence, of course, goes beyond investigation; it is affirmative action taken to neutralize hostile agents.

The Bureau believed its wartime counterattacks on foreign agents to be effective–and what works against one enemy will work against another. In the atmosphere of the Cold War, the American Communist Party was viewed as a deadly threat to national security.

In 1956, the Bureau decided that a formal counterintelligence program, coordinated from headquarters, would be an effective weapon in the fight against Communism. The first COINTELPRO was therefore initiated.

The CPUSA COINTELPRO accounted for more than half of all approved proposals. The Bureau personnel involved believed that the success of the program—one action was described as "the most effective single blow ever dealt the organized communist movement"—made counterintelligence techniques the weapons of choice whenever the Bureau assessed a new and, in its view, equally serious threat to the country.

As noted earlier, law enforcement frustration also played a part in the origins of each COINTELPRO. In each case, Bureau witnesses testified that the lack of adequate statutes, uncooperative or ineffective local police, or restrictive court rulings had made it impossible to use traditional law enforcement methods against the targeted groups.

Additionally, a certain amount of empire building may have been at work. Under William C. Sullivan, the Domestic Intelligence Division greatly expanded its jurisdiction. Klan matters were transferred in 1964 to the Intelligence Division from the General Investigative Division; black nationalist groups were added in 1967; and, just as the Old Left appeared to be dying out, the New Left was gradually added to the work of the Division's Internal Security Section in the late 1960s.

Finally, it is significant that the five domestic COINTELPROs were started against the five groups which were the subject of intensified investigative programs. Of course, the fact that such intensive investigative programs were started at all reflects the Bureau's process of threat assessment: the greater the threat, the more need to know about it (intelligence) and the more impetus to counter it (covert action). More important, however, the mere existence of the additional information gained through the investigative programs inevitably demonstrated those particular organizational or personal weaknesses which were vulnerable to disruption. COINTELPRO demonstrates the dangers inherent in the overbroad collection of domestic intelligence; when information is available, it can be—and was—improperly used.

B. The Programs

Before examining each program in detail, some general observations may be useful. Each of the five domestic COINTELPROs had certain traits in common. As noted above, each program used techniques learned from the Bureau's wartime efforts against hostile foreign agents. Each sprang from frustration with the perceived inability of law enforcement to deal with what the Bureau believed to be a serious threat to the country. Each program depended on an intensive intelligence effort to provide the information used to disrupt the target groups.

The programs also differ to some extent. The White Hate program, for example, was very precisely targeted; each of the other programs spread to a number of groups which do not appear to fall within any clear parameters. In fact, with each subsequent COINTELPRO, the targeting became more diffuse.

The White Hate COINTELPRO also used comparatively few techniques which carried a risk of serious physical, emotional, or economic damage to the targets, while the Black Nationalist COINTELPRO used such techniques extensively. The New Left COINTELPRO, on the other hand, had the highest proportion of proposals aimed at preventing the exercise of free speech. Like the progression in targeting, the use of dangerous, degrading, or blatantly unconstitutional techniques also appears to have become less restrained with each subsequent program.

1. CPUSA.—The first official COINTELPRO program, against the Communist Party, USA, was started in August 1956 with Director

Hoover's approval. Although the formal program was instituted in 1956, COINTELPRO-type activities had gone on for years. The memorandum recommending the program refers to prior actions, constituting "harassment," which were generated by the field during the course of the Bureau's investigation of the Communist Party. These prior actions were instituted on an *ad hoc* basis as the opportunity arose. As Sullivan testified, "[Before 1956] we were engaged in COINTELPRO tactics, divide, confuse, weaken in diverse ways, an organization. . . . [Before 1956] it was more sporadic. It depended on a given office. . . . "

In 1956, a series of field conferences was held to discuss the development of new security informants. The Smith Act trials and related proceedings had exposed over 100 informants, leaving the Bureau's intelligence apparatus in some disarray. During the field conferences, a formal counterintelligence program was recommended, partly because of the gaps in the informant ranks.

Since the Bureau had evidence that until the late 1940s the CPUSA had been "blatantly" involved in Soviet espionage, and believed that the Soviets were continuing to use the Party for "political and intelligence purposes," there was no clear line of demarcation in the Bureau's switch from foreign to domestic counterintelligence. The initial areas of concentration were the use of informants to capitalize on the conflicts within the Party over Nikita Khrushchev's denunciation of Stalin; to prevent the CP's efforts to take over (via a merger) a broad-based socialist group; to encourage the Socialist Workers Party in its attacks on the CP; and to use the IRS to investigate underground CP members who either failed to file, or filed under false names.

As the program proceeded, other targets and techniques were developed, but until 1960 the CPUSA targets were Party members, and the techniques were primarily aimed at the Party organization (factionalism, public exposure, etc.)

2. The 1960 Expansion.—In March 1960, CPUSA COINTELPRO field offices received a directive to intensify counterintelligence efforts to prevent Communist infiltration ("COMINFIL") of mass organizations, ranging from the NAACP to a local scout troop. The usual technique would be to tell a leader of the organization about the alleged Communist in its midst, the target, of course, being the alleged Communist rather than the organization. In an increasing number of cases, however, both the alleged Communist and the organization were targeted, usually by planting a news article about Communists active in the organization. For example, a newsman was given information about Communist participation in a SANE march, with the express purpose being to discredit SANE as well as the participants, and another newspaper was alerted to plans of Bettina Aptheker to join a United Farm Workers picket line. The 1960 "COMINFIL" memorandum marks the beginning of the slide from targeting CP members to those allegedly under CP "influence" (such civil rights leaders as Martin Luther King, Jr.) to "fellow travelers" (those taking positions supported by the Communists, such as school integration, increased minority hiring, and opposition to HUAC.)

3. Socialist Workers Party.—The Socialist Workers Party ("SWP") COINTELPRO program was initiated on October 12, 1961, by the headquarters supervisor handling the SWP desk (but with Hoover's concurrence) apparently on a theory of even-handed treatment: if the Bureau has a program against the CP, it was only fair to have one against the Trotskyites. (The COINTELPRO unit chief, in response to a question about why the Bureau targeted the SWP in view of the fact that the SWP's hostility to the Communist Party had been useful in disrupting the CPUSA, answered, "I do not think that the Bureau discriminates against subversive organizations.")

The program was not given high priority—only 45 actions were approved—and was discontinued in 1969, two years before the other four programs ended. (The SWP program was then subsumed in the New Left COINTELPRO.) Nevertheless, it marks an important departure from the CPUSA COINTELPRO: although the SWP had contacts with foreign Trotskyite groups, there was no evidence that the SWP was involved in espionage. These were, in C. D. Brennan's phrase, "home grown tomatoes." The Bureau has conceded that the SWP has never been engaged in organizational violence, nor has it taken any criminal steps toward overthrowing the country.

Nor does the Bureau claim the SWP was engaged in revolutionary acts. The Party was targeted for its rhetoric; significantly, the originating letter points to the SWPs "open" espousal of its line "through running candidates for public office" and its direction and/or support of "such causes as Castro's Cuba and integration problems arising in the South." Further, the American people had to be alerted to the fact that "the SWP is not just another socialist group but follows the revolutionary principles of Marx, Lenin, and Engels as interpreted by Leon Trotsky."

Like the CPUSA COINTELPRO, non-Party members were also targeted, particularly when the SWP and the Young Socialist Alliance (the SWP's youth group) started to co-sponsor antiwar marches.

4. White Hate.—The Klan COINTELPRO began on July 30, 1964, with the transfer of the "responsibility for development of informants and gathering of intelligence on the KKK and other hate groups" from the General Investigative Division to the Domestic Intelligence Division. The memorandum recommending the reorganization also suggested that "counterintelligence and disruption tactics be given further study by DID and appropriate recommendations made."

Accordingly, on September 2, 1964, a directive was sent to seventeen field offices instituting a COINTELPRO against Klan-type and hate organizations "to expose, disrupt, and otherwise neutralize the activities of the various Klans and hate organizations, their leadership, and adherents." Seventeen Klan organizations and nine "hate" organizations (e.g., American Nazi Party, National States Rights Party, etc.) were listed as targets. The field offices were also instructed specifically to consider "Action Groups"—"the relatively few individuals in each organization who use strong arm tactics and violent actions to achieve their ends." However, counterintelligence proposals were not to be limited to these few, but were to include any influential member if the opportunity arose. As the unit chief stated:

> The emphasis was on determining the identity and exposing and neutralizing the violence prone activities of "Action Groups," but also it was important to expose the unlawful activities of other Klan organizations. We also made an effort to deter or counteract the propaganda and to deter violence and to deter recruitment where we could. This was done with the view that if we could curb the organization, we could curb the action or the violence within the organization.

The White Hate COINTELPRO appears to have been limited, with few exceptions, to the original named targets. No "legitimate" right wing organizations were drawn into the program, in contrast with the earlier spread of the CPUSA and SWP programs to non-members. This precision has been attributed by the Bureau to the superior intelligence on "hate" groups received by excellent informant penetration.

Bureau witnesses believe the Klan program to have been highly effective. The unit chief stated:

> I think the Bureau got the job done. . . . I think that one reason we were able to get the job done was that we were able to use counterintelligence techniques. It is possible that we eventually could have done the job without counterintelligence techniques. I am not sure we could have done it as well or as quickly.

This view was shared by George C. Moore, Section Chief of the Racial Intelligence Section, which had responsibility for the White Hate and Black Nationalist COINTELPROs:

> I think from what I have seen and what I have read, as far as the counterintelligence program on the Klan is concerned, that it was effective. I think it was one of the most effective programs I have ever seen the Bureau handle as far as any group is concerned.

5. Black Nationalist-Hate Groups.—In marked contrast to prior COINTELPROs, which grew out of years of intensive intelligence investigation, the Black Nationalist COINTELPRO and the racial intelligence investigative section were set up at about the same time in 1967.

Prior to that time, the Division's investigation of "Negro matters" was limited to instances of alleged Communist infiltration of civil rights groups and to monitoring civil rights protest activity. However, the long, hot summer of 1967 led to intense pressure on the Bureau to do something to contain the problem, and once again, the Bureau heeded the call.

The originating letter was sent out to twenty-three field offices on August 25, 1967, describing the program's purpose as

> . . . to expose, disrupt, misdirect, discredit, or otherwise neutralize the activities of black nationalist, hate-type organizations and groupings, their leadership, spokesmen, membership, and supporters, and to counter their propensity for violence and civil disorder. . . . Efforts of the various groups to consolidate their forces or to recruit new or youthful adherents must be frustrated.

Initial group targets for "intensified attention" were the Southern Christian Leadership Conference, the Student Nonviolent Coordinating Committee, Revolutionary Action Movement, Deacons for Defense and Justice, Congress of Racial Equality, and the Nation of Islam. Individuals named targets were Stokely Carmichael, H. "Rap" Brown, Elijah Muhammad, and Maxwell Stanford. The targets were chosen by conferring with Headquarters personnel supervising the racial cases; the list was not intended to exclude other groups known to the field.

According to the Black Nationalist supervisor, individuals and organizations were targeted because of their propensity for violence or their "radical or revolutionary rhetoric [and] actions":

> Revolutionary would be [defined as] advocacy of the overthrow of the Government. . . . Radical [is] a loose term that might cover, for example, the separatist view of the Nation of Islam, the influence of a group called U.S. Incorporated. . . . Generally, they wanted a separate black nation. . . . They [the NOI] advocated formation of a separate black nation on the territory of five Southern states.

The letter went on to direct field offices to exploit conflicts within and between groups; to use news media contacts to disrupt, ridicule, or discredit groups; to preclude "violence-prone" or "rabble rouser" leaders of these groups from spreading their philosophy publicly; and to gather information on the "unsavory backgrounds"—immorality, subversive activity, and criminal activity—of group members.

According to George C. Moore, the Southern Christian Leadership Conference was included because

> . . . at that time it was still under investigation because of the communist infiltration. As far as I know, there were not any violent propensities, except that I note . . . in the cover memo [expanding the program] or somewhere, that they mentioned that if Martin Luther King decided to go a certain way, he could cause some trouble. . . . I cannot explain it satisfactorily . . . this is something the section inherited.

On March 4, 1968, the program was expanded from twenty-three to forty-one field offices. The letter expanding the program lists five long-range goals for the program:

(1) to prevent the "coalition of militant black nationalist groups," which might be the first step toward a real "Mau Mau" in America;

(2) to prevent the rise of a "messiah" who could "unify, and electrify," the movement, naming specifically Martin Luther King, Stokely Carmichael, and Elijah Muhammad;

(3) to prevent violence on the part of black nationalist groups, by pinpointing "potential troublemakers" and neutralizing them "before they exercise their potential for violence";

(4) to prevent groups and leaders from gaining "respectability" by discrediting them to the "responsible" Negro community, to the white community (both the responsible community and the "liberals"—the distinction is the Bureau's), and to Negro radicals; and

(5) to prevent the long-range growth of these organizations, especially among youth, by developing specific tactics to "prevent these groups from recruiting young people."

6. The Panther Directives.—The Black Panther Party ("BPP") was not included in the first two lists of primary targets (August 1967 and March 1968) because it had not attained national importance. By November 1968, apparently the BPP had become sufficiently active to be considered a primary target. A letter to certain field offices with BPP activity dated November 25, 1968, ordered recipient offices to submit "imaginative and hard-hitting counterintelligence measures aimed at crippling the BPP." Proposals were to be received every two weeks. Particular attention was to be given to capitalizing upon the differences between the BPP and US, Inc. (Ron Karenga's group), which had reached such proportions that "it is taking on the aura of gang warfare with attendant threats of murder and reprisals."

On January 30, 1969, this program against the BPP was expanded to additional offices, noting that the BPP was attempting to create a better image. In line with this effort, Bobby Seale was conducting a "purge" of the party, including expelling police informants. Recipient offices were instructed to take advantage of the opportunity to further plant the seeds of suspicion concerning disloyalty among ranking officials.

Bureau witnesses are not certain whether the Black Nationalist program was effective. Mr. Moore stated:

> I know that the . . . overall results of the Klan [COINTELPRO] was much more effective from what I have been told than the Black

> Extremism [COINTELPRO] because of the number of informants in the Klan who could take action which would be more effective. In the Black Extremism Group . . . we got a late start because we did not have extremist activity [until] '67 and '68. Then we had to play catch-up. . . . It is not easy to measure effectiveness. . . . There were policemen killed in those days. There were bombs thrown. There were establishments burned with Molotov cocktails. . . . We can measure that damage. You cannot measure over on the other side, what lives were saved because somebody did not leave the organization or suspicion was sown on his leadership and this organization gradually declined and [there was] suspicion within it, or this organization did not join with [that] organization as a result of a black power conference which was aimed towards consolidation efforts. All we know, either through their own ineptitude, maybe it emerged through counterintelligence, maybe, I think we like to think that that helped to do it, that there was not this development. . . . What part did counterintelligence [play?] We hope that it did play a part. Maybe we just gave it a nudge."

7. New Left.—The Internal Security Section had undergone a slow transition from concentrating on the "Old Left"—the CPUSA and SWP—to focusing primarily on the activities of the "New Left"—a term which had no precise definition within the Bureau. Some agents defined "New Left" functionally, by connection with protests. Others defined it by philosophy, particularly antiwar philosophy.

On October 28, 1968, the fifth and final COINTELPRO was started against this undefined group. The program was triggered in part by the Columbia campus disturbance. Once again, law enforcement methods had broken down, largely (in the Bureau's opinion) because college administrators refused to call the police on campus to deal with student demonstrations. The atmosphere at the time was described by the Headquarters agent who supervised the New Left COINTELPRO:

> During that particular time, there was considerable public, Administration—I mean governmental Administration—[and] news media interest in the protest movement to the extent that some groups, I don't recall any specifics, but some groups were calling for something to be done to blunt or reduce the protest movements that were

> disrupting campuses. I can't classify it as exactly an hysteria, but there was considerable interest [and concern]. That was the framework that we were working with. . . . It would be my impression that as a result of this hysteria, some governmental leaders were looking to the Bureau.

And, once again, the combination of perceived threat, public outcry, and law enforcement frustration produced a COINTELPRO.

According to the initiating letter, the counterintelligence program's purpose was to "expose, disrupt, and otherwise neutralize" the activities of the various New Left organizations, their leadership, and adherents, with particular attention to Key Activists, "the moving forces behind the New Left." The final paragraph contains an exhortation to a "forward look, enthusiasm, and interest" because of the Bureau's concern that "the anarchist activities of a few can paralyze institutions of learning, induction centers, cripple traffic, and tie the arms of law enforcement officials all to the detriment of our society." The internal memorandum recommending the program further sets forth the Bureau's concerns:

> Our Nation is undergoing an era of disruption and violence caused to a large extent by various individuals generally connected with the New Left. Some of these activists urge revolution in America and call for the defeat of the United States in Vietnam. They continually and falsely allege police brutality and do not hesitate to utilize unlawful acts to further their so-called causes.

The document continues:

> The New Left has on many occasions viciously and scurrilously attacked the Director and the Bureau in an attempt to hamper our investigation of it and to drive us off the college campuses.

Based on those factors, the Bureau decided to institute a new COINTELPRO.

8. New Left Directives.—The Bureau's concern with "tying the hands of law enforcement officers," and with the perceived weakness of college administrators in refusing to call police onto the campus, led to a May 23, 1968, directive to all participating field offices to gather information on three categories of New Left activities:

> (1) false allegations of police brutality, to "counter the wide-spread charges of police brutality that invariably arise following student-police encounters";
>
> (2) immorality, depicting the "scurrilous and depraved nature of many of the characters, activities, habits, and living conditions representative of New Left adherents"; and
>
> (3) action by college administrators, "to show the value of college administrators and school officials taking a firm stand," and pointing out "whether and to what extent faculty members rendered aid and encouragement."

The letter continues, "Every avenue of possible embarrassment must be vigorously and enthusiastically explored. It cannot be expected that information of this type will be easily obtained, and an imaginative approach by your personnel is imperative to its success."

The order to furnish information on "immorality" was not carried out with sufficient enthusiasm. On October 9, 1968, headquarters sent another letter to all offices, taking them to task for their failure to "remain alert for and to seek specific data, depicting the depraved nature and moral looseness of the New Left" and to "use this material in a vigorous and enthusiastic approach to neutralizing them." Recipient offices were again instructed to be "particularly alert for this type of data" and told:

> As the current school year commences, it can be expected that the New Left with its anti-war and anti-draft entourage will make every effort to confront college authorities, stifle military recruiting, and frustrate the Selective Service System. Each office will be expected, therefore, to afford this program continuous effective attention in order that no opportunity will be missed to destroy this insidious movement.

As to the police brutality and "college administrator" categories, the Bureau's belief that getting tough with students and demonstrators would solve the problem, and that any injuries which resulted were deserved, is reflected in the Bureau's reaction to allegations of police brutality following the Chicago Democratic Convention.

On August 28, 1968, a letter was sent to the Chicago field office instructing it to "obtain all possible evidence that would disprove these charges" [that the Chicago police used undue force] and to "consider measures by which cooperative news media may be used to counteract these allegations." The administrative "note" (for the file) states:

> Once again, the liberal press and the bleeding hearts and the forces on the left are taking advantage of the situation in Chicago surrounding the Democratic National Convention to attack the police and organized law enforcement agencies. . . . We should be mindful of this situation and develop all possible evidence to expose this activity and to refute these false allegations.

In the same vein, on September 9, 1968, an instruction was sent to all offices which had sent informants to the Chicago convention demonstrations, ordering them to debrief the informants for information "indicating incidents were staged to show police reacted with undue force and any information that authorities were baited by militants into using force." The offices were also to obtain evidence of possible violations of anti-riot laws.

The originating New Left letter had asked all recipient offices to respond with suggestions for counterintelligence action. Those responses were analyzed and a letter sent to all offices on July 6, 1968, setting forth twelve suggestions for counterintelligence action which could be utilized by all offices. Briefly the techniques are:

(1) preparing leaflets designed to discredit student demonstrators, using photographs of New Left leadership at the respective universities. "Naturally, the most obnoxious pictures should be used";
(2) instigating "personal conflicts or animosities" between New Left leaders;
(3) creating the impression that leaders are "informants for the Bureau or other law enforcement agencies";
(4) sending articles from student newspapers or the "underground press" which show the depravity of the New Left to university officials, donors, legislators, and parents. "Articles showing advocation of the use of narcotics and free sex are ideal";

(5) having members arrested on marijuana charges;
(6) sending anonymous letters about a student's activities to parents, neighbors, and the parents' employers. "This could have the effect of forcing the parents to take action";
(7) sending anonymous letters or leaflets describing the "activities and associations" of New Left faculty members and graduate assistants to university officials, legislators, Boards of Regents, and the press. "These letters should be signed 'A Concerned Alumni,' or 'A Concerned Taxpayer' ";
(8) using "cooperative press contacts" to emphasize that the "disruptive elements" constitute a "minority" of the students. "The press should demand an immediate referendum on the issue in question";
(9) exploiting the "hostility" among the SDS and other New Left groups toward the SWP, YSA, and Progressive Labor Party;
(10) using "friendly news media" and law enforcement officials to disrupt New Left coffeehouses near military bases which are attempting to "influence members of the Armed Forces";
(11) using cartoons, photographs, and anonymous letters to "ridicule" the New Left; and
(12) using "misinformation" to "confuse and disrupt" New Left activities, such as by notifying members that events have been cancelled.

As noted earlier, the lack of any Bureau definition of "New Left" resulted in targeting almost every anti-war group, and spread to students demonstrating against anything. One notable example is a proposal targeting a student who carried an "obscene" sign in a demonstration protesting administration censorship of the school newspaper, and another student who sent a letter to that paper defending the demonstration. Another article regarding "free love" on a university campus was anonymously mailed to college administrators and state officials since free love allows "an atmosphere to build up on campus that will be a fertile field for the New Left."

None of the Bureau witnesses deposed believes the New Left COINTELPRO was generally effective, in part because of the imprecise targeting.

III. THE GOALS OF COINTELPRO: PREVENTING OR DISRUPTING THE EXERCISE OF FIRST AMENDMENT RIGHTS

The origins of COINTELPRO demonstrate that the Bureau adopted extralegal methods to counter perceived threats to national security and public order because the ordinary legal processes were believed to be insufficient to do the job. In essence, the Bureau took the law into its own hands, conducting a sophisticated vigilante operation against domestic enemies.

The risks inherent in setting aside the laws, even though the purpose seems compelling at the time, were described by Tom Charles Huston in his testimony before the Committee:

> The risk was that you would get people who would be susceptible to political considerations as opposed to national security considerations, or would construe political considerations to be national security considerations, to move from the kid with a bomb to the kid with a picket sign, and from the kid with the picket sign to the kid with the bumper sticker of the opposing candidate. And you just keep going down the line.

The description is apt. Certainly, COINTELPRO took in a staggering range of targets. As noted earlier, the choice of individuals and organizations to be neutralized and disrupted ranged from the violent elements of the Black Panther Party to Martin Luther King, Jr., who the Bureau concedes was an advocate of nonviolence; from the Communist Party to the Ku Klux Klan; and from the advocates of violent revolution such as the Weathermen, to the supporters of peaceful social change, including the Southern Christian Leadership Conference and the Inter-University Committee for Debate on Foreign Policy.

The breadth of targeting springs partly from a lack of definition for the categories involved, and partly from the Bureau's belief that dissident speech and association should be prevented because they were incipient steps toward the possible ultimate commission of an act which might be criminal. Thus, the Bureau's self-imposed role as protector of the existing political and social order blurred the line between targeting criminal activity and constitutionally protected acts and advocacy.

The clearest example of actions directly aimed at the exercise of constitutional rights are those targeting speakers, teachers, writers or publications, and meetings or peaceful demonstrations. Approximately 18 percent of all approved COINTELPRO proposals fell into these categories.

The cases include attempts (sometimes successful) to get university and high school teachers fired; to prevent targets from speaking on campus; to stop chapters of target groups from being formed; to prevent the distribution of books, newspapers, or periodicals; to disrupt news conferences; to disrupt peaceful demonstrations, including the SCLC's Washington Spring Project and Poor People's Campaign, and most of the large antiwar marches; and to deny facilities for meetings or conferences.

{ . . . }

IV. COINTELPRO TECHNIQUES

The techniques used in COINTELPRO were—and are—used against hostile foreign intelligence agents. Sullivan's testimony that the "rough, tough, dirty business" of foreign counterintelligence was brought home against domestic enemies was corroborated by George Moore, whose Racial Intelligence Section supervised the White Hate and Black Nationalist COINTELPROs:

> You can trace [the origins] up and back to foreign intelligence, particularly penetration of the group by the individual informant. Before you can engage in counterintelligence you must have intelligence. . . . If you have good intelligence and know what it's going to do, you can seed distrust, sow misinformation. The same technique is used in the foreign field. The same technique is used, misinformation, disruption, is used in the domestic groups, although in the domestic groups you are dealing in '67 and '68 with many, many more across the country . . . than you had ever dealt with as far as your foreign groups.

The arsenal of techniques used in the Bureau's secret war against domestic enemies ranged from the trivial to the life-endangering. Slightly more than a quarter of all approved actions were intended to promote factionalization within groups and between groups; a roughly equal number of actions involved the creation and dissemination of propaganda. Other techniques involved the use of federal, state, and local agencies in selective law enforcement, and other use (and abuse) of government processes;

disseminating derogatory information to family, friends, and associates; contacting employers; exposing "communist infiltration" or support of target groups; and using organizations which were hostile to target groups to disrupt meetings or otherwise attack the targets.

A. Propaganda

The Bureau's COINTELPRO propaganda efforts stem from the same basic premise as the attacks on speaking, teaching, writing and meeting: propaganda works. Certain ideas are dangerous, and if their expression cannot be prevented, they should be countered with Bureau-approved views. Three basic techniques were used: (1) mailing reprints of newspaper and magazine articles to group members or potential supporters intended to convince them of the error of their ways; (2) writing articles for or furnishing information to "friendly" media sources to "expose" target groups; and (3) writing, printing, and disseminating pamphlets and fliers without identifying the Bureau as the source.

1. Reprint Mailings

The documents contain case after case of articles and newspaper clippings being mailed (anonymously, of course) to group members. The Jewish members of the Communist Party appear to have been inundated with clippings dealing with Soviet mistreatment of Jews. Similarly, Jewish supporters of the Black Panther Party received articles from the BPP newspaper containing anti-Semitic statements. College administrators received reprints of a *Reader's Digest* article and a *Barron's* article on campus disturbances intended to persuade them to "get tough."

Perhaps only one example need be examined in detail, and that only because it clearly sets forth the purpose of propaganda reprint mailings. Fifty copies of an article entitled "Rabbi in Vietnam Says Withdrawal Not the Answer," described as "an excellent article in support of United States foreign policy in Vietnam," were mailed to certain unnamed professors and members of the Vietnam Day Committee "who have no other subversive organizational affiliations." The purpose of the mailing was "to convince [the recipients] of the correctness of the U.S. foreign policy in Vietnam."

Reprint mailings would seem to fall under Attorney General {Edward} Levi's characterization of much of COINTELPRO as "foolishness." They violate no one's civil rights, but should the Bureau be in the anonymous propaganda business?

2. "Friendly" Media

Much of the Bureau's propaganda efforts involved giving information or articles to "friendly" media sources who could be relied upon not to reveal the Bureau's interests. The Crime Records Division of the Bureau was responsible for public relations, including all headquarters contacts with the media. In the course of its work (most of which had nothing to do with COINTELPRO) the Division assembled a list of "friendly" news media sources—those who wrote pro-Bureau stories. Field offices also had "confidential sources" (unpaid Bureau informants) in the media, and were able to ensure their cooperation.

The Bureau's use of the news media took two different forms: placing unfavorable articles and documentaries about targeted groups, and leaking derogatory information intended to discredit individuals.

A typical example of media propaganda is the headquarters letter authorizing the Boston Field Office to furnish "derogatory information about the Nation of Islam (NOI) to established source [name excised]":

> Your suggestions concerning material to furnish [name] are good. Emphasize to him that the NOI predilection for violence, preaching of race hatred, and hypocrisy, should be exposed. Material furnished [name] should be either public source or known to enough people as to protect your sources. Insure the Bureau's interest in this matter is completely protected by [name].

In another case, information on the Junta of Militant Organizations ("JOMO," a Black Nationalist target) was furnished to a source at a Tampa television station. Ironically, the station manager, who had no knowledge of the Bureau's involvement, invited the Special Agent in Charge, his assistant, and other agents to a preview of the half-hour film which resulted. The SAC complimented the station manager on his product, and suggested that it be made available to civic groups.

A Miami television station made four separate documentaries (on the Klan, Black Nationalist groups, and the New Left) with materials secretly supplied by the Bureau. One of the documentaries, which had played to an estimated audience of 200,000, was the subject of an internal memorandum "to advise of highly successful results of counterintelligence exposing the black extremist Nation of Islam."

> [Excised] was elated at the response. The station received more favorable telephone calls from viewers than the switchboard could handle. Community leaders have commented favorably on the program, three civic organizations have asked to show the film to their members as a public service, and the Broward County Sheriff's Office plans to show the film to its officers and in connection with its community service program.
>
> This exposé showed that NOI leaders are of questionable character and live in luxury through a large amount of money taken as contributions from their members. The extreme nature of NOI teachings was underscored. Miami sources advised the exposé has caused considerable concern to local NOI leaders who have attempted to rebut the program at each open meeting of the NOI since the program was presented. Local NOI leaders plan a rebuttal in the NOI newspaper. Attendance by visitors at weekly NOI meetings has dropped 50%. This shows the value of carefully planned counterintelligence action.

The Bureau also planted derogatory articles about the Poor People's Campaign, the Institute for Policy Studies, the Southern Students Organizing Committee, the National Mobilization Committee, and a host of other organizations it believed needed to be seen in their "true light."

3. Bureau-Authored Pamphlets and Fliers

The Bureau occasionally drafted, printed, and distributed its own propaganda. These pieces were usually intended to ridicule their targets, rather than offer "straight" propaganda on the issue. Four of these fliers are reproduced in the following pages.

FLY UNITED?

NEW MOBE

S.W.P.

BALLS!

Dig.it. It's time to pull the chain, brothers and sisters. If the peace movement in Amerika is to survive, the crap influence of the Socialist Workers Party and its bastard youth group - Young Socialist Alliance - must be flushed from New Mobe once and for all. Stagnant zeros like Freddie Halstead and Harry Ring, both members of the SWP Nat'l Committee, must be dumped. Let's get rid of the Carol Lipmans, Gus Horowitzs and the Joanna Misniks along with other SWP shits! DEMAND AN END TO SWP BALLING! Write New Mobe today at Suite 900, 1029 Vermont Ave., N.W., Washington, D.C.

Memorandum from New York Field Office to FBI Headquarters, 1/14/70; memorandum from FBI Headquarters to New York Field Office, 1/20/70.

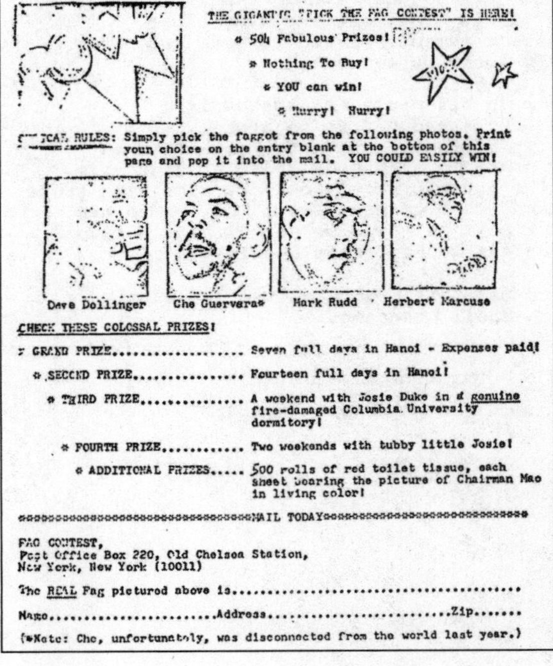

THE GIGANTIC "PICK THE FAG CONTEST" IS HERE!

* 504 Fabulous Prizes!
* Nothing To Buy!
* YOU can win!
* Hurry! Hurry!

OFFICIAL RULES: Simply pick the faggot from the following photos. Print your choice on the entry blank at the bottom of this page and pop it into the mail. YOU COULD EASILY WIN!

Dave Dollinger — Che Guervara* — Mark Rudd — Herbert Marcuse

CHECK THESE COLOSSAL PRIZES!

* GRAND PRIZE.................... Seven full days in Hanoi - Expenses paid!
* SECOND PRIZE................ Fourteen full days in Hanoi!
* THIRD PRIZE.................. A weekend with Josie Duke in a genuine fire-damaged Columbia University dormitory!
* FOURTH PRIZE............ Two weekends with tubby little Josie!
* ADDITIONAL PRIZES..... 500 rolls of red toilet tissue, each sheet bearing the picture of Chairman Mao in living color!

********************************MAIL TODAY********************************

FAG CONTEST,
Post Office Box 220, Old Chelsea Station,
New York, New York (10011)

The REAL Fag pictured above is.......................................

Name........................Address..........................Zip.......

(*Note: Che, unfortunately, was disconnected from the world last year.)

Memorandum from New York Field Office to FBI Headquarters, 2/7/69; memorandum from FBI Headquarters to New York Field Office, 2/14/69.

FLASH FLASH FLASH FLASH FLASH FLASH

DESPERATE DAVE DANGLES DINGUS

Murderously Mangles MOBE

Washington, D. C. Jan. 20 - Speaking in his usual high pitched voice, Dave Dellinger, National Chairman of the National Mobilization Committee (MOBE), today claimed that the anti-inaugural demonstrations called by his organization had been responsible in getting the Paris peace talks going again.

Dellinger made this startling disclosure before an audience of newsmen in the dingy Hawthorne School which housed many of his followers. A cluster of the latter stood behind their Guru sniffling and fingering wilted flowers. Dellinger, looking pale - more fairy-like than ever - tried to control the squeaks in his voice to no avail. "How many demonstrators did MOBE bring to the inaugural?", he was asked.

"At least 10,000, " he answered.

"Bullshit", was heard in several sections of the room.

Dellinger shuffled his notes. " Let's make that 5,000."

"Bullshit".

"Would you believe 3,000?" Silence. Dave rolled his eyes at the ceiling. "I'm not going to play at numbers, " he chirped. "What matters is that MOBE accomplished so much. We did get the peace talks going. We did break some windows in the National Geographic Society building. Despite police brutality, our brave people managed to throw cans and sticks at the President." His voice went higher - sounding like glass bells in a soft summer breeze. "We shook the establishment, gentlemen."

Associated Press stood up. "We understand MOBE is broke. That you lost control of the thing. That SDS and many other organizations in the peace movement refused to back you. That you have no idea how MOBE funds were spent."

Dellinger put a finger in his mouth and sucked it reflectively. Some minutes passed before he spoke. "MOBE is solvent, boys. As of this morning, we have $1.54 in the treasury. The price of peace is high." He tried to look grim. "SDS, of course, is just a bunch of dirty college kids with grass for brains. We didn't want them or need them." He formed his lips into a cute bow. "I must go now. We're hitching a ride back to New York today unless we can raise bus fare."

He shoved four fingers into his mouth and was led slowly from the room humming "We Shall Overcome."

Memorandum from New York Field Office to FBI Headquarters, 1/21/69; memorandum from FBI Headquarters to New York Field Office, 1/24/69.

Memorandum from New York Field Office to FBI Headquarters, 8/5/69; memorandum from FBI Headquarters to New York Field Office, 8/11/69.

B. Effects to Promote Enmity and Factionalism Within Groups or Between Groups

Approximately 28% of the Bureau's COINTELPRO efforts were designed to weaken groups by setting members against each other, or to separate groups which might otherwise be allies, and convert them into mutual enemies. The techniques used included anonymous mailings (reprints, Bureau-authored articles and letters) to group members criticizing a leader or an allied group; using informants to raise controversial issues; forming a "notional"—a Bureau-run splinter group—to draw away membership from the target organization; encouraging hostility up to and including gang warfare, between rival groups; and the "snitch jacket."

1. Encouraging Violence Between Rival Groups

The Bureau's attempts to capitalize on active hostility between target groups carried with them the risk of serious physical injury to the targets. As the Black Nationalist supervisor put it:

> It is not easy [to judge the risks inherent in this technique]. You make the best judgment you can based on all the circumstances and you always have an element of doubt where you are dealing with individuals that I think most people would characterize as having a degree of instability.

The Bureau took that risk. The Panther directive instructing recipient officers to encourage the differences between the Panthers and U.S., Inc., which were "taking on the aura of gang warfare with attendant threats of murder and reprisals," is just one example.

A separate report on disruptive efforts aimed at the Panthers will examine in detail the Bureau's attempts to foment violence. These efforts included anonymously distributing cartoons which pictured the U.S. organization gloating over the corpses of two murdered Panthers, and suggested that other BPP members would be next, and sending a New Jersey Panther leader the following letter which purported to be from an SDS member:

> To Former Comrade [name]
>
> As one of "those little bourgeois, snooty nose"—"little schoolboys"—"little sissies" Dave Hilliard spoke of in the "Guardian" of 8/16/69, I would like to say that you and the rest of you black racists can go to hell. I stood shoulder to shoulder with Carl Nichols last year in Military Park in Newark and got my a— whipped by a Newark pig all for the cause of the wineheads like you and the rest of the black pussycats that call themselves Panthers. Big deal; you have to have a three hour educational session just to teach those . . . (you all know what that means don't you! It's the first word your handkerchief head mamma teaches you) how to spell it.
>
> Who the hell set you and the Panthers up as the vanguard of the revolutionary and disciplinary group. You can tell all those wineheads you associate with that you'll kick no one's ". . . a—," because you'd have to take a three year course in spelling to know what an a— is and three more years to be taught where it's located.
>
> Julius Lester called the BPP the vanguard (that's leader) organization so international whore Cleaver calls him racist, now when full allegiance is not given to the Panthers, again racist. What the hell do you want? Are you getting this? Are you lost? If you're not digging then you're really hopeless.
>
> Oh yes! We are not concerned about Hilliard's threats.
>
> Brains will win over brawn. The way the Panthers have retaliated against US is another indication. The score: US–6: Panthers–0.

> Why, I read an article in the Panther paper where a California Panther sat in his car and watched his friend get shot by Karenga's group and what did he do? He run back and write a full page story about how tough the Panthers are and what they're going to do. Ha Ha—B— S—.
>
> Goodbye [name] baby—and watch out. Karenga's coming.
> "Right On" as they say.

An anonymous letter was also sent to the leader of the Blackstone Rangers, a Chicago gang "to whom violent type activity, shooting, and the like, are second nature," advising him that "the brothers that run the Panthers blame you for blocking their thing and there's supposed to be a hit out for you." The letter was intended to "intensify the degree of animosity between the two groups" and cause "retaliatory action which could disrupt the BPP or lead to reprisals against its leadership."

> Editor:
>
> What's with this bull— SDS outfit? I'll tell you what they has finally showed there true color White. They are just like the commies and all the other white radical groups that suck up to the blacks and use us. We voted at our meeting in Oakland for community control over the pigs but SDS says no. Well we can do with out them mothers. We can do it by ourselfs.
>
> OFF THE PIGS POWER TO THE PEOPLE
> Soul Brother Jake

In another case, the Bureau tried to promote violence, not between violent groups, but between a possibly violent person and another target. The field office was given permission to arrange a meeting between an SCLC officer and the leader of a small group described as "anti-Vietnam black nationalist [veterans'] organization." The leader of the veterans' group was known to be upset because he was not receiving funds from the SCLC. He was also known to be on leave from a mental hospital, and the Bureau had been advised that he would be recommitted if he were arrested on any charge. It was believed that "if the confrontation occurs at SCLC headquarters," the veterans' group leader "will lose his temper, start a fight," and the "police will be called in." The purpose was to "neutralize" the leader by causing his commitment to a mental hospital, and to gain "unfavorable publicity for the SCLC."

At least four assaults—two of them on women—were reported as "results" of Bureau actions. The San Diego field office claimed credit for three of them. In one case, US members "broke into" a BPP meeting and "roughed up" a woman member.

In the second instance, a critical newspaper article in the Black Panther paper was sent to the US leader. The field office noted that "the possibility exists that some sort of retaliatory actions will be taken against the BPP." The prediction proved correct; the field office reported that as a result of this mailing, members of US assaulted a Panther newspaper vendor. The third assault occurred after the San Diego Police Department, acting on a tip from the Bureau that "sex orgies" were taking place at Panther headquarters, raided the premises. (The police department conducted a "research project," discovered two outstanding traffic warrants for a BPP member, and used the warrants to gain entry.) The field office reported that as a "direct result" of the raid, the woman who allowed the officers into the BPP headquarters had been "severely beaten up" by other members.

In the fourth case, the New Haven field office reported that an informant had joined in a "heated conversation" between several group members and sided with one of the parties "in order to increase the tension." The argument ended with members hitting each other. The informant "departed the premises at this point, since he felt that he had been successful, causing a flammable situation to erupt into a fight."

2. Anonymous Mailings

The Bureau's use of anonymous mailings to promote factionalism range from the relatively bland mailing of reprints or fliers criticizing a group's leaders for living ostentatiously or being ineffective speakers, to reporting a chapter's infractions to the group's headquarters intended to cause censure or disciplinary action.

Critical letters were also sent to one group purporting to be from another, or from a member of the group registering a protest over a proposed alliance.

For instance, the Bureau was particularly concerned with the alliance between the SDS and the Black Panther Party. A typical example of anonymous mailing intended to separate these groups is a letter sent to the Black Panther newspaper.*

In a similar vein, is a letter mailed to Black Panther and New Left leaders.

> Dear Brothers and Sisters,
>
> Since when do us Blacks have to swallow the dictates of the honky SDS? Doing this only hinders the Party progress in gaining Black control over Black people. We've been — over by the white facists pigs and the Man's control over our destiny. We're sick and tired of being severly brutalized, denied our rights and treated like animals by the white pigs. We say to hell with the SDS and its honky intellectual approaches which only perpetuate control of Black people by the honkies.
>
> The Black Panther Party theory for community control is the only answer to our problems and that is to be followed and enforced by all means necessary to insure control by Blacks over all police departments regardless of whether they are run by honkies or uncle toms.
>
> The damn SDS is a paper organization with a severe case of diarrhea of the mouth which has done nothing but feed us lip service. Those few idiots calling themselves weathermen run around like kids on halloween. A good example is their "militant" activities at the Northland Shopping Center a couple of weeks ago. They call themselves revolutionaries but take a look at who they are. Most of them come from well heeled families even by honky standards. They think they're helping us Blacks but their futile, misguided and above all white efforts only muddy the revolutionary waters.
>
> The time has come for an absolute break with any non-Black group and especially those — SDS and a return to our pursuit of a pure black revolution by Blacks for Blacks.
>
> Power!
> Off the Pigs !!!!

* Editors' note: In a rare oversight, the text of this anonymous letter to the "Black Panther newspaper" is not reproduced in the original published report.

These examples are not, of course, exclusive, but they do give the flavor of the anonymous mailings effort.

3. Interviews

Interviewing group members or supporters was an overt "investigative" technique sometimes used for the covert purpose of disruption. For example, one field office noted that "other [BPP] weaknesses that have been capitalized on include interviews of members wherein jealousy among the members has been stimulated and at the same time has caused a number of persons to fall under suspicion and be purged from the Party."

In another case, fourteen field offices were instructed to conduct simultaneous interviews of individuals known to have been contacted by members of the Revolutionary Union. The purpose of the coordinated interviews was "to make possible affiliates of the RU believe that the organization is infiltrated by informants on a high level."

In a third instance, a "black nationalist" target attempted to organize a youth group in Mississippi. The field office used informants to determine "the identities of leaders of this group and in interviewing these leaders, expressed to them [the target's] background and his true intentions regarding organizing Negro youth groups." Agents also interviewed the target's landlords and "advised them of certain aspects of [his] past activities and his reputation in the Jackson vicinity as being a Negro extremist." Three of the landlords asked the target to move. The same field office reported that it had interviewed members of the Tougaloo College Political Action Committee, an "SNCC affiliated" student group. The members were interviewed while they were home on summer vacation. "Sources report that these interviews had a very upsetting effect on the PAC organization and they felt they have been betrayed by someone at Tougaloo College. Many of the members have limited their participation in PAC affairs since their interview by Agents during the summer of 1968."

4. Using Informants to Raise Controversial Issues

The Bureau's use of informants generally is the subject of a separate report. It is worth noting here, however, that the use of informants to take advantage of ideological splits in an organization dates back to the first COINTELPRO. The originating CPUSA document refers to the use of informants to capitalize on the discussion within the Party following Khrushchev's denunciation of Stalin.

Informants were also used to widen rifts in other organizations. For instance, an informant was instructed to imply that the head of one faction of the SDS was using group funds for his drug habit, and that a second leader embezzled funds at another school. The field office reported that "as a result of actions taken by this informant, there have been fist fights and acts of name calling at several of the recent SDS meetings." In addition, members of one faction "have made early morning telephone calls" to other SDS members and "have threatened them and attempted to discourage them from attending SDS meetings."

In another case, an informant was used to "raise the question" among his associates that an unmarried, 30-year-old group leader "may be either a bisexual or a homosexual." The field office believed that the question would "rapidly become a rumor" and "could have serious results concerning the ability and effectiveness of [the target's] leadership."

5. Fictitious Organizations

There are basically three kinds of "notional" or fictitious organizations. All three were used in COINTELPRO attempts to factionalize.

The first kind of "notional" was the organization whose members were all Bureau informants. Because of the Committee's agreement with the Bureau not to reveal the identities of informants, the only example which can be discussed publicly is a proposal which, although approved, was never implemented. That proposal involved setting up a chapter of the W.E.B. DuBois Club in a Southern city which would be composed entirely of Bureau informants and fictitious persons. The initial purpose of the chapter was to cause the CPUSA expense by sending organizers into the area, cause the Party to fund Bureau coverage of out-of-town CP meetings by paying the informants' expenses, and receive literature and instructions. Later, the chapter was to begin to engage in deviation from the Party line so that it would be expelled from the main organization "and then they could claim to be the victim of a Stalinist type purge." It was anticipated that the entire operation would take no more than 18 months.

The second kind of "notional" was the fictitious organization with some unsuspecting (non-informant) members. For example, Bureau informants set up a Klan organization intended to attract membership away from the United Klans of America. The Bureau paid the informant's personal expenses in setting up the new organization, which had, at its height, 250 members.

The third type of "notional" was the wholly fictitious organization, with no actual members, which was used as a pseudonym for mailing letters or pamphlets. For instance, the Bureau sent out newsletters from something called "The Committee for Expansion of Socialist Thought in America," which attacked the CPUSA from the "Marxist right" for at least two years.

6. Labeling Targets as Informants

The "snitch jacket" technique—neutralizing a target by labeling him a "snitch" or informant, so that he would no longer be trusted—was used in all COINTELPROs. The methods utilized ranged from having an authentic informant start a rumor about the target member, to anonymous letters or phone calls, to faked informants' reports.

When the technique was used against a member of a nonviolent group, the result was often alienation from the group. For example, a San Diego man was targeted because he was active in draft counseling at the city's Message Information Center. He had, coincidentally, been present at the arrest of a Selective Service violator, and had been at a "crash pad" just prior to the arrest of a second violator. The Bureau used a real informant to suggest at a Center meeting that it was "strange" that the two men had been arrested by federal agents shortly after the target became aware of their locations. The field office reported that the target had been "completely ostracized by members of the Message Information Center and all of the other individuals throughout the . . . area . . . associated with this and/or related groups."

In another case, a local police officer was used to "jacket" the head of the Student Mobilization Committee at the University of South Carolina. The police officer picked up two members of the Committee on the pretext of interviewing them concerning narcotics. By prearranged signal, he had his radio operator call him with the message, "[name of target] just called. Wants you to contact her. Said you have her number." No results were reported.

The "snitch jacket" is a particularly nasty technique even when used in peaceful groups. It gains an added dimension of danger when it is used—as, indeed, it was—in groups known to have murdered informers.

For instance, a Black Panther leader was arrested by the local police with four other members of the BPP. The others were released, but the leader remained in custody. Headquarters authorized the field office to circulate the rumor that the leader "is the last to be released" because "he is cooperating with and has made a deal with the Los Angeles Police Department to furnish them information concerning the BPP." The target of the first proposal then received an anonymous phone call stating that his own arrest was caused by a rival leader.

In another case, the Bureau learned that the chairman of the New York BPP chapter was under suspicion as an informant because of the arrest of another member for weapons possession. In order to "cast further suspicion on him" the Bureau sent anonymous letters to BPP headquarters in the state, the wife of the arrested member, and a local member of CORE, saying "Danger—Beware-Black Brothers, [name of target] is the fink who told the pigs that [arrested members] were carrying guns." The letter also gave the target's address.

In a third instance, the Bureau learned through electronic surveillance of the BPP the whereabouts of a fugitive. After his arrest, the Bureau sent a letter in a "purposely somewhat illiterate type scrawl" to the fugitive's half-brother:

> Brother:
>
> Jimmie was sold out by Sister [name—the BPP leader who made the phone call picked up by the tap] for some pig money to pay her rent. When she don't get it that way she takes Panther money. How come her kid sells the paper in his school and no one bothers him. How comes Tyler got busted up by the pigs and her kid didn't. How comes the FBI pig fascists knew where to bust Lonnie and Minnie way out where they were.
>
> —Think baby.

In another example, the chairman of the Kansas City BPP chapter went to Washington in an attempt to testify before a Senate subcommittee about information he allegedly possessed about the transfer of firearms from the Kansas City Police Department to a retired Army General. The attempt did not succeed; the committee chairman adjourned the hearing and then asked the BPP member to present his information to an aide. The Bureau then authorized an anonymous phone call to BPP headquarters "to the effect that [the target] was paid by the committee to testify, that he has cooperated fully with this committee, and that he intends to return at a later date to furnish additional testimony which will include complete details of the BPP operation in Kansas City."

In the fifth case, the Bureau had so successfully disrupted the San Diego BPP that it no longer existed. One of the former members, however, was " 'politicking' for the position of local leader if the group is ever reorganized." Headquarters authorized the San Diego field office to send anonymous notes to "selected individuals within the black community of San Diego" to "initiate the rumor that [the target], who has aspirations of becoming the local Black Panther Party Captain, is a police informant."

In a sixth case, a letter alleging that a Washington, D.C., BPP leader was a police informant was sent "as part of our continuing effort to foment internal dissension within ranks of Black Panther Party":

> Brother:
>
> I recently read in the Black Panther newspaper about that low dog Games down in Texas who betrayed his people to the pigs and it reminded me of a recent incident that I should tell you about. Around the first part of Feb. I was locked up at the local pigpen when the pigs brought in this dude who told me he was a Panther. This dude who said his name was [deleted] said he was vamped on by six pigs and was brutalized by them. This dude talked real bad and said he had killed pigs and was going to get more when he got out, so I thought he probably was one of you. The morning after [name] was brought in a couple of other dudes in suits came to see him and called him out of the cell and he was gone a couple of hours. Later on these dudes came back again to see him. [Name] told me the dudes were his lawyers but they smelled like pig to me. It seems to me that you might want to look into this because I know you don't want anymore low-life dogs helping the pigs brutalize the people. You don't know me and I'm not a Panther but I want to help with the cause when I can.
>
> A lumpen brother

In a seventh case, the "most influential BPP activist in North Carolina" had been photographed outside a house where a "shoot out" with local police had taken place. The photograph, which appeared in the local newspaper, showed the target talking to a policeman. The photograph and an accompanying article were sent to BPP headquarters in Oakland, California, with a handwritten note, supposedly from a female BPP member known to be "disenchanted" with the target, saying, "I think this is two pigs oinking."

Although Bureau witnesses stated that they did not authorize a "snitch jacket" when they had information that the group was *at that time* actually killing suspected informants, they admitted that the risk was there whenever the technique was used.

> It would be fair to say there was an element of risk there which we tried to examine on a case by case basis.

Moore added, "I am not aware of any time we ever labeled anybody as an informant, that anything [violent] ever happened as a result, and that is something that could be measured." When asked whether that was luck or lack of planning, he responded, "Oh, it just happened that way, I am sure."

C. Using Hostile Third Parties Against Target Groups

The Bureau's factionalism efforts were intended to separate individuals or groups which might otherwise be allies. Another set of actions is a variant of that technique; organizations already opposed to the target groups were used to attack them.

The American Legion and the Veterans of Foreign Wars, for example, printed and distributed under their own names Bureau-authored pamphlets condemning the SDS and the DuBois Clubs. In another case, a confidential source who headed an anti-Communist organization in Cleveland, and who published a "self-described conservative weekly newspaper," the *Cleveland Times,* was anonymously mailed information on the Unitarian Society of Cleveland's sponsorship of efforts to abolish the House Committee on Un-American Activities. The source had "embarrassed" the Unitarian minister with questions about the alleged Communist connections of other cosponsors "at public meetings."

It was anticipated that the source would publish a critical article in her newspaper, which "may very well have the result of alerting the more responsible people in the community" to the nature of the movement and "stifle it before it gets started."

The source newspaper did publish an article entitled "Locals to Aid Red Line," which named the Minister, among others, as a local sponsor of what it termed a "Communist dominated plot" to abolish the House Committee.

One group, described as a "militant anticommunist right wing organization, more of an activist group than is the more well-known John Birch Society," was used on at least four separate occasions. The Bureau developed a long-range program to use the organization in "counterintelligence activity" by establishing a fictitious person named "Lester Johnson" who sent letters, made phone calls, offered financial support, and suggested action:

> In view of the activist nature of this organization, and their lack of experience and knowledge concerning the interior workings of the [local] CP, [the field office proposes] that efforts be made to take over their activities and use them in such a manner as would be best calculated by this office to completely disrupt and neutralize the [local] CP, all without [the organization] becoming aware of the Bureau's interest in its operation.

"Lester Johnson" used the organization to distribute fliers and letters opposing the candidacy of a lawyer running for a judgeship and to disrupt a dinner at which an alleged Communist was to speak. "Johnson" also congratulated the organization on disrupting an anti-draft meeting at a Methodist Church, furnishing further information about a speaker at the meeting, and suggested that members picket the home of a local "communist functionary."

Another case is slightly different from the usual "hostile third party" actions, in that both organizations were Bureau targets. "Operation Hoodwink" was intended to be a long-range program to disrupt both La Cosa Nostra (which was not otherwise a COINTELPRO target) and the Communist Party by "having them expend their energies attacking each other." The initial project was to prepare and send a leaflet, which purported to be from a Communist Party leader to a member of a New York "family" attacking working conditions at a business owned by the family member.

D. Disseminating Derogatory Information to Family, Friends, and Associates

Although this technique was used in relatively few cases it accounts for some of the most distressing of all COINTELPRO actions. Personal life information, some of which was gathered expressly to be used in the programs, was then disseminated, either directly to the target's family through an anonymous letter or telephone call, or indirectly, by giving the information to the media.

Several letters were sent to spouses; three examples follow. The names have been deleted for privacy reasons.

The first letter was sent to the wife of a Grand Dragon of the United Klans of America ("Mrs. A"). It was to be "typed on plain paper in an amateurish fashion."

My Dear Mrs. (A),

I write this letter to you only after a long period of praying to God. I must cleanse my soul of these thoughts. I certainly do not want to create problems inside a family but I owe a duty to the klans and its principles as well as to my own menfolk who have cast their divine lot with the klans.

Your husband came to [deleted] about a year ago and my menfolk blindly followed his leadership, believing him to be the savior of this country. They never believed the stories that he stole money from the klans in [deleted] or that he is now making over $25,000 a year. They never believed the stories that your house in [deleted] has a new refrigerator, washer, dryer and yet one year ago, was threadbare. They refuse to believe that your husband now owns three cars and a truck, including the new white car. But I believe all these things and I can forgive them for a man wants to do for his family in the best way he can.

I don't have any of these things and I don't grudge you any of them neither. But your husband has been committing the greatest of the sins of our Lord for many years. He has taken the flesh of another unto himself.

Yes, Mrs. A, he has been committing adultery. My menfolk say they don't believe this but I think they do. I feel like crying. I saw her with my own eyes. They call her Ruby. Her last name is something like [deleted] and she lives in the 700 block of [deleted] Street in [deleted.] I know this. I saw her strut around at a rally with her lustfilled eyes and smart aleck figure.

I cannot stand for this. I will not let my husband and two brothers stand side by side with your husband and this woman in the glorious robes of the klan. I am typing this because I am going to send copys to Mr. Shelton and some of the klans leaders that I have faith in. I will not stop until your husband is driven from [deleted] and back into the flesh-pots from wherein he came.

I am a loyal klanswoman and a good churchgoer. I feel this problem affects the future of our great country. I hope I do not cause you harm by this and if you believe in the Good Book as I do, you may soon receive your husband back into the fold. I pray for you and your beautiful little children and only wish I could tell you who I am. I will soon, but I am afraid my own men would be harmed if I do.

A God-fearing klanswoman

The second letter was sent to the husband ("Mr. B") of a woman who had the distinction of being both a New Left and Black Nationalist target; she was a leader in the local branch of the Women's International League for Peace and Freedom, "which group is active in draft resistance, antiwar rallies and New Left activities," and an officer in ACTION, a biracial group which broke off from the local chapter of the Congress of Racial Equality and which "engaged in numerous acts of civil disruption and disobedience."

Two informants reported that Mr. B had been making suspicious inquiries about his wife's relationship with the Black males in ACTION. The local field office proposed an anonymous letter to the husband which would confirm his suspicions, although the informants did not know whether the allegations of misconduct were true. It was hoped that the "resulting marital tempest" would "result in ACTION losing: their [officer] and the WILPF losing a valuable leader, thus striking a major blow against both organizations."

Accordingly, the following letter, written in black ink, was sent to the husband:

Dear Mr. B

Look man I guess your old lady doesn't get enough at home or she wouldn't be shucking and jiving with our Black Men in ACTION, you dig? Like all she wants to integrate is the bed room ~~and we~~ Black Sisters ain't gonna take no second best from our men. . . So lay it on her, man— or get her the hell off Newstead.

A Soul Sister

Memorandum from FBI Headquarters to New York Field Office, 8/11/69.

A letter from the field office to headquarters four months later reported as a "tangible result" of the letter that the target and her husband had recently separated, following a series of marital arguments:

> This matrimonial stress and strain should cause her to function much less effectively in ACTION. While the letter sent by the [field office] was probably not the sole cause of this separation, it certainly contributed very strongly.

The third letter was sent to the wife of a leader of the Black Liberators ("Mrs. C"). She was living in their home town with their two daughters while he worked in the city. Bureau documents describe Mrs. C. as a "faithful, loving wife, who is apparently convinced that her husband is performing a vital service to the Black world. . . . She is to all indications an intelligent, respectable young mother, who is active in the AME Methodist Church."

The letter was "prepared from a penmanship, spelling style to imitate, that of the average Black Liberator member. It contains several accusations which should cause [X's] wife great concern." It was expressly intended to produce "ill feeling and possibly a lasting distrust" between X and his wife; it was hoped that the "concern over what to do about it" would "detract from his time spent in the plots and plans of his organization."

The letter was addressed to "Sister C":

~~Sister C~~

C Us Black Liberators are trained to
respect Black Women and special are wifes
and girls. Brother C keeps tellen
the Brothers this but he dont treat you
that way. I only been in the organisatoin
12 months but C been maken it here with
Sister Marva Bass & Sister Tony and than he gives
~~us the jive bout~~ their better in bed then you
and how he keeps you off his back
by senden you a little dough ever now an then.
He says he gotta send you money
the Draft board gonna shack him in the army
or somethin. This aint rite and were sayen that
is treaten you wrong —

A Black Liberator

The Petersen Committee said that some COINTELPRO actions were "abhorrent in a free society." This technique surely falls within that condemnation.

E. Contacts with Employers

The Bureau often tried to get targets fired, with some success. If the target was a teacher, the intent was usually to deprive him of a forum and to remove what the Bureau believed to be the added prestige given a political cause by educators. In other employer contacts, the purpose was either to eliminate a source of funds for the individual or (if the target was a donor) the group, or to have the employer apply pressure on the target to stop his activities.

For example, an Episcopal minister furnished "financial and other" assistance to the Black Panther Party in his city. The Bureau sent an anonymous letter to his bishop so that the church would exert pressure on the minister to "refrain from assistance to the Black Panther Party." Similarly, a priest who allowed the Black Panther Party to use his church for its breakfast program was targeted; his bishop received both an anonymous letter and three anonymous phone calls. The priest was transferred shortly thereafter.

In another case, a black county employee was targeted because he had attended a fund raiser for the Mississippi Summer Project and, on another occasion, a presentation of a Negro History Week program. Both functions had been supported by "clandestine CP members." The employee, according to the documents, had no record of subversive activities; "he and his wife appear to be genuinely interested in the welfare of Negroes and other minority groups and are being taken in by the communists." The Bureau chose a curiously indirect way to inform the target of his friends' Party membership; a local law enforcement official was used to contact the County Administrator in the expectation that the employee would be "called in and questioned about his left-wing associates."

The Bureau made several attempts to stop outside sources from funding target operations. For example, the Bureau learned that SNCC was trying to obtain funds from the Episcopal Church for a "liberation school." Two carefully spaced letters were sent to the Church which falsely alleged that SNCC was engaged in a "fraudulent scheme" involving the anticipated funds. The letters purported to be from local businessmen approached by SNCC to place fictitious orders for school supplies and divide the money when the Church paid the bills. Similar letters were sent to the Interreligious Foundation for Community Organizing, from which SNCC had requested a grant for its "Agrarian Reform Plan." This time, the letters alleged kickback approaches in the sale of farm equipment and real estate.

Other targets include an employee of the Urban League, who was fired because the Bureau contacted a confidential source in a foundation which funded the League; a lawyer known for his representation of "subversives," whose nonmovement client received an anonymous letter advising it not to employ a "well-known Communist Party apologist"; and a television commentator who was transferred after his station and superiors received an anonymous protest letter. The commentator, who had a weekly religious program, had expressed admiration for a black nationalist leader and criticized the United States' defense policy.

F. Use and Abuse of Government Processes

This category, which comprises 9 percent of all approved proposals, includes selective law enforcement (using Federal, state, or local authorities to arrest, audit, raid, inspect, deport, etc.); interference with judicial proceedings, including targeting lawyers who represent "subversives"; interference with candidates or political appointees; and using politicians and investigating committees, sometimes without their knowledge, to take action against targets.

1. Selective Law Enforcement

Bureau documents often state that notifying law enforcement agencies of violations committed by COINTELPRO targets is not counterintelligence, but part of normal Bureau responsibility. Other documents, however, make it clear that "counterintelligence" was precisely the purpose. "Be alert to have them arrested," reads a New Left COINTELPRO directive to all participating field offices. Further, there is clearly a difference between notifying other agencies of information that the Bureau happened across in an investigation—in plain view, so to speak—and instructing field offices to find evidence of violations—any violations—to "get" a target. As George Moore stated:

> Ordinarily, we would not be interested in health violations because it is not my jurisdiction, we would not waste our time. But under this program, we would tell our informants perhaps to be alert to any health violations or other licensing requirements or things of that nature, whether there were violations and we would see that they were reported.

State and local agencies were frequently informed of alleged statutory violations which would come within their jurisdiction. As noted above, this was not always normal Bureau procedure.

A typical example of the attempted use of local authorities to disrupt targeted activities is the Bureau's attempt to have a Democratic Party fundraiser raided by the state Alcoholic Beverage Control Commission. The function was to be held at a private house: the admission charge included "refreshments." It was anticipated that alcoholic beverages would be served. A confidential source in the ABC Commission agreed to send an agent to the fundraiser to determine if liquor was being served and then to conduct a raid. (In fact, the raid was cancelled for reasons beyond the Bureau's control. A prior raid on the local fire department's fundraiser had given rise to considerable criticism and the District Attorney issued an advisory opinion that such affairs did not violate state law. The confidential source advised the field office that the ABC would not, after all, raid the Democrats because of "political ramifications.")

In the second case, the target was a "key figure" Communist. He had a history of homosexuality and was known to frequent a local hotel. The Bureau requested that the local police have him arrested for homosexuality; it was then intended to publicize the arrest to "embarrass the Party." Interestingly, the Bureau withdrew its request when the target stopped working actively for the Party because it would no longer cause the intended disruption. This would appear to rebut the Bureau's contention that turning over evidence of violations to local authorities was not really COINTELPRO at all, but just part of its job.

2. Interference with Judicial Process

The Bureau's attempts to interfere with judicial processes affecting targets are particularly disturbing because they violate a fundamental principle of our system of government. Justice is supposed to be blind. Nevertheless, when a target appeared before a judge, a jury, or a probation board, he sometimes carried an unknown burden; the Bureau had gotten there first.

Three examples should be sufficient. A university student who was a leader of the Afro American Action Committee had been arrested in a demonstration at the university. The Bureau sent an anonymous letter to the county prosecutor intended to discredit her by exposing her "subversive connections"; her adoptive father was described as a Communist Party member. The Bureau believed that the letter might aid the prosecutor in his case against the student. Another anonymous letter containing the same information was mailed to a local radio announcer who had an "open mike" program critical of local "leftist" activity. The letter was intended to further publicize the "connection" between the student and the Communist Party.

In the second example, a Klan leader who had been convicted on a weapons charge was out on bail pending appeal. He spoke at a Klan rally, and the Bureau arranged to have newsmen present. The resulting stories and photographs were then delivered to the appellate judges considering his case.

The third instance involved a real estate speculator's bequest of over a million dollars to the three representatives of the Communist Party who were expected to turn it over to the Party. The Bureau interviewed the probate judge sitting on the case, who was "very cooperative" and promised to look the case over carefully. The judge asked the Bureau to determine whether the widow would be willing to "take any action designed to keep the Communist Party from getting the money." The Bureau's efforts to gain the widow's help in contesting the will proved unsuccessful.

3. Candidates and Political Appointees

The Bureau apparently did not trust the American people to make the proper choices in the voting booth. Candidates who, in the Bureau's opinion, should not be elected were therefore targeted. The case of the Democratic fundraiser discussed earlier was just one example.

Socialist Workers Party candidates were routinely selected for counterintelligence, although they had never come close to winning an election. In one case, a SWP candidate for state office inadvertently protected herself from action by announcing at a news conference that she had no objections to premarital sex; a field office thereupon withdrew its previously approved proposal to publicize her common law marriage.

Other candidates were also targeted. A Midwest lawyer whose firm represented "subversives" (defendants in the Smith Act trials) ran for City Council. The lawyer had been active in the civil rights movement in the South, and the John Birch Society in his city had recently mailed a book called "It's Very Simple—The True Story of Civil Rights" to various ministers, priests, and rabbis. The Bureau received a copy of the mailing list from a source in the Birch Society and sent an anonymous follow-up letter to the book's recipients noting the pages on which the candidate had been mentioned and calling their attention to the "Communist background" of this "charlatan." The Bureau also sent a fictitious-name letter to a television station on which the candidate was to appear, enclosing a series of informative questions it believed should be asked. The candidate was defeated. He subsequently ran (successfully, as it happened) for a judgeship.

Political appointees were also targeted. One target was a member of the board of the NAACP and the Democratic State Central Committee. His brother, according to the documents, was a communist, and the target had participated in some Party youth group activities fifteen years earlier. The target's appointment as secretary of a city transportation board elicited an anonymous letter to the Mayor, with carbons to two newspapers, protesting the use of "US taxpayers' money" in the appointment of a "known Communist" to a highly paid job; more anonymous letters to various politicians, the American Legion, and the county prosecutor in the same vein; and a pseudonymous letter to the members of the transportation board, stating that the Mayor had "saddled them with a Commie secretary because he thinks it will get him a few Negro votes."

4. Investigating Committees

State and Federal legislative investigating committees were occasionally used to attack a target, since the committees' interests usually marched with the Bureau's.

Perhaps the most elaborate use of an investigating committee was the framing of a complicated "snitch jacket." In October 1959, a legislative committee held hearings in Philadelphia, "ostensibly" to show a resurgence of CP activity in the area. The Bureau's target was subpoenaed to appear before the committee but was not actually called to testify. The field office proposed that local CP leaders be contacted to raise the question of "how it was possible for [the target] to escape testifying" before the committee; this "might place suspicion on him as being cooperative" with the investigators and "raise sufficient doubt in the minds of the leaders regarding [the target] to force him out of the CP or at least to isolate and neutralize him." Strangely enough, the target was not a bona fide CP member; he was an undercover infiltrator for a private anti-Communist group who had been a source of trouble for the FBI because he kept getting in their way.

A more typical example of the use of a legislative committee is a series of anonymous letters sent to the chairman of a state investigating committee that was designated to look into New Left activities on the state's college campuses. The target was an activist professor, and the letters detailed his "subversive background."

G. Exposing "Communist Infiltration" of Groups

This technique was used in approximately 4 percent of all approved proposals. The most common method involved anonymously notifying the group (civil rights organization, PTA, Boy Scouts, etc.) that one or more of its members was a "Communist," so that it could take whatever action it deemed appropriate. Occasionally, however, the group itself was the COINTELPRO target. In those cases, the information went to the media, and the intent was to link the group to the Communist Party.

For example, one target was a Western professor who was the immediate past president of a local peace center, "a coalition of anti-Vietnam and antidraft groups." He had resigned to become chairman of the state's McCarthy campaign organization, but it was anticipated that he would return to the peace center after the election. According to the documents, the professor's wife had been a Communist Party member in the early 1950s. This information was furnished to a newspaper editor who had written an editorial branding the SDS and various black power groups as "professional revolutionists." The information was intended to "expose these people at this time when they are receiving considerable publicity to not only educate the public to their character, but disrupt the members" of the peace organization.

In another case, the Bureau learned through electronic surveillance of a civil rights leader's plans to attend a reception at the Soviet Mission to the United Nations. (The reception was to honor a Soviet author.) The civil rights leader was active in a school boycott which had been previously targeted; the Bureau arranged to have news photographers at the scene to photograph him entering the Soviet mission.

Other instances include furnishing information to the media on the participation of the Communist Party Presidential candidate in a United Farm Workers' picket line "confidentially" telling established sources of three Northern California newspapers that the San Francisco County CP Committee had stated that the Bay area civil rights groups would "begin working" on the area's large newspapers "in an effort to secure greater employment of Negroes"; and furnishing information on Socialist Workers Party participation in the Spring Mobilization Committee to End the War in Vietnam to "discredit" the antiwar group by tying it "into the subversive movement."

V. COMMAND AND CONTROL: THE PROBLEM OF OVERSIGHT

A. Within the Bureau

1. Internal Administration

The Bureau attempted to exercise stringent internal controls over COINTELPRO. All counterintelligence proposals had to be approved by headquarters. Every originating COINTELPRO document contains a strong warning to the field that "no counterintelligence action may be initiated by the field without specific Bureau authorization." The field would send a proposal under the COINTELPRO caption to the Seat of Government—the Bureau term for headquarters—where it would be routed to the Section Chief of the section handling the particular COINTELPRO program.

The recommendation would then be attached to the proposal, beginning the process of administrative review. The lowest level on which a proposal could be approved was the Assistant Director, Domestic Intelligence Division, to whom the Section Chief reported *via* the Branch Chief. More often, the proposal would go through the Assistant to the Director and often to the Director himself.

{ . . . }

B. Outside the Bureau: 1956–1971

There is no clear answer to the question whether anyone outside the Bureau knew about COINTELPRO. One of the hallmarks of COINTELPRO was its secrecy. No one outside the Bureau was to know it existed. A characteristic instruction appeared in the Black Nationalist originating letter:

> You are also cautioned that the nature of this new endeavor is such that under no circumstances should the existence of the program be made known outside the Bureau and appropriate within-office security should be afforded to sensitive operations and techniques considered under the program.

Thus, for example, anonymous letters had to be written on commercially purchased stationery; newsmen had to be so completely trustworthy that they were guaranteed not to reveal the Bureau's interest; and inquiries of law enforcement officials had to be under investigative pretext. In approving or denying any proposal, the primary consideration was preventing "embarrassment to the Bureau." Embarrassment is a term of art. It means both public relations embarrassment—criticism—and any revelation of the Bureau's investigative interest to the subject, which may then be expected to take countermeasures.

This secrecy has an obvious impact on the oversight process. There is some question whether anyone with oversight responsibility outside the Bureau was informed of COINTELPRO. In response to the Committee's request, the Bureau has assembled all documents available in its files which indicate that members of the executive and legislative branches were so informed.

1. Executive Branch

On May 8, 1958, Director Hoover sent two letters, one to the Honorable Robert Cutler, Special Assistant to President Eisenhower, and the other to Attorney General William Rogers, containing the same information. The Attorney General's letter is captioned "COMMUNIST PARTY,

USA-INTERNAL SECURITY." The letters are fairly explicit notification of the CPUSA COINTELPRO:

> In August of 1956, this Bureau initiated a program designed to promote disruption within the ranks of the Communist Party (CP) USA. . . . Several techniques have been utilized to accomplish our objectives.

The letters go on to detail use of informants to engage in controversial discussions, after which "acrimonious debates ensued, suspicions were aroused, and jealousies fomented"; and anonymous mailings of anti-communist material, both reprinted and Bureau-prepared, to active CP members. (Two examples of the Bureau's product were enclosed.) "Tangible accomplishments" achieved by the program were "disillusionment and defection among Party members and increased factionalism at all levels." However, the only techniques disclosed were use of informants and anonymous propaganda mailings. There is no record of any reply to these letters.

On January 10, 1961, letters from the Director were sent to Dean Rusk, Robert Kennedy, and Byron R. White, who were about to take office as Secretary of State, Attorney General, and Deputy Attorney General, respectively. The letters enclosed a top-secret summary memorandum setting forth the overall activities of the Communist Party, USA, and stated, "Our responsibilities in the internal security field and our counterattack against the CPUSA are also set out in this memorandum."

The five-page memorandum contains one section entitled "FBI Counterattack." This section details penetration of the Party at all levels with security informants; use of various techniques to keep the Party off-balance and disillusioned; infiltration by informants; intensive investigation of Party members; and prosecution. Only one paragraph of that report appears at all related to the Bureau's claim that the CPUSA COINTELPRO was disclosed:

> As an adjunct to our regular investigative operations, we carry on a carefully planned program of counterattack against the CPUSA which keeps it off balance. Our primary purpose in this program is to bring about disillusionment on the part of individual members which is carried on from both inside and outside the Party organization. [Sentence on use of informants to disrupt excised for security reasons.]

> In certain instances we have been successful in preventing communists from seizing control of legitimate mass organizations and have discredited others who were secretly operating inside such organizations. For example, during 1959 we were able to prevent the CPUSA from seizing control of the 20,000-member branch of the National Association for the Advancement of Colored People in Chicago, Illinois.

The only techniques disclosed were use of informants and COMINFIL exposure. There is no record of any replies to these letters.

On September 2, 1965, letters were sent to the Honorable Marvin Watson, Special Assistant to President Johnson and Attorney General Katzenbach (whose letter was captioned "PENETRATION AND DISRUPTION OF KLAN ORGANIZATIONS—RACIAL MATTERS"). These two-page letters refer to the Bureau's success in solving a number of cases involving racial violence in the South. They then detail the development of a large number of informants and the value of the information received from them.

One paragraph deals with "disruption":

> We also are seizing every opportunity to disrupt the activities of Klan organizations. Typical is the manner in which we exposed and thwarted a "kick back" scheme a Klan group was using in one southern state to help finance its activities. One member of the group was selling insurance to other Klan members and would deposit a generous portion of the premium refunds in the Klan treasury. As a result of action we took, the insurance company learned of the scheme and cancelled all the policies held by Klan members, thereby cutting off a sizable source of revenue which had been used to finance Klan activities.

Notifying an insurance company of a kick-back scheme involving its premiums is not a "typical" COINTELPRO technique. It falls within that grey area between counterintelligence and ordinary Bureau responsibilities. Nevertheless, the statement that the Bureau is "seizing every opportunity to disrupt the activities of Klan organizations" is considered by the Bureau to be notification of the White Hate COINTELPRO, even though it does not distinguish between the inevitable and sometimes proper disruption of intensive investigation and the intended disruption of covert action.

On September 3, 1965, Mr. Katzenbach replied to the Director's letter with a two-paragraph memorandum captioned "Re: Your memorandum of September 2, regarding penetration and disruption of Klan organizations." The body of the memorandum makes no reference to disruption, but praises the accomplishments of the Bureau in the area of Klan penetration and congratulates Director Hoover on the development of his informant system and the results obtained through it. The letter concludes:

> It is unfortunate that the value of these activities would in most cases be lost if too extensive publicity were given to them; however, perhaps at some point it may be possible to place these achievements on the public record, so that the Bureau can receive its due credit.

The Bureau interpreted this letter as approval and praise of its White Hate COINTELPRO. Mr. Katzenbach has said that he has no memory of this document, nor of the response. He testified that during his term in the Department he had never heard the terms "COINTEL" or COINTELPRO, and that while he was familiar with the Klan investigation, he was not aware of any improper activities such as letters to wives. Mr. Katzenbach added:

> It never occurred to me that the Bureau would engage in the sort of sustained improper activity which it apparently did. Moreover, given these excesses, I am not surprised that I and others were unaware of them. Would it have made sense for the FBI to seek approval for activities of this nature—especially from Attorneys General who did not share Mr. Hoover's political views, who would not have been in sympathy with the purpose of these attacks, and who would not have condoned the methods?

The files do not reveal any response from Mr. Watson.

On December 19, 1967, Director Hoover sent a letter to Attorney General Ramsey Clark, with a copy to Deputy Attorney General Warren Christopher, captioned "KU KLUX KLAN INVESTIGATIONS—FBI ACCOMPLISHMENTS" and attaching a ten-page memorandum with the same caption and a list of statements and publications regarding the Ku Klux Klan "and the FBI's role in investigating Klan matters." The memorandum was prepared "pursuant to your conversation with Cartha DeLoach of this Bureau concerning FBI coverage and penetration of the Ku Klux Klan."

The memo is divided into eleven sections: Background, Present Status, FBI Responsibility, Major Cases, Informants, Special Projects, Liaison with Local Authorities, Klan Infiltration of Law Enforcement, Acquisition of Weapons and Dynamite of the Ku Klux Klan, Interviews of Klansmen, and Recent Developments.

The first statement in the memorandum which might conceivably relate to the White Hate COINTELPRO appears under the heading "FBI Responsibility":

> . . . We conduct intelligence investigations with the view toward infiltrating the Ku Klux Klan with informants, neutralizing it as a terrorist organization, and deterring violence.

The Bureau considers the word "neutralize" to be a COINTELPRO key word.

Some specific activities which were carried out within the Bureau under the COINTELPRO caption are then detailed under the heading "Special Projects." The use of Bureau informants to effect the removal of Klan officers is set forth under the subheadings "Florida," "Mississippi," and "Louisiana." More significantly, the "Florida" paragraph includes the statement that, "We have found that by the removal of top Klan officers and provoking scandal within the state Klan organization through our informants, the Klan in a particular area can be rendered ineffective." This sentence, although somewhat buried should, if focused upon, have alerted the recipients to actions going beyond normal investigative activity. Other references are more vague, referring only to "containing the growth" or "controlling the expansion" of state Klans. There is no record of any reply to this letter, which Clark does not remember receiving:

> Did [these phrases in the letter] put me on notice? No. Why? I either did not read them, or if I did read them, didn't read them carefully. . . . I think I didn't read this. I think perhaps I had asked for it for someone else, and either bucked it on to them or never saw it.

He added, "I think that any disruptive activities, such as those you reveal, regarding the COINTEL program and the Ku Klux Klan, should be absolutely prohibited and subjected to criminal prosecution."

Finally, on September 17, 1969, a letter was sent to Attorney General Mitchell, with copies to the Deputy Attorney General and the Assistant Attorneys General of the Criminal Division, Internal Security Division, and Civil Division, captioned "INVESTIGATION OF KLAN ORGANIZATIONS-RACIAL MATTERS (KLAN)," which informs the recipients of the "significant progress we have recently made in our investigation of the Ku Klux Klan." The one-page letter states that, "during the last several months, while various national and state leaders of the United Klan of America remain in prison, we have attempted to negate the activities of the temporary leaders of the Ku Klux Klan."

The only example given is the "careful use and instruction of selected racial informants" to "initiate a split within the United Klans of America." This split was evidenced by a Klan rally during which "approximately 150 Klan membership cards were tacked to a cross and burned to signify this breach."

The letter concludes, "We will continue to give full attention to our responsibilities in an effort to accomplish the maximum possible neutralization of the Klan." There is no record of any replies to these letters.

While the only documentary evidence that members of the executive branch were informed of the existence of any COINTELPRO has been set forth above, the COINTELPRO unit chief stated that he was certain that Director Hoover orally briefed every Attorney General and President, since he wrote "squibs" for the Director to use in such briefings. He could not, however, remember the dates or subject matter of the briefings, and the Bureau was unable to produce any such "squibs" (which would not, in any case, have been routinely saved). Cartha DeLoach, former Assistant to the Director, testified that he "distinctly" recalled briefing Attorney General Clark, "generally . . . concerning COINTELPRO." Clark denied that DeLoach's testimony was either true or accurate, adding "I do not believe that he briefed me on anything even, as he says, generally concerning COINTELPRO, whatever that means." The Bureau has failed to produce any memoranda of such oral briefings, although it was the habit of both Director Hoover and DeLoach to write memoranda for the files in such situations.

{ . . . }

3. Legislative Branch

The Bureau has furnished excerpts from briefing papers prepared for the Director in his annual appearances before the House Appropriations Subcommittee. During the hearings pertaining to fiscal years 1958, 1959, 1960, 1961, 1963, 1966, and 1967, these briefing papers were given to the Director to be used in top secret, off-the-record testimony relating to the CPUSA and White Hate COINTELPROs. No transcripts are available of the actual briefings, and it is, therefore, not possible to determine whether the briefing papers were used at all, or, conversely, whether the Director went beyond them to give additional information. Additionally, portions of the briefing papers are underlined by hand and portions have been crossed out, also by hand. Some sections are both underlined and crossed out. The Bureau has not been able to explain the meaning of the underlining or cross marks. However, if the briefing papers were used as written, the Subcommittee was informed of the existence of the CPUSA and Klan COINTELPROs.

{...}

VI. EPILOGUE

On April 1, 1976, Attorney General Levi announced the establishment of a special review committee within the Department of Justice to notify COINTELPRO victims that they were the subjects of FBI activities directed against them. Notification will be made "in those instances where the specific COINTELPRO activity was improper, actual harm may have occurred, and the subjects are not already aware that they were the targets of COINTELPRO activities."

The review committee has established guidelines for determining which COINTELPRO activities were "improper," but it will be difficult to make that determination without giving an official imprimatur to questionable activities which do not meet the notification criteria. For example, there is little point in notifying all recipients of anonymous reprint mailings that they received their copy of a *Reader's Digest* article from the FBI, but the Department should not suggest that the activity itself is a proper Bureau function. Other acts which fall within the "grey area" between COINTELPRO and aggressive investigation present similar problems.

Nevertheless, a Departmental notification program is an important step toward redressing the wrongs done, and carries with it some additional benefits. For the first time, Departmental attorneys will review the original files, rather than relying on Bureau-prepared summaries. Further, the Department will have acknowledged—finally—that COINTELPRO was wrong. Official repudiation of the programs is long overdue.

The American people need to be assured that never again will an agency of the government be permitted to conduct a secret war against those citizens it considers threats to the established order. Only a combination of legislative prohibition and Departmental control can guarantee that COINTELPRO will not happen again. The notification program is an auspicious beginning.

3.

Dr. Martin Luther King, Jr., Case Study

I. INTRODUCTION

From December 1963 until his death in 1968, Martin Luther King, Jr., was the target of an intensive campaign by the Federal Bureau of Investigation to "neutralize" him as an effective civil rights leader. In the words of the man in charge of the FBI's "war" against Dr. King:

> No holds were barred. We have used [similar] techniques against Soviet agents. [The same methods were] brought home against any organization against which we were targeted. We did not differentiate. This is a rough, tough business.

The FBI collected information about Dr. King's plans and activities through an extensive surveillance program, employing nearly every intelligence-gathering technique at the Bureau's disposal. Wiretaps, which were initially approved by Attorney General Robert F. Kennedy, were maintained on Dr. King's home telephone from October 1963 until mid-1965; the SCLC headquarters telephones were covered by wiretaps for an even longer period. Phones in the homes and offices of some of Dr. King's close advisers were also wiretapped. The FBI has acknowledged 16 occasions on which microphones were hidden in Dr. King's hotel and motel rooms in an "attempt" to obtain information about the "private activities of King and his advisers" for use to "completely discredit" them.

FBI informants in the civil rights movement and reports from field offices kept the Bureau's headquarters informed of developments in the civil rights field. The FBI's presence was so intrusive that one major figure in the civil rights movement testified that his colleagues referred to themselves as members of "the FBI's golden record club." The FBI's formal program to discredit Dr. King with Government officials began with the distribution of a "monograph" which the FBI realized could "be regarded as a personal attack on Martin Luther King," and which was subsequently described by a Justice Department official as "a personal diatribe . . . a personal attack without evidentiary support."

Congressional leaders were warned "off the record" about alleged dangers posed by Reverend King. The FBI responded to Dr. King's receipt of the Nobel Peace Prize by attempting to undermine his reception by foreign heads of state, and American ambassadors in the countries that he planned to visit. When Dr. King returned to the United States, steps were taken to reduce support for a huge banquet and a special "day" that were being planned in his honor.

The FBI's program to destroy Dr. King as the leader of the civil rights movement entailed attempts to discredit him with churches, universities, and the press. Steps were taken to attempt to convince the National Council of Churches, the Baptist World Alliance and leading Protestant ministers to halt financial support of the Southern Christian Leadership Conference (SCLC), and to persuade them that "Negro leaders should completely isolate King and remove him from the role he is now occupying in civil rights activities." When the FBI learned that Dr. King intended to visit the Pope, an agent was dispatched to persuade Francis Cardinal Spellman to warn the Pope about "the likely embarrassment that may result to the Pope should he grant King an audience." The FBI sought to influence universities to withhold honorary degrees from Dr. King. Attempts were made to prevent the publication of articles favorable to Dr. King and to find "friendly" news sources that would print unfavorable articles. The FBI offered to play for reporters' tape recordings allegedly made from microphone surveillance of Dr. King's hotel rooms.

The FBI mailed Dr. King a tape recording made from its microphone coverage. According to the Chief of the FBI's Domestic Intelligence Division, the tape was intended to precipitate a separation between Dr. King and his wife in the belief that the separation would reduce Dr. King's stature. The tape recording was accompanied by a note which Dr. King and his advisers interpreted as a threat to release the tape recording unless Dr. King committed suicide. The FBI also made preparations to promote someone "to assume the role of leadership of the Negro people when King has been completely discredited."

The campaign against Dr. King included attempts to destroy the Southern Christian Leadership Conference by cutting off its sources of funds. The FBI considered, and on some occasions executed, plans to cut off the support of some of the SCLC's major contributors, including religious organizations, a labor union, and donors of grants such as the Ford Foundation. One FBI field office recommended that the FBI send letters to the SCLC's donors over Dr. King's forged signature warning them that the SCLC was under investigation by the Internal Revenue Service. The IRS files on Dr. King and the SCLC were carefully scrutinized for financial irregularities. For over a year, the FBI unsuccessfully attempted to establish that Dr. King had a secret foreign bank account in which he was sequestering funds.

The FBI campaign to discredit and destroy Dr. King was marked by extreme personal vindictiveness. As early as 1962, Director Hoover penned on an FBI memorandum, "King is no good." At the August 1963 March on Washington, Dr. King told the country of his dream that "all of God's children, black men and white men, Jews and Gentiles, Protestants and Catholics, will be able to join hands and sing in the words of the old Negro spiritual, 'Free at last, free at last. Thank God almighty, I'm free at last.'" The FBI's Domestic Intelligence Division described this "demagogic speech" as yet more evidence that Dr. King was "the most dangerous and effective Negro leader in the country." Shortly afterward, *Time* magazine chose Dr. King as the "Man of the Year," an honor which elicited Director Hoover's comment that "they had to dig deep in the garbage to come up with this one." Hoover wrote "astounding" across the memorandum informing him that Dr. King had been granted an audience with the Pope despite the FBI's efforts to prevent such a meeting. The depth of Director Hoover's bitterness toward Dr. King, a bitterness which he had effectively communicated to his subordinates in the FBI, was apparent from the FBI's attempts to sully Dr. King's reputation long after his death. Plans were made to "brief" congressional leaders in 1969 to prevent the passage of a "Martin Luther King Day." In 1970, Director Hoover told reporters that Dr. King was the "last one in the world who should ever have received" the Nobel Peace Prize.

{ . . . }

The FBI conducted its investigation of Dr. King and the SCLC under an FBI manual provision—called COMINFIL—permitting the investigation of legitimate noncommunist organizations, suspected by the FBI of having been infiltrated by communists, to determine the extent, if any, of communist influence. The FBI's investigation was based on its concern that Dr. King was being influenced by two persons—hereinafter referred to as Adviser A and Adviser B—that the Bureau believed were members of the Communist Party.

Officials in the Justice Department relied on the FBI's representations that both of these advisers were communists, that they were in a position to influence Dr. King, and that Adviser A in fact exercised some influence in preparing Dr. King's speeches and publications. Burke Marshall, Assistant Attorney General for Civil Rights from 1961–1965, testified that he "never had any reason to doubt [the FBI's] allegations concerning [Adviser A]." He recalled that the charges about Adviser A were "grave and serious," and said that he believed Attorney General Kennedy had permitted the investigation to proceed because:

> Stopping the investigation in light of those circumstances would have run the risk that there would have been a lot of complaints that the Bureau had been blocked for political reasons from investigating serious charges about communist infiltration in the civil rights movement.

Edwin Guthman, Press Secretary for the Justice Department from 1961 through 1964, testified that Attorney General Robert Kennedy "viewed this as a serious matter," that he did not recall "that any of us doubted that the FBI knew what it was talking about," and that although the question of whether Adviser A was influencing Dr. King was never fully answered "we accepted pretty much what the FBI reported as being accurate."

We have been unable to reach a conclusion concerning the accuracy of the FBI's charges that the two Advisers were members of the Communist Party, USA or under the control of the Party during the FBI's COMINFIL investigation. However, FBI files do contain information that Adviser A and Adviser B had been members of the Communist Party at some point prior to the opening of the COMINFIL investigation in October 1962. FBI documents provided to the Committee to support the Bureau's claim that both men were members of the Communist Party at the time the COMINFIL investigation was opened are inconclusive. Moreover, the FBI has stated that it cannot provide the Committee with the full factual basis for its charges on the grounds that to do so would compromise informants of continuing use to the Bureau.

Without access to the factual evidence, we are unable to conclude whether either of those two Advisers was connected with the Communist Party when the "case" was opened in 1962, or at any time thereafter. We have seen no evidence establishing that either of those Advisers attempted to exploit the civil rights movement to carry out the plans of the Communist Party.

In any event, the FBI has stated that at no time did it have any evidence that Dr. King himself was a communist or connected with the Communist Party. Dr. King repeatedly criticized Marxist philosophies in his writing and speeches. The present Deputy Associate Director of the FBI's Domestic Intelligence Division, when asked by the Committee if the FBI ever concluded that Dr. King was a communist, testified, "No, sir, we did not."

{ . . . }

Allegations of communist influence on Dr. King's organization must not divert attention from the fact that, as the FBI now states, its activities were unjustified and improper. In light of the Bureau's remarks about Dr. King, its reactions to his criticisms, the viciousness of its campaign to destroy him, and its failure to take comparable measures against the Advisers that it believed were communists, it is highly questionable whether the FBI's stated motivation was valid. It was certainly not justification for continuing the investigation of Dr. King for over six years, or for carrying out the attempts to destroy him.

Our investigation indicates that FBI officials believed that some of Dr. King's personal conduct was improper. Part of the FBI's efforts to undermine Dr. King's reputation involved attempts to persuade Government officials that Dr. King's personal behavior would be an embarrassment to them. The Committee did not investigate Dr. King's personal life, since such a subject has no proper place in our investigation. Moreover, in order to preclude any further dissemination of information obtained during the electronic surveillances of Dr. King, the Committee requested the FBI to excise from all documents submitted to the Committee any information which was so obtained. We raise the issue of Dr. King's private life here only because it may have played a part in forming the attitudes of certain FBI and administration officials toward Dr. King.

Many documents which we examined contained allegations about the political affiliations and morality of numerous individuals. We have attempted to be sensitive to the privacy interests of those individuals, and have taken care not to advance the effort to discredit them. We have excised many of the Bureau's characterizations from the documents quoted in this report. In some cases, however, in order fully to explain the story, it was judged necessary to quote extensively from Bureau reports, even though they contain unsupported allegations. We caution the reader not to accept these allegations on their face, but rather to read them as part of a shameful chapter in the nation's history.

The reader is also reminded that we did not conduct an investigation into the assassination of Dr. King. In the course of investigating the FBI's attempts to discredit Dr. King, we came across no indication that the FBI was in any way involved in the assassination.

II. THE COMINFIL INVESTIGATION

In October 1962 the FBI opened its investigation of the Southern Christian Leadership Conference and of its president, Dr. Martin Luther King, Jr. The investigation was conducted under an FBI manual provision captioned "COMINFIL"—an acronym for communist infiltration—which authorized investigations of legitimate noncommunist organizations which the FBI believed to be influenced by communist party members in order to determine the extent of the alleged communist influence. These wide-ranging investigations were conducted with the knowledge of the Attorney General and were predicated on vague executive directives and broad statutes.

The FBI kept close watch on Dr. King and the SCLC long before opening its formal investigation. FBI Director J. Edgar Hoover reacted to the formation of the SCLC in 1957 by reminding agents in the field of the need for vigilance:

> In the absence of any indication that the Communist Party has attempted, or is attempting, to infiltrate this organization you should conduct no investigation in this matter. However, in view of the stated

> purpose of the organization, you should remain alert for public source information concerning it in connection with the racial situation.

In May 1962 the FBI had included Dr. King on "Section A of the Reserve Index" as a person to be rounded up and detained in the event of a "national emergency." During this same period the FBI ordered its field offices to review their files for "subversive" information about Dr. King and to submit that information to FBI headquarters in reports "suitable for dissemination."

The Bureau had apparently also been engaged in an extensive surveillance of Dr. King's civil rights activities since the late 1950s under an FBI program called "Racial Matters." This program, which was unrelated to COMINFIL, required the collection of "all pertinent information" about the "proposed or actual activities" of individuals and organizations "in the racial field." Surveillance of Dr. King's civil rights activities continued under the Racial Matters program after the COMINFIL case was opened. Indeed, the October 1962 memorandum which authorized the COMINFIL case specifically provided that "any information developed concerning the integration or racial activities of the SCLC must [also] be reported [under a] Racial Matters caption."

The first FBI allegations that the Communist Party was attempting to infiltrate the SCLC appeared in a report from the FBI to Attorney General Robert F. Kennedy, dated January 8, 1962. The report stated that one of Dr. King's advisers—hereinafter referred to as "Adviser A"—was a "member of the Communist Party, USA." Within a few months FBI reports were describing another of Dr. King's associates—hereinafter referred to as "Adviser B"—as a "member of the National Committee of the Communist Party." The allegations concerning these two individuals formed the basis for opening the COMINFIL investigation in October 1962.

{ . . . }

Despite the goals and procedures outlined in the COMINFIL section of the FBI Manual, the Bureau's investigation of Dr. King did not focus on whether any of his advisers were acting under Communist Party discipline and control or were working to enable the Communist Party to influence or control the SCLC. The microphone which had been installed in Adviser A's office in March 1962 was discontinued before the COMINFIL investigation began, and, although wiretap coverage of Adviser A continued—and even intensified—the information obtained appears to have related solely to his advice to Dr. King concerning the civil rights movement and not at all to the alleged Communist Party origins of that advice. Two FBI reports prepared in succeeding years which summarize the FBI's information about Adviser A do not contain evidence substantiating his purported relationship with the Communist Party.

{ . . . }

The FBI sent frequent reports about Dr. King's plans and activities to officials in both the Justice Department and the White House from the initiation of the COMINFIL investigation until Dr. King's death in 1968. Despite the fact that the investigation of Dr. King failed to produce evidence that Dr. King was a communist, or that he was being influenced to act in a way inimical to American interests, no responsible Government official ever asked the FBI to terminate the investigation. Their inaction appears to have stemmed from the belief that it was safer for the FBI to conduct the investigation than to stop the Bureau and run the risk of charges that the FBI was being muzzled for political reasons.

Burke Marshall testified that the "charges" made by the Bureau against Adviser A "were grave and serious." The Kennedy Administration had been outspoken in its support of Dr. King, and ordering the FBI to terminate its investigation would, in Marshall's opinion, "have run the risk" that there would have been a lot of complaints that the Bureau had been blocked for political reasons from investigating serious charges about communist infiltration in the civil rights movement.

Edwin O. Guthman, Press Chief for the Justice Department under Attorney General Kennedy, testified that Robert Kennedy viewed the charges about Adviser A:

> as a serious matter and not in the interest of the country and not in the interest of the civil rights movement. . . . The question of whether he was influencing King and his contacts with King, that was a matter which was not fully decided, but in those days we accepted pretty much what the FBI reported as being accurate.

Guthman testified that he was told by Kennedy in 1968 that Kennedy had approved wiretap coverage of Dr. King's home and of two SCLC offices in October 1963 because "he felt that if he did not do it, Mr. Hoover would move to impede or block the passage of the Civil Rights Bill . . . and that he felt that he might as well settle the matter as to whether [Adviser A] did have the influence on King that the FBI contended. . . . " Attorney General Kennedy's reasons for approving the wiretaps are discussed at length in a subsequent chapter. Of relevance here is the support which Guthman's observations lend to Marshall's recollection that Attorney General Kennedy permitted the COMINFIL investigation to continue from concern about the truth of the FBI's charges and about the political consequences of terminating the investigation.

The Johnson Administration's willingness to permit the FBI to continue its investigation of Dr. King also appears to have involved political considerations. Bill Moyers, President Johnson's assistant, testified that sometime around the spring of 1965 President Johnson "seemed satisfied that these allegations about Martin Luther King were not founded." Yet President Johnson did not order the investigation terminated. When asked the reasons, Moyers explained that President Johnson:

> was very concerned that his embracing the civil rights movement and Martin Luther King personally would not backfire politically. He didn't want to have a southern racist Senator produce something that would be politically embarrassing to the President and to the civil rights movement. We had lots of conversations about that. . . . Johnson, as everybody knows, bordered on paranoia about his enemies or about being trapped by other people's activities over which he had no responsibility.

Intelligence reports submitted by the Bureau to the White House and the Justice Department contained considerable intelligence of potential value to the Kennedy and Johnson Administrations. The Attorneys General were informed of meetings between Dr. King and his advisers, including the details of advice that Dr. King received, the strategies of the civil rights movement, and the attitude of civil rights leaders toward the Administrations and their policies. The implications of this inside knowledge were graphically described by one of Dr. King's legal advisers, Harry Wachtel:

> The easiest example I can give is that if I'm an attorney representing one side, negotiating and trying to achieve something, and if the Attorney on the other side has information about what my client was

> thinking and what we were talking about, it would become a devastatingly important impediment to our negotiation, our freedom of action.

Burke Marshall, however, described the Bureau's reports about Dr. King and the SCLC as "of no use: it was stupid information." He elaborated:

> I was in touch with Martin King all the time about all kinds of information that went way beyond what was reported by the Bureau about what he was going to do, where he was going to be, the wisdom of what he was going to do, who he was going to do it with, what the political situation was. The Southern Christian Leadership Conference and Dr. King were in some sense close associates of mine. [Information of the type included in FBI reports] was all information that I would have had anyway.

III. CONCERN INCREASES IN THE FBI AND THE KENNEDY ADMINISTRATION OVER ALLEGATIONS OF COMMUNIST INFLUENCE IN THE CIVIL RIGHTS MOVEMENT, AND THE FBI INTENSIFIES THE INVESTIGATION: JANUARY 1962–OCTOBER 1963

Introduction and Summary

This chapter explores developments in the Martin Luther King case from the period preceding the FBI's opening of the COMINFIL investigation in October 1962 through the FBI's decision to intensify its investigation of suspected communist influence in the civil rights movement in October 1963. Particular emphasis is placed on the internal reasons for the FBI's intensification of its investigation of Dr. King and on the interplay between the Justice Department and the FBI during this period.

In summary, the evidence described in this chapter establishes that the FBI barraged the Justice Department with a stream of memoranda concerning the Communist Party's interest in the civil rights movement and Dr. King's association with two individuals, referred to in this report as Advisers A and B, who were alleged to have strong ties to the Party. In response to the Bureau's warnings, the Justice Department endeavored to convince Dr. King to sever his relations with those individuals, but met with only mixed success. Dr. King continued to turn to Adviser A for advice;

Adviser B, whose association with Dr. King and allegedly with the Communist Party had been picked up by the press in late 1962, publicly announced his resignation from the SCLC in early July 1963, although he apparently continued to associate with Dr. King on an informal basis.

During hearings over the administration's proposed public accommodations bill in July 1963, critics of the bill charged that the civil rights movement, and Dr. King in particular, were influenced by Communists. Dr. King's plans for a civil rights march on Washington in August were receiving increasing publicity. On July 16, the Attorney General raised with the FBI's Justice Department liaison, Courtney Evans, the possibility of a wiretap on Dr. King and one of his legal advisers.

The following day the FBI sent an analysis of its COMINFIL information to the Justice Department. The administration decided to continue its public support of Dr. King. During the ensuing week, the President informed the press that there was no evidence that civil rights demonstrations were Communist-inspired; the Attorney General announced that the FBI had no evidence that any civil rights leaders were controlled by Communists; and the Attorney General rejected the FBI's request for authority to wiretap Dr. King.

In August 1963, the Justice Department received a report from the FBI which apparently contained allegations extremely unfavorable to Dr. King. The Attorney General told Courtney Evans that he faced impeachment if the report was "leaked," and demanded that it be resubmitted with a cover memorandum detailing the factual basis for the allegation. The memorandum submitted in response to that request contained no information concerning Dr. King that had not already been known to the Attorney General in July, but the Attorney General permitted the investigation to proceed.

In late July 1963, the FBI opened a file entitled "Communist Influence in Racial Matters," and closely monitored preparations for the August 28 Civil Rights March on Washington. The FBI's Domestic Intelligence Division informed Director Hoover shortly before the March that Communist influence in the civil rights movement was negligible. The Director disagreed. The head of the Domestic Intelligence Division, William Sullivan, responded by recommending more intense FBI surveillance of the civil rights movement.

A. The Justice Department Warns Dr. King About Advisers A and B: January 1962–June 1963

The Kennedy administration's concern over FBI allegations that Communists were influencing the civil rights movement led the Justice Department to make several attempts to persuade Dr. King to sever his relations with Advisers A and B. In January 1962, Hoover first warned Attorney General Kennedy that Advisor A, a member of the Communist Party, U.S.A., "is allegedly a close adviser to the Reverend Martin Luther King." Shortly afterwards, Assistant Attorney General Burke Marshall of the Justice Department's Civil Rights Division told Dr. King that the Bureau claimed Adviser A was a communist and advised that they break off relations. According to an FBI memorandum, Deputy Attorney General Byron R. White also considered speaking with Dr. King about Adviser A, but decided against doing so when told by the FBI that revealing too much of the FBI's information might tip off Dr. King or Adviser A to the identity of certain FBI informants.

Dr. King gave no indication of breaking off relations with Advisor A, who was a close friend and trusted advisor. He did, however, apparently consider the adverse effects on the civil rights movement that his association with Adviser B might cause. In June 1962 the FBI intercepted a conversation in which Adviser A recommended that Dr. King informally use Adviser B as his executive assistant, noting that "as long as Adviser B did not have the title of Executive Director, there would not be as much lightning flashing around him." Dr. King was reported to have agreed, remarking that "no matter what a man was, if he could stand up now and say he is not connected, then as far as I am concerned, he is eligible to work for me."

On October 8, 1962, the FBI's Domestic Intelligence Division prepared a memorandum summarizing accounts that had previously appeared in newspapers concerning Adviser B's alleged Communist background and his association with Dr. King. The Division forwarded the memorandum to Cartha D. DeLoach, head of the Crime Records Division, the FBI's public relations arm, for "possible use by his contacts in the news media field in such Southern states as Alabama where Dr. King has announced that the next targets for integration of universities are located." DeLoach's signature and the notation, "handled, Augusta (illegible), Atlanta, 1–/19" appear on the recommendation.

The article was apparently disseminated, because an October 25,

1962, article in the *Augusta Chronicle* described Adviser B as a member of the CPUSA's National Committee who was serving as Dr. King's "Acting Executive Director." Dr. King publicly responded, on October 30, that "no person of known Communist affiliation" could serve on the staff of the SCLC and denied any knowledge that Adviser B had Communist affiliations. Dr. King also announced Adviser B's temporary resignation from the SCLC pending an SCLC investigation of the allegations.

A stream of memoranda from the FBI, however, warned the Justice Department that Adviser B continued as an associate of Dr. King despite his apparent resignation from the SCLC. In December, Director Hoover was cautioning the Attorney General that Adviser B continued to "represent himself as being affiliated with the New York Office of the SCLC and, during late November and early December 1962, was actively engaged in the work of this organization." A few days later, the Attorney General was informed that Advisers A and B were planning a "closeted . . . critical review" with Dr. King concerning the direction of the civil rights movement. Kennedy penned on the memorandum: "Burke—this is not getting any better."

In early February 1963, Dr. King asked the Justice Department for a briefing on Adviser B's background, apparently in response to newspaper articles about Adviser B resulting from the Bureau's campaign to publicize Adviser B's relationship with Dr. King. Assistant Attorney General Marshall noted in a memorandum that he had "been in touch with the Attorney General on this matter and is anxious to have it handled as soon as possible." Sometime later in February, Marshall spoke with Dr. King about severing his association with Advisers A and B. Memoranda from Director Hoover to the Justice Department during the ensuing months, however, emphasized that Dr. King was maintaining a close relationship with both men. Those memoranda to the Justice Department contained no new information substantiating the charges that either was a member of the Communist Party, or that either was carrying out the Party's policies.

The Attorney General's concern over Dr. King's association with the two advisers continued. A memorandum by Hoover states that on June 17, 1963:

> The Attorney General called and advised he would like to have Assistant Attorney General Burke Marshall talk to Martin Luther King and tell Dr. King he has to get rid of [Advisers A and B], that he should not have any contact with them directly or indirectly.

> I pointed out that if Dr. King continues this association, he is going to hurt his own cause as there are more and more Communists trying to take advantage of [the] movement and bigots down South who are against integration are beginning to charge Dr. King is tied in with Communists. I stated I thought Marshall could very definitely say this association is rather widely known and, with things crystalizing for them now, nothing could be worse than for Dr. King to be associated with it.

Marshall subsequently spoke with Dr. King about Advisers A and B. In a follow-up memorandum written several months later Marshall stated:

> I brought the matter to the attention of Dr. King very explicitly in my office on the morning of June 22 prior to a scheduled meeting which Dr. King had with the President. This was done at the direction of the Attorney General, and the President separately [and] strongly urged Dr. King that there should be no further connection between Adviser B and the Southern Christian Leadership Conference. Dr. King stated that the connection would be ended.

Dr. King later told one of his associates that the President had told him "there was an attempt (by the FBI) to smear the movement on the basis of Communist influence. The President also said, 'I assume you know you're under very close surveillance.'"

Marshall's and the President's warnings did not go unheeded. On July 3, 1963, Dr. King sent the Attorney General a copy of a letter to Adviser B bearing that date. In that letter, Dr. King stated that an investigation by the SCLC had proven the charges concerning Adviser B's association with the Communist Party groundless, but that his permanent resignation was necessary because "the situation in our country is such that . . . any allusion to the left brings forth an emotional response which would seem to indicate that SCLC and the Southern Freedom Movement are Communist inspired."

{ . . . }

E. The FBI Intensifies Its Investigation of Alleged Communist Influence in the Civil Rights Movement: July–September 1963

On July 18, 1963, in response to intelligence reports that the Communist Party was encouraging its members to participate actively in the forthcoming March on Washington, the FBI opened a file captioned "Communist Influence in Racial Matters." Field offices were advised:

> It is reasonable to assume that the future will witness a strong effort on the part of the CPUSA to inject itself into and to exploit the struggle for equal rights for Negroes. Therefore, during the investigation of the CPUSA, each recipient office should be extremely alert to data indicating interest, plans, or actual involvement of the Party in the current Negro movement. This matter should be given close attention and the Bureau kept currently advised.

The results of voluminous reports from field offices around the country concerning the plans of the Communist Party and "other subversive groups" were summarized by the Domestic Intelligence Division in a report dated August 22, 1963. That report concluded that there was no evidence that the March "was actually initiated by or is controlled by the CP," although the Party had publicly endorsed the March and had urged members to "clandestinely participate" in order to "foster the illusion that the CP is a humanitarian group acting in the interest of the Negro." The Party's tactics were summarized:

> CP leaders have stressed the fact that the March is not the be all and end all in itself. Events which subsequently flow from the March will be of utmost importance, such as following up in contacts now being made by CP members working in support of the demonstration. Utilizing the March, the Party has three basic general objectives:
>
> (1) Participation by CP members through legitimate organizations.
>
> (2) Attempt to get the Party line into the hands of sympathizers and supporters of the March through distribution of "The Worker" and Party pamphlets.

(3) Utilize the March as a stepping stone for future Party activity through contacts now being made by Party members involved in the March.

The next day the Domestic Intelligence Division submitted to the Director a 67-page Brief detailing the CPUSA's efforts to exploit the American Negro, and finding virtually no successes in these efforts. A synopsis observed:

(1) "The 19 million Negroes in the United States today constitute the largest and most important racial target of the Communist Party, USA. Since 1919, communist leaders have devised countless tactics and programs designed to penetrate and control Negro population." The "colossal efforts" focused around "equal opportunity," and efforts were presently being made with "limited degrees of success" to infiltrate legitimate Negro organizations. "*[T]here is no known substantial implementation of Communist Party aims and policies among Negroes in the labor field.*"

(2) "*While not the instigator and presently unable to direct or control* the coming Negro August 28 March on Washington, D.C., communist officials are *planning* to do all possible to advance communist aims in a supporting role."

(3) "Despite tremendous sums of money and time spent by the Communist Party, USA, on the American Negro during the past 44 years, the *Party has failed to reach its goal with the Negroes.*"

(4) "There has been *an obvious failure of the Communist Party of the United States to appreciably infiltrate, influence, or control large numbers of American Negroes in this country.* . . . The Communist Party in the next few years may fail dismally with the American Negro as it has in the past. On the other hand, it may make prodigious strides and great success with the American Negroes, to the serious detriment of our national security. Time alone will tell."

William Sullivan, who then headed the Domestic Intelligence Division of the FBI, testified that this "Brief" precipitated a dispute between Director Hoover and the Domestic Intelligence Division over the extent of communist influence in the civil rights movement, and that the resulting "intensification" was part of an attempt by the Intelligence Division to regain Hoover's approval. The documentary evidence bearing on the internal FBI dispute is set forth below, with Sullivan's explanation of what occurred. Sullivan's comments, however, should be considered in light of the intense personal feud that subsequently developed between Sullivan and Director Hoover, and which ultimately led to Sullivan's dismissal from the Bureau. While Sullivan testified that the intensified investigation of the SCLC was the product of Director Hoover's prodding the Domestic Intelligence Division to conform its evidence to his preconceptions, the documentary evidence may also be read as indicating that the Domestic Intelligence Division was manipulating the Director in a subtle bureaucratic battle to gain approval for expanded programs.

Sullivan testified that a careful review of the files in preparation for writing the "Brief" revealed no evidence of "marked or substantial" Communist infiltration of the movement, and that he had instructed his assistant to "state the facts just as they are" and "then let the storm break." Sullivan said he had known that Hoover would be displeased with his conclusions because Hoover was convinced the civil rights movement was strongly influenced by communists. Sullivan's prediction was borne out by Hoover's observations, scrawled across the bottom of the memorandum:

> This memo reminds me vividly of those I received when Castro took over Cuba. You contended then that Castro and his cohorts were not communists and not influenced by communists. Time alone proved you wrong. I for one can't ignore the memoes . . . re King, Advisers A and B . . . et al. as having only an infinitesimal effect on the efforts to exploit the American Negro by the Communists.

Sullivan recalled:

> This [memorandum] set me at odds with Hoover. . . . A few months went by before he would speak to me. Everything was conducted by exchange of written communications. It was evident that we had to change our ways or we would all be out on the street.

The Director penned sarcastic notes on subsequent memoranda from the Domestic Intelligence Division. In the margin of a report that over 100 Communist Party members were planning to participate in the March on Washington, the Director wrote, "just infinitesimal!" A preliminary report on possible communist influence on the March noted that Party functionaries were pleased with the March, believed it would impress Congress, and that a "rally of similar proportions on the subject of automation could advance the cause of socialism in the United States." Director Hoover remarked, "I assume CP functionary claims are all frivolous." Sullivan testified:

> The men and I discussed how to get out of trouble. To be in trouble with Mr. Hoover was a serious matter. These men were trying to buy homes, mortgages on homes, children in school. They lived in fear of getting transferred, losing money on their homes, as they usually did. In those days the market was not soaring, and children in school, so they wanted another memorandum written to get us out of this trouble we were in. I said I would write the memorandum this time. The onus always falls on the person who writes a memorandum.

On August 30, Sullivan wrote his apologetic reply:

> The Director is correct. We were completely wrong about believing the evidence was not sufficient to determine some years ago that Fidel Castro was not a communist or under communist influence. On investigating and writing about communism and the American Negro, we had better remember this and profit by the lesson it should teach us.
>
> . . . Personally, I believe in the light of King's powerful demagogic speech yesterday he stands head and shoulders over all other Negro leaders put together when it comes to influencing great masses of Negroes. We must mark him now, if we have not done so before, as the most dangerous Negro of the future in this Nation from the standpoint of communism, the Negro and national security.
>
> . . . [I]t may be unrealistic to limit ourselves as we have been doing to legalistic proofs or definitely conclusive evidence that would stand up in testimony in court or before Congressional Committees that the Communist Party, USA, does wield substantial influence over Negroes which one day could become decisive.
>
> . . . .
>
> We regret greatly that the memorandum did not measure up to what the Director has a right to expect from our analysis.

Sullivan testified concerning this memorandum:

> Here again we had to engage in a lot of nonsense which we ourselves really did not believe in. We either had to do that or we would be finished.

The memorandum stated that "The history of the Communist Party, U.S.A., is replete with its attempts to exploit, influence and recruit the Negro." After reading this entry, Sullivan testified:

> These are words that are very significant to me because I know what they mean. We build this thing . . . and say all this is a clear indication that the Party's favorite target is the Negro today. When you analyze it, what does it mean? How often has it been able to hit the target? . . . We did not discuss that because we would have to say they did not hit the target, hardly at all.

In an apparent further effort to please the Director, Sullivan recommended, on September 16, 1963, "increased coverage of communist influence on the Negro." His memorandum noted that "all indications" pointed toward increasing "attempts" by the Party to exploit racial unrest. The field was to "intensify" coverage of communist influence on Negroes by giving "fullest consideration to the use of all possible investigative techniques."

> Further, we are stressing the urgent need for imaginative and aggressive tactics to be utilized through our Counterintelligence Program—these designed to attempt to neutralize or disrupt the Party's activities in the Negro field.

Hoover rejected this proposal with the remarks:

> No. I can't understand how you can so agilely switch your thinking and evaluation. Just a few weeks ago you contended that the Communist influence in the racial movement was ineffective and infinitesimal. This—notwithstanding many memos of specific instances of infiltration. Now you want to load the Field down with more coverage in spite of your recent memo depreciating C.P. influence in racial movement.

> I don't intend to waste time and money until you can make up your minds what the situation really is.

Sullivan testified that he had interpreted Hoover's note to mean that the Director was:

> egging us on, to come back and say, "Mr. Hoover, you are right, we are wrong. There is communist infiltration of the American Negro. We think we should go ahead and carry on an intensified program against it." He knew when he wrote this, he knew precisely what kind of reply he was going to get.

Sullivan responded in a memorandum to the Deputy Associate Director, Alan Belmont:

> On returning from a few days leave I have been advised of the Director's continued dissatisfaction with the manner in which we prepared a Brief on [communist influence in racial matters] and subsequent memoranda on the same subject matter. This situation is very disturbing to those of us in the Domestic Intelligence Division and we certainly want to do everything possible to correct our shortcomings . . . The Director indicated he would not approve our last SAC letter until there was a clarification and a meeting of minds relative to the question of the extent of communist influence over Negroes and their leaders. . . .
>
> As we know, facts by themselves are not too meaningful, for they are somewhat like stones tossed in a heap as contrasted to the same stones put in the form of a sound edifice. It is obvious that *we did not put the proper interpretation upon the facts which we gave to the Director.* [Emphasis added.]
>
> As previously stated, we are in complete agreement with the Director that communist influence is being exerted on Martin Luther King, Jr., and that King is the strongest of the Negro leaders. . . . [W]e regard Martin Luther King to be the most dangerous and effective Negro leader in the country.
>
> May I repeat that our failure to measure up to what the Director expected of us in the area of Communist-Negro relations is a subject of very deep concern to us in the Domestic Intelligence Division. We

> are disturbed by this and ought to be. I want him to know that we will do everything that is humanly possible to develop all facts nationwide relative to communist penetration and influence over Negro leaders and their organizations.

Sullivan resubmitted his proposed intensification instructions to the field. This time the Director agreed.

The intensification was put into effect by an SAC letter dated October 1, 1963, which contained the usual allusion to "efforts" and "attempts" by the Communist Party to influence the civil rights movement, but which said nothing about the absence of results:

> The history of the Communist Party, USA (CPUSA), is replete with its *attempts to exploit, influence and recruit* the Negro. The March on Washington, August 28, 1963, was a striking example as Party leaders early put into motion *efforts* to accrue gains for the CPUSA from the March. The presence at the March of around 200 Party members, ranging from several national functionaries headed by CPUSA General Secretary Gus Hall to many rank-and-file members, is clear indication of the Party's favorite target (the Negro) today.
>
> All indications are that the March was not the "end of the line" and that the Party will *step up its efforts* to exploit racial unrest and in every possible way claim credit for itself relating to any "gains" achieved by the Negro. A clear-cut indication of the Party's *designs* is revealed in secret information obtained from a most sensitive source that the Party plans to hold a highly secretive leadership meeting in November, 1963, which will deal primarily with the Negro situation. The Party has closely guarded *plans* for Gus Hall to undertake a "barnstorming" trip through key areas of the country to meet Party people and thus better prepare himself for the November meeting.
>
> In order for the Bureau to cope with the Party's efforts and thus fulfill our responsibilities in the security field, it is necessary that we at once intensify our coverage of communist influence on the Negro. Fullest consideration should be given to the use of all possible investigative techniques in the investigation of the CPUSA, those communist fronts through which the Party channels its influence, and the many individual Party members and dupes. There is also an urgent need for

> imaginative and aggressive tactics to be utilized through our Counterintelligence Program for the purpose of attempting to neutralize or disrupt the Party's activities in the Negro field. Because of the Bureau's responsibility for timely dissemination of pertinent information to the Department and other interested agencies, it is more than ever necessary that all facets of this matter receive prompt handling.

The instruction to use "all possible investigative techniques" appears to have dictated the intensification of the COMINFIL investigation of the SCLC.

This was consistent with Sullivan's assurance to Director Hoover at the end of September that "we will do everything that is humanly possible to develop all facts nationwide relative to the Communist penetration and influence over Negro leaders and their organizations."

The emphasis on "imaginative and aggressive tactics" to disrupt Communist Party activities in the Negro field appears to have involved an expansion of the COINTELPRO operation already underway against the Communist Party. In 1956, the Bureau had initiated a COINTELPRO operation against the Communist Party, USA, with the goal of "feeding and fostering" internal friction within the Party. The program was soon expanded to include "preventing communists from seizing control of legitimate mass organizations, and . . . discrediting others who [are] secretly operating inside such organizations." The October 1, 1963 "intensification" instruction emphasized this latter objective of disruption.

The intensification order appears to have been more a product of preconceptions and bureaucratic squabbles within the FBI than a response to genuine concerns based on hard evidence that communists might be influencing the civil rights movement. Because Director Hoover is deceased, the Committee was able to obtain only one side of the story. Sullivan's version depicts the Domestic Intelligence Division executing an about-face after Director Hoover rejected its conclusion that evidence did not indicate significant communist influence, reinterpreting its original data to reach conclusions the Director wanted to hear, and then basing its recommendations for action on the new "analysis." However, the memoranda could also support a contention that the Domestic Intelligence Division misled Director Hoover in order to maneuver him into supporting expanded domestic intelligence programs.

IV. ELECTRONIC SURVEILLANCE OF DR. MARTIN LUTHER KING AND THE SOUTHERN CHRISTIAN LEADERSHIP CONFERENCE

Introduction and Summary

In October 1963, Attorney General Robert Kennedy approved an FBI request for permission to install wiretaps on phones in Dr. King's home and in the SCLC's New York and Atlanta offices to determine the extent, if any, of "communist influence in the racial situation." The FBI construed this authorization to extend to Dr. King's hotel rooms and the home of a friend. No further authorization was sought until mid-1965, after Attorney General Katzenbach required the FBI for the first time to seek renewed authorization for all existing wiretaps. The wiretaps on Dr. King's home were apparently terminated at that time by Attorney General Katzenbach; the SCLC wiretaps were terminated by Attorney General Ramsey Clark in June 1966.

In December, 1963—three months after Attorney General Kennedy approved the wiretaps—the FBI, without informing the Attorney General, planned and implemented a secret effort to discredit Dr. King and to "neutralize" him as the leader of the civil rights movement. One of the first steps in this effort involved hiding microphones in Dr. King's hotel rooms. Those microphones were installed without Attorney General Kennedy's prior authorization or subsequent notification, neither of which were required under practices then current. The FBI continued to place microphones in Dr. King's hotel rooms until November 1965. Attorney General Katzenbach was apparently notified immediately after the fact of the placement of three microphones between May and November 1965. It is not clear why the FBI stopped its microphone surveillance of Dr. King, although its decision may have been related to concern about public exposure during the Long Committee's investigation of electronic surveillance.

This chapter examines the { . . . } evidence surrounding the motives for their use, and the degree to which Justice Department and White House officials were aware of the FBI's electronic surveillance of Dr. King.

{ . . . }

B. Wiretap Surveillance of Dr. King and the SCLC: October 1963–June 1966

On September 6, 1963, Assistant Director William Sullivan first recommended to Director Hoover that the FBI install wiretaps on Dr. King's home and the offices of the Southern Christian Leadership Conference. Sullivan's recommendation was apparently part of an attempt to improve the Domestic Intelligence Division's standing with the Director by convincing him that Sullivan's Division was concerned about alleged communist influence on the civil rights movement and that the Division intended, as Sullivan subsequently informed the Director, to "do everything that is humanly possible" in conducting its investigation.

Sullivan's recommendation was viewed with scepticism by the FBI leadership since Attorney General Kennedy had rejected a similar proposal two months earlier. Associate Director Clyde Tolson noted on the memorandum containing Sullivan's proposal: "I see no point in making this recommendation to the Attorney General in view of the fact that he turned down a similar recommendation on July 22, 1963." Director Hoover scrawled below Tolson's note: "I will approve though I am dizzy over vacillation as to influence of CPUSA."

In late September 1963 the FBI conducted a survey and concluded that wiretap coverage of Dr. King's residence and of the New York SCLC office could be implemented without detection. On October 7, citing "possible communist influence in the racial situation," Hoover requested the Attorney General's permission for a wiretap "on King at his current address or at any future address to which he may move" and "on the SCLC office at the current New York address or to any other address to which it may be moved." Attorney General Kennedy signed the request on October 10 and, on October 21, also approved the FBI request for coverage of the SCLC's Atlanta office.

{ . . . }

Wiretaps were installed on the SCLC's New York office on October 24, 1963, and at Dr. King's home and the SCLC's Atlanta office on November 8, 1963. The FBI made an internal evaluation of the wiretaps in December 1963 and decided on its own to extend the wiretaps for three months. Reading the Attorney General's authorization broadly, the FBI construed permission to wiretap Dr. King "at his current address or at any future address" to include hotel room phones and the phone at the home of friends with whom he temporarily stayed. The FBI installed wiretaps, without seeking further authorization, on the following occasions:

Location	Installed	Discontinued
King's Atlanta Home	Nov. 8, 1963	Apr. 30, 1965
A friend's home	Aug. 14, 1964	Sept. 8, 1964
Hyatt House Motel, Los Angeles	Apr. 24, 1964	Apr. 26, 1964
Hyatt House Motel, Los Angeles	July 7, 1964	July 9, 1964
Claridge Hotel, Atlantic City	Aug. 22, 1964	Aug. 27, 1964
SCLC Atlanta headquarters	Nov. 8, 1963	June 21, 1966
SCLC New York headquarters	Oct. 24, 1963 July 13, 1964	Jan. 24, 1964 July 31, 1964

The Committee was not able to ascertain why Attorney General Kennedy approved the FBI's request for wiretaps in October 1963 after refusing an identical request in July 1963. Burke Marshall, Kennedy's assistant in charge of civil rights affairs, testified that he could not recall ever having discussed the matter with the Attorney General. It was his opinion, however, that the decision had been influenced by events arising out of concern about possible communist influence in the civil rights movement that had been widely publicized during the hearings on the Public Accommodations Act in the summer of 1963. Marshall recalled that Dr. King had made a "commitment" to the Attorney General and to the President to "stop having any communication" with Advisers A and B. Subsequently,

> information came in, not as far as Adviser B, but as far as Adviser A was concerned, that that commitment was not lived up to, and I have assumed since, although I do not remember discussing it with Robert

> Kennedy, that the reason that he authorized the tap . . . was that he wanted to find out what was going on.
>
> From his point of view, Martin Luther King had made a commitment on a very important matter . . . [and] King had broken that commitment. So therefore the Attorney General wanted to find out whether [Adviser A] did in fact have influence over King, what he was telling King, and so forth.

Marshall's answer to a question concerning whether anyone in the Justice Department ever considered asking the FBI to discontinue the investigation of Dr. King also sheds some light on why the Attorney General might have decided to approve the wiretaps:

> Not that I know of. [The FBI's allegations concerning Adviser A] were grave and serious, and the inquiries from the Senate and from the public, both to the President and to the Attorney General, as well as the Bureau, had to be answered and they had to be answered fully. Stopping the investigation in light of those circumstances would have run the risk that there would have been a lot of complaints that the Bureau had been blocked for political reasons from investigating serious charges about communist infiltration in the civil rights movement.

Edwin O. Guthman, the Justice Department Public Relations Chief during Robert Kennedy's tenure as Attorney General, told the Committee that he had spoken with then Senator Robert Kennedy about the wiretap when it was revealed in a Jack Anderson story in 1968. According to Guthman, Robert Kennedy told him:

> he had been importuned or requested by the FBI over a period of time to wiretap the phones of Dr. King, specifically wiretap the phones, as I recollect, at the headquarters of the Southern Christian Leadership Conference and, I think, Martin Luther King's home, but I'm not certain about that. . . .
>
> Robert Kennedy said that he finally agreed in the fall of 1963 to give the FBI permission to wiretap the phones, and my clear recollection on this is that his feeling was that if he did not do it, Mr. Hoover would move to impede or block the passage of the civil rights bill,

> which had been introduced in the summer of 1963, and that he felt that he might as well settle the matter as to whether (Adviser A) did have the influence on King that the FBI contended. . . . My recollection is that there had been a number of conversations with King by Burke Marshall and Robert Kennedy, and I think President Kennedy had indicated to King that he ought not to have anything to do with (Adviser A). My understanding and recollection is that King said he would, and then each time the FBI would come back and say, he's still in contact with (Adviser A). . . . Robert Kennedy viewed this as a serious matter and not in the interest of the country and not in the interest of the civil rights movement, if the FBI information was accurate.

Guthman testified that he could not recall Kennedy's elaborating on the steps that he had feared Director Hoover would take against the civil rights legislation if he had not agreed to the wiretap, but gave his own opinion that "Hoover's influence on the Hill could be considerable and it could have been a form of public statement or conferring with Senators in that area."

It is also not clear why Attorney General Kennedy insisted that the wiretaps be evaluated after 30 days and then failed to complain when the FBI neglected to send him an evaluation. Evans, after reviewing his memorandum stating that the Attorney General required the FBI to evaluate the wiretaps after 30 days, testified that he assumed the Attorney General had "expected the Bureau to . . . submit the results of that evaluation to him." When asked if the Attorney General had ever inquired into whether the evaluation had been made, Evans testified:

> I am reasonably certain he never asked me. I would point out, however, that the assassination of President Kennedy followed these events reasonably close in point of time, and this disrupted the operation of the Office of the Attorney General.

In March 1965 Attorney General Nicholas Katzenbach requested the FBI to submit all of its wiretaps for reauthorization. He testified:

> In late April 1965, in accordance with this program, I received a request from the Bureau to continue a tap on Dr. King's personal phone. I ordered it discontinued. It is, however, possible that a request for the continuation of a preexisting tap on the headquarters of the

> Southern Christian Leadership Conference was made about the same time, and I may have approved that tap. I do not recall the date or the circumstances which would have led me to do so.

Documents provided to the Committee by the FBI reflect that in early April 1965 the Atlanta office informed headquarters that it was discontinuing the wiretap on Dr. King's home because he was moving. On April 19 the Director authorized a survey to determine if a wiretap could be placed on the phone in Dr. King's new residence with "full security." The Director's memorandum also stated that "After receipt of results of survey and Atlanta's recommendations, a memorandum will be prepared along with any necessary correspondence with the Attorney General." A memorandum from the Atlanta office the next month states: "On [May 6, 1965], Mr. Sullivan telephonically advised that the installation of this Tesur [technical surveillance] was not authorized at this time."

The Bureau has been unable to find a record of any discussions between FBI officials and Attorney Katzenbach concerning this wiretap, and there are no memoranda in the Bureau files which indicate the reason that the wiretap on Dr. King's new home was not authorized.

The FBI terminated the wiretap on the New York SCLC office in January 1964, only two months after it had been installed, "for lack of productivity." The wiretap was reinstalled in July 1964 and discontinued later that month because "the office moved." No further wiretaps were placed on the New York office.

The wiretap on the Atlanta SCLC office was reviewed by Attorney General Katzenbach on October 27, 1965, and received his approval. A Bureau memorandum recommending continuation of the coverage in April 1966 was returned with a notation by Katzenbach, dated June 20, 1966, stating: "I think this coverage should be discontinued, particularly in light of possible charges of a criminal nature against [certain SCLC employees]." Technical coverage was discontinued the following day.

Attorney General Ramsey Clark turned down two requests by the FBI for wiretaps on the phones of the SCLC, once on January 3, 1968, and again on January 17, 1969. Clark wrote the Director concerning the 1968 request:

> I am declining authorization of the requested installation of the above telephone surveillance at the present time. There has not been an adequate demonstration of a direct threat to national security.

Clark's refusal to authorize an SCLC wiretap in 1969 occurred two days before he left office, at the termination of the Johnson Administration. Less than a month later the Director informed the Atlanta office that an SCLC wiretap "is in line to be presented to the new Attorney General, and a survey, with full security assured . . . is desirable." FBI files contain no indication of the disposition of this final request.

C. Microphone Surveillance of Dr. King: January 1964–November 1965

From January 1964 through November 1965, the FBI installed at least 15 hidden microphones in hotel and motel rooms occupied by Martin Luther King. The FBI has told the Committee about the following microphone surveillances:

—Willard Hotel, Washington, D.C. (Jan. 5, 1964).
—Shroeder Hotel, Milwaukee (Jan. 27, 1964).
—Hilton Hawaiian Village, Honolulu (Feb.18, 1964).
—Ambassador Hotel, Los Angeles (Feb. 20, 1964).
—Hyatt House Motel, Los Angeles (Feb. 22, 1964).
—Statler Hotel, Detroit (Mar. 19, 1964).
—Senator Motel, Sacramento (Apr. 23, 1964).
—Hyatt House Motel, Los Angeles (July 7, 1964).
—Manger Hotel, Savannah, Ga. (Sept. 28, 1964).
—Park Sheraton Hotel, New York (Jan. 8, 1965).
—Americana Hotel, New York (Jan. 28, 1965).
—Sheraton Atlantic Hotel, New York (May 12, 1965).
—Astor Hotel, New York (Oct. 14, 1965).
—New York Hilton Hotel, New York (Oct. 28, 1965).
—Americana Hotel, New York (Nov. 29, 1965).

1. Reasons for the FBI's Microphone Surveillance of Dr. King.

The wiretaps on Dr. King's home telephone and the phones of the SCLC offices were authorized by the Attorney General for the stated purpose of determining whether suspected communists were influencing the course of the civil rights movement. FBI documents indicate that the microphone coverage (which was initiated without the knowledge of the Attorney Generals, in conformance with practice then current) was originally designed not only to pick up information bearing on possible Communist influence over Dr. King, but also to obtain information for use in the FBI's secret effort to discredit Dr. King as the leader of the civil rights movement. By 1965, references to discrediting efforts had been dropped, and documents requesting authorization for microphones mentioned only the purpose of obtaining information about possible communist influences. The details of the Bureau's efforts to undermine Dr. King are discussed in the ensuing chapters.

The first microphones were installed about two weeks after a December 23, 1963, FBI conference at which methods of "neutralizing" Dr. King were explored. Microphone surveillance was again discussed at an all-day conference at FBI Headquarters in February 1964, attended by representatives of the FBI laboratory "preparatory to effecting coverage of the activities of Martin Luther King, Jr., and his associates in Honolulu." Justifying the need for microphone coverage, the Chief of the FBI's Internal Security Section wrote that the FBI was "attempting" to obtain information about "the [private] activities of Dr. King and his associates" so that Dr. King could be "completely discredited."

The FBI memorandum authorizing the placement of the first microphone on Dr. King—at the Willard Hotel in early January 1964—gave as a basis "the intelligence and counterintelligence possibilities which thorough coverage of Dr. King's activities might develop . . . " The Willard Hotel "bug" yielded 19 reels of tape. A memorandum summarizing the tapes was sent to the Director with William Sullivan's recommendation that it be shown to Walter Jenkins, President Johnson's Special Assistant, "inasmuch as Dr. King is seeking an appointment with President Johnson." Cartha D. DeLoach, Assistant to the Director, showed the summary memorandum to Jenkins, and later wrote:

> I told Jenkins that the Director indicated I should leave this attachment with him if he desired to let the President personally read it. Jenkins mentioned that he was sufficiently aware of the facts that he could verbally advise the President of the matter. Jenkins was of the opinion that the FBI could perform a good service to the country if this matter could somehow be confidentially given to members of the press. I told him the Director had this in mind, however, he also believed we should obtain additional information prior to discussing it with certain friends.

The FBI was apparently encouraged by the intelligence afforded by "bugs" and by the White House's receptiveness to that type of information. A microphone was installed at the Shroeder Hotel in Milwaukee two weeks later, but was declared "unproductive" because "there were no activities of interest developed." Dr. King's visit to Honolulu in mid-February 1964 was covered by a squad of surveillance experts brought in for the occasion from San Francisco. One of these experts was described in a Bureau memorandum as the "most experienced, most ingenious, most unruffled, most competent sound man for this type of operation in the San Francisco Office"; another was chosen because he had "shown unusual ingenuity, persistence, and determination in making microphone installations"; and a third had "been absolutely fearless in these types of operations for over twelve years." More than twenty reels of tape were obtained during Dr. King's stay in Honolulu and his sojourn in Los Angeles immediately afterward. Director Hoover agreed to send a copy of a memorandum describing the contents of the tapes to Jenkins and Attorney General Kennedy in order to:

> remove all doubt from the Attorney General's mind as to the type of person King is. It will probably also eliminate King from any participation in [a memorial for President Kennedy which the Attorney General was helping to arrange].

Dr. King's stay in Los Angeles in July 1964 was covered by both wiretaps and microphones in his hotel room. The wiretap was intended to gain intelligence about Dr. King's plans at the Republican National Convention. Microphone surveillance was requested to attempt to obtain information useful in the campaigns to discredit him. Sullivan's memorandum describing the coverage was sent to Hoover with a recommendation against dissemination to the White House or the Attorney General:

> as in this instance it is merely repetitious and does not have nearly the impact as prior such memoranda. We are continuing to follow closely King's activities and giving consideration to every possibility for future similar coverage that will add to our record on King so that in the end he might be discredited and thus be removed from his position of great stature in the Negro community.

Hoover wrote on the memorandum, "Send to Jenkins." The summary memorandum and a cover letter were sent to Jenkins on July 17.

It should also be noted that Dr. King's activities at the Democratic National Convention in Atlantic City, New Jersey, in August 1964 were closely monitored by the FBI. Microphones were not installed on that occasion, although wiretaps were placed on Dr. King's hotel room phone. The stated justification for the wiretap was the investigation of possible communist influence and the fact that Dr. King "may indulge in a hunger fast as a means of protest." A great deal of potentially useful political information was obtained from this wiretap and disseminated to the White House.

The memorandum authorizing microphone coverage of Dr. King's room in Savannah, Georgia, during the annual SCLC conference in September and October 1964 described surveillance as necessary because it was "expected that attempts will again be made to exert influence upon the SCLC and in particular on King by communists." The seven "bugs" in Dr. King's rooms during visits to New York from January to November 1965 were justified in contemporaneous internal FBI memoranda by anticipated meetings of Dr. King with several people whom the FBI claimed had affiliations with the Communist Party. No mention was made of the possibility of obtaining private life material in memoranda concerning these "bugs."

{...}

V. THE FBI'S EFFORT TO DISCREDIT DR. MARTIN LUTHER KING: 1964

Introduction and Summary

In December 1963, a meeting was convened at FBI headquarters to discuss various "avenues of approach aimed at neutralizing King as an effective Negro leader." Two weeks later, FBI agents planted the first microphones in Dr. King's hotel rooms in an "attempt" to obtain information about the private "activities of Dr. King and his associates" so that Dr. King could be "completely discredited." That same week, the head of the Domestic Intelligence Division recommended the promotion of a new "national Negro leader" who could "overshadow King and be in the position to assume the role of the leadership of the Negro people when King has been completely discredited."

The FBI's effort to discredit Dr. King and to undermine the SCLC involved plans touching on virtually every aspect of Dr. King's life. The FBI scrutinized Dr. King's tax returns, monitored his financial affairs, and even tried to establish that he had a secret foreign bank account. Religious leaders and institutions were contacted in an effort to undermine their support of him, and unfavorable material was "leaked" to the press. Bureau officials contacted members of Congress, and special "off the record" testimony was prepared for the Director's use before the House Appropriations Committee. Efforts were made to turn White House and Justice Department Officials against Dr. King by barraging them with unfavorable reports and, according to one witness, even offering to play for a White House official tape recordings that the Bureau considered embarrassing to King.

This chapter examines not only the Bureau's efforts to discredit Dr. King, but the degree to which officials in other branches of the Government were responsible for those actions. A few months before the FBI held its December 1963 conference at which its program against Dr. King was apparently formulated, the Director distributed a "monograph" about Dr. King to the heads of several Governmental agencies. Attorney General Kennedy ordered it immediately withdrawn. During the course of the following year, the FBI sent several intelligence reports bearing on Dr. King's private life to the White House and Justice Department. Although government officials outside the FBI were not aware of the extent of the FBI's efforts to discredit Dr. King, officials of the Justice Department and of the White House did know that the FBI had offered tape recordings and derogatory information about Dr. King to reporters. The Attorney General went no further than complaining to the President and accepting a Bureau official's representation that the allegations were not true. President Johnson not only failed to order the Bureau to stop, but indeed cautioned it against dealing with certain reporters who had complained of its conduct.

A. The FBI Disseminates the First King "Monograph" and Attorney General Kennedy Orders It Recalled: October 1963

On October 15, 1963, William Sullivan forwarded to Assistant Director Alan Belmont for his approval a monograph entitled "Communism and the Negro Movement-A Current Analysis." He proposed that it be distributed to the Attorney General, the White House, CIA, State Department,

Defense Department, and Defense Department intelligence agencies. Sullivan testified that the purpose of the monograph was to "discredit King."

Belmont submitted the monograph to the Director with a note stating:

> The attached analysis of Communism and the Negro movement is highly explosive. It can be regarded as a personal attack on Martin Luther King. There is no doubt it will have a heavy impact on the Attorney General and anyone else to whom we disseminate. . . .
>
> The memorandum makes good reading and is based on information from reliable sources. We may well be charged, however, with expressing opinions and conclusions, particularly with reference to some of the statements about King.
>
> This memorandum may startle the Attorney General, particularly in view of his past association with King, and the fact that we are disseminating this outside the Department. He may resent this. Nevertheless, the memorandum is a powerful warning against Communist influence in the Negro movement, and we will be carrying out our responsibility by disseminating it to the people indicated in the attached memorandum.

The monograph was distributed on October 18, 1963. One week later, the Attorney General called Courtney Evans and stated that he had just learned that the Army had received a copy of a report about Dr. King's alleged communist activities. Evans reported to Belmont:

> He was obviously irritated. He went on to ask if the Army got copies of all reports submitted to him. . . . The Attorney General asked what responsibilities the Army had in relation to the communist background of Martin Luther King. I told the Attorney General . . . that the Army had an interest in communist activities particularly in relation to racial matters because the military had to be called on if civil disturbances arising out of such matters went beyond the ability of civilian authorities. This explanation seemed to serve no purpose.

Director Hoover recorded in a memorandum of the same date:

> The Attorney General called and advised me there was a lot of talk at the Pentagon regarding the document. . . . The Attorney General

> anticipated that this information would leak out as the military didn't like the Negroes.
>
> The Attorney General felt we should get back all copies of the document. I told him . . . we would get them from all agencies to which they were disseminated. . . . I also told him if any newspapers asked about this, no comment would be made and no mention would be made that such a document existed.

All copies were recovered by October 28.

Burke Marshall, Assistant Attorney General in charge of the Civil Rights Division under Robert Kennedy, told the Committee that the monograph was:

> a personal diatribe . . . a personal attack without evidentiary support on the character, the moral character and person of Dr. Martin Luther King, and it was only peripherally related to anything substantive, like whether or not there was communist infiltration or influence on the civil rights movement. . . . It was a personal attack on the man and went far afield from the charges [of possible communist influence].

Marshall recalled that he had been very "irritated" about the monograph and that the Attorney General had "thought it was outrageous." He remembered that the Attorney General had ordered the monograph withdrawn, but did not know if the Attorney General had taken any further steps to reprimand the Bureau.

B. The FBI Plans Its Campaign to Discredit Dr. King: December 23, 1963

On December 23, 1963, a nine-hour conference was held at FBI headquarters to discuss Martin Luther King. In attendance were Assistant Director Sullivan, Internal Security Section Chief Frederick Baumgardner, three other FBI headquarters officials, and two agents from the FBI's Atlanta Field Office.

A prepared list of twenty-one proposals was presented and discussed. The proposals raised the possibility of "using" ministers, "disgruntled" acquaintances, "aggressive" newsmen, "colored" agents, Dr. King's housekeeper, and even suggested using Dr. King's wife or "placing a good looking female plant in King's office." An account of the meeting written by William Sullivan emphasized that the Bureau must take a "discreet approach" in developing information about Dr. King for use "at an opportune time in a counterintelligence move to discredit him." It was generally agreed that the Bureau should make use of "all available investigative techniques coupled with meticulous planning, boldness, and ingenuity, tempered only with good judgment," but that "discretion must not reach the point of timidity."

Sullivan's memorandum reported that the following decisions were made at the conference:

> (1) We must determine and check out all of the employees of the SCLC.
>
> (2) We must locate and monitor the funds of the SCLC.
>
> (3) We must identify and check out the sources who contribute to the SCLC.
>
> (4) We must continue to keep close watch on King's personal activities.
>
> (5) We will, at the proper time when it can be done without embarrassment to the Bureau, expose King as an opportunist who is not a sincere person but is exploiting the racial situation for personal gain.
>
> (6) We will explore the possibility of utilizing additional specialized investigative techniques at the SCLC office.

Sullivan described the purpose of the meeting as

> To explore how best to carry on our investigation to produce the desired results without embarrassment to the Bureau. Included in our discussion was a complete analysis of the avenues of approach aimed at neutralizing King as an effective Negro leader and developing evidence concerning King's continued dependence on communists for guidance and direction.

Precisely what prompted the Bureau to decide upon this drastic new approach is still unclear.

William Sullivan was asked by the Committee whether tactics, such as placing female "plants," were common practices of the FBI. Sullivan testified that they were:

> common practice among intelligence services all over the world. This is not an isolated phenomenon. . . . This is a common practice, rough, tough, dirty business. Whether we should be in it or not, that is for you folks to decide. We are in it. . . . No holds were barred. We have used that technique against Soviet agents. They have used it against us.
>
> *Question.* The same methods were brought home?
>
> Mr. SULLIVAN. Brought home against any organization against which we were targeted. We did not differentiate. This is a rough, tough business
>
> Senator MONDALE. Would it be safe to say that the techniques we learned in fighting . . . true espionage in World War II came to be used against some of our own American citizens?
>
> Mr. SULLIVAN. That would be a correct deduction.

Sullivan testified that the plans formulated at the December 24, 1963 meeting were in accord with "Mr. Hoover's policy." After reviewing the memoranda, Sullivan emphasized,

> I want to make this clear, this is not an isolated phenomenon, that this was a practice of the Bureau down through the years. I might say it often became a real character assassination.

Sullivan was asked by the Committee whether he or any other employees of the Bureau ever objected to using these tactics. Sullivan responded:

> Not to my recollection. . . . I was not ready at that time to collide with him. Everybody in the Division went right along with Hoover's policy. I do not recall anybody ever raising a question.
>
> . . . never once did I hear anybody, including myself, raise the question, is this course of action which we have agreed upon lawful, is it legal, is it ethical or moral? We never gave any thought to this realm of reasoning, because we were just naturally pragmatists. The one thing we were concerned about will this course of action work, will it get us what we want, will we reach the objective that we desire to reach?
>
> As far as legality is concerned, morals or ethics, was never raised by myself or anybody else. . . . I think this suggests really in government we are amoral.

On December 29, 1963, less than a week after the FBI conference, *Time* magazine chose Dr. King as the "Man of the Year," describing him as the "unchallenged voice of the Negro people . . . [who] has infused the Negroes themselves with the fiber that gives their revolution its true stature." Hoover wrote across the memorandum informing him of this honor: "They had to dig deep in the garbage to come up with this one."

C. William Sullivan Proposes a Plan to Promote a New Negro Leader: January 1964

On January 6, 1964—about two weeks after the FBI's conference to plan methods of "neutralizing" Dr. King's influence and to gather information about Dr. King's personal life—the FBI installed the microphone in Dr. King's room at the Willard Hotel. As explained in the preceding chapter, additional microphones soon followed; physical and photographic surveillance was initiated; special Headquarters "briefings" were held; "dry runs" were planned; and the most sophisticated and experienced Bureau personnel were deployed to gather information that might be used in a concerted effort to destroy Dr. King's influence.

Two days after the installation of the Willard Hotel microphones, Assistant Director William Sullivan proposed that the FBI select a new "national Negro leader" as Dr. King's successor. In proposing the plan, Sullivan stated:

> It should be clear to all of us that Martin Luther King must, at some propitious point in the future, be revealed to the people of this country and to his Negro followers as being what he actually is—a fraud, demagogue and scoundrel. When the true facts concerning his activities are presented, such should be enough, if handled properly, to take him off his pedestal and to reduce him completely in influence. When this is done, and it can be and will be done, obviously much confusion will reign, particularly among the Negro people.
>
> . . . The Negroes will be left without a national leader of sufficiently compelling personality to steer them in the proper direction. This is what could happen, but need not happen if the right kind of a national Negro leader could at this time be gradually developed so as to overshadow Dr. King and be in the position to assume the role of the leadership of the Negro people when King has been completely discredited.

> For some months I have been thinking about this matter. One day I had an opportunity to explore this from a philosophical and sociological standpoint with [an acquaintance] whom I have known for some years. . . . I asked [him] to give the matter some attention and if he knew any Negro of outstanding intelligence and ability to let me know and we would have a discussion. [He] has submitted to me the name of the above-captioned person. Enclosed with this memorandum is an outline of [the person's] biography which is truly remarkable for a man so young. On scanning this biography, it will be seen that [he] does have all the qualifications of the kind of a Negro I have in mind to advance to positions of national leadership. . . .
>
> If this thing can be set up properly without the Bureau in any way becoming directly involved, I think it would be not only a great help to the FBI but would be a fine thing for the country at large. While I am not specifying at this moment, there are various ways in which the FBI could give this entire matter the proper direction and development. There are highly placed contacts of the FBI who might be very helpful to further such a step. These can be discussed in detail later when I have probed more fully into the possibilities.

When Sullivan was shown this memorandum by the Committee, he testified:

> I'm very proud of this memorandum, one of the best memoranda I ever wrote. I think here I was showing some concern for the country.

Sullivan sought the Director's approval "to explore this whole matter in greater detail." The Director noted his own "o.k." and added:

> I am glad to see that "light" has finally, though dismally delayed, come to the Domestic Int. Div. I struggled for months to get over the fact that the communists were taking over the racial movement but our experts here couldn't or wouldn't see it.

It is uncertain whether the FBI took steps to implement Sullivan's plan. The FBI files contain no additional memoranda on the subject. The successor for Dr. King proposed in Sullivan's memorandum has told the

Committee that he was never contacted by the FBI, and that he was not aware of the FBI's plans for him or of any attempts by the FBI to promote him as a civil rights leader.

D. FBI Headquarters Orders the Field Offices to Intensify Efforts to Discredit Dr. King: April–August 1964

On April 1, 1964, in response to a suggestion from the Atlanta field office for another conference in Washington to plan strategy against Dr. King, FBI Headquarters ordered the Atlanta and New York offices to:

> give the matter of instant investigation a thorough analysis with a view toward suggesting new avenues of investigation and intensification in areas already being explored. Bear in mind the main goals of this matter; namely, determining the extent of the communist influence in racial matters and taking such *action as is appropriate to neutralize or completely discredit the effectiveness of Martin Luther King, Jr., as a Negro leader*. . . . [Emphasis added.]

Headquarters listed several areas "having potential for further inquiry":

> possibilities of anonymous source contacts; possibilities of utilizing contacts in the news media field; initiating discreet checks relative to developing background information on employees of the Southern Christian Leadership Conference (SCLC); remaining alert to the possibility of capitalizing on any disgruntled SCLC employee; the possibility of developing information concerning any financial dealings of King which may be illegal; and the development of subversive information pertaining to SCLC employees.

The Atlanta Office responded with several ideas for "how the effectiveness of King can be neutralized or discredited":

— Determining whether a "rift" was developing between Dr. King and Roy Wilkins, head of the NAACP, and if so, using newspapers friendly to the Bureau to "feed pertinent subversive connections and dealings of King to Wilkins."

— "Furnishing to friendly newspapers on an anonymous basis, certain specific leads where he may develop the necessary data so that he may further write critical news stories."
— "Discreetly investigate the background of twelve key (SCLC) employees and associates in an effort to obtain some weakness that could be used for counter-intelligence activities."
— "Injection of false information with certain discontented (SCLC) employees."
— Sending letters to SCLC's financial donors, written on SCLC stationery fabricated in the FBI laboratory and bearing Dr. King's signature, advising the donors that the IRS was checking SCLC's tax records. "It is believed that such a letter of this type from SCLC may cause considerable concern and eliminate future contributions."
— Placing a pretext call to an SCLC creditor to impress him with the "financial plight" of the SCLC so that he "may be incited into collection efforts."
— Examining Dr. King's checking accounts and credit card accounts to develop information about his financial affairs.
— Making a survey to determine whether to install a "trash cover" of the SCLC office in Atlanta.

The Atlanta office also assured the Bureau that it would continue to explore the possibility of technical coverage of an Atlanta apartment frequently used by Dr. King, although coverage would involve several security problems.

Shortly after these proposals were submitted, the Director expressed "the Bureau's gratitude" to the Atlanta agents for their "aggressive imagination looking toward more and better ways of meeting the problems involved" in the investigation.

The New York office submitted only a few new suggestions, asserting that "It is felt that [our] coverage is adequate." To this the Director replied:

> The Bureau cannot adjudge as adequate any coverage which does not positively provide to the Bureau 100 percent of the intelligence relating to the communist influence in racial matters. Obviously, we are not securing all the information that is pertinent and needs to be secured. Our coverage, therefore, is not deemed adequate.

With respect to the New York office's conclusions about a civil rights leader and associate of Dr. King, who was also under close Bureau scrutiny for alleged "subversive" ties, the Director wrote:

> The Bureau does not agree with the expressed belief of the New York office that [ ] is not sympathetic to the Party cause. While there may not be any direct evidence that [ ] is a communist, neither is there any substantial evidence that he is anticommunist.

Surprisingly, the Bureau did not even comment on the statement of the New York office that Adviser A was "not now under CP discipline in the civil rights field."

In June 1964 a special unit was established in the Bureau's Internal Security Section to handle exclusively "the overall problem of communist penetration with the racial movement." The memorandum justifying the special unit pointed out that "urgency for the FBI to 'stay ahead' of the situation is tied to pending civil rights legislation and foreseeable ramifications arising out of the complex political situations in an election year where civil rights and social disturbances will play a key role in campaign efforts and possible election results."

In August the Bureau issued new instructions directing the field "to broaden its efforts relating to communist influences in the racial field." The term "communist," the field was told, "should be interpreted in its broadest sense as including persons not only adhering to the principles of the CPUSA itself, but also to such splinter and offshoot groups as the Socialist Workers Party, Progressive Labor and the like." The Director pointed out:

> The news media of recent months mirror the civil rights issue as probably the number one domestic issue in the political spectrum. There are clear and unmistakable signs that we are in the midst of a social revolution with the racial movement as its core. The Bureau, in meeting its responsibilities in this area, is an integral part of this revolution . . .

The Special Unit that had been established in June was made a permanent unit.

E. Steps Taken by the FBI in 1964 to Discredit Dr. King

The FBI's program to "neutralize" Martin Luther King as the leader of the civil rights movement went far beyond the planning and collection stage. The Committee has discovered the following attempts by the FBI to discredit Dr. King in 1964.

1. Attempts to Discredit Dr. King with the White House

As set forth in the preceding chapter, a memorandum summarizing the contents of the Willard Hotel tapes was shown to presidential assistant Walter Jenkins in January 1964 "inasmuch as King is seeking an appointment with President Johnson." The summary of information obtained from surveillance at the Willard, Honolulu, and Los Angeles hotels was sent to the White House and to the Attorney General in March 1964 in order to "remove all doubt from the Attorney General's mind as to the type of person King is." A third memorandum derived from microphone surveillance was sent to the White House in July.

2. Attempts to Discredit Dr. King with the Congress

In January 1964, Director Hoover gave off-the-record testimony before the House Appropriations Committee. His precise comments are not known. The briefing paper prepared for his appearance by the Domestic Intelligence Division, however, indicates that Director Hoover was prepared to represent to the Committee that Dr. King's advisers were communists and that Dr. King engaged in improper behavior.

The Director's off-the-record briefing had an immediate impact. The FBI was soon told that the members of the Committee were "very concerned regarding the background" of Dr. King, and that some members of the Committee felt that the President should be requested to instruct the USIA to withdraw a film dealing favorably with the August 1963 March on Washington. They were reported to be "particularly disturbed and irked at the fact that Martin Luther King appears to predominate the film."

In March 1964 Cartha DeLoach, Assistant to the Director, reported that he had been approached by Representative Howard Smith (D-Va.), Chairman of the House Rules Committee. According to DeLoach's memorandum, Representative Smith said that he had heard about the Director's remarks before the Appropriations Committee. Congressman Smith was reported to have asked for information for a speech about Dr. King on the floor of the House. DeLoach declined to furnish the required information, but recommended to the Director that Congressman Smith might be useful in the future because a speech by him about Dr. King would be picked up by "newspapers all over the Nation."

In a television interview several years later, Congressman Rooney stated:

> Now you talk about the FBI leaking something about Martin Luther King. I happen to know all about Martin Luther King, but I have never told anybody.
>
> INTERVIEWER. How do you know everything about Martin Luther King?
>
> Representative ROONEY. From the Federal Bureau of Investigation.
>
> INTERVIEWER. They've told you—gave you information based on tapes or other sources about Martin Luther King?
>
> Representative ROONEY. They did.
>
> INTERVIEWER. Is that proper?
>
> Representative ROONEY. Why not?

3. Attempts to Discredit Dr. King with Universities

In early March 1964, the Bureau learned that Marquette University in Milwaukee, Wisconsin, contemplated awarding Dr. King an honorary degree. A memorandum noted:

> It is shocking indeed that the possibility exists that King may receive an Honorary Degree from the same institution which honored the Director with such a degree in 1950. . . . By making pertinent information available to [a University official] at this time, on a strictly confidential basis, we will be giving the University sufficient time to enable it to take positive action in a manner which might avoid embarrassment to the University.

The university official was briefed by an FBI agent on Dr. King's background and assured the Bureau that Dr. King would not be considered for an honorary degree. The result of this FBI project is unclear.

In April 1964, the FBI learned that Dr. King had been offered an honorary degree by Springfield College. DeLoach visited Senator Leverett Saltonstall, who was a member of the Board of the College, in an effort to convince him to influence the College to withdraw its offer. According to DeLoach, Senator Saltonstall promised to speak with an official of the College. The College official was reported to have subsequently visited DeLoach, but to have said that he would be unable to "uninvite" Dr. King because the information concerning Dr. King had to be held in confidence, and the board of trustees was governed by "liberals."

4. Attempts to Discredit Dr. King with Churches

On June 12, 1964, William Sullivan wrote a memorandum stating that he had been contacted by the General Secretary of the National Council of the Churches of Christ. Sullivan reported that, "I took the liberty of advising [him] confidentiality of the fact that. Dr. Martin Luther King not only left a great deal to be desired from the standpoint of Communism, but also from the standpoint of personal conduct." Sullivan observed:

> I think that we have sowed an idea here which may do some good. I will follow up on the matter very discreetly to see what desirable results may emanate therefrom.

Sullivan met again with the General Secretary in mid-December 1964 and reported that the General Secretary had assured him "steps have been taken by the National Council of the Churches of Christ to make certain from this time on that Martin Luther King will never get 'one single dollar' of financial support from the National Council." Sullivan reported that the Secretary stated that he had discussed Dr. King's background with some "key" protestant clergymen who were "horrified." Sullivan also noted that the Secretary said that he also intended to discuss the matter with Roy Wilkins to persuade Wilkins "that Negro leaders should completely isolate King and remove him from the role he is now occupying in civil rights activities."

On December 8, 1964, the Director authorized the disclosure of information about Dr. King's personal life to an influential member of the Baptist World Alliance (BWA), so that he could pass the information along to the General Secretary of BWA, and to BWA Program Committee members, to prevent the Committee from inviting Dr. King to address the BWA's 1965 Congress in Miami Beach. The Director rejected a proposal, however, for "arranging for [certain BWA members] to listen to sources we have concerning this matter."

5. Attempts to Discredit Dr. King with the Pope

On August 31, 1964, the FBI learned that Dr. King, who was going to be touring Europe in September, might have plans to visit the Pope. Internal Security Section Chief Baumgardner observed:

> It would be shocking indeed for such an unscrupulous character as King to receive an audience with the Pope. It is believed that if a plan to see the Pope is in the making, it ought to be nipped in the bud. We have considered different possibilities for meeting this problem and believe that the best one would be to have Assistant Director Malone of the New York office personally contact Francis Cardinal Spellman and on a highly confidential basis bring to the Cardinal's attention the fact that King is to visit Rome. . . .
>
> Malone should be able to impress upon the Cardinal the likely embarrassment that may result to the Pope should he grant King an audience and King is later discredited.

On September 8, Baumgardner reported:

> Malone called today and stated that he had discussed the situation with Cardinal Spellman over the weekend and he said that the Cardinal took instant steps to advise the Vatican against granting any audience to King. . . . Cardinal Spellman is going to Rome next week . . . and thus will be on the scene personally and further insure that the Pope is not placed in an embarrassing position through any contact with King.

The FBI's efforts were to no avail. The Pope met with Dr. King. The Director wrote across the memoranda informing him of that meeting, "astounding," and "I am amazed that the Pope gave an audience to such a [excised by FBI]." The Director then initiated inquiries into the reason for the failure of this project.

6. The Attempt to Discredit Dr. King During His Receipt of the Nobel Peace Prize

On October 14, 1964, Martin Luther King was named to win the Nobel Peace Prize. He received the prize in Europe on December 10, 1965. The FBI took measures to dampen Dr. King's welcome, both in Europe and on his return home.

On November 22, 1964—two weeks before Dr. King's trip to receive the prize—the Domestic Intelligence Division assembled a thirteen-page updated printed version of the monograph which Attorney General Kennedy had ordered recalled in October 1963. A copy was sent to Bill Moyers, Special Assistant to the President, on December 1, 1964, with a letter requesting his advice concerning whether the monograph should also be distributed to "responsible officials in the Executive Branch." Moyers gave his permission on December 7, and copies were distributed to the heads of several executive agencies.

Information about Dr. King's private life was also made available to United Nations representatives Adlai Stevenson and Ralph Bunche, who the Bureau had learned were being considered as possible participants at the December 1964 "welcome home" reception for Dr. King.

Three days after Vice President-elect Humphrey participated in one of the "welcome home" receptions for Dr. King in New York, the Bureau sent him a copy of the updated King monograph and a separate memorandum entitled "Martin Luther King, Jr.: His Personal Conduct." On December 8, 1964, the Bureau decided to brief Governor Nelson Rockefeller about Dr. King's private life and alleged Communist associations, apparently to dissuade the Governor from taking part in ceremonies commending Dr. King for having received the Nobel Prize.

Upon learning that Dr. King might meet with a certain foreign leader, FBI headquarters instructed the FBI representative in that country to brief the proper authorities about Dr. King. The United States ambassadors in London and Oslo were briefed about Dr. King because "the Ambassadors might consider entertaining King while he is in Europe to receive the Nobel Peace Prize" and it might be possible to "forestall such action by the Ambassadors if they were briefed." The ambassadors in Stockholm and Copenhagen were also briefed because "King is also to visit those cities."

On November 10, 1964, the FBI learned that the United States Information Agency was considering requesting Dr. King to engage in a one-week lecture tour in Europe following his receipt of the Nobel Prize. Hoover approved the Domestic Intelligence Division's recommendation that USIA be furnished with the latest critical Bureau reports about Dr. King.

7. Attempts to Block Dr. King's Publications

On September 11, 1964, the FBI learned that Dr. King intended to publish an article in a major national publication. The Domestic Intelligence Division noted that it did not know "what line King will take in the article or what its specific stands will be," but, nonetheless recommended that "it would be well to prevent any publication of his views."

The task of preventing publication was assigned to an agent with contacts at the magazine who had "forestalled" the publication of an article by Dr. King in that magazine earlier in 1964.

The agent subsequently reported that he had contacted an official of the magazine in late September. According to the agent, the official had agreed to "endeavor to assist" the FBI, and had been briefed about King, but was unable to block publication because a contractual agreement had already been made. The FBI did apparently have some influence at the magazine, however, because a memorandum reporting the incident concludes:

> In connection with this [magazine] article by King, our sources have indicated that since he was awarded the Nobel Peace Prize he has attempted through some of his associates to change the [magazine] article in an effort to soften criticism made by him against other civil rights groups and leaders. King feared that such criticism would cause difficulties in the civil rights movement. The [magazine], however, has resisted King's efforts to make these changes.

In February 1964, the Director alerted the field offices that Dr. King was writing a new book, and noted that "it is entirely possible that with the publication of the book the Bureau may desire to take some action, possibly in the counterintelligence area or otherwise, which may be designed to discredit King or otherwise neutralize his effectiveness. . . ."

The field offices were instructed to maintain information relating to the preparation and publication of the hook. The FBI files indicate that this information was collected, but it is not clear whether it was ever used.

8. Attempt to Undermine the National Science Foundation's Cooperation with the SCLC

The FBI sent the National Science Foundation (NSF) a copy of the second printed monograph on King in order to convince the NSF to remove the SCLC from "the NSF program to obtain qualified Negro students from southern schools."

9. Unsuccessful FBI Attempts to Locate Financial Improprieties

In early January 1964, the Chief of the Internal Security Section of the Domestic Intelligence Division, Frederick J. Baumgardner, recommended that "examination of recent income tax returns of King might well reveal information which could assist the Bureau in its efforts to discredit King or neutralize his effectiveness." The Intelligence Division subsequently acquired from the Internal Revenue Service copies of income tax returns for the prior five years of Dr. King, the SCLC, and the Gandhi Society, an organization which the FBI stated "augmented" the fund-raising activities of the SCLC. The Intelligence Division of the IRS told the Bureau that "IRS had very carefully scrutinized King's returns in the past but had not been able to establish a cause of action against him." However, the IRS assured the FBI that Dr. King's current returns would be scrutinized "very carefully to determine whether any violations appear." None did.

Undeterred, the Director informed the field offices that "the Bureau believes that more than ever it would be most desirable to identify any bank where [King] may have an account . . . and consider an audit of such account."

One effort to uncover derogatory information about Dr. King was conceived by the Supervisor in charge of the King case during a golf game. A remote acquaintance of the Supervisor mentioned that he had heard from a friend that an acquaintance had said that Dr. King had a numbered account in a foreign bank with a balance of over one million dollars. The Supervisor suggested to Sullivan:

> If we can prove that King is hoarding large sums of money, we would have available possibly the best information to date which could be used to discredit him, especially in the eyes of his own people . . . we may take the action to discredit King ourselves through friendly news

sources, or the like, or we might turn the information over to the Internal Revenue Service for possible criminal prosecution.

The plan was approved by Director Hoover and an inquiry was initiated. By December 1965, the investigation into a possible foreign bank account was described by the Director as "the most important presently pending" facet of the King investigation. The investigation was dropped shortly afterward, however, when it developed that the initial source of the allegation informed the FBI that "it was merely a wild conclusion that had been previously drawn by someone whose identity he does not now recall."

{ . . . }

VI. THE HOOVER-KING CONTROVERSY BECOMES PUBLIC AND A TRUCE IS CALLED: APRIL–DECEMBER 1964

Summary

Director Hoover's dislike for Dr. King, which had been known within the Bureau since early 1962, became a matter of public record in November 1964 when Director Hoover described Dr. King at a meeting with women reporters as the "most notorious liar" in the country. Dr. King responded that the Director was obviously "faltering" under the responsibilities of his office. The FBI immediately intensified its secret campaign against Dr. King, offering to play the tapes from microphone surveillance of Dr. King to reporters and to leak stories concerning him to the press. The FBI also sent a tape recording made from the microphone surveillance to Dr. King, with a warning which Dr. King and his close associates interpreted as an invitation to suicide.

The public aspects of the dispute peaked in December 1964, shortly before Dr. King went to Europe to receive the Nobel Peace Prize. Dr. King publicly announced that it was time for the controversy to end, and arranged a meeting with Director Hoover to seal a truce. The FBI's public criticism stopped, but the Bureau's secret campaign to discredit Dr. King continued. Believing that Dr. King's downfall would severely harm the entire movement for racial equality, several prominent civil rights figures met with FBI officials to voice their concern and seek assurances from the FBI that the attacks on Dr. King would stop.

A. First Steps in the Public Controversy April–November 1964

Although the FBI had been covertly engaged in a massive campaign to discredit Dr. King for several months, the fact that the FBI was the source of allegations about communist influence in the-civil rights movement did not become public until the release of Director Hoover's off-the-record testimony before the House Appropriations Committee in April 1964. The Director was quoted in the press as having testified that "'Communist influence does exist in the Negro movement' and can influence 'large masses' of people." Dr. King immediately issued a forceful reply:

> It is very unfortunate that Mr. J. Edgar Hoover, in his claims of alleged communist infiltration in the civil rights movement, has allowed himself to aid and abet the salacious claims of southern racists and the extreme right-wing elements.
>
> We challenge all who raise the "red" issue, whether they be newspaper columnists or the head of the FBI himself—to come forward and provide real evidence which contradicts this stand of the SCLC. We are confident that this cannot be done.
>
> We affirm that SCLC is unalterably opposed to the misguided philosophy of communism.
>
> It is difficult to accept the word of the FBI on communist infiltration in the civil rights movement, when they have been so completely ineffectual in resolving the continued mayhem and brutality inflicted upon the Negro in the deep south. It would be encouraging to us if Mr. Hoover and the FBI would be as diligent in apprehending those responsible for bombing churches and killing little children as they are in seeking out alleged communist infiltration in the civil rights movement.

In early May 1964, Director Hoover made the following response to a question from United Press International concerning whether any communists were in positions of leadership in the civil rights movement:

> Let me first emphasize that I realize the vast majority of Negroes have rejected and recognize communism for what it is. . . .

> The existence and importance of the communist influence in the Negro movement should not be ignored or minimized, nor should it be exaggerated. The Communist Party will use its forces either in the open forum of public opinion or through its sympathizers who do not wear the badge of communism but who spout some of the same ideas carried in the Communist Party line. This is the influence which is capable of moving large masses of loyal and dedicated citizens toward communist objectives while being lured away from the true issues involved. It is up to the civil rights organizations themselves to recognize this and face up to it.

On May 11, Dr. King appeared on the news program, "Face the Nation." He denied communists had infiltrated decision-making positions in the civil rights movement or the SCLC and remarked that it was "unfortunate" that "such a great man" as Director Hoover had made allegations to that effect. Dr. King added that the Director should more appropriately have remarked on how surprising it was that so few Negroes had turned to communism in light of the treatment they had received. Dr. King said that the Justice Department had warned him of only one suspected communist in the SCLC, and that he had fired that individual.

The feud between Director Hoover and Dr. King heightened on November 18, 1964, with the Director's public allegation that Dr. King was the "most notorious liar" in the country. Director Hoover made that comment during a meeting with women reporters in the context of explaining how FBI agents were assigned in civil rights cases. According to a memorandum of the meeting written by DeLoach:

> [The Director] stated it was a common belief in some circles that Special Agents in the South were all, without exception, southern born agents. As a matter of fact, 70% of the agents currently assigned to the South were born in the North. He stated that the "notorious" Martin Luther King had attempted to capitalize on this matter by claiming that all agents assigned to the Albany, Georgia, Resident Agency were southern born agents. As a matter of fact, 4 out of 5 of the agents assigned to the Albany, Georgia, Resident Agency were northern born. The Director stated he had instructed me to get in touch with Reverend King and line up an appointment so that King

> could be given the true facts. He stated that King had refused to give me an appointment and, therefore, he considered King to be the most "notorious liar" in the country.

When the reporters asked Director Hoover for more details about Dr. King,

> he stated, off the record, "He is one of the lowest characters in the country." There was an immediate inquiry as to whether he could be quoted on the original statement that Martin Luther King was a liar and he stated, "Yes-that is public record."

Nicholas Katzenbach, who was then Acting Attorney General, testified that he talked with Director Hoover about that press conference and

> [Hoover] told me that it was not his practice to have press conferences, had not done so in the past, and would not do so again in the future. Perhaps the depth of his feeling with respect to Dr. King was revealed to me by his statement that he did not understand all the publicity which the remark had attracted because he had been asked a simple question and given a simple truthful answer.

Some of Dr. King's advisers drafted a strong response, one of which would have "blown Hoover out of the water, calling him every name in the book." Before they had an opportunity to release the statement, Dr. King, who was then in Bimini, issued the following public reply:

> I cannot conceive of Mr. Hoover making a statement like this without being under extreme pressure. He has apparently faltered under the awesome burden, complexities and responsibilities of his office.

Dr. King also sent a telegram to Director Hoover, which was made public, stating:

> I was appalled and surprised at your reported statement maligning my integrity. What motivated such an irresponsible accusation is a mystery to me.
>
> I have sincerely questioned the effectiveness of the F.B.I. in racial incidents, particularly where bombings and brutalities against

> Negroes are at issue. . . . I will be happy to discuss this question with you at length in the near future. Although your statement said you have attempted to meet with me, I have sought in vain for any record of such a request.

Dr. King also criticized Director Hoover in a press interview on the same day for "following the path of appeasement of political powers in the South."

The Domestic Intelligence Division prepared an analysis of the allegations in Dr. King's telegram, emphasizing the events two years earlier which the FBI had interpreted as a refusal by Dr. King to be interviewed. Sullivan recommended against replying to Dr. King's charges or meeting with Dr. King. The Director penned his agreement on Sullivan's memorandum:

> O.K. But I can't understand why we are unable to get the true facts before the public. We can't even get our accomplishments published. We are never taking the aggressive, but above lies remain unanswered.

The following day, the FBI mailed a tape recording from the Willard Hotel microphone surveillance to Dr. King accompanied by a letter which Dr. King and his associates interpreted as an invitation to suicide.

B. Tapes Are Mailed to King: November 21, 1964

Sometime in mid-November 1964, a decision was made at FBI Headquarters to mail a tape recording made during microphone surveillance of Dr. King to the SCLC office in Atlanta. William Sullivan, who was responsible for the project, testified that he first learned of the plan when Alan Belmont, Assistant to the Director, told him that Director Hoover wanted one of the King tapes mailed to Coretta King to precipitate their separation, thereby diminishing Dr. King's stature. Belmont told Sullivan that the FBI laboratory would "sterilize the tape to prevent its being traced to the Bureau." Sullivan was to have the tape mailed from a southern state.

Sullivan told the Committee that he had opposed the plan because it would warn Dr. King that his activities were being covered by microphones. According to Sullivan, Belmont agreed that the plan was unwise, but said that he had no power to stop it because the orders had come from Hoover and Tolson.

The FBI technician who prepared the tape told the Committee that he had been ordered to produce a "composite" tape from coverage of hotel rooms in Washington, D.C., San Francisco, and Los Angeles. After the tape was completed, a copy was left with Sullivan.

Sullivan testified that he ordered a "tight-lipped . . . reliable" agent to fly to Tampa, Florida, to mail a package to Coretta King. He did not tell the agent that the package contained the King tape. The agent testified that he flew to Miami and then called Sullivan, who instructed him to address the package to Martin Luther King, Jr. The agent said that he mailed the package from a post office near the Miami airport. A travel voucher provided to the Committee by the FBI indicates that the agent flew to Miami on November 21, 1964.

Congressman Andrew Young, who was then Dr. King's assistant, recalled that the tape arrived at the SCLC Headquarters in Atlanta sometime before December 1964. Congressman Young said that the office personnel assumed the tape contained another of Dr. King's speeches; it was stored for a while, and later sent to Dr. King's home along with several other tapes. Dr. King, Congressman Young, and some others listened to the tape sometime after Dr. King had returned from receiving the Nobel Peace Prize, probably in January 1965. Congressman Young testified that he probably destroyed the tape several years later.

Congressman Young recalled that the tape was of "very poor quality, very garbled," but that at least part of it appeared to have been made during a conversation between Dr. King and other civil rights leaders at the Willard Hotel. He testified that none of the comments on the tape related to the commission of a crime or to "affection" for communism. "It was personal conversation among friends."

According to Congressman Young a letter had accompanied the tape, stating that the tape would be released in 34 days and threatening "there is only one thing you can do to prevent this from happening." Congressman Young said that when he and Dr. King read the letter, "we assumed that the letter and the tape had been mailed 34 days before the receipt of the Nobel Prize, and that this was a threat to expose Martin just before he received the Nobel Prize." Congressman Young testified:

> I think that the disturbing thing to Martin was that he felt somebody was trying to get him to commit suicide, and because it was a tape of a meeting in Washington and the postmark was from Florida, we

assumed nobody had the capacity to do that other than the Federal Bureau of Investigation.

Both Young and Ralph Abernathy, who also heard the tape and read the letter, interpreted it as inviting Dr. King to take his own life.

William Sullivan testified that he could not recall such a letter. The FBI provided the Committee with a copy of a letter which was found in Sullivan's office files following his discharge in 1971. The letter stated in part:

> King, look into your heart. You know you are a complete fraud and a greater liability to all of us Negroes. White people in this country have enough frauds of their own but I am sure they don't have one at this time that is any where near your equal. You are no clergyman and you know it. I repeat that you are a colossal fraud and an evil, vicious one at that. . . .
>
> King, like all frauds your end is approaching. You could have been our greatest leader. . . . But you are done. Your "honorary" degrees, your Nobel Prize (what a grim farce) and other awards will not save you. King, I repeat you are done. . . .
>
> The American public, the church organizations that have been helping—Protestants, Catholics and Jews will know you for what you are—an evil beast. So will others who have backed you. You are done.
>
> King, there is only one thing left for you to do. You know what it is. You have just 34 days in which to do (this exact number has been selected for a specific reason, it has definite practical significance). You are done. There is but one way out for you. You better take it before your filthy fraudulent self is bared to the nation.

Andrew Young stated that the last paragraph of this letter was identical with the letter that had been sent to the SCLC headquarters, but that the other portions of the letter appeared to be an earlier draft of the letter that he had seen. Sullivan testified that he did not recall ever having seen the document, although it was "possible" that he had something to do with it and simply cannot remember. Sullivan also testified that he could not recall any conversations at the FBI concerning the possibility of Dr. King's committing suicide. After reading the last paragraph of the letter, he conceded that it could be interpreted as an invitation to suicide, although so far as

Sullivan knew, the FBI's goal was simply to convince Dr. King to resign from the SCLC, not to kill himself.

When asked by the Committee what had ultimately happened to the letter received by Reverend King, Andrew Young testified:

> I'm not really sure about this now, but I think we discussed something about a letter with DeLoach—I'm not certain whether it was DeLoach or the local FBI agents—and they said they would be glad to look into it. They said, whenever we got any of these kind of threatening letters, to send them to them, and they would be glad to investigate. That letter may have been sent back to DeLoach.

C. Attempts by the FBI to "Leak" to Reporters Tape Recordings Embarrassing to Dr. King

After Director Hoover denounced Dr. King as a "notorious liar" in mid-November, the FBI apparently made several attempts to "leak" tape recordings concerning Dr. King to newsmen. One offer involving the Bureau Chief of a national news publication has been discussed at length in the preceding chapter. David Kraslow, another reporter, has told a Committee staff member that one of his "better sources at the Bureau" offered him a transcript of a tape recording about Dr. King. Kraslow said that his source read him a portion of the transcript on the phone, and claimed that it came from a "bug" operated by a Southern police agency. Kraslow said that he declined the offer. It is not known how many other reporters were approached by the FBI during that period; Nicholas Katzenbach testified that at least one other reporter had informed him of a similar Bureau offer, and other witnesses, such as James Farmer, have mentioned additional "leaks" from the Bureau.

{ . . . }

VII. THE FBI PROGRAM AGAINST DR. KING: 1965–1968

The public dispute between Dr. King and Director Hoover ended with their December 1, 1964, meeting. The Bureau's covert attempts to discredit Dr. King and undermine his influence in the civil rights movement did not cease, however, but continued unabated until Dr. King's death. Although the intensity of the FBI's campaign against Dr. King appears to have been reduced somewhat in 1966 and 1967, Dr. King's public stand against the war in Vietnam in mid-1967 revived the FBI's attempt to link Dr. King and the SCLC with communism.

A. Major Efforts to Discredit Dr. King: 1965–1968

1. Attempts to Discredit Dr. King with Churches

On February 1, 1965, The Domestic Intelligence Division learned that Dr. King was scheduled to speak at the Davenport, Iowa, Catholic Interracial Council's banquet and receive a "Pacem in Terris" award in memory of Pope John. Internal Security Section chief Frederick Baumgardner observed, "it is shocking indeed that King continues to be honored by religious groups." Baumgardner recommended that Assistant Director Malone contact Francis Cardinal Spellman and suggest that "in the end it might well be embarrassing to the Catholic Church for having given honors to King." The Director noted on the memorandum, "I see no need to further approach Spellman"; he was apparently alluding to the unsuccessful attempt to sabotage Dr. King's audience with the Pope through Spellman's intervention. There is no record of any further action.

In February 1966 Dr. King held a press conference following a meeting with the Reverend John P. Cody, Archbishop of the Chicago Diocese of the Roman Catholic Church, and announced that he and Cody were in agreement on general civil rights goals and that he hoped priests and nuns in Chicago would participate in SCLC programs. The Domestic Intelligence Division subsequently recommended that a special agent acquainted with the Archbishop brief him about Dr. King to aid "the Archbishop in determining the degree of cooperation his archdiocese will extend to King's program in Chicago and [to] result in a lessening of King's influence in Chicago."

The Archbishop was briefed on February 24, 1966, "along the lines discussed with Assistant Director Sullivan." The agent who conducted the briefing wrote that he felt "certain that [Cody] will do everything possible to neutralize King's effect in this area."

In April 1966 the FBI Legal Attache in Paris requested permission to inform the pastor of the American Church in Paris of Dr. King's background "in an effort to convince him that his continued support of

Martin Luther King may result in embarrassment for him and the American Church in Paris." The pastor was briefed on May 9, 1966. According to the agent who conducted the briefing, the pastor was skeptical about the FBI allegations, but promised to keep the information in mind for future dealings with Dr. King.

2. Attempts to Discredit Dr. King with Heads of Government Agencies

In March 1965 the FBI contacted former Florida Governor LeRoy Collins. Collins was then Director of the Community Relations Service, Department of Commerce, a position the Bureau viewed as "something of a 'mediator' in problems relating to the racial field." The FBI told Collins that Corretta King had criticized his participation in developments in Selma, Alabama, and had said that Collins was "blinded by prejudice." A copy of the December 1964 monograph about Dr. King was also sent to Collins, "in view of [his] important position relative to the racial movement."

Also in March 1965 the FBI learned that the Internal Revenue Service intended to invite Dr. King as one of 19 guest lecturers at a series of seminars on Equal Employment Opportunities. When the IRS requested routine name checks on the 19 individuals, Director Hoover approved a Domestic Intelligence Division request to send the IRS a copy of the December 1964 monograph; normal procedures were followed in checking the other 18 people.

In December 1966 Domestic Intelligence Director William Sullivan reported that he had met with Ambassador U. Alexis Johnson during a tour of the FBI's Legal Attache Office in Japan and was surprised to learn that Johnson was unaware of allegations that communists were influencing Dr. King. Sullivan recommended that Johnson be sent a copy of the monograph about Dr. King "because of his position." Director Hoover approved the plan, and a copy of the monograph was sent to the FBI Legal Attache in Tokyo for hand-delivery to the Ambassador.

Dr. King publicly announced his opposition to American involvement in the war in Vietnam in a speech at New York's Riverside Church on April 4, 1967. Six days later, Charles Brennan of the Domestic Intelligence Division recommended the circulation of an updated draft of the King monograph to the White House. Brennan's memorandum states that the revised monograph contained allegations about communist influence over Dr. King as well as personally derogatory allegations.

Director Hoover approved and copies of the revised monograph were sent to the White House, the Secretary of State, the Secretary of Defense, the Director of the Secret Service, and the Attorney General. A copy was subsequently sent to the Commandant of the Marine Corps, who had been interested in "King's activities in the civil rights movement but recently had become quite concerned as to whether there are any subversive influences which have caused King to link the civil rights movement with the anti-Vietnam War movement." The Domestic Intelligence Division recommended that a copy be given to the Marine Commandant because "it is felt would definitely be to the benefit of [the Commandant] and to the Bureau. . . . "

In February 1968, FBI Headquarters learned that Dr. King planned a "Washington Spring Project" for April 1968. According to a Domestic Intelligence Division memorandum, the Director suggested that the King monograph be again revised. That memorandum noted:

> Bringing this monograph up-to-date and disseminating it at high level prior to King's "Washington Spring Project" should serve again to remind top-level officials in Government of the wholly disreputable character of King.
>
> . . . Because of the importance of doing a thorough job on this, we will conduct an exhaustive field review to bring together the most complete and up-to-date information and to present it in a hard-hitting manner.

The revised monograph, dated March 12, 1968, was disseminated to the White House, the Attorney General, and the heads of various government intelligence agencies.

3. Attempts to Discredit Dr. King by Using the Press

Despite Cartha DeLoach's assurances to Andrew Young and Ralph Abernathy that the FBI would never disseminate information to the press, the Bureau continued its efforts to cultivate "friendly" news sources that would be willing to release information unfavorable to Dr. King. Ralph McGill, the pro-civil rights editor of the *Atlanta Constitution,* was a major focus of the Bureau's attentions. The Bureau apparently first furnished McGill with derogatory information about Dr. King as part of an attempt to dissuade community leaders in Atlanta from participating in a banquet planned to honor Dr. King upon his return from the Nobel Prize ceremonies. After a meeting with McGill, William Sullivan reported that McGill said that he had stopped speaking favorably of Dr. King, that he had refused to take an active part in preparing for the banquet, and that he had even taken steps to undermine the banquet. McGill's version of what transpired will never be known, since McGill is deceased. According to Sullivan's memorandum, however:

> Mr. McGill told me that following my first discussion with him a few weeks ago he contacted a banker friend in Atlanta who was helping to finance the banquet to be given King next Wednesday night. The banker was disturbed and said he would contact some other bankers also involved and see if support could be quietly withdrawn. McGill's friend and some of the bankers did take steps to withdraw but this was very quickly relayed to bankers in Haiti who were on the threshold of an important financial deal with the Atlanta, Georgia, bankers. They took the position that if the Atlanta bankers did not support the Martin Luther King party, their financial deal with these Georgia bankers was off. . . . As a result they got cold feet and decided to go ahead with financing King's party.
>
> McGill told me that . . . a Catholic leader in Georgia, an Episcopal clergyman and a Jewish rabbi are also quite active in support of this party for King. . . . I told him that . . . he might want to explore very confidentially and discreetly the subject matter with these three men. . . . McGill told me that he thinks it is too late now, especially in view of the financial interest of the Georgia bankers in the Haiti deal, to prevent the banquet from taking place. However, McGill said he would do what he could to encourage key people to limit their praise and support of King as much as possible.
>
> McGill also told me that he is taking steps through [a Negro leader] to get key Negro leaders to unite in opposition to King and to gradually force him out of the civil rights movement if at all possible.

The FBI subsequently told the White House that McGill:

> believes that the very best thing that could happen would be to have King step completely out of the civil rights movement and public life for he feels that if this is not done, sooner or later King will be publicly exposed. Mr. McGill believes that an exposure of King will do irreparable harm to the civil rights movement in which he, Mr. McGill, and others are so interested and have worked so hard for; and likewise it will do injury to different citizens of the country who have been supporting King.

In late May 1965, a reporter from United Press International requested the Bureau for information about Dr. King for use in a series of articles about the civil rights leader. The Special Agent in Charge in Atlanta recommended that the Bureau give the reporter both public source and confidential information about Dr. King because the reporter "is the UPI's authority in the South on the Negro movement and his articles carry a great deal of influence and [the SAC did not believe] that he would prepare anything flattering or favorable to King." The Director approved a recommendation that the reporter be supplied with a public source document and with a "short summation" of allegations concerning communist influence over Dr. King to be used "merely for orientation purposes."

In October 1966, the Domestic Intelligence Division recommended that an article "indicting King for his failure to take a stand on the [black power] issue and at the same time exposing the degree of communist influence on him" be given to a newspaper contact "friendly" to the Bureau, "such as . . . [the] Editor of *U.S. News and World Report*."

> It is felt that the public should again be reminded of this communist influence on King, and the current controversy among civil rights leaders makes this timely to do so.

Attached to the memorandum was a proposed article which noted that the efforts of several civil rights leaders to denounce "Black Power" had been "undermined by one man in the civil rights movement who holds in his hands the power to silence the rabble rousers and to give the movement renewed momentum." The article attributed Dr. King's equivocation to his advisers, who were alleged to have had affiliations with the Communist Party or organizations associated with the Party. Dr. King's decision to oppose the Vietnamese war was also attributed to these advisers.

One project involving the mass media which the FBI felt had been particularly successful was its attempt to prevent Dr. King from obtaining contributions from James Hoffa of the Teamsters Union. In October 1966, the FBI discovered that Dr. King planned to meet with Hoffa, but that Dr. King had wanted to avoid publicity because, in the words of the Bureau:

> Disclosure of King's transparent attempt to blackmail Hoffa with the large Negro membership of Hoffa's union, to solve the Southern Christian Leadership Conference's financial problems, would cause an uproar among leaders of organizations having large Negro memberships. pointing out their own vulnerability to such a squeeze by any unscrupulous civil rights leader. This potential collusion between large labor unions and the civil rights movement, could also react to the detriment of the Negro in that through large financial donations, an unscrupulous labor leader could subvert the legitimate aims and objectives of the civil rights movement to his own purposes.

The Crime Records Division prepared an article for public release raising the question of "who really gets squeezed when these two pythons get together." The Domestic Intelligence Division also recommended:

> a Bureau official be designated now to alert friendly news media of the meeting once the meeting date is learned so that arrangements can be made for appropriate press coverage of the planned meeting to expose and disrupt it.

Director Hoover's "O.K." appears below the recommendation.

On discovering that the meeting was about to occur, the Crime Records Division notified a reporter for the *New York Daily News* and a national columnist. "News photographers and wire services are also being alerted to give coverage . . . "

A Crime Records Division memorandum on the following day reported that "in view of publicity in the New York Daily News regarding this proposed meeting, King and his aides had decided that it would be unwise to meet with Hoffa." The Bureau then notified reporters that Dr. King was coming to Washington, D.C. The reporters "cornered" Dr. King as he came off the plane and quizzed him about the proposed meeting. The Crime Records Division reported these events to the Director with the assessment that "our counterintelligence aim to thwart King from receiving money from the Teamsters has been quite successful to date." Director Hoover initiated the memorandum reporting this news, "Excellent."

In March 1967 Director Hoover approved a recommendation by the Domestic Intelligence Division to furnish "friendly" reporters questions to ask Dr. King. The Intelligence Division believed that Dr. King would be particularly "vulnerable" to questions concerning his opposition to the war in Vietnam, and recommended that a reporter be selected to interview Dr. King "ostensibly to question King about his new book," but with the objective of bringing out the foreign policy aspects of Dr. King's philosophy.

> This could then be linked to show that King's current policies remarkably parallel communist efforts. This would cause extreme embarrassment to King.

In October 1967 the Domestic Intelligence Division recommended that an editorial in a Negro magazine, which criticized Dr. King for his stance on the Vietnam war, be given to "friendly news sources." The purpose of the dissemination was to "publicize King as a traitor to his country and his race" and to "reduce his income" from a series of shows given by Harry Belafonte to earn funds for the SCLC. The recommendation was approved by the Director and is marked "Handled 10/28/67."

4. Attempts to Discredit Dr. King with Major Political and Financial Leaders

In March 1965 the FBI learned that a "Martin Luther King Day" was being planned in a major city. The Domestic Intelligence Division recommended that the Special Agent in Charge "personally meet with the Governor and brief him concerning King" in order to "induce him to minimize the affair and especially the award for King."

The Domestic Intelligence Division memorandum was initialed by the Director and bears the handwritten notation, "handled 3-5-65, WCS[ullivan]."

In October 1966 the FBI learned that Dr. King had met with McGeorge

Bundy, then Director of the Ford Foundation, and received a tentative offer of a grant for the SCLC. The Domestic Intelligence Division decided that officials of the Foundation might not be aware of the "subversive backgrounds of King's principal advisers," but that if they were briefed, "this might preclude any assistance being granted." Director Hoover approved a plan to have a former FBI agent, who was then a vice president of the Ford Motor Company, approach Bundy. The ex-agent was contacted, briefed on Dr. King, and according to DeLoach, "stated he would personally contact Bundy in an effort to put a stop to King receiving any funds from the Ford Foundation."

In a memorandum dated October 26, 1966, DeLoach reported that the ex-agent had contacted Bundy, but that Bundy had refused to talk with him about Dr. King, saying that he would only talk with a person having first-hand knowledge about Dr. King, and would not listen to rumors. DeLoach recommended that the FBI not directly approach Bundy, since "it is doubtful that contact with him by the FBI will convince him one way or another." Director Hoover wrote on DeLoach's memorandum, "Yes. We would get nowhere with Bundy."

5. Attempts to Discredit Dr. King with Congressional Leaders

According to a memorandum by Assistant to the Director DeLoach, Speaker of the House John McCormack requested a briefing about Dr. King's background and activities in August 1965. DeLoach reported that he briefed McCormack for 45 minutes about Dr. King's private life and about possible communist influence over Dr. King. According to DeLoach, McCormack stated that "he now recognized the gravity of the situation and that something obviously must be done about it." McCormack was not interviewed by the committee staff.

Not all Congressional inquiries about Dr. King, however, were answered by the Bureau. For example, in January 1968, DeLoach reported that he had met with Senator Robert C. Byrd at the Senator's request. DeLoach's memorandum of the meeting states that the Senator expressed concern over Dr. King's plan for demonstrations in Washington, D.C., during the summer and said that it was time Dr. King "met his Waterloo." DeLoach's memorandum states that Senator Byrd asked if the FBI would prepare a speech about Dr. King which he could deliver on the floor of the Senate. DeLoach declined to provide any information that was not on the public record, although he did promise to keep the Senator informed of new public source items. The Committee staff did not interview Senator Byrd.

B. COINTELPRO Operations Against Dr. King and His Associates

The FBI elevated its activities against Dr. King and his associates to the status of formal counterintelligence programs (COINTELPRO) during this period. In July 1966, the Director instructed the New York field office that "immediate steps should be taken to discredit, expose, or otherwise neutralize Adviser A's role as a clandestine communist." An agent was assigned full-time to "carefully review the [Adviser A] case file seeking possible counterintelligence approaches." He reported that there was no derogatory information on Adviser A's personal life, and that the only "effective way to neutralize [him] is by public exposure" of his alleged Communist Party associations. None of the FBI's efforts against Adviser A appear to have met success.

The FBI considered initiating a formal COINTELPRO to discredit Dr. King and Dr. Benjamin Spock in May 1967 when rumors developed concerning the possibility that King and Spock might run as "peace" candidates in the 1968 presidential election. The New York field office recommended postponing the effort to expose "communist connections" of persons associated with King and Spock until they had formally announced their candidacy. The Chicago field office proposed waiting until the summer of 1968, reasoning that by then the Administration would have either resolved the Vietnam conflict or, if not, the Communist Party would be emphasizing the peace theme, and exposure of Communist Party links with the King-Spock campaign "would doubtlessly be appreciated by the Administration." While the Chicago field office felt that the Bureau should not "rule out" the use of "flyers, leaflets, cards and bumper stickers" to discredit the King-Spock ticket, it recommended "the use of a political columnist or reporter for this purpose." Apparently no steps were taken to implement the plan.

In August 1967 the Bureau initiated a COINTELPRO captioned "Black Nationalist-Hate Groups." This program is extensively described in the Staff Report on COINTELPRO. The document initiating the program states:

> The purpose of this new counterintelligence endeavor is to expose, disrupt, misdirect, discredit, or otherwise neutralize the activities of black-nationalist, hate-type organizations and groupings, their leadership, spokesmen, membership and supporters, and to counter their propensity for violence and civil disorder.
>
> Intensified attention under this program should be afforded to the activities of such groups as the Student Nonviolent Coordinating Committee, *Southern Christian Leadership Conference,* Revolutionary Action Movement, the Deacons for Defense and Justice, Congress of Racial Equality, and the Nation of Islam. [Emphasis added.]

The Domestic Intelligence Division expanded the Black Nationalist-Hate Groups COINTELPRO in February 1968. The instructions to the field offices listed as a "goal":

> Prevent the rise of a "messiah" who could unify and electrify the militant black nationalist movement. Malcolm X might have been such a "messiah"; he is the martyr of the movement today. Martin Luther King, Stokely Carmichael, and Elijah Muhammad all aspire to this position. Elijah Muhammad is less of a threat because of his age. King could be a real contender for this position should he abandon his supposed "obedience" to "white, liberal doctrines" (nonviolence) and embrace black nationalism. . . .

The SCLC was retained as a "primary target" of the COINTELPRO, and Martin Luther King's name was added to the list of persons who were targets.

The supervisor of the Black Nationalist COINTELPRO, told the Committee that he could recall no counterintelligence activities directed against the SCLC, but that several were taken against Dr. King.

C. The FBI's Efforts to Discredit Dr. King During His Last Months

Between 1965 and early 1967, the files indicate that Bureau concern about Dr. King had decreased. This concern was revived by Dr. King's April 4, 1967, speech at New York's Riverside Church, in which he opposed the Administration's position in Vietnam. The FBI interpreted this position as proof he "has been influenced by communist advisers," and noted that King's remarks were "a direct parallel of the communist position on Vietnam." A week after the speech the FBI sent the White House and the Justice Department a revised edition of the printed King monograph.

In early December 1967 Dr. King announced plans to hold demonstrations in major American cities, including Washington, D.C., to spur Congress into enacting civil rights legislation. The FBI followed closely developments in Dr. King's "Washington Spring Project" forwarding to the White House information concerning Adviser A's fund-raising activities and Dr. King's plans to tape a lecture series for a foreign television system, allegedly to raise funds for the project.

In February 1968 the FBI again revised the King monograph and distributed it to certain officials in the Executive Branch. The Domestic Intelligence Division memorandum recommending the new monograph stated that its dissemination "prior to King's 'Washington Spring Project' should serve again to remind top-level officials in Government of the wholly disreputable character of King."

In early March, the Bureau broadened its Black Nationalist-Hate Groups COINTELPRO explicitly to include Dr. King. Toward the end of the month, the FBI began to disseminate information to the press "designed to curtail success of Martin Luther King's fund raising campaign for the Washington Spring Project." The first of many plans included circulating a story

> that King does not need contributions from the 70,000 people he solicited. Since the churches have offered support, no more money is needed and any contributed would only be used by King for other purposes. This item would need nation-wide circulation in order to reach all the potential contributors and curtail their donations.

On March 25, the Bureau approved a plan to mail an anonymous letter to a civil rights leader in Selma, Alabama, who was "miffed" with Dr. King, and a copy of that letter to a Selma newspaper, hoping that the newspaper might interview the leader about its contents. The Bureau described the purpose of the letter as calling

> to the attention of [the civil rights leader] that King is merely using the Negroes of the Selma area for his own personal aggrandizement;

> that he is not genuinely interested in their welfare, but only in their donations; that in all probability the individuals going to Washington for the Spring Project will be left stranded without suitable housing or food. The letter should also play up the possibility of violence.

There is no indication in FBI files that the letter was mailed.

During the latter part of March, Dr. King went to Memphis, Tennessee, where a strike by Sanitation Workers had erupted into violent riots.

A March 28, 1968, Domestic Intelligence Division memorandum stated:

> A sanitation strike has been going on in Memphis for some time. Martin Luther King, Jr., today led a march composed of 5,000 to 6,000 people through the streets of Memphis. King was in an automobile preceding the marchers. As the march developed, acts of violence and vandalism broke out including the breaking of windows in stores and some looting. This clearly demonstrates that acts of so-called nonviolence advocated by King cannot be controlled. The same thing could happen in his planned massive civil disobedience for Washington in April.
>
> ACTION
>
> Attached is a blind memorandum pointing out the above, which if you approve, should be made available by Crime Records Division to cooperative news media sources.

The memorandum carried Director Hoover's "O.K." and the notation, "handled on 3/28/68."

On March 29, 1968, the Domestic Intelligence Division recommended that the following article be furnished to a cooperative news source:

> Martin Luther King, during the sanitation workers' strike in Memphis, Tennessee, has urged Negroes to boycott downtown white merchants to achieve Negro demands. On 3/29/68 King led a march for the sanitation workers. Like Judas leading lambs to slaughter King led the marchers to violence, and when the violence broke out, King disappeared.
>
> The fine Hotel Lorraine in Memphis is owned and patronized exclusively by Negroes but King didn't go there for his hasty exit. Instead King decided the plush Holiday Inn Motel, white owned,

operated and almost exclusively patronized, was the place to "cool it." There will be no boycott of white merchants for King, only for his followers.

On April 4, Dr. King returned to Memphis. This time he registered at the Lorraine Hotel. We have discovered no evidence that the FBI was responsible for Dr. King's move to the Lorraine Hotel.

D. Attempts to Discredit Dr. King's Reputation After His Death

The FBI's attempts to discredit Dr. King did not end with his death. In March 1969 the Bureau was informed that Congress was considering declaring Dr. King's birthday a national holiday, and that members of the House Committee on Internal Security might be contacting the Bureau for a briefing about Dr. King. The Crime Records Division recommended briefing the Congressmen because they were "in a position to keep the bill from being reported out of Committee" if "they realize King was a scoundrel." DeLoach noted: "This is a delicate matter—but can be handled very cautiously." Director Hoover wrote, "I agree. It must be handled *very cautiously.*"

In April 1969 FBI Headquarters received a recommendation for a counterintelligence program from the Atlanta Field Office. The nature of the proposed program has not been revealed to the Committee. A memorandum concerning the plan which the Bureau has given to the Committee, however, notes that the plan might be used "in the event the Bureau is inclined to entertain counterintelligence action against Coretta Scott King and/or the continuous projection of the public image of Martin Luther King. . . . " The Director informed the Atlanta office that "the Bureau does not desire counterintelligence action against Coretta King of the nature you suggest at this time."

CONCLUSION

Although it is impossible to gauge the full extent to which the FBI's discrediting programs affected the civil rights movement, the fact that there was impact is unquestionable.

Rumors circulated by the FBI had a profound impact on the SCLC's ability to raise funds. According to Congressman Andrew Young, a personal friend and associate of Dr. King, the FBI's effort against Dr. King and the SCLC "chilled contributions. There were direct attempts at some of our larger contributors who told us that they had been told by agents that Martin had a Swiss bank account, or that Martin had confiscated some of the monies from the March on Washington for his personal use. None of that was true." Harry Wachtel, one of Dr. King's legal counsels who handled many of the financial and fund-raising activities of the SCLC, emphasized that the SCLC was always in need of funds. "Getting a grant or getting a contribution is a very fragile thing. A grant delayed has a very serious impact on an organization whose financial condition was pretty rough." Wachtel testified that the SCLC continually had to overcome rumors of poor financial management and communist connections.

> The material . . . stayed in the political bloodstream all the way through to the time of Dr. King's death, and even after. In our efforts to build a King Center, it was around. It was like a contamination.

The SCLC leadership assumed that anything said in meetings or over the telephone would be intercepted by wiretaps, bugs, or informants. Ironically, the FBI memorandum reporting that a wiretap of the SCLC's Atlanta office was feasible stated:

> In the past when interviews have been conducted in the office of Southern Christian Leadership Conference certain employees when asked a question, in a half joking manner and a half serious manner replied, "You should know that already, don't you have our wires tapped?" It is noted in the past, State of Georgia has conducted investigations regarding subject and Southern Christian Leadership Conference.

Harry Wachtel commented on the impact of constant surveillance on members of the SCLC:

> When you live in a fishbowl, you act like you're in a fishbowl, whether you do it consciously or unconsciously. . . . I can't put specifics before you, except to say that it beggars the imagination not to believe that the SCLC, Dr. King, and all its leaders were not chilled or inhibited from all kinds of activities, political and even social.

Wachtel also pointed out the ramifications stemming from the Government's advance knowledge of what civil rights leaders were thinking:

> It is like political intelligence. It did not chill us from saying it, but it affected the strategies and tactics because the people you were having strategies and tactics about were privy to what you were about. They knew your doubts. . . . Take events like strategies in Atlantic City. . . . Decision-making concerning which way to go, joining one challenge or not, supporting a particular situation, or not, had to be limited very strongly by the fact that information which was expressed by telephone, or which could even possibly be picked up by bugging, would be in the hands of the President.

Perhaps most difficult to gauge is the personal impact of the Bureau's programs. Congressman Young told the Committee that while Dr. King was not deterred by the attacks which are now known to have been instigated in part by the FBI, there is "no question" but that he was personally affected:

> It was a great burden to be attacked by people he respected, particularly when the attacks engendered by the FBI came from people like Ralph McGill. He sat down and cried at the New York Times editorial about his statement on Vietnam, but this just made him more determined. It was a great personal suffering, but since we don't really know all that they did, we have no way of knowing the ways that they affected us.

4.

Warrantless FBI Electronic Surveillance

I. INTRODUCTION

Technological developments in this century have rendered the most private conversations of American citizens vulnerable to interception and monitoring by government agents. The electronic means by which the Government can extend its "antennae" are varied: microphones may be secretly planted in private locations or on mobile informants; so-called "spike mikes" may be inserted into the wall of an adjoining room; and parabolic microphones may be directed at speakers far away to register the sound waves they emit. Telephone conversations may be overheard without the necessity of attaching electronic devices to the telephone itself or to the lines connecting the telephone with the telephone company. An ordinary telephone may also be turned into an open microphone—a "miketel"—capable of intercepting all conversations within hearing range even when the telephone is not in use.

Even more sophisticated technology permits the Government to intercept any telephone, telegram, or telex communication which is transmitted at least partially through the air, as most such communications now are. This type of interception is virtually undetectable and does not require the cooperation of private communications companies.

Techniques such as these have been used, and continue to be used, by intelligence agencies in their intelligence operations. Since the early part of this century the FBI has utilized wiretapping and "bugging" techniques in both criminal and intelligence investigations. In a single year alone

(1945), the Bureau conducted 519 wiretaps and 186 microphone surveillances (excluding those conducted by means of microphones planted on informants). Until 1972, the Bureau used wiretaps and bugs against both American citizens and foreigners within the United States—without judicial warrant—to collect foreign intelligence, intelligence and counterintelligence information, to monitor "subversive" and violent activity, and to determine the sources of leaks of classified information. The FBI still uses these techniques without a warrant in foreign intelligence and counterintelligence investigations.

The CIA and NSA have similarly used electronic surveillance techniques for intelligence purposes. The CIA's Office of Security, for example, records a total of fifty-seven individuals who were targeted by telephone wiretaps or microphones within the United States between the years 1947 and 1968. Of these, thirty were employees or former employees of the CIA or of another federal agency who were presumably targeted for security reasons; four were United States citizens unconnected with the CIA or any federal agency. One of the primary responsibilities of the National Security Agency (NSA) is to collect foreign "communications intelligence." To fulfill this responsibility, it has electronically intercepted an enormous number of international telephone, telegram, and telex communications since its inception in the early 1950s.

Electronic surveillance techniques have understandably enabled these agencies to obtain valuable information relevant to their legitimate intelligence missions. Use of these techniques has provided the Government with vital intelligence, which would be difficult to acquire through other means, about the activities and intentions of foreign powers, and has provided important leads in counterespionage cases. By their very nature, however, electronic surveillance techniques also provide the means by which the Government can collect vast amounts of information, unrelated to any legitimate governmental interest, about large numbers of American citizens. Because electronic monitoring is surreptitious, it allows Government agents to eavesdrop on the conversations of individuals in unguarded moments, when they believe they are speaking in confidence. Once in operation, electronic surveillance techniques record not merely conversations about criminal, treasonable, or espionage-related activities, but all conversations about the full range of human events. Neither the most mundane nor the most personal nor the most political expressions of the speakers are immune from interception. Nor are these techniques sufficiently precise to limit the conversations overheard to those of the intended subject of the surveillance: anyone who speaks in a bugged room and anyone who talks over a tapped telephone is also overheard and recorded.

The very intrusiveness of these techniques implies the need for strict controls on their use, and the Fourth Amendment protection against unreasonable searches and seizures demands no less. Without such controls, they may be directed against entirely innocent American citizens, and the Government may use the vast range of information exposed by electronic means for partisan political and other improper purposes. Yet in the past the controls on these techniques have not been effective; improper targets have been selected and politically useful information obtained through electronic surveillance has been provided to senior administration officials.

Until recent years, Congress and the Supreme Court set few limits on the use of electronic surveillance. When the Supreme Court first considered the legal issues raised by wiretapping, it held that the warrantless use of this technique was not unconstitutional because the Fourth Amendment's warrant requirement did not extend to the seizure of conversations. This decision, the 1928 case of *Olmstead v. United States,* 277 U.S. 438, arose in the context of a criminal prosecution, and it left agencies such as the Bureau of Prohibition and the Bureau of Investigation (the former name of the FBI) free to engage in the unrestricted use of wiretapping in both criminal and intelligence investigations.

Six years later, Congress imposed the first restrictions on wiretapping in the Federal Communications Act of 1934, which made it a crime for "any person" to intercept and divulge or publish the contents of wire and radio communications. The Supreme Court subsequently construed this section to apply to federal agents as well as ordinary citizens, and held that evidence obtained directly or indirectly from the interception of wire and radio communications was inadmissible in court. But Congress acquiesced in the Justice Department's interpretation that these cases did not prohibit wiretapping *per se,* only the divulgence of the contents of wire communications outside the federal establishment, and government wiretapping for purposes other than prosecution continued.

The Supreme Court reversed its holding in the *Olmstead* case in 1967, holding in *Katz* v. *United States,* 389 U.S. 347 (1967), that the Fourth Amendment's warrant requirement did apply to electronic surveillances. But it expressly declined to extend this holding to cases "involving the national security." Congress followed suit the next year in the Omnibus Crime

Control Act of 1968, which established a warrant procedure for electronic surveillance in criminal cases but included a provision that neither it nor the Federal Communications Act of 1934 "shall limit the constitutional power of the President"—a provision which has been relied upon by the Executive Branch as permitting "national security" electronic surveillances.

In 1972, the Supreme Court again addressed the issue of warrantless electronic surveillance. It held in *United States* v. *United States District Court,* 407 U.S. 297 (1972), that the constitutional power of the President did not extend to authorizing warrantless electronic surveillance in cases involving threats to the "domestic security." The Court distinguished—but remained silent on—the question of warrantless electronic surveillance where there was a "significant connection with a foreign power, its agents or agencies."

Without effective guidance by the Supreme Court or Congress, executive branch officials developed broad and ill-defined standards for the use of warrantless electronic surveillance. Vague terms such as "subversive activities," "national interest," "domestic security," and "national security" were relied upon to electronically monitor many individuals who engaged in no criminal activity and who, by any objective standard, represented no genuine threat to the security of the United States.

The secrecy which has enshrouded the warrantless use of this technique, moreover, facilitated the occasional violation of the generally meager procedural requirements for warrantless electronic surveillance. Since the early 1940s, for example, Justice Department policy has required the approval of the Attorney General prior to the institution of wiretaps; such approval has been required prior to the institution of microphone surveillances since 1965. This requirement has often been ignored for wiretaps and bugs, and it was not even applied to NSA's electronic monitoring system and its program for "Watch Listing" American citizens. From the early 1960s until 1973, NSA compiled a list of individuals and organizations, including more than one thousand American citizens and domestic groups, whose communications were segregated from the mass of communications intercepted by the Agency, transcribed, and frequently disseminated to other agencies for intelligence purposes. The Americans on the list, many of whom were active in the anti-war and civil rights movements, were placed there by the FBI, CIA, Secret Service, Defense Department, and the Bureau of Narcotics and Dangerous Drugs without judicial warrant, without prior approval by the Attorney General, and without a determination that they satisfied the executive branch standards for warrantless electronic surveillance. For many years in fact, no Attorney General even knew of this project's existence.

Electronic monitoring by the National Security Agency and the CIA, however, is outside the scope of this Report. This Report focuses exclusively on the FBI's use of electronic surveillance; NSA's monitoring system is described at length in the Committee's Report on NSA. Because the legal issues and the FBI's policy and practice regarding consensual monitoring devices such as "body recorders" are distinct from those of nonconsensual wiretaps and microphone installations, the Report is also confined to the latter forms of electronic surveillance.

{ . . . }

IV. AN OVERVIEW OF FBI ELECTRONIC SURVEILLANCE PRACTICES

{ . . . } This section attempts to provide an overview of FBI electronic surveillance practices. Without purporting to explore the full range of FBI electronic surveillance practices, a limited number of key areas are highlighted in order to suggest the manner in which electronic surveillances are conducted.

{ . . . }

A. Extent of FBI Electronic Surveillance: 1940–1975

While FBI use of warrantless electronic surveillance has not been as pervasive as many other investigative techniques such as informants, both wiretaps and bugs have been strategically utilized in a large number of intelligence investigations. The Bureau's reliance on these techniques was greatest during World War II and the immediate postwar period. During the 1960s and early 1970s, internal FBI policy placed a ceiling on the number of simultaneous electronic surveillances conducted by the Bureau. This self-restriction did not act to curtail all use of this technique, but it apparently frustrated intelligence officials in the FBI and other agencies who sought—unsuccessfully—a change in this policy through the Huston Plan in 1970. In recent years, judicial decisions have severely restricted the use of warrantless electronic surveillance against domestic targets, although wiretaps and bugs still continue to be commonly used in the area of foreign intelligence and counterintelligence.

1. Annual Totals for Wiretaps and Microphone Installations

According to Justice Department records, the annual totals of warrantless FBI wiretaps and microphones in operation between 1940 and 1974 were as follows:

Year	Telephone wiretaps	Microphones	Year	Telephone wiretaps	Microphones
1940	6	6	1958	166	70
1941	67	25	1959	120	75
1942	304	88	1960	115	74
1943	475	193	1961	140	85
1944	517	198	1962	198	100
1945	519	186	1963	244	83
1946	364	84	1964	260	106
1947	374	81	1965	233	67
1948	416	67	1966	174	10
1949	471	75	1967	113	0
1950	270	61	1968	82	9
1951	285	75	1969	123	14
1952	285	63	1970	102	19
1953	300	52	1971	101	16
1954	322	99	1972	108	32
1955	214	102	1973	123	40
1956	164	71	1974	190	42*
1957	173	73			

*Attorney General Edward H. Levi testimony, Nov. 6, 1975, hearings, vol. 5, pp. 68–70. The statistics before 1968 encompass electronic surveillance for both intelligence and law enforcement purposes. Those after 1968, when the Omnibus Crime Control Act was enacted, include surveillances for intelligence purposes only; electronic surveillance for law enforcement purposes were thereafter subject to the warrant procedures required by the Act.

Comparable figures for the year 1975, through October 29, are: 121 telephone wiretaps and 24 microphone installations.

It should be noted that these figures are cumulative for each year; that is, a wiretap on an individual in one year which continued into a second year is recorded in both years. The figures are also duplicative to some extent, since a telephone wiretap or microphone which was installed, then discontinued, and later reinstated is counted as a new surveillance upon reinstatement.

{ . . . }

V. WARRANTLESS FBI ELECTRONIC SURVEILLANCE OF FOREIGN INTELLIGENCE AND COUNTERINTELLIGENCE TARGETS WITHIN THE UNITED STATES

Foreign agents and foreign establishments within the United States have often been, and continue to be, the targets of warrantless FBI electronic surveillance. In general, the Fourth Amendment questions raised by electronic surveillance of foreigners are not as serious as those raised by the targeting of American citizens, and surveillance of foreign targets may be less susceptible to the types of abuses that have often been associated with wiretapping and bugging of American citizens. Because Americans are often overheard on "foreign" taps and bugs, however, and because American citizens may also be the indirect targets of "foreign" surveillances, the rights of Americans may nonetheless be affected even by surveillance of foreign targets.

Apparently, most warrantless electronic surveillances conducted by the FBI in the past fifteen years have fallen into this broad category. Foreign establishments and foreigners living within the United States have been the subject of wiretaps and bugs far more frequently than have American citizens connected with domestic organizations, for purposes ranging from the collection of foreign intelligence and counterintelligence information to the detection of terrorist activity. Since the 1972 *Keith* decision, which invalidated "domestic security" warrantless electronic surveillances, the proportion of foreign targets has been even greater. As of November 1975, for example, all existing warrantless electronic surveillances were directed against foreigners.

{ . . . }

VI. WARRANTLESS FBI ELECTRONIC SURVEILLANCE OF AMERICAN CITIZENS

American citizens and domestic organizations have also been the direct targets of FBI wiretaps and bugs for intelligence purposes. Indeed, the use of these techniques against Americans for such purposes has a long history. In 1941, for example, Attorney General Francis Biddle approved a wiretap on the Los Angeles Chamber of Commerce under the standard of "persons suspected of subversive activities." Four years later, a high official in the Truman administration and a former aide to President Roosevelt were both the subject of warrantless electronic surveillance.

Between 1960 and 1972 numerous American citizens and domestic organizations were targeted for electronic surveillance. Most of these warrantless wiretaps and bugs were predicated on the need to protect the country against "subversive" and/or violent activities; many were based on the perceived need to discover the source of leaks of classified information; and an undetermined number of American citizens were wiretapped for other reasons such as the desire to obtain foreign intelligence or counterintelligence information.

The *Keith* decision in 1972 sharply restricted the grounds for wiretapping and bugging which had been asserted previously, although it did not prohibit warrantless electronic surveillance of American citizens for foreign intelligence or counterintelligence purposes when a substantial connection is shown to exist between the American individual or group and a foreign power. No Americans were the subjects of this technique as of November 1975, but a small number of Americans have been electronically monitored since the *Keith* case on the basis of such a foreign connection.

This section focuses on warrantless electronic surveillance of American citizens during the 1960 to 1972 period. It contains a general description of surveillances which were instituted because of the perceived "subversive" or violent nature of the targets, because of leaks of classified information, and on various other grounds.

{ . . . }

A. Electronic Surveillance Predicated on Subversive Activity

Numerous American citizens and domestic organizations have been wiretapped and bugged because their activities, while not necessarily violent, were regarded as sufficiently "subversive" to constitute a threat to the security of the United States. In many of these cases, it was believed that the individuals or groups were controlled or financed by, or otherwise connected with, a hostile foreign power. In other cases, the surveillances were based only on the possibility that the targets, whether consciously or not, were being influenced by persons believed to be acting under the direction of a foreign power; such surveillance typically occurred in the context of COMINFIL (Communist infiltration) investigations.

The Communist Party, USA, provides the clearest example of a group that was selected for electronic surveillance on the ground of foreign-connected "subversive" activities. In addition to a wiretap on the Headquarters of the Communist Party, the FBI conducted wiretaps in the following target categories:

Communist Party Functionaries

Communist Party Propaganda Outlet

Communist Party Front Group

Communist Party Member

Communist Party Affiliate

Communist Party Publication

Microphone surveillances are recorded in these categories:

Communist Party Functionaries

Communist Party Front Groups

Communist Party Propaganda Outlets

Communist Party Front Groups Organizer

Communist Party Function

Communist Party Members

Communist Party Publications

Coverage of Communist Party Meeting

Communist Party Youth Activist

Communist Party Labor Group

Communist Party Youth Group

Communist Party Affiliate

Coverage of Communist Party Conference

Communist Party Apologist

Other groups adhering to a communist ideology have also been electronically monitored for similar reasons. According to FBI records, wiretaps were used in cases involving a "Marxist-Leninist Group Affiliate," a "Marxist-Leninist Group Leader," and a "Marxist-Leninist Group Functionary." Microphone surveillances were also conducted against a "Basic Revolutionary Group Founder," a "Marxist-Oriented Youth Group," a "Trotskyite Organization," a "Basic Revolutionary Group," an "Organizer of a Basic Revolutionary Group," "Marxist-Leninist Groups," a "Basic Revolutionary Front Group," a "Basic Revolutionary Front Functionary," a "Marxist-Leninist Front Group," and a "Marxist-Oriented Racial Organization." One "Trotskyite Organization Meeting" was also bugged.

Several groups which were believed to have a connection with the Communist Party in Cuba and China have been targeted as well. Into this category fell wiretaps which were directed against a "Pro-Castro Organization," a "Pro-Castro Movement Leader," a "Pro-Castro Group Functionary," and a "Pro-Chicom [Chinese Communist] Propaganda Outlet"; and microphones directed against "Pro-Castro Organizations," a "Pro-Chicom Group," and a "Pro-Cuban American Group which travelled to Cuba."

The "subversive activities" predicate was stretched furthest when used to support electronic surveillance of American citizens and domestic organizations not primarily because their own activities were considered to be subversive but because they were believed to be adversely influenced, whether consciously or not, by persons acting under the direction of a foreign power. One example of reliance on such a rationale is seen in the wiretapping and bugging of Dr. Martin Luther King, Jr., and several of his associates. In October 1963, Attorney General Robert Kennedy authorized wiretaps on the residence and two office telephones of Dr. King on the ground of possible Communist infiltration into the Southern Christian Leadership

Conference, of which Dr. King was President. The possibility that two of Dr. King's advisors may have been associated with the Communist Party, USA, led to four additional wiretaps on King and a total of fifteen microphone installations in his hotel rooms during 1964 and 1965. Apparently as part of this COMINFIL (Communist infiltration) investigation, several of King's associates were also wiretapped and bugged.

At least three other organizations have been targeted for electronic surveillance primarily on the ground of possible Communist infiltration. One such organization, believed to have been influenced by the Communist Party, USA, was wiretapped in 1962. In 1965, Attorney General Nicholas Katzenbach approved wiretaps on both the Student Non-Violent Coordinating Committee (SNCC) and the Students for a Democratic Society (SDS) for similar reasons; the former group had also been the subject of a microphone surveillance in 1964.

B. Electronic Surveillance Predicated on Violent Activity

Allegations of violent activity, or the threat of violent activity, have also served as the predicate for numerous warrantless electronic surveillance of Americans.

Most of the wiretaps and bugs which were instituted for this reason have been directed against "black extremists" and "black extremist organizations." In 1957, for example, Attorney General Herbert Brownell authorized a wiretap on Elijah Muhammad, a leader of the Nation of Islam, because of the organization's alleged "violent nature." This tap, which was never re-authorized until 1964, was finally terminated in 1966. A wiretap was also placed on Malcolm X, another Nation of Islam leader, in 1964 for essentially the same reason. Similarly, Attorney General Katzenbach approved a wiretap on a "black extremist leader" of the Revolutionary Action Movement in 1965. During the first half of the 1960s, microphone surveillance was also directed against a "black separatist group" (one surveillance in 1960 and 1961; two separate surveillances each year from 1962 until 1965) and a "black separatist group functionary" (from 1961 until 1965).

The possibility of violent activity also led to wiretaps on the Black Panther Party and one of its leaders in 1969. Both of these taps continued into 1970, when wiretaps on a "black extremist group affiliate" and two (non-white) "racial extremist groups" were added to the list. 1971 apparently represented the high point of wiretapping "black extremists": in that year, there were wiretaps on the Black Panther Party (six separate taps as of March 29, 1971), two (non-white) "racial extremist groups," two individuals described as "militant black extremist group members" (one of whom was a member of SNCC), two individuals described as "militant black extremist group functionaries," and a "racial group member." A wiretap was also authorized to cover a "meeting of a militant [black] group." In 1972, wiretaps continued to be used against the Black Panther Party and one of its leaders, a (non-white) "racial extremist group," a "militant black extremist group member," and a "militant black extremist group functionary." Microphone surveillances during the Nixon Administration years were directed against the Black Panther Party in 1970 and a "Black Extremist Group Functionary" (Huey Newton, a leader of the Black Panther Party) from 1970 to 1972.

Electronic surveillance based on a "violent activity" predicate was certainly not confined to "black extremists," however. In the early and mid-1960s, wiretaps were placed on Ku Klux Klan members for similar reasons. Two "leaders of a racist organization," one of whom was a Klan member suspected of involvement in the bombing of a black church in Birmingham, Alabama, were wiretapped in 1963 and 1964. Another Ku Klux Klan member was wiretapped in 1964 and 1965. FBI records also disclose the bugging of The National States Rights Party in 1962.

White radical organizations were also the subjects of electronic surveillance in the late 1960s and early 1970s on the grounds of violent or potentially violent activity. A "New Left Campus Group" was both wiretapped and bugged in 1969, and the wiretap continued into 1970. Three anti-war organizations which were involved in planning the November 1969 "March on Washington" were also wiretapped in 1969. In 1970, the Headquarters of the Worker Student Alliance (an affiliate of SDS) and an individual who was a contact for the Weatherman organization were wiretapped. The tap on the Worker Student Alliance continued into 1971 and was supplemented in that year by wiretaps on a "New Left Activist," a "domestic protest group," and a "violence prone faction of a domestic protest group" (two separate wiretaps). Additional wiretaps and microphone surveillances during the years 1969 to 1972 fall into the categories: "Investigation of Clandestine Underground Group Dedicated to Strategic Sabotage"; "Weatherman Organization Publication"; "Publication of Clandestine Underground Group Dedicated to Strategic Sabotage"; "Leader of Revolutionary Group"; and "Weather Underground Support Apparatus."

For several years during the 1960s, Puerto Rican nationalist groups and their members were also electronically monitored because of their alleged proclivity towards violence. FBI records reveal wiretaps on a "Puerto Rican Independence Group" in 1960 and 1962; and on a "Puerto Rican Independence Group Member" in 1965. Microphone surveillances were placed on a "Contact of Puerto Rican Nationalist Party" in 1960; a "Puerto Rican Independence Group Office" in 1963, 1964, and 1965; a "Puerto Rican Revolutionary" in 1963; and "Pro-Puerto Rican Independence Group Activists" in 1964 and 1965.

Other organizations were the subject of electronic surveillance because they were seen as violent advocates of the interests of a foreign power or group. (To the extent an actual connection with a hostile foreign power was perceived, they would also be considered "subversive.") These organizations, which were, or may have been, composed at least in part of American citizens, are described by the following categories: "Pro-Arab Group," "Arab Terrorist Affiliate," "Pro-Palestine Group," "Militant Pro-Chicom [Chinese Communist] Group," "West Coast Fundraising Front for Arab Terrorist Groups," "Arab Terrorist Activist Affiliates," and "Co-Conspirators in Plot to Kidnap a Prominent Anti-Castro Cuban Exile."

C. Electronic Surveillance Predicated on Leaks of Classified Information

Another purpose of warrantless electronic surveillance of American citizens during the period 1960 to 1972 was to determine the source of perceived leaks of classified information. At least eight separate investigations into perceived leaks resulted in the wiretapping or bugging of nearly thirty American citizens, yet Bureau memoranda reveal no case in which the source of any leak was discovered by means of electronic surveillance. These investigations are described below.

Lloyd Norman: 1961.—On June 27, 1961, Attorney General Robert Kennedy informed FBI Director Hoover that the most recent issue of *Newsweek* magazine contained an article about American military plans in Germany, which, the administration believed, was based on classified information. According to an FBI memorandum, Kennedy stated that the President had called him to see if it would be possible to determine who was responsible for the apparent leak. On the same day, and without specific authorization from the Attorney General, the FBI placed a wiretap on the residence of Lloyd Norman, the *Newsweek* reporter who wrote the article. Kennedy was informed about the tap on June 28, and formally approved it on June 30. It was discontinued on July 3, 1961, when "Norman left Washington, D.C., for the west coast on a month's vacation [and] the only person left at Norman's residence [was] his son."

Hanson Baldwin: 1962.—A July 1962 *New York Times* article about Soviet missile systems by Hanson Baldwin, which the administration also believed was based on classified information, led to the installation of wiretaps on the residences of both Baldwin and a *New York Times* secretary. According to contemporaneous Bureau memoranda, these wiretaps were instituted without the prior written approval of the Attorney General, and one of them—the tap on the secretary—was instituted without the Attorney General's prior knowledge. Formal written approval for these wiretaps was obtained on July 31, 1962, however, three days after the tap on Baldwin was installed and four days after the tap on his secretary was installed. The wiretap on the secretary continued until August 15, 1962; that on Baldwin until August 29, 1962.

Former FBI Special Agent: 1962.—Warrantless electronic surveillance predicated on classified information leaks continued with the wiretapping of a former Bureau agent who "disclosed information of a confidential nature concerning investigations conducted by [the] Bureau" in a public forum on October 18, 1962. According to an internal memorandum, the coverage lasted from October 18, 1962, until October 26, 1962, and was repeated in January 1963. On October 19, 1962, Attorney General Kennedy was advised that the Bureau desired to place coverage on this agent; he was apparently not informed that coverage had already been effected the day before. Kennedy's written approval was granted on October 26, the day the surveillance was terminated. The surveillance was reinstituted in January: a Bureau memorandum dated January 9, 1963, simply states:

> Mr. Belmont called to say [FBI Assistant Director Courtney] Evans spoke to the Attorney General re placing the tech on [   ] again, and the Attorney General said by all means do this. Mr. Belmont has instructed New York to do so.

The authorization for the second surveillance therefore appears to have been oral. Coverage of this agent was permanently suspended on September 9, 1963.

High Executive Official: 1963.—Because of the possibility that a high-ranking executive official may have provided classified information not to the press but to a foreign intelligence officer, the FBI requested the Attorney General in February 1963 to authorize a wiretap on the residence telephone of this official. According to the request which was sent to Attorney General Kennedy, "The President expressed personal interest in receiving information concerning the current relationship between [the official] and representatives of [a foreign country]."

The Attorney General approved the request, and it was instituted three days later. It was discontinued on June 14, 1963, when the target travelled abroad; reinstituted on July 14, 1963; and permanently discontinued on November 6, 1963, "because of lack of productivity."

Editor of an Anti-Communist Newsletter: 1965.—The publication in an anti-Communist newsletter of information believed to be classified led to the wiretapping of both the editor of the newsletter and an attorney in the Washington, D.C., area with whom the editor was in frequent contact. These surveillances were approved in writing by Attorney General Nicholas Katzenbach in April and June of 1965, respectively, and each began about three weeks after approval.

In November 1965, the FBI recommended discontinuance of the taps because "[w]e have not developed any data since outset of investigation which would show that [the targets] are currently receiving information from individuals in the Executive Branch of the Government. In fact, we now believe that it is highly unlikely that our technical coverage will develop such information in the future."

According to a memorandum sent to the Attorney General, the tap on the lawyer was discontinued on November 2, 1965, and that on the editor on November 10, 1965.

Joseph Kraft: 1969.—The basic facts surrounding the wiretapping and microphone surveillance of columnist Joseph Kraft are a matter of public record. In June 1969, possibly in response to a leak from the National Security Council, John Ehrlichman instructed John Caulfield and John Ragan, two individuals associated with the White House "Plumbers" and unconnected with the FBI, to place a wiretap on the Washington, D.C., residence of Mr. Kraft. This tap was removed one week later, when the columnist left Washington on an extended trip to Europe. W. C. Sullivan, then Assistant Director of the FBI, subsequently followed Mr. Kraft abroad, apparently on instructions from Mr. Hoover and Mr. Ehrlichman. Overseas, Sullivan arranged with a foreign security agency to conduct electronic surveillance of Kraft in his hotel room: when the installation of a telephone tap proved to be impossible because of the "elaborate switchboard" of the hotel, a microphone was placed in his room instead. The results of this coverage, which lasted from July 3 to July 7, 1969, were transmitted back to Mr. Hoover personally through the FBI's Legal Attache at the American Embassy.

In November and December of that year, Mr. Kraft was again the target of FBI surveillance: the Washington Field Office conducted physical surveillance of the columnist from November 5 until December 12. In addition, Director Hoover requested approval from Attorney General Mitchell for a wiretap on Mr. Kraft on November 5, but approval was never granted and the wiretap never installed.

The "Seventeen Wiretaps": 1969–1971.—The wiretaps which were directed against seventeen government employees and newsmen between May 1969 and February 1971 have been the subject of civil litigation and extensive Congressional inquiries. In view of the pending civil litigation, the Committee has not attempted to duplicate the depositions which bear on the authorization of these wiretaps. The basic facts as recorded in FBI documents and public record testimony, however, may be summarized as follows:

On May 9, 1969, a story by William Beecher concerning American bombing raids in Cambodia appeared in the *New York Times.* According to a contemporaneous internal memorandum from J. Edgar Hoover to senior FBI officials, Henry Kissinger telephoned him that morning requesting the Bureau to "make a major effort to find out where [the story] came from." Kissinger called Mr. Hoover twice more that day, once to request that additional articles by Beecher be included in the inquiry and once to request that the investigation be handled discreetly "so no stories will get out." Before 5:00 p.m. on May 9, Hoover telephoned Kissinger to inform him that initial FBI inquiries suggested that Morton Halperin, a staff member of the National Security Council, could have been in a position to leak the information upon which Beecher was believed to have based his article. Hoover noted that Halperin "knew Beecher and that he [Hoover] considered [Halperin] a part of the Harvard clique, and, of course, of the Kennedy era."

According to Hoover, "Dr. Kissinger said he appreciated this very much and he hoped I would follow it up as far as we can take it and they will destroy whoever did this if we can find him, no matter where he is."

Dr. Kissinger has testified that he had been asked at a White House meeting, which, he believed, may have occurred in late April 1969 and which was attended by the President, the Attorney General, and J. Edgar Hoover, "to supply the names of key individuals having access to sensitive information which had leaked [even before the Cambodia story]." He noted that at this meeting "Director Hoover identified four persons as security risks and suggested that these four be put under surveillance initially." Among the persons so identified was Morton Halperin. Kissinger said that when the Cambodia story was published on May 9, "I called Mr. Hoover at President Nixon's request to express the President's and my concern about the seriousness of the leak appearing that date and to request an immediate investigation." He also stated that in these telephone conversations, "I do not recall any discussion of wiretapping. At that time, my understanding was that the wiretapping program had been authorized and that, therefore, Mr. Hoover or his staff had the right to use wiretapping in their investigations. I do not recall any discussions as to when the program would actually be put into effect." He further testified that "[i]n view of the President's authorization, Mr. Hoover evidently chose to institute the wiretaps after my calls to him on May 9, regarding the national security significance of the Beecher story in the *New York Times* of the same date."

The wiretap on Halperin was installed without the written approval of the Attorney General, in late afternoon on May 9, 1969. The next morning, Alexander Haig personally visited William Sullivan at FBI Headquarters. According to a memorandum from Sullivan to Cartha DeLoach, Haig requested that wiretaps be placed on four individuals, including Halperin, who were members of the National Security Council staff and Defense Department employees. Haig stated that this request "was being made on the highest authority" and "stressed that it is so sensitive it demands handling on a need-to-know basis, with no record maintained." According to Sullivan, Haig said that "if possible, it would be even more desirable to have the matter handled without going to the [Justice] Department."

Alexander Haig testified that Dr. Kissinger had instructed him to see

Mr. Sullivan and to act as the "so-called liaison as this program was instituted, I believe, authorized by the President, the Director, and the Attorney General." He further stated that Dr. Kissinger provided him with the names to take to Sullivan and that he had the "impression" that the names were "cleared and concurred in by" the President or his representative, the Director, and the Attorney General. Haig denied that he requested the Bureau not to maintain a record of the surveillances, noting that "the point I would recall making very clearly was the extreme sensitivity of this thing, and the avoidance of unnecessary paperwork, which would make this program subject to compromise." He also testified that he does not recall urging Sullivan to avoid going to the Justice Department.

On May 12, a formal request was sent by the Director to Attorney General Mitchell for wiretaps on all four individuals (one of which had been in operation for three days); Mitchell approved; and the additional taps were subsequently instituted.

Over the course of the next one and one-half years, thirteen more individuals became the subjects of wiretaps in this same program. Bureau documents reflect the following authorizations from Attorney General Mitchell:

—May 20, 1969: Two members of the staff of the National Security Council
—May 29, 1969: A reporter for the *London Sunday Times*
—June 4, 1969: A reporter for the *New York Times*
—July 23, 1969: A White House domestic affairs adviser
—August 4, 1969: A White House speech writer
—September 10, 1969: A correspondent for CBS News
—May 4, 1970: A Deputy Assistant Secretary of State; a State Department official of "Ambassador" rank; and a Brigadier General with the Defense Department
—May 13, 1970: Two additional staff members of the National Security Council
—December 14, 1970: A second White House domestic affairs adviser.

The longest of these wiretaps was the one on Halperin: it continued for twenty-one months, until February 10, 1971, and was apparently terminated at the insistence of Director Hoover, who was about to testify before the House Appropriations Committee. Other wiretaps lasted for periods of time varying from six weeks to twenty months.

Charles Radford: 1971–1973.—The December 1971 publication of an article by Jack Anderson which described private conversations between President Nixon and Henry Kissinger led to a total of four wiretaps on American citizens to determine the source of this apparent leak. According to an internal Bureau memorandum, Attorney General Mitchell personally contacted Deputy Associate FBI Director W. Mark Felt on December 22, 1971, and orally instructed him to institute a wiretap on Charles E. Radford II. Radford, a Navy Yeoman who was assigned to the Joint Chiefs of Staff, was apparently a primary suspect because he had frequent contact with the White House and the National Security Council and belonged to the same church as Jack Anderson. Mitchell informed Felt that this request originated with the President and noted that no prosecution was contemplated. The FBI was not requested to conduct a full investigation of the leak, only to wiretap Radford. After obtaining approval from J. Edgar Hoover, Felt secured the institution of the wiretap on Radford's residence on December 23.

On the basis of certain telephone contacts Radford subsequently made, additional wiretaps were placed on the residences of two of Radford's friends, one a former Defense Attache, the other a State Department employee. These wiretaps were instituted on January 5 and January 14, respectively, and both continued until Feb 17. When Radford was transferred to the Naval Reserve Training Center near Portland, Oregon, the Attorney General requested a wiretap on the home of Radford's step-father, with whom he was to stay until he could locate a home of his own. This coverage was instituted immediately, and although Radford moved into his own residence by February 15, when another wiretap was installed on his new home, the tap on his step-father was not terminated until April 11, 1972. Coverage was also instituted on the training center where Radford worked on February 7, 1972, and like the tap on his step-father it continued until April 11.

The tap on Radford's Oregon residence was not terminated until June 20, 1972—one day after the Supreme Court's decision in the *Keith* case. One Bureau official wrote that "it was not discontinued on 6/19/72, as others falling under the *Keith* rule had been, since we were awaiting a decision from the White House."

In violation of Justice Department procedures, none of these Radford wiretaps was ever authorized by the Attorney General in writing. Two of the wiretaps apparently did not even receive the explicit oral approval of the

Attorney General. An internal Bureau memorandum states that the surveillance of the State Department employee and the wiretap on the Naval Reserve Training Center were both requested by David Young, an assistant to John Ehrlichman, who merely informed the Bureau that the requests originated with Ehrlichman and had the Attorney General's concurrence.

Thus, between 1960 and 1972, nearly thirty American citizens ostensibly suspected of leaking classified information were wiretapped by the FBI without a warrant in the United States; another was the subject of an FBI microphone surveillance abroad. No fewer than seven of these targets were journalists or newsmen. At least ten of the wiretaps were instituted without the prior written approval of the Attorney General, which was required in every case. Although the taps generated a significant amount of both personal and political information—much of which was disseminated to the highest levels in the White House—Bureau memoranda do not reveal that the wiretaps succeeded in identifying a single person who had leaked national security information.

D. Electronic Surveillance Predicated on Other Grounds

In the course of at least three separate investigations between 1960 and 1972, Americans were the targets of FBI electronic surveillance for purposes which cannot easily be categorized as collecting information about subversive or violent activities or about leaks of classified material. Two of these cases—the "Sugar Lobby" and the Jewish Defense League surveillances, described below—related to foreign concerns. The Sugar Lobby investigation was apparently instituted to gather foreign intelligence information seen as necessary for the conduct of foreign affairs and to detect alleged attempts of foreign representatives to influence American officials. A wiretap on the Jewish Defense League (JDL) and one of its members, while requested primarily on the ground of "violent activities," was defended in a subsequent civil action as similarly necessary to gather information important to United States foreign relations.

The third case occurred in connection with the Warren Commission's review of events surrounding President John F. Kennedy's assassination. In 1964, the FBI installed one wiretap (with the approval of the Attorney General) and two microphone surveillances at the specific request of this Commission in order to obtain information about the assassination.

The "Sugar Lobby" Wiretaps: 1961–1962.—On February 9, 1961, Attorney General Robert Kennedy requested the FBI to initiate an investigation for the purpose of:

> develop[ing] intelligence data which would provide President Kennedy a picture of what was behind pressures exerted on behalf of [a foreign country] regarding sugar quota deliberations in Congress . . . in connection with pending sugar legislation.

This investigation lasted for approximately nine weeks, and was reinstituted for a three-month period in mid-1962. At its height, the investigation involved a total of twelve telephone wiretaps, three microphone surveillances, and physical surveillances of eleven separate individuals. Six of the wiretaps were directed against American citizens, who included three executive branch employees, a Congressional staff member, and two registered lobbying agents for foreign interests, one of whom was an attorney whose office telephone was wiretapped. One of the microphone surveillances was directed at a United States Congressman.

The expiration of existing import quotas for sugar in 1961 provided the backdrop against which these events were set. In early 1961, the intelligence community had learned that officials of a foreign government "intensely desired passage of a sugar bill by the U.S. Congress which would contain quotas favorable to [that government]." This fact had significant ramifications on American foreign policy. According to a CIA memorandum addressed to the President's national security advisor:

> It is thought by some informed observers that the outcome of the sugar legislation which comes up for renewal in the U.S. Congress in March 1961 will be all-important to the future of U.S.-[foreign country] relations.

There was also a possibility that unlawful influence was involved. In early February, the FBI discovered that representatives of the foreign government might have made monetary payments or given gifts to influence certain Congressmen, Senators, and executive branch officials.

Because of the foreign intelligence interest involved, and on the ground that "the administration has to act if money or gifts are being passed by the [foreign representatives]," Robert Kennedy authorized a number of wiretaps on foreign targets and domestic citizens who were believed to be involved in the situation. Specifically, he approved wiretaps on the following American citizens: three officials of the Agriculture Department (residence telephones only); the clerk of the House Agriculture Committee (residence telephone only); and a registered agent of the foreign country (both residence and business telephones).

In the course of this investigation, the Bureau determined that Congressman Harold D. Cooley, the Chairman of the House Agriculture Committee, planned to meet with representatives of the foreign country in a hotel room in New York City, in mid-February 1961. At the instruction of Director Hoover, the New York Field Office installed a microphone in Cooley's hotel room to record this meeting, and the results were disseminated to the Attorney General.

Under the Justice Department policy that was in effect at this time, the Bureau was not required to obtain the prior written approval of the Attorney General for microphone surveillance, and none was obtained in this case. It is not certain, moreover, that Attorney General Kennedy was ever specifically informed that Congressman Cooley was the target of a microphone surveillance: a review of this case by Bureau agents in 1966 concluded that "our files contain no clear indication that the Attorney General was specifically advised that a microphone surveillance was being utilized . . . " It was noted, however, that on the morning of February 17, 1961—after the microphone was in place but an hour or two before the meeting actually occurred—the Director spoke with the Attorney General and, according to Hoover's contemporaneous memorandum, advised him that the Cooley meeting was to take place that day and that "we are trying to cover it." Hoover also wrote that he "stated [to the Attorney General] this New York situation is interesting and if we can get it covered we will have a full record of it," and that "the Attorney General asked that he be kept advised. . . . " As noted above, Kennedy did receive a summary of the results of the meeting, although no specific reference was made to the technique employed.

The 1961 "Sugar Lobby" investigation did discover that possibly unlawful influence was being exerted by representatives of the foreign country involved, but it did not reveal that money was actually being passed to any executive or legislative branch official. All of the electronic surveillances but two (both of which were on foreign targets) were discontinued in April 1961, about two weeks after the administration's own sugar bill passed the Senate.

The investigation was reinstituted in June 1962, however, when the

Bureau learned that representatives of the same foreign country might be influencing Congressional deliberations concerning an amendment to the sugar quota legislation. On June 26, 1962, the Bureau requested authority for wiretaps on five foreign establishments plus the office telephones of an attorney who was believed to be an agent for the foreign country and, again, the residence telephone of the Clerk of the House Agriculture Committee. Robert Kennedy approved all of these taps on July 9, and they were instituted about one week later.

After one month of operation, the wiretaps on one foreign establishment and the Clerk of the House Agriculture Committee had "produced no information of value" and were consequently discontinued. While there is no indication that the other wiretaps produced evidence of actual payoffs, they did reveal that possibly unlawful influence was again being exerted by the foreign government and internal Bureau permission was obtained to continue them for another sixty days, after which time they were presumably terminated.

Jewish Defense League: 1970 and 1971.—On September 14, 1970, the FBI requested a wiretap on six telephone lines of the New York Headquarters of the Jewish Defense League, an organization composed of American citizens who opposed, through both peaceful and violent means, the Soviet Union's treatment of Jewish citizens. Attorney General John Mitchell approved the wiretap on September 15; it was instituted on October 1 and continued for one month. It was re-authorized for two three-month periods on January 4, 1971, and March 31, 1971. Coverage was terminated July 3, 1971.

According to Attorney General Mitchell, the JDL wiretap was "deemed essential to protect this nation and its citizens against hostile acts of a foreign power and to obtain foreign intelligence information deemed essential to the security of the United States." More specifically, he contended that the activities of the Jewish Defense League toward official representatives of the Soviet Union, which had allegedly included acts of violence such as bombing the offices of a Soviet trade organization and the Soviet airlines, risked "the possibility of international embarrassment or Soviet retaliation against American citizens in Moscow," especially in light of vigorous protests by the Soviet Union. The wiretap was approved in order to obtain "advance knowledge of any activities of the JDL" which might have such repercussions; its re-authorization was sought and obtained on the ground that it had "furnished otherwise unobtainable information, well in advance of public statements by the JDL, thereby allowing for adequate countermeasures to be taken by appropriate police and security forces."

Criminal indictments were returned against several JDL members in May 1971, and shortly thereafter the prosecution revealed the existence of the wiretap to the defendants. In the context of the criminal case, the Government characterized the JDL wiretap as a "domestic security wiretap" and conceded that it was unlawful. The "foreign intelligence" predicate, however, was raised by Attorney General Mitchell and other civil defendants in the civil action—*Zweibon v. Mitchell*—subsequently filed by sixteen members of JDL who were overheard on the wiretap.

The District Court in the *Zweibon* case agreed with Attorney General Mitchell that the JDL wiretap was in fact related to United States foreign affairs and held that its authorization by the Attorney General was a proper exercise of the constitutional power of the President and his designees. On appeal, the Court of Appeals did not reexamine the District Court's finding that the wiretap was originally predicated on foreign affairs needs because it held that even if one accepts the foreign relationship predicate, the wiretapping of American citizens who are neither the agents of nor collaborators with a foreign power is unconstitutional under the Fourth Amendment.

{. . .}

In summary electronic surveillance has proven to be a valuable technique for the collection of foreign intelligence and counterintelligence information within the legitimate mandate of the FBI. But the history of the use of this technique by the Bureau also proves that its dangers are equally great: without precise standards and effective checks to restrain its use, innocent American citizens may be its victims; without rigid means of restricting the dissemination of information generated through electronic surveillance, Government officials may learn the most personal—and the most political—expressions and beliefs of its targets.

5.

Warrantless Surreptitious Entries

FBI "Black Bag" Break-Ins and Microphone Installations

I. INTRODUCTION

A. FBI Policy and Practice

Since 1948 the FBI has conducted hundreds of warrantless surreptitious entries to gather domestic and foreign intelligence, despite the questionable legality of the technique and its deep intrusion into the privacy of targeted individuals. Before 1966, the FBI conducted over two hundred "black bag jobs." These warrantless surreptitious entries were carried out for intelligence purposes *other than* microphone installation, such as physical search and photographing or seizing documents. Since 1960, more than five hundred warrantless surreptitious *microphone installations* against intelligence and internal security targets have been conducted by the FBI, a technique which the Justice Department still permits. Almost as many surreptitious entries were conducted in the same period against targets of criminal investigations.

Although several Attorneys General were aware of the FBI practice of break-ins to install electronic listening devices, there is no indication that the FBI informed any Attorney General about its use of "black bag jobs."

Surreptitious entries were performed by teams of FBI agents with special training in subjects such as "lock studies." Their missions were authorized in writing by FBI Director Hoover or his deputy, Clyde Tolson. A "Do Not File" procedure was utilized, under which most records of surreptitious entries were destroyed soon after an entry was accomplished.

The use of surreptitious entries against domestic targets dropped drastically after J. Edgar Hoover banned "black bag jobs" in 1966. In 1970, the relaxation of restraints on domestic intelligence techniques such as surreptitious entries was proposed in the Huston Plan. Hoover opposed this proposal, although he expressed a willingness to follow the Huston Plan, if directed to do so by the Attorney General.

{ . . . }

II. OPERATIONAL PROCEDURE, AUTHORIZATION, AND TARGETING

A. Internal Procedure and Authorization

The only internal FBI memorandum located by the Select Committee which discussed the policy for surreptitious entries stated:

> We do not obtain authorization for "black bag" jobs from outside the Bureau. Such a technique involves trespassing and is clearly illegal; therefore, it would be impossible to obtain any legal sanction for it. Despite this, "black bag" jobs have been used because they represent an invaluable technique in combating subversive activities of a clandestine nature aimed directly at undermining and destroying our nation.

The FBI described the procedure for authorization of surreptitious entries as follows:

> When a Special Agent in Charge (SAC) of a field office considered surreptitious entry necessary to the conduct of an investigation, he would make his request to the appropriate Assistant Director at FBIHQ, justifying the need for an entry and assuring it could be accomplished safely with full security. In accordance with instructions of Director J. Edgar Hoover, a memorandum outlining the facts of the request was prepared for approval of Mr. Hoover, or Mr. Tolson, the Associate Director. Subsequently, the memorandum was filed in the Assistant Director's office under a "Do Not File" procedure, and thereafter destroyed. In the field office, the SAC maintained a record of approval as a control device in his office safe. At the next

> yearly field office inspection, a review of these records would be made by the Inspector to insure that the SAC was not acting without prior FBIHQ approval in conducting surreptitious entries. Upon completion of this review, these records were destroyed.

One FBI agent who performed numerous "black bag jobs" stated that he obtained approval from some officer at FBI headquarters, although not always the Director, before performing a study of the feasibility of an entry. He said that a feasibility study was intended to determine: whether the entry could be accomplished in a secure manner, who owned the building and whether a key could be obtained. Floor plans of the building were often procured. If a building owner appeared to be a "patriotic citizen," FBI agents would approach him for assistance in entering a unit of his building—"show our credentials and wave the flag." If the FBI agents decided that they would be unable to obtain the building owner's consent to enter the target's premises, the agents would examine the building and the area to determine the feasibility of a break-in.

The FBI agent stated that if an entry was considered feasible he would write a memorandum to "Director, FBI" and, in response, would invariably receive an authorizing memorandum from headquarters initialled "JEH" [J. Edgar Hoover]. Another FBI agent who frequently participated in break-ins stated that the directives for such operations were sometimes initialled by Hoover and usually initialled by the Assistant Director in charge of the Domestic Intelligence Division.

One agent, who served on a special squad responsible for installing electronic surveillance devices, stated that in the majority of cases he was able to obtain a key to the target's premises, either from a landlord, hotel manager, or neighbor. In other cases, he simply entered through unlocked doors. He stated that only in a small proportion of the cases to which he was assigned was it necessary to pick a lock. Once a bug was planted, it was generally necessary for Bureau agents to monitor the conversations from a location close to the targeted premises.

Selected FBI agents received training courses in the skills necessary to perform surreptitious entries. An FBI technician provided formal instruction in "lock studies" as in-service training for experienced agents; "specialized lock-training" was also provided to each agent who received training in electronic surveillance at "sound school." These courses were conducted at the direction of the Assistant Director in charge of the Bureau Laboratory. The Unit Chief who taught the courses stated that he had participated in numerous "black bag jobs" in which his only role was to open locks and safes; all other activities were performed by other agents accompanying him. He said that he would ordinarily receive an incentive award for a successful entry.

One agent involved in surreptitious entries stated that he never knowingly conducted an entry for, or with the assistance of, a local police force; nor was he aware of any information being provided by the FBI to local police about an entry.

The agent said that he performed two microphone installations against CIA employees at the request of the CIA. He also stated that he was never accompanied on an entry operation by a CIA officer.

B. Targets: Counterintelligence and Domestic Subversives

The FBI has identified two broad categories of targets for surreptitious entries from 1942 to April 1968: (1) groups and individuals connected with foreign intelligence and espionage operations; and (2) "domestic subversive and white hate groups."

A Domestic Intelligence Division memorandum summarized the fruits obtained from surreptitious entries against domestic groups:

> We have on numerous occasions been able to obtain material held highly secret and closely guarded by subversive groups and organizations which consisted of membership lists and mailing lists of these organizations.

The memorandum also cited a warrantless surreptitious entry against the Ku Klux Klan as an example of the utility of the technique:

> Through a "black bag" job, we obtained the records in the possession of three high-ranking officials of a Klan organization. . . . These records gave us the complete membership and financial information concerning the Klan's operation which we have been using most effectively to disrupt the organization and, in fact, to bring about its near disintegration.

A former FBI agent has stated that the locations of break-in operations included the residences of targets of investigation as well as organizational headquarters.

The FBI was "unable to retrieve an accurate accounting" of the number of warrantless surreptitious entries from their files: "there is no central index, file, or document . . . no precise record of entries" due to the "Do Not File procedure." Relying upon a general review of files and upon the recollections of FBI agents at headquarters, the Bureau estimated that, in the "black bag job" category (warrantless surreptitious entries for purposes other than microphone installation):

> There were at least 239 surreptitious entries conducted against at least fifteen domestic subversive targets from 1942 to April 1968. In addition, at least three domestic subversive targets were the subject of numerous entries from October 1952 to June 1966.

"An entry against one white hate group" was also reported. One example of a "domestic subversive target" against whom numerous entries were conducted is the Socialist Workers Party, which may have been targeted for as many as ninety-two break-ins during the period from 1960 to 1966.

To have a more complete picture of the extent of "black bag" operations, two other FBI estimates, also based on incomplete records, must be considered along with this partial accounting of the number of "black bag job" entries against domestic subversive groups. First, the Bureau estimated that between 1960 and 1975, 509 surreptitious microphone installations took place against 420 separate "targets of counterintelligence, internal security, and intelligence collection investigations." It is impossible to determine from the FBI estimates exactly how many of these installations involved a surreptitious entry because other techniques were also utilized, such as installing a microphone prior to the occupancy of the target or encapsulating it in an article which was sent into the premises. It is also impossible to determine the number of these targets who were American citizens.

Second, the FBI estimated that between 1960 and 1975, there were 491 surreptitious entries to install electronic surveillance devices against 396 targets of criminal investigations.

C. Operations Directed Against the Socialist Workers Party

Recently disclosed FBI memoranda pertaining to surreptitious entries directed at the Socialist Workers Party (SWP) in 1960–1966 provide additional details on FBI procedures. Most of the documents were to be filed in the "Personal Folder" of the Special Agent in Charge of the New York field office.

The "purpose of assignment" for surreptitious entries against an SWP affiliate, the Young Socialist Alliance (YSA), was described as follows:

> To locate records and information relating to the national organization of the YSA, [and] the identity of national members located throughout the country. Also it is anticipated that records of the local organization will be made available.

To carry out this assignment, the FBI prepared memoranda which contained detailed plans for post-midnight burglarizing of YSA headquarters. The FBI's entry plans included descriptions of "security aspects" such as building floor plans, locks, lighting, surrounding streets, entrances, and the occupants' living habits.

The FBI's Los Angeles field office obtained "photographs of material maintained in the office of James P. Cannon, National Chairman of the SWP," including letters to and from Cannon. The field office reports about this material carried the warning:

> EXTREME CAUTION SHOULD BE EXERCISED IN UTILIZING INFORMATION FURNISHED BY [DELETED] IN ORDER THAT THE IDENTITY OF THIS HIGHLY CONFIDENTIAL SOURCE IS NOT COMPROMISED.

Several of the reports were "classified" because disclosure could "compromise effectiveness of the source." Moreover, upon receipt of this information, FBI headquarters advised the Los Angeles field office:

> Due to the sensitive nature of [deleted], which may become a further source of valuable information concerning the Socialist Worker's

> Party, any data obtained from that source should be paraphrased when submitted to the Bureau or other offices in memorandum form suitable for dissemination.

The Bureau apparently required such paraphrasing because it contemplated the dissemination outside the FBI of data obtained from surreptitious entries.

The material photographed by the FBI included membership lists, photographs of members, contribution lists, and correspondence concerning members' public participation in United States presidential campaigns, academic debates, and civil rights and antiwar organizing. For example, the following items were among those photographed by Bureau agents at the national offices of the Socialist Worker's Party:

> —"Items of correspondence between SWP National Headquarters and various branches detailing plans to obtain petition signatures to get on the ballot in 1960 elections."
>
> —"Letter sent by [SWP leader] to President Eisenhower (1/21/60) against loyalty program."
>
> —"SWP members active in trade unions—identity of union and members disclosed."
>
> —"Letter dated 6/1/60 setting forth the topic of speech to be given by . . . SWP Vice-Presidential candidate at opening of tour at Detroit, and listing complete schedule of cities to be visited thereafter in nationwide tour."
>
> —"Correspondence identifying contributors to SWP election campaign fund."
>
> —"Letter proposing picket activity at Democratic Convention."
>
> —"List naming all students at each session of Trotsky School from beginning in 1947 to the present."
>
> —"Letter setting forth that [deleted] was cancelling balance of her national tour because her husband . . . had suffered a stroke."
>
> —"Correspondence re arrangements for [deleted] to debate at Yale University."
>
> —"Letter announcing death of [deleted] . . . and plans for NY memorial meeting."
>
> —"Letter of Young Socialist Alliance (YSA) of 5/23/61 organizing Northern support for Southern students in integration struggle."

—"Note from SWP member . . . requesting new key to headquarters so he could continue delivering newspapers there when he finished work at night."

—"Letter . . . detailing health status of . . . Nat'l Chairman."

—"Several current items of correspondence to and from SWP members active in integration activities in Georgia."

—"Letters from National office to all branches re March on Washington."

—"Voluminous correspondence from many areas re SWP getting on the ballot in 1964 Presidential elections."

—"Complete tour schedule for SWP Presidential candidates Sept.–Oct. 1964."

—"Plans of [deleted] to write a book."

—"Reports on SWP participation in March on Washington (against the Vietnam War)."

—"Correspondence re new veterans anti-war organization."

—"Current photographs of SWP members."

—"Correspondence re new anti-war front in Cleveland."

—"Confidential address book of National-international Trotskyites."

In addition to these items, the FBI obtained information about other activities of SWP members, leaders and affiliates, including publishing plans, financial status, international travels and contacts, legal defense strategy, and the political conflicts within the party. For example, information about "proposed legal maneuvers" by a committee to aid indicted Young Socialist Alliance members in Bloomington, Indiana, was obtained by the FBI.

The number of documents photographed during a single operation reached as high as 220 and regularly was above 100.

III. FBI POLICY AND THE QUESTION OF AUTHORIZATION OUTSIDE THE BUREAU

A. FBI Policy: The Hoover Termination of "Black Bag Jobs"

After apparently approving hundreds of warrantless surreptitious entries, J. Edgar Hoover changed the FBI policy in 1966. In response to a Domestic Intelligence Division memorandum of July 19, 1966, outlining the procedures used for approval and reporting on "black bag jobs," Hoover appended the following handwritten note: "No more such techniques must be used." Six months later, Hoover formalized this directive in a memorandum:

> I note that requests are still being made by Bureau officials for the use of "black bag" techniques. I have previously indicated that l do not intend to approve any such requests in the future, and, consequently, no such recommendations should be submitted for approval of such matters. This practice, which includes also surreptitious entrances upon premises of any kind, will not meet with my approval in the future.

The FBI's accounting of surreptitious entries indicated that Hoover's prohibition applied only to "black bag jobs." Break-ins to install microphones were not banned. Moreover, Hoover's order did not finally terminate "black bag jobs" against foreign targets. Despite Hoover's directive, there is evidence that at least one "black bag job" directed against a "domestic subversive target" took place between 1966 and 1968.

B. Presidential and Attorney General Authorization

1. The Huston Plan: Proposal to Lift the Ban

In 1970, a plan for the inter-agency coordination of domestic intelligence activity was presented to President Nixon. The "Huston Plan" proposed, among other things, that restrictions against "black bag" entries "should be modified to permit selective use of this technique against foreign intelligence targets and other urgent and high priority internal security targets." Presidential assistant Tom Charles Huston, the proponent of this plan, which received the support of many high officials in the intelligence community, was of the opinion that "black bag jobs" were illegal but should be utilized nonetheless:

> Use of this technique is clearly illegal: it amounts to burglary. It is also highly risky and could result in great embarrassment if exposed. However, it is also the most fruitful tool and can produce the type of intelligence which cannot be obtained in any other fashion.

> The FBI, in Mr. Hoover's younger days, used to conduct such operations with great success and with no exposure. The information secured was invaluable.
>
> . . . .
>
> Surreptitious entry of facilities occupied by subversive elements can turn up information about identities, methods of operation, and other invaluable investigative information which is not otherwise obtainable. This technique would be particularly helpful if used against the Weathermen and Black Panthers.

In a memorandum to Attorney General John Mitchell, J. Edgar Hoover expressed his "clear-cut opposition to the lifting of the various restraints" proposed in the Huston Plan, but he also indicated a willingness to participate in the plan if it were adopted:

> [T]he FBI is prepared to implement the instructions of the White House at your direction. Of course, we would continue to seek your specific authorization, where appropriate, to utilize the various sensitive investigative techniques involved in individual cases.

Although President Nixon granted approval for the Huston Plan, he revoked this approval within five days, in part because of Hoover's opposition.

2. Justice Department Policy

{ . . . }

(c) Present Policy.—The Justice Department under Attorney General Edward H. Levi has addressed, for the first time, the legal issues arising from "black bag jobs." This occurred in a statement submitted by Acting Assistant Attorney General John C. Keeney in the appeal of the conviction of John Ehrlichman for the break-in by the White House "plumbers: at the office of Daniel Ellsberg's psychiatrist. Assessing the "plumbers" break-in, the Justice Department declared:

> The physical entry here was plainly unlawful . . . because the search was not controlled as we have suggested it must be, there was no proper authorization, there was no delegation to a proper officer, and

> there was no sufficient predicate for the choice of the particular premises invaded.

At the same time, however, the Justice Department defended the President's constitutional authority to conduct warrantless surreptitious entries in limited circumstances and with proper executive authorization:

> It is the position of the Department that such activities must be very carefully controlled. There must be solid reason to believe that foreign espionage or intelligence is involved. In addition, the intrusion into any zone of expected privacy must be kept to the minimum and there must be personal authorization by the President or the Attorney General. The Department believes that activities so controlled are lawful under the Fourth Amendment.
>
> In regard to warrantless searches related to foreign espionage or intelligence, the Department does not believe there is a constitutional difference between searches conducted by wire-tapping and those involving physical entries into private premises. One form of search is no less serious than another. It is and has long been the Department's view that warrantless searches involving physical entries into private premises are justified.

The Justice Department and the FBI have not terminated the use of warrantless surreptitious entry for electronic surveillance purposes in cases of "foreign espionage or intelligence." Warrantless surreptitious entry for other forms of search is not presently being conducted but, as indicated in the Justice Department statement, has not been ruled out as a matter of policy in foreign intelligence cases. The FBI has stated that "microphone surveillances have been continued and in some instances physical entry of the premises has been necessary" against foreign counterintelligence targets. In addition, "a small number" of surreptitious entries which apparently did not involve microphone installation "were conducted in connection with foreign counterintelligence investigations having grave impact on the security of the nation." Entries for the purpose of installing electronic surveillance devices have also provided an opportunity to conduct other forms of search. The Bureau has stated:

> Based on available records and discussions with FBI personnel, it has been determined that in connection with microphone surveillances in the United States, there have been occasions when observations and recordings were made of pertinent information contained within the premises.

According to the FBI, this "opportunity" has been "exploited" exclusively against foreign agents.

Warrantless surreptitious entries against American citizens who have "no significant connection with a foreign power, its agents or agencies" are undoubtedly unconstitutional. The constitutional issues arising from warrantless surreptitious entries against foreign agents within the United States have not been definitely resolved by the courts. The Committee recommends as a matter of policy that all governmental search and seizure "should be conducted only upon authority of a judicial warrant" issued in narrowly defined circumstances and with procedural safeguards "to minimize the acquisition and retention of non-foreign intelligence information about Americans."

6.

CIA Intelligence Collection About Americans

CHAOS and the Office of Security

I. INTRODUCTION

One of the main controversies raised by recent practices of the Central Intelligence Agency is the question of intelligence collection about Americans. Unlike the FBI, the CIA was intended to focus on foreign intelligence matters. Charges have been made, however, suggesting that the CIA spied on thousands of Americans and maintained files on many more, all in violation of its statutory charter.

Senate Resolution 21, establishing the Select Committee, authorized inquiry into the extent of covert intelligence efforts against Americans and their legality under CIA's charter. It specifically authorized review of the need for new legislation to protect American citizens and to clarify the authority of CIA. This included the tension under present law between the authority of the Director of Central Intelligence to protect sources and methods of intelligence, on the one hand, and the prohibition on CIA exercising police powers and internal security functions, on the other.

This report discusses the results of a staff inquiry into the major CIA programs which involved collection of information about Americans: the CHAOS, MERRIMAC and RESISTANCE programs and the special security investigations undertaken by the Office of Security.

A. CHAOS

The most extensive program of alleged "domestic spying" by CIA on Americans was the "CHAOS" program. CHAOS was the centerpiece of a major CIA effort begun in 1967 in response to White House pressure for intelligence about foreign influence upon American dissent. The CHAOS mission was to gather and evaluate all available information about foreign links to racial, antiwar and other protest activity in the United States. CHAOS was terminated in 1974.

The CHAOS office participated in the preparation of some half dozen major reports for higher authorities, all of which concluded that no significant role was being played by foreign elements in the various protest movements. This repeatedly negative finding met with continued skepticism from the White House under two administrations and pressures for further inquiry. In response to this skepticism CHAOS continued to expand its coverage of Americans in order to increase White House confidence in the accuracy of its findings.

A second major element of the CHAOS operation was to pursue specific inquiries from the FBI about the activity of particular Americans traveling abroad.

CHAOS received a great deal of information regarding Americans from CIA stations abroad, as well as from the FBI itself. In addition, CHAOS eventually received such information from its own agents who participated in domestic dissident activity in America in order to develop radical "credentials" as cover for overseas assignment. CHAOS also obtained information about Americans from other domestic CIA components, from the CIA mail opening project and from a National Security Agency international communications intercept program.

In the process, the CHAOS project amassed thousands of files on Americans, indexed hundreds of thousands of Americans into its computer records, and disseminated thousands of reports about Americans to the FBI and other government offices. Some of the information concerned the domestic activity of those Americans.

B. MERRIMAC and RESISTANCE

The MERRIMAC and RESISTANCE programs were both run by the CIA Office of Security, a support unit of the CIA charged with safeguarding its personnel, facilities and information.

Project MERRIMAC involved the infiltration by CIA agents of Washington-based peace groups and black activist groups. The stated purpose of that program was simply to obtain early warning of demonstrations and other physical threats to the CIA. The collection requirements, however, were broadened to include general information about the leadership, funding and activities and policies of the targeted groups.

Project RESISTANCE was a broad effort to obtain general background information for predicting violence which might create threats to CIA installations, recruiters or contractors and for security evaluation of CIA applicants. From 1967 until 1973, the program compiled information about radical groups around the country, particularly on campuses. Much of the reporting to headquarters by field offices was from open sources such as newspapers. But additional information was obtained from cooperating police departments, campus officials and other local authorities, some of whom, in turn, were using more active collection techniques such as informants.

In addition, both MERRIMAC and RESISTANCE supplied information for the CHAOS program.

C. Special Security Investigations

Finally, there was a group of specific security investigations undertaken either to find the source of news leaks, or to determine whether government employees were involved in espionage or otherwise constituted security risks. Investigations were made of former CIA employees, employees of other government agencies, newsmen and other private individuals in this country. Physical surveillance, electronic surveillance, mail and tax return inspection, and surreptitious entry have been used on various occasions.

They were not part of a particularly organized program, and were conducted on a case-by-case basis. But they raise questions about what kinds of security investigations are within the CIA's lawful authority, and also about what kinds of techniques are permissible, even when such investigations are authorized.

D. The Investigation

The Committee staff investigation of each of these areas has included interviews, depositions, and documentary review of available files.

Each of these areas had been examined intensively by the Rockefeller Commission on CIA Activities within the United States before the Select Committee was given access to the files and to some of the persons involved.

The Committee staff conducted an independent review of these programs. At the same time, an effort was made to avoid duplication of the extensive testimonial record already made by the Commission, and to take additional testimony only when necessary to clarify the record or to explore additional issues which arose. Hence, this report includes citations to both testimony given to the Select Committee and the Rockefeller Commission.

{ . . . }

E. Summary of the Issues

Before turning to the description of these programs, the remainder of this introduction summarizes the issues which these programs present for congressional decision.

Three themes are fundamental. First, to what extent did any of these activities exceed the lawful authority of the CIA under its charter in the 1947 National Security Act? The answer is not always clear; the statute's legislative history is often obscure at best.

Second, what should be the extent of the CIA's authority in the future? Whatever the limits of present law, now is the time to reassess which intelligence operations impinging upon Americans are appropriate for the CIA, and which best left to others.

Finally, in reviewing the CHAOS program, particularly, the Congress must look beyond judging past legality or reallocating functions among Federal agencies. For the American citizen, the fact that his Government keeps a file on his associations, or monitors his travel and his advocacy of dissent, is far more important than the question of which office in the bureaucracy is doing it. Ultimately the activity discussed in this report bears on the question of what kinds of intelligence operations are proper undertakings for any part of the Government.

{ . . . }

PART II: HISTORY AND OPERATION OF CHAOS

A. Background

Operation CHAOS was not an intelligence mission sought by the CIA. Presidents Johnson and Nixon pressed the Director of CIA, Richard Helms, to determine the extent of hostile foreign influence on domestic unrest among students, opponents of the Vietnam war, minorities and the "New Left." By all the testimony and available evidence, it was this pressure which led to the creation and expansion of a special office in the CIA to coordinate the efforts to respond.

The decisions to initiate the CHAOS program and, subsequently, to expand the effort, were made in the context of increasing domestic unrest in the United States.

The nonviolent policy of civil rights efforts in the first half of the Sixties was being challenged by militant "Black Power" advocates urging confrontation with the white majority. On July 29, 1967, following serious disturbances in the Nation's cities, which comprised the worst period of racial riots in American history, President Johnson had established the National Commission on Civil Disorders (the "Kerner Commission") to investigate their origins.

Organized demonstrations and international conferences protesting America's role in the Vietnamese war also became an increasing concern to the Government.

In April 1967, there were large antiwar demonstrations in San Francisco and New York. In May the International War Crimes Trials, sponsored by Bertrand Russell in regard to U.S. activity in Vietnam, began in Stockholm. In July 1967, there was a major international conference of peace groups in Stockholm. In September, a wide range of American activists in domestic peace groups, student and black organizations met with groups from other countries who were opposed to American involvement in Vietnam, including North Vietnam, in Bratislava, Czechoslovakia. Finally, on October 21, 1967, there were large scale protest activities in Washington, including a march on the Pentagon, and worldwide demonstrations of support for opposition to continued American involvement in Vietnam.

Government concern about domestic unrest continued throughout 1968, with riots following the death of Martin Luther King in April, continuing student violence at campuses from coast to coast, stepped-up antiwar protest activity, and violence at the National Democratic Party Convention in Chicago.

During the remaining five years for which the CHAOS program lasted, 1969–1974, racial disorders diminished but the intensity of antiwar demonstration and student violence increased and then subsided after 1972.

B. Authorization of CHAOS

Against this backdrop of unrest, the CIA's systematic investigation of possible foreign involvement began with two assignments made by Director Richard Helms in the late summer and fall of 1967.

In August, Helms established a program to coordinate and improve the CIA's coverage abroad of American dissidents. Helms does not claim a specific presidential request for a new CIA program in this area. Rather, Helms testified that he was acting in general response to President Johnson's insistent interest in the extent of foreign influence on domestic dissidents. Helms testified that:

> President Johnson was after this all the time. I don't recall any specific instructions in writing from his staff, particularly, but this was something that came up almost daily and weekly.

Helms summarized his response to the presidential overtures:

> But what I am attempting to say is that when a President keeps asking if there is any information, "how are you getting along with your examination," "have you picked up any more information on these subjects," it isn't a direct order to do something, but it seems to me it behooves the Director of Central Intelligence to find some way to improve his performance, or improve his Agency's performance. And the setting up of this unit was what I conceived to be a proper action in an effort to see if we couldn't improve the Agency's performance in this general field

The Deputy Director of Plans, Thomas Karamessines, also testified to his understanding of the White House pressures precipitating CHAOS.

As a result, Helms sought to have the CIA try to pull together all the pertinent information already being received and to use the resources available for better intelligence coverage.

Within CIA, there is no written directive from Helms to Karamessines, his deputy for the Plans Directorate, to establish the CHAOS program. The first recorded authorization is an August 15, 1967, memorandum from Karamessines to James Angleton, Chief of the Counterintelligence Staff.

Karamessines' memorandum refers to discussions earlier that day among himself, Angleton and Helms and asks Angleton to designate a staff officer to run the program. The memorandum contemplated the conduct of operations to collect intelligence. It also acknowledged the program's "domestic counterintelligence aspects," and the need for dissemination of the information obtained to domestic agencies. The memorandum requested:

> b. The exclusive briefing of specific division chiefs and certain selected officers in each division, on the aims and objectives of this intelligence collection program with definite domestic counterintelligence aspects.
>
> c. The establishment of some sort of system by Dick Ober (or whatever officer you select) for the orderly coordination of the operations to be conducted, with the responsibility for the actual conduct of the operations vested in the specific area divisions.
>
> d. The identification of a limited dissemination procedure which will afford these activities high operational security while at the same time getting the information to the appropriate departments and agencies which have the responsibility domestically.

Angleton chose Richard Ober to head what became the Special Operations Group within the Counterintelligence Staff. Ober had already been involved in a more limited inquiry into possible foreign links to American dissidents.

In the beginning of 1967, *Ramparts* magazine had published an exposé of various CIA activities and relationships with private institutions in America. Ober had been investigating the possibility of ties between foreign intelligence services and persons associated with the magazine, or their friends. He had begun to build a computerized file on dissident activists in America with some connection to the *Ramparts* organization. By the time he was given the more general CHAOS assignment in August 1967, Ober estimates he had indexed several hundred Americans and had created perhaps fifty actual files. However, there was no indication that the *Ramparts* inquiry was expected to lead to a larger investigation of American protest.

Ober first sought to pull together the Agency's holdings and information readily available here and abroad which would be pertinent to his assigned inquiry.

The scope of that inquiry had not been defined in Karamessines' August 15 memorandum, which was simply entitled "Overseas Coverage of Subversive Student and Related Matters." The first direct statement of the target was included in an August 31 cable to the field describing the collection requirement:

> In light of recent and current events which of major interest and deep concern to highest levels here, Headquarters has established program for keeping tabs on radical students and U.S. Negro expatriates as well as travelers passing through certain select areas abroad. Objective is to find out extent to which Soviets, Chicoms and Cubans are exploiting our domestic problems in terms of espionage and subversion. High sensitivity is obvious.

The cable also advised that a special reporting channel had been established with a cryptonym limiting distribution at Headquarters of any traffic. The recipient chiefs of station were told to control knowledge of the program and the information collected and to destroy the cable itself after reading. Cable distribution was to be limited at Headquarters to the Division Chiefs controlling the station or base involved, Angleton and Karamessines or his deputy.

C. The November 1967 Peace Movement Study

CIA's inquiry into foreign ties of American dissidents intensified at the end of October 1967. This time, responding to a specific White House request, Helms directed CIA to produce a study on the "International Connections of the U.S. Peace Movement." Presumably, this request was precipitated by the October 21 demonstrations and arrests at the Pentagon and the worldwide antiwar demonstrations on the same day.

Ober testified that the scope of his own operation soon came to include antiwar activists, as well as student radicals and black nationalists. But it was his participation in the October CIA study for the President which firmly set Vietnam protest as a major target of the CHAOS office's efforts.

The study was written by the Intelligence Directorate of the Agency. Ober coordinated the Plans Directorate contribution and the receipt of material from the FBI and other Federal agencies.

Both the "peace movement" and "foreign connections" were broadly defined. According to Ober's memorandum of his meeting with the Directorate of Intelligence officers in charge of the study, American organizations "affiliated with the overall Peace Movement" as well as peace organizations themselves, were to be included. "Foreign connections" were defined to include associations with the American Communist Party.

With the approval of Angleton, Karamessines and Helms, Ober sent a second reporting requirement to the stations, this time asking for information on foreign connections to the peace movement. The information was to be handled in another restricted channel separate from the one provided for responses to the August inquiry on radical students and black activists. The November 1967 cable to multiple addresses told the stations:

> Headquarters is participating in high level interdepartmental survey of international connections of anti-Vietnam war movement in U.S. For purposes this study, we are attempting to establish nature and extent of illegal and subversive connections that may exist between US organizations or activists involved and communist, communist front or other anti-American and foreign elements abroad. *Such connections might range from casual contacts based merely on mutual interest* to closely controlled channels for party directives. [Emphasis added.]

Since Director Helms had asked for the report within two weeks, the stations were asked only to furnish information on hand or readily available.

The conclusions of the review were essentially negative. The study noted that the diversity and loose structure of the peace movement in America permitted the more active leaders to coordinate some of the activities on an international scale and it cited the simultaneous demonstrations on October 21, both here and abroad. But the CIA found little evidence of actual foreign direction or control, or evidence that any international dialogue went beyond consultation and coordination.

However, these conclusions were explicitly tentative. Director Helms' letter of transmittal to the President states reservations about the adequacy of the intelligence community's coverage of the target:

> From this intimate review of the bulk of the material on hand in Washington, we conclude that there are significant holes in the story. We lack information on certain aspects of the movement which could only be met by levying requirements on the FBI.
>
> First we found little or no information on the financing of the principal peace movement groups. Specifically, we were unable to uncover any sources of funds for the costly travel schedules of prominent peace movement coordinators, many of whom are on the wing almost constantly.
>
> Second we could find no evidence of any contact between the most prominent peace movement leaders and foreign embassies, either in the U.S. or abroad. Of course, there may not be any such contact, but on the other hand, we are woefully short of information on the day-to-day activities and itineraries of these men.
>
> Finally, there is little information available about radical peace movement groups on U.S. college campuses. These groups are, of course, highly mobile and sometimes even difficult to identify, but their more prominent leaders are certainly visible and active enough for monitoring.

D. Operation of the CHAOS Program and Related CIA Projects

The assignment of responsibility to Ober in August 1967, and the CIA's study of the peace movement in November, set the initial pattern of the Agency's inquiry into foreign powers and American dissidents.

Ober's office served as the focal point and clearinghouse for Agency efforts on this question, and along with the analysts in the Intelligence Directorate, provided the expertise for Director Helms to respond to the White House interest.

As it developed, the CHAOS mission included three related tasks:

> (1) to coordinate and expand CIA's own collection of relevant information and to obtain pertinent material from other government agencies;

(2) to process, control and retain the information as it became available;

(3) to provide the results for dissemination by CIA to the White House, other high-level offices and interested agencies.

At the same time, CHAOS performed a second role. It serviced the FBI's own requirements for information about foreign contacts and travel of Americans. Ober regarded responding to the Bureau's requests for coverage of Americans abroad as an accepted part of his responsibilities.

1. Gathering Information

The two main sources of information received by CHAOS were the CIA's stations abroad, and the FBI at home.

For example, the CIA received all of the FBI's reports on the American peace movement.

The material received from the FBI included information about foreign travel, contacts, and communications of Americans. Much of it was simply information about individual activists or groups and their domestic activities. In many instances, FBI reports would contain both kinds of information.

By June 1970, these FBI reports were pouring into CHAOS at the rate of over 1,000 a month.

The background information on individuals provided by the FBI served as a "data base" of names, and intelligence about the associations between different dissident elements. This background information could be used to develop leads, and to understand the significance of reports directly relating to foreign contacts.

The other basic source of information was the reporting from the CIA's overseas stations. Using the special reporting channel, the stations supplied reports from their own assets and also supplied whatever CHAOS information was obtained from the liaison with local intelligence services.

On June 25, 1968, a message was sent to various European stations advising that recent high level discussions had underscored the need for increasing the coverage of American black, student and antiwar dissidents abroad. The stations were asked to engage friendly foreign intelligence services more fully in that effort. Headquarters said that foreign intelligence services covering their own dissidents might be able to provide more information on the foreign contacts of American citizens.

This cable was followed shortly by another multi-station message which repeated the general reporting requirement as follows:

> As many of you know, Headquarters is engaged in a sensitive high priority program concerning foreign contacts with US individuals and organizations of the "Radical Left." Included in this category are radical students, antiwar activists, draft resisters and deserters, black nationalists, anarchists and assorted "New Leftists." The objective is to discover the extent to which Soviets, ChiComs, Cubans and other Communist countries are exploiting our domestic problems in terms of subversion and espionage. Of particular interest is any evidence of foreign direction, control, training or funding.

The cable also directed even tighter control over the reporting procedures. The two previously separate channels for reporting information on antiwar and on black or student activists were combined into the single restricted handling cryptonym "CHAOS."

Information supplied CHAOS by the stations was of two types. First there was the general outstanding requirement for any intelligence pertinent to the CHAOS mission as defined in the basic cable instructions. Second, the stations were asked to respond to specific inquiries. Such requests from Ober might relate to an upcoming international conference or the activities of particular foreign persons suspected of being involved in efforts to influence American unrest. Frequently these special inquiries were triggered by travel of particular Americans to the area and a CHAOS request for coverage of their activities and contacts.

2. Processing, Storage and Control of CHAOS Information

As the material flowed into CHAOS from stations, domestic CIA components, and the FBI, it was analyzed, indexed and filed. Every name of individuals and organizations was extracted and referenced in the central CHAOS computer system known as "HYDRA." This system served as the reference index to all of the office's holdings.

If a report on one individual referred to others, their names would be indexed also. Any information which was received about an individual for whom CHAOS maintained a file, went into his file. There was no winnowing of the material before its entry into the permanent record system of CHAOS.

Once the information was indexed and filed, the HYDRA computer system permitted its prompt retrieval. By checking a name in HYDRA, one could find all the cables, memoranda or other documents referring to that individual, whether he was the subject of the material or merely mentioned in passing. It should be emphasized, however, that CHAOS did not maintain a separate file on every American whose name was indexed in the computer. In many instances the computer would refer a searcher to the file of another person, or some other CHAOS holdings in which the subject individual was mentioned, but there was not enough material to open a file. Thus, there were an estimated 300,000 Americans indexed in HYDRA, but only an estimated 7,500 Americans for whom actual files were maintained.

The tight control maintained over communication of CHAOS information from the CIA's stations was continued at Headquarters. The special reporting channel and restricted handling assured that the cable traffic would be seen only by a few high-level officials in the area divisions of the Plans Directorate, Karamessines, Angleton and their deputies or designees.

Tight security was maintained over the information deemed most sensitive, even within the CHAOS office itself. The information in the HYDRA computer system was compartmented into several layers of increasing sensitivity and correspondingly more restricted access. Only CHAOS officers cleared for access to the more restricted streams of information could retrieve the items on an individual which involved sensitive sources and methods or other tightly held intelligence.

3. Reporting by CIA

CIA disseminated the information gathered on foreign ties of American dissidents in three forms: major studies prepared for the President; special reports for the White House and other senior officials on individual items of information; and routine reporting to the FBI.

(a) Studies.—On November 20, 1967, at the request of Director Helms, the CIA began an investigation of "Demonstration Techniques" both here and abroad.

On December 21, 1967, Helms sent President Johnson a follow up review of the November Study on the United States Peace Movement.

On January 5, 1968, Helms sent to the White House an interim study of "Student Dissent and Its Techniques in the U.S.," "which is part of our continuing examination of this general matter. It is an effort to identify the locus of student dissent and how widespread it is." The forty-page paper dealt exclusively with American student activists and the bulk of it contained much the same kind of material on the Students for a Democratic Society (SDS) that formed the chapter of "Restless Youth" CIA produced a year later.

"Student Dissent" briefly noted that Communist front groups did not control the student organizations, and that American student groups had not forged significant links with foreign radicals. The report concentrated on domestic matters and analyzed the makeup, strength, motivation, strategy and views of the American students. It concluded, for example, that

> Except on the issue of selective service, the student community appears generally to support the Administration more strongly than the population as a whole.

The last analytical study prepared for President Johnson, "Restless Youth," was finished in the fall of 1968. "Restless Youth" is a detailed sociological and political analysis of student unrest throughout the world. It found common sources of alienation and hostility to established institutions in many countries, but concluded that, in each nation, student dissent was essentially homegrown and not stimulated by an international conspiracy.

The version sent to the White House included a section on the SDS in the United States. Helms' cover memorandum to the President stated:

> Some time ago you requested that I make occasional round-up reports on youth and student movements worldwide. Responding to this request and guided by comments and suggestions from Walt Rostow, we have prepared the attached study. You will, of course, be aware of the peculiar sensitivity which attached to the fact that CIA has prepared a report on student activities both here and abroad.

Helms did not testify that the White House had requested the section on domestic student protest. Rather, he said that since the White House had wanted a study of possible international orchestration of protest activity, it did not seem sensible to leave out the American scene, so it was included.

The section on the United States was drawn largely from public sources. An updated, unabridged version was sent to Henry Kissinger for President Nixon in February of the following year. Helms stated his concern more explicitly in the transmittal letter for that version:

> Herewith is a survey of student dissidence worldwide as requested by the President. In an effort to round out our discussion of this subject, we have included a section on American students. This is an area not within the charter of this Agency, so I need not emphasize how extremely sensitive this makes the paper. Should anyone learn of its existence, it would prove most embarrassing for all concerned.

This first series of studies for the White House were all prepared by the CIA's Intelligence Directorate, with continuing assistance from CHAOS in providing material from overseas stations, other CIA components, and the FBI. The CHAOS office, itself, only began to produce the studies itself following further White House requests in the summer of 1969, discussed below. Copies of the material collected for the 1967 and 1968 studies on the Peace movement and on student dissent, however, were also indexed and retained by the CHAOS operation for its own files.

(b) Special Reports.—In addition to the formal studies CIA prepared for the President, Ober prepared occasional reports, so-called "M" memoranda, of particularly sensitive or timely intelligence items for high level distribution to the White House, the Attorney General, Secretary of State, and similar officials. During the entire history of CHAOS there were 34 such M memoranda.

The content of M memoranda varied. They included, for example, information that a foreign government was making a grant to a dissident protest group in America; information regarding a reported kidnapping and murder plot against high government officials; and information about speeches made by radical leaders while abroad. Essentially these were one-shot reports about some contact or cooperation between foreign elements and American radicals, rather than an analysis of such links.

One or two of the earliest memoranda did deal with plans for domestic protests. In connection with the anticipated demonstrations in Washington at the end of October 1967, Helms had requested all available information to be furnished the administration:

> In any event, I want to be sure that any information you gentlemen acquire through whatever channels, is promptly passed to appropriate Federal authorities, including the White House, the Secret Service, the FBI, and anyone else who counts. I am under the impression that this "do" may turn out to be a humdinger, and I want to insure that we have clean hands in passing along any information that *we turn up in the normal course of business.* [Emphasis added.]

On October 10, the CIA distributed a memorandum to the White House, recounting "unevaluated information" about alleged plans for racial disturbances at the time of the October 21 demonstrations and the alleged involvement of a particular black leader.

Richard Ober, at the request of Director Helms, also provided the Kerner Commission with a series of 26 reports. The Executive Order establishing the Commission had directed all agencies, to the extent permitted by law, to provide information and otherwise assist its efforts. The material supplied by the CIA primarily consisted of reports on overseas travel and statements by American black leaders and allegations of foreign efforts to exacerbate racial unrest in America. However, they included some of the early memoranda on reported plans for domestic disorders, which appear to be from domestic sources and to have little relevance to the question of foreign links.

(c) Dissemination to the FBI.—By far the main tangible product of CHAOS was extensive dissemination of raw reports to the FBI. Information deemed of interest to the Bureau was put in memorandum form and sent through special channels directly from the CHAOS office to the FBI. In many instances it was information about Americans which CHAOS had sought in response to a specific FBI request. Most typically, the Bureau would notify Ober that it wished coverage of Americans whose overseas travel it had learned about in advance.

In addition, CHAOS obtained information pursuant to its general collection requirements from stations abroad, and wholly domestic information about dissident activities obtained in the course of its operations. This, too, was disseminated to the FBI, if it was deemed pertinent to the Bureau's concerns about such Americans. Ober testified that he regarded any names in reports sent to CHAOS by the FBI a standing requirement from the FBI for information which CHAOS obtained about those persons.

E. 1969 Expansion of CHAOS

The CHAOS operation was expanded and given renewed impetus in 1969, when the new Nixon administration expressed the same concern about foreign influence on domestic unrest as had its predecessors.

1. The Review of CHAOS for the President

On June 20, 1969, Tom Huston, Staff Assistant to the President, asked the CIA for a review of its progress:

> The President has directed that a report on foreign Communist support of revolutionary protest movements in this country be prepared for his study. . . . "Support" should be liberally construed to include all activities by foreign Communists designed to encourage or assist revolutionary protest movements in the United States.
>
> On the basis of earlier reports submitted to the President on a more limited aspect of this problem, it appears that our present intelligence collection capabilities in this area may be inadequate.

Huston asked for both a substantive review and a survey of the effectiveness of resources the CIA was employing, and what gaps might exist "because of either inadequate resources or a low priority of attention." This study was the first one actually produced by the CHAOS office.

The review was completed within 10 days. Deputy Director {Robert E.} Cushman summarized the results in his letter of transmittal:

> 2. The information collected by this Agency provides evidence of only a very limited amount of foreign Communist assistance to revolutionary protest movements in the United States. There is very little reporting on Communist assistance in the form of funding or training and no evidence of Communist direction or control of any United

> States revolutionary protest movement. The bulk of our information illustrates Communist encouragement of these movements through propaganda methods.
>
> 3. Since the summer of 1967, this Agency has been attempting to determine through its sources abroad, whether or not there is any significant Communist direction or assistance to revolutionary groups in the United States. We have been collaborating closely in this effort with the Federal Bureau of Investigation and disseminating information to it. Existing Agency collection resources are being employed wherever feasible and new sources are being sought through independent means as well as with the assistance of foreign intelligence services and the Federal Bureau of Investigation. Of course, the Katzenbach guidelines have inhibited our access to certain persons who might have information on efforts by Communist intelligence services to exploit revolutionary groups in the United States.

Two additional studies were prepared by CHAOS, which were essentially revisions of this 1969 review. In 1970, as part of the CIA contribution to the work of the Interdepartmental Committee on Intelligence which led to the so-called "Huston Plan," CHAOS prepared an update of the 1969 study. A similar revised version was prepared in 1971.

The 1971 report, "Definition and Assessment of Existing Internal Security Threat—Foreign," concluded that hostile foreign governments were committed to exploiting United States unrest as much as possible. But, apart from a few isolated instances, the study concluded that the main "assistance" was still in the form of exhortation and encouragement through international conferences and statements of support by foreign figures. The summary of foreign Communist influence on the New Left and radical student groups stated:

> There is no evidence, based on available information and sources, that foreign governments, organizations, or intelligence services now control U.S. New Left movements and/or are capable at the present time of directing these movements for the purpose of instigating open insurrection or disorders; for initiating and supporting terrorist or sabotage activities; or for fomenting unrest and subversion in the United States Armed Forces, among government employees, or in labor unions, colleges and universities, and mass media.

. . . .

> In summary, foreign funding, training, propaganda, and other support does not now play a major role in the U.S. New Left. International fronts and conferences help to promote New Left causes, but at present the U.S. New Left is basically self-sufficient and moves under its own impetus.

The conclusions with regard to black activists were the same.

Following the Huston memorandum of June 1969, questioning the adequacy of the CIA's efforts, the CHAOS program was expanded to develop better sources of information, and an improved capability to process it.

In September, Helms issued a memorandum regarding CHAOS to the heads of the Directorates. Helms told the Deputy Directors that he had:

> recently reviewed the Agency's efforts to monitor those international activities of radicals and black militants which may affect the national security. I believe that we have the proper approach in discharging this sensitive responsibility, while strictly observing the statutory and de facto proscriptions on Agency domestic involvements.

The memo acknowledged overlapping interests of several CIA components in this area but made clear that Ober had the principal operational responsibility for coordinating collection efforts. Helms specifically requested that Ober be provided with trained analysts to process a large backlog of undigested data and skilled operations officers.

In the fall of 1969, CHAOS began to develop two additional programs to increase its sources of information. The first was a domestic collection program undertaken by the Domestic Contact Service. In the second, CHAOS developed its own agents, who were trained in the United States and then sent on reporting missions abroad.

2. Domestic Contact Service

In early 1969, Domestic Contact Service (DCS) was receiving an increasing volume of field reports on Black militant activity. Some of the material related to possible foreign association and had been routinely sent in by the field offices. On March 10, 1969, in order to channel and control this material, DCS opened a new case on "Activities of Black Militants" here and abroad.

Because of references to foreign contacts, DCS sent some of the reports to the Counterintelligence Staff and they were routed to Ober, who sought additional material.

In October 1969, Ober formally briefed DCS officials. A subsequent memorandum to DCS field offices, jointly drafted by DCS and CHAOS representatives, expanded projects to the same five subject categories used by CHAOS: black militants; radical youth groups; radical underground press; antiwar groups; and deserter/draft resister movements. The directive advised that:

> CI's interest is primarily to ascertain the details, if any, of any foreign involvement/support/guidance/training/funding/or exploitation of above groups and movements, particularly through coverage of foreign travel, contacts and activities of the Americans involved.

Over 200 reports and other items were supplied by DCS to CHAOS between 1969 and 1973. Much of the material included information relating to foreign contacts of Americans; some contained "operational leads" to potential sources who might be willing to collect information when they went overseas. Other items consisted largely of information about domestic organization and activity.

DCS officials thought they were expected to supply domestic information about dissidents for use as background data, as well as any leads to foreign connections.

There was no express reference to a domestic information collection requirement in the directive sent to DCS field offices in December 1969. But the Deputy Chief of CHAOS testified that his office had indicated their appreciation to DCS for such material, which helped build the CHAOS data base.

Moreover, whatever the formal written requirements, CHAOS made specific requests for domestic materials and, in other instances, made follow up requests based on items which DCS field offices had sent in. For example, CHAOS asked the Chicago Field Office for information on the "28 co-conspirators" of 12 SDS members who had been locally indicted for the Weathermen riots in Chicago the previous fall. This was supplied, as well as subsequent coverage of the legal proceedings.

Another CHAOS request resulted in a DOS field office obtaining from confidential sources a large report prepared by a state investigating commission on radical demonstrations in that state.

The CHAOS office thanked DCS for one early report on the domestic political activities of a black leader and asked for any additional information available.

In the beginning of 1971, however, after expressions of uncertainty about the program from the field, DCS officials sought a revised written requirement stating both a primary interest in foreign-related information and a secondary CHAOS interest in background information of a domestic nature.

DCS claimed this was merely intended to confirm the prior practice based on oral requests from CHAOS.

> The draft directive stated that: . . . The second type of information concerns the activities of US radical groups but does not contain any obvious foreign implications. Such information is considered of primary interest to the FBI under its domestic security charter. DCS however has been directed to collect both types of information, with the emphasis on that pertaining to foreign involvement.

Ober refused to approve the new directive. As a result, DCS closed the old case, and opened a new one under a narrower directive. DCS reporting was to be "focused exclusively upon the collection of information suggesting *foreign involvement* in U.S. radical activities." [Emphasis in original.] Purely domestic information was to be passed locally to the FBI.

Though nowhere near as voluminous as domestic reports received by CHAOS from the FBI, the DCS material was one of the main additional sources of "domestic intelligence" in the CHAOS files.

3. CHAOS Agents

The other main source of "domestic intelligence" about Americans which went into CHAOS files came from agents being run by the CHAOS project and a few from a related foreign intelligence operation run in close coordination with CHAOS.

The effort to develop assets targeted fully on CHAOS information began right after the White House review of the Agency's CHAOS effort in the fall of 1969. Previously, overseas reporting had come from assets already working for the various stations on other assignments. Those station assets continued to supply CHAOS information even after Ober obtained his own agent program.

Over 40 potential recruits were evaluated. About half of these were referred by the FBI, for whom they had already worked. Most of those referred by the FBI ultimately were used on a single assignment. Seven recruits developed unilaterally by the CIA also were used as CHAOS agents.

CHAOS agents participated in radical activity here as part of their preparation for assignments overseas. In the process, they supplied detailed information on domestic activities of Americans.

While here, the agents spent at least several weeks, and, in some cases, much longer, immersed in the radical community. This not only enhanced their radical credentials and increased their familiarity with persons and groups they might be reporting on from abroad. It also afforded their case officer with an opportunity to train them, assess their progress, test the possibility they were a plant, and evaluate how CHAOS could best use them abroad. This was done by extensive debriefing of the agents on a periodic basis.

According to {Charles} Marcules, the agents in training were asked to report to him in detail on their activities, persons with whom they had been meeting and so forth.

In all of these instances, the information about individuals in dissident groups, the plans and policies of the organizations and other domestic information, as well as any leads to possible foreign connections went not only into the case file of the agent in training but also into the general CHAOS files on those individuals and groups.

4. Project 2

A separate intelligence project which also involved the use of radical credentials by American agents furnished CHAOS with additional information about American dissidents. "Project 2" was developed in 1969 and implemented in 1970 by a particular area division at CIA. It was designed ultimately to penetrate certain foreign intelligence targets through these agents, or to have them spot others who could accomplish such infiltration.

Most of the assets developed their leftist coloration by entering universities in the United States after an initial period of basic agent training. When in school, they participated in the radical community. While preparing for their future assignments, the agents filed detailed reports and were also debriefed by their case officer. In the process, they provided considerable information on their associates, dissident organizations, demonstration plans and sometimes personal information. One asset submitted a 60-page report for a three week period which included detailed information on demonstrations, group meetings, and general accounts of such activity as Women's Liberation efforts in the area.

From the outset, the project's potential usefulness to CHAOS was recognized. All of the agent reports and debriefing contact reports were provided to CHAOS for its files.

Once abroad on their basic intelligence mission, moreover, the Project 2 agents were explicitly directed to acquire CHAOS information as well. One memorandum regarding the overseas assignment of a Project 2 agent stated:

> His mission will be to spot, assess and develop leftists in the Maoist spectrum. . . . He will also report on CHAOS developments in [the target country].

One Project 2 agent became affiliated with an American dissident group in the foreign country which was directing its activities at personnel of American bases in that area. He began to report on both the native "radical left and the American radical left."

5. Provision to CHAOS of NSA and Mail Intercepts

When CHAOS was in full scale operation, it also was receiving information from the CIA's mail intercept program and the interception of international communications by the National Security Agency. The CIA mail project was run by another unit within the Counterintelligence Staff. CHAOS supplied that office with a list of 41 individuals and organizations for specific inclusion in the so-called "watch list" used as one basis for intercepting international mail. The names provided by CHAOS were to be sent to the point of interception in the field, and not merely to be used to screen mail which had independently been selected and had already arrived at the project office in Headquarters.

CHAOS also supplied lists of individuals and organizations to the

National Security Agency for inclusion in its "watch list." In addition, CHAOS had access to more general distributions of communications intelligence involving Americans which were received by the CIA from NSA.

F. Reduction, Limitation and Termination of CHAOS

1. Reduced Reporting Priority

With the decline of student demonstrations and antiwar activity in the latter part of 1972, the intensity of the CHAOS effort declined. A cable to several stations advised that general reporting of information regarding foreign contacts of the New Left was no longer a high priority, although routine coverage was to be maintained in order to preserve a "residual counteraction capability for possible future use." The cable noted that a high priority would continue with regard to foreign connections of New Left individuals or groups advocating or engaging in violence.

2. Reaction to Inspector General's Survey

At the end of 1972, the CHAOS program was subject to a high-level review. In the fall of 1972, an Inspector General survey of overseas stations for a particular region raised questions about CHAOS. The survey team was not permitted to review specific CHAOS files and operations, either in the field or at Headquarters. However, questions voiced to the team by station personnel in several countries resulted in a separate memorandum from the Inspector General, William Broe, to the Executive Director. Broe summarized the policy concerns expressed about CHAOS:

> Even though there is a general belief that CIA involvement is directed primarily at foreign manipulation and subversive exploitation of U.S. citizens, we also encountered general concern over what appeared to constitute a monitoring of the political views and activities of Americans not known to be or suspected of being involved in espionage. Occasionally, stations were asked to report on the whereabouts and activities of prominent persons . . . *whose comings and goings were not only in the public domain but for whom allegations of subversion seemed sufficiently nebulous to raise renewed doubts as to the nature and legitimacy of the CHAOS program.* [Emphasis added.]

On a practical level, the stations had complained about the burden of seeking information from the liaison service on behalf of the FBI when the local or nearby FBI representative had also requested the same information from the liaison directly.

Broe's memorandum caused a review of the CHAOS operation by Karamessines, Helms, William Colby, who was then the Executive Director/Comptroller of the CIA, and other senior officials. In addition to improving coordination with the FBI and briefing overseas officers with a misunderstanding of CHAOS, Helms also directed that thereafter:

> A clear priority is to be given in this general field to the subject of terrorism. This should bring about a reduction in the intensity of attention to political dissidents in the United States not, or not apt to be, involved in terrorism. On a secondary level, continued discreet coverage will be maintained of counterintelligence matters, including the possible manipulation of American citizens by foreign intelligence services or their actions abroad of counterintelligence interest.

Ober had already taken on the additional duties of coordinating the CIA's efforts to combat international terrorism the previous summer. In 1973, the CHAOS program was transferred from the Counterintelligence Staff to the newly formed Operations Staff within the Plans Directorate.

On May 9, 1973, CIA Director James Schlesinger requested an inventory of all "questionable activities" in which the CIA might have engaged. One such activity on which reports were sent to the Director was CHAOS. On August 29, 1973, William Colby, who had succeeded Schlesinger as Director, issued a series of instructions regarding the questioned programs and activities. His directive in regard to CHAOS limited the CIA's own operations to focus more narrowly on collecting information about foreign nationals and organizations, rather than the Americans with whom they might be in contact:

> MEMORANDUM
> *Subject: CHAOS*
> CHAOS is restricted to the collection abroad of information on foreign activities related to domestic matters. *CIA will focus clearly on the foreign organizations and individuals involved and only incidentally on their American contacts. As a consequence, CIA will not take on the primary*

responsibility for following Americans abroad, although CIA can accept a request by the FBI to be passed to an appropriate liaison service in a foreign country for the surveillance of such an American and the transmission of the results back to the FBI. It must be plainly demonstrated in each such transmission that the CIA is merely a channel of communication between the FBI and the appropriate foreign service and is not to be directly engaged in the surveillance or other action against the American involved. [Emphasis added.]

3. Termination of CHAOS

CHAOS was terminated as a specified collection program on March 5, 1974, by order of Director Colby. The cable announcing this to the stations also stated guidelines for future activity involving Americans:

1. This message is to notify you of the termination of the CHAOS program and to provide guidelines under which HQS has been operating for some time on certain activities formerly included in CHAOS.

2. Guidelines: All collection takes place abroad. Collection is restricted to information on foreign activities related to domestic matters. CIA will focus clearly on the foreign organizations and individuals involved and only incidentally on their American contacts. In doing this, following will apply:

A. Whenever information is uncovered as a byproduct result of CIA foreign-targeted intelligence or counterintelligence operations abroad which makes Americans abroad suspect for security or counterintelligence reasons, the information will be reported by CIA in the following manner:

(1) With respect to private American citizens abroad, such information will be reported to the FBI.

(2) With respect to official U.S. personnel abroad, such information will be reported to their parent agency's security authorities, and to the FBI if appropriate.

In both such cases, under this sub-paragraph, specific CIA operations will not be mounted against such individuals; CIA responsibilities thereafter will be restricted to reporting any further intelligence or counterintelligence aspects of the specific case which come to CIA attention as a by-product of its continuing foreign

> targeted operational activity. If the FBI, on the basis of the receipt of the CIA information, however, specifically requests further information on terrorist or counterintelligence matters relating to the private American citizens involved in the specific case, CIA will respond according to the guidance in subparagraph B below. In performing these functions CIA will be discharging its responsibilities for primary foreign counterintelligence collection abroad, particularly as assigned under paragraphs 1B and 3B of NSCID 5.
>
> B. CIA may respond to written requests by the FBI for clandestine collection abroad by CIA of information on foreign terrorist or counterintelligence matters involving private American citizens. Such collection activity may involve both liaison services and unilateral operations. In the case of liaison services, whenever feasible it should be plainly demonstrated in the transmission of the request to such liaison services that CIA is acting as a channel of communication between the FBI and the appropriate foreign service. Any unilateral operational activity will require specific prior approval of the DDO and the DCI will be advised thereof. Pertinent information obtained will be provided by CIA to the FBI.

A new restricted channel cryptonym was provided for the controlled reporting and handling of information relating to Americans which was furnished pursuant to these guidelines.

At the same time, domestic offices of the CIA were sent a copy of the cable to stations with the additional guidance that the cable was specifically restricted to information obtained abroad:

> If as a byproduct of ongoing activities, incidental information is received on U.S. citizens and it is determined that such information is inimical to U.S. interests or the Base feels that the incidental information should be reported to Headquarters, they should do so via appropriate staff channels with [a priority] indicator. Headquarters will make the final determination as to disposition of any information which is received.

{ . . . }

PART IV. OFFICE OF SECURITY PROGRAMS

The concerns about domestic unrest, which led to the CHAOS program, also caused the CIA to undertake other programs through the Office of Security, the support unit of the CIA charged with protecting its personnel, facilities and operations. The Office of Security has responsibility for both physical security measures and questions of personnel security.

The Office conducts routine background investigations of prospective personnel. It has also developed files on individuals and organizations in the course of investigating individual security cases of alleged penetration or attempted penetration of CIA employees.

In 1967, the Office began two efforts which were not focused on particular security cases. Rather, they were designed to collect information about groups which might pose a threat to the Agency's physical security through violent demonstrations or other disruptive activities.

By the mid-1960s, student unrest had led to increased harassment of government recruiters, including those of CIA, at campuses throughout the country. In the fall of 1968, the CIA recruiting office at the University of Michigan was destroyed by a bomb.

A. Project RESISTANCE

Project RESISTANCE developed out of a narrower program designed to provide direct support to CIA recruiters visiting college campuses. In February 1967, the Office of Security had directed its field offices to report on the possibilities of violence or harassment at those schools which CIA recruiters planned to visit. Subsequently, pursuant to this directive, the field offices provided information on expected opposition to government recruiting, or to CIA in particular, and made appropriate security arrangements with campus officials if the recruitment effort took place.

The broader RESISTANCE program was initiated by the Deputy Director of the CIA for support, whose directorate included the Office of Security and who previously had been a Director of Security, himself. In December 1967, he requested the Office of Security to study campus dissidence on a systematic basis. The Deputy Director suggested that there was an increased pattern of similar activity among student protest movements and directed the Office to examine their aims, causes, attitudes and the extent of their support among the nation's students. The collection requirement sent to the field officers in a telegram from headquarters asked for local news clippings about campus demonstrations related both to local grievances or to national issues such as the Vietnam War.

Because of the volume of material reported by the field offices, a special unit, the Targets Analysis Branch, was established in May 1968, to process and digest the information.

The testimony and the files indicate no use of infiltrations by CIA in connection with this program. The overwhelming bulk of the information continued to be press clippings passed on to headquarters. However, the field offices also obtained information from confidential sources in the local community such as campus officials and police authorities.

For example, one field office indicated that it had already obtained information from the local law enforcement authorities and advised of additional opportunities to obtain from other police departments reports of their informants with local dissident groups. Headquarters advised the office to utilize such sources when the information was offered to CIA.

On some occasions, the field offices were specifically requested to obtain information about particular activities or individuals, through information obtained directly by CIA personnel and material developed through confidential sources.

The analyses provided by the RESISTANCE project were criticized at one point by the Office of Security analyst who had initiated the program for primarily focusing on publicly available information:

> The RESISTANCE output should not attempt to duplicate or compete with the media on such reporting. Rather it should draw on such open sources for material needed to link together the data acquired from other sources.

By the end of 1970, the Director of the Office of Security felt that some of the field offices might be going too far in developing information from cooperating confidential sources. At the beginning of 1971, limiting instructions to the field offices directed restraint in the development of information:

> No attempts should be made to recruit new informants or sources such as campus or police officials for the express purpose of obtaining information regarding dissident groups, individuals, or activities.

> No new requirements for information should be levied on existing sources.
>
> The above limitations do not preclude acceptance of information gratuitously offered by informants or sources and field personnel should continue to be on the alert for non-solicited information which might contribute to the protection of the Agency personnel, projects or installations.

The Targets Analysis Branch also received FBI reports.

Although the initial impetus for RESISTANCE was an effort to evaluate campus activities, the Targets Analysis Branch broadened its inquiry to include analyses of protest activities in Washington and other centers of protest.

The incoming material was digested and indexed. Eventually the project developed an estimated 600–700 files and indexed an estimated 12,000 to 16,000 names. Apart from specific spot reports and evaluations of particular groups requested by other components of the Office of Security, the main product of the operation was weekly Situation Reports, summarizing and analyzing past events and projecting a calendar of upcoming events which might involve violence or disruption directed at government facilities.

The knowledge of organizations was also made available to the Personnel Office for purposes of evaluating membership in such groups by prospective employees.

The project was terminated at the end of June 1973.

B. Project MERRIMAC

The second general effort by the Office of Security to protect the CIA from threats posed by domestic disorder was Project MERRIMAC. MERRIMAC involved the participation of CIA assets in dissident groups in the Washington metropolitan area in order to obtain advance warning of demonstrations which posed a threat to CIA facilities and also to collect other intelligence about the groups and their members.

There is no record of MERRIMAC having been authorized at the outset by Director Helms. The Director of the Office of Security, Howard Osborn, testified that Helms had indicated his concern about the security of the CIA facilities in the face of dissident activities in the period prior to the formal commencement of MERRIMAC in early 1967. And Helms believes that he approved the project at some point.

In February 1967, Osborn inquired whether a proprietary company used by the Office of Security could monitor the activity of certain groups in Washington in order to provide advance information about demonstrations directed against CIA properties.

Shortly thereafter, the proprietary was directed to obtain such information. At the beginning of April, it was specifically asked to have its assets collect intelligence on the April antiwar demonstrations in Washington, D.C.

The Office of Security initially chose four "indicator organizations"—the Women's Strike for Peace, the Washington Peace Center, the Congress of Racial Equality, and the Student Nonviolent Coordinating Committee—deemed to be bellwethers of the likely nature of protest activity and the potential threat it might pose to the CIA.

The proprietary used only a few assets at first, including one regular employee and several others hired on a part-time basis. None of the assets were sophisticated agents, although they eventually received some training. They were construction workers or persons in similar trades and their relatives. Most of their work continued on a part-time basis, in addition to their regular employment, throughout the duration of MERRIMAC.

Initially, the assets were asked to monitor the organizations in order to report information only about planned demonstrations which might threaten the Agency. In June, however, the collection requirement was expanded to include information about the organizations' financial operations and sources of support.

In the fall of 1967, in anticipation of the peace demonstrations in Washington, MERRIMAC sought to obtain information about the leadership and plans of organizations participating in the National Mobilization Committee to End the War, as well as information about all the participant organizations.

The scope of the information requested continued to increase. The assets were asked to report any information about the plans and attitudes of groups revealed at meetings, their associations with other groups, sources of support, and an account of what was said at the meetings, in addition to information specifically relating to threatened action against the CIA. In addition, other organizations were added to the list of covered groups. By August 1968, ten groups were targeted by MERRIMAC for such coverage.

Thus, although the primary purpose remained advance warning of threats to the Agency, the program expanded into a general collection effort whose results were made available to other components in the CIA, and in many instances, to the FBI. As Osborn put it:

> Now I would be less than candid and less than honest with you to say that over the course of this project we reported pretty much of everything we got [sic]. I am not going to try to kid you. But the primary purpose of the project was self-protection physical security and I think we probably exceeded that.

In some instances the agents conducted surveillance of particular dissident leaders and activists of special interest to the CIA. Photographs were taken of persons attending meetings, or license plates, and persons were trailed home in order to identify them. Some of the assets also made contributions to the organizations at a low level necessary for credible participation.

Information obtained from MERRIMAC agents was made available to CHAOS. Osborn testified that the broadening scope of MERRIMAC was due in part to the requests from the CHAOS office to the Office of Security for general information about dissident groups.

> I think it started out legitimately concerned with the physical security of installations and I think it expanded, as these things often do, in light of the intense interest in the requirements by Mr. Ober and by a lot of other people. I think it just kind of grew in areas that it perhaps shouldn't have.

Osborn testified that most of the requests for specific information beyond the threat of immediate situations came from inquiries by the CHAOS office.

The last reports from MERRIMAC agents found in CIA files were gathered in late 1968. However, CIA has confirmed that the program lasted until September 1970.

In August 1973, Director Colby issued a directive as part of the Agency's review of "questionable activities" regarding the activity which had involved MERRIMAC. The Directive stated:

It is appropriate for the Office of Security to develop private sources among CIA employees. It is not appropriate for CIA to penetrate domestic groups external to CIA, even for the purpose of locating threats to the Agency. Notice of such threat should be reported to the appropriate law enforcement bodies and CIA will cooperate with them in any action required which does not involve direct CIA participation in covert clandestine operations against U.S. citizens in the United States.

{ . . . }

PART II

FOREIGN AND MILITARY INTELLIGENCE

EDITORS' NOTE: *The four chapters in this section are derived from Books I and III of the original Church Committee Report, as well as the committee's "Interim Report on Assassination Plots." Together they demonstrate how U.S. foreign intelligence agencies—the CIA and NSA, in particular—carried out field operations, developed surveillance projects, and engaged in covert action campaigns that violated fundamental principles of human rights.*

7.

Introduction

I. PREFACE

The Senate Select Committee on Intelligence Activities has conducted a fifteen-month-long inquiry, the first major inquiry into intelligence since World War II. The inquiry arose out of allegations of substantial, even massive wrongdoing within the "national intelligence" system. This final report provides a history of the evolution of intelligence, an evaluation of the intelligence system of the United States, a critique of its problems, recommendations for legislative action and recommendations to the executive branch. The Committee believes that its recommendations will provide a sound framework for conducting the vital intelligence activities of the United States in a manner which meets the nation's intelligence requirements and protects the liberties of American citizens and the freedoms which our Constitution guarantees.

The shortcomings of the intelligence system, the adverse effects of secrecy, and the failure of congressional oversight to assure adequate accountability for executive branch decisions concerning intelligence activities were major subjects of the Committee's inquiry. Equally important to the obligation to investigate allegations of abuse was the duty to review systematically the intelligence community's overall activities since 1945, and to evaluate its present structure and performance.

An extensive national intelligence system has been a vital part of the United States government since 1941. Intelligence information has had an important influence on the direction and development of American foreign policy and has been essential to the maintenance of our national security. The Committee is convinced that the United States requires an intelligence system which will provide policymakers with accurate intelligence and analysis. We must have an early warning system to monitor potential military threats by countries hostile to United States interests. We need a strong intelligence system to verify that treaties concerning arms limitation are being honored. Information derived from the intelligence agencies is a necessary ingredient in making national defense and foreign policy decisions. Such information is also necessary in countering the efforts of hostile intelligence services, and in halting terrorists, international drug traffickers and other international criminal activities. Within this country certain carefully controlled intelligence activities are essential for effective law enforcement.

The United States has devoted enormous resources to the creation of a national intelligence system, and today there is an awareness on the part of many citizens that a national intelligence system is a permanent and necessary component of our government. The system's value to the country has been proven and it will be needed for the foreseeable future. But a major conclusion of this inquiry is that congressional oversight is necessary to assure that in the future our intelligence community functions effectively, within the framework of the Constitution.

The Committee is of the view that many of the unlawful actions taken by officials of the intelligence agencies were rationalized as their public duty. It was necessary for the Committee to understand how the pursuit of the public good could have the opposite effect. As Justice Brandeis observed:

> Experience should teach us to be most on our guard to protect liberty when the Government's purposes are beneficent. Men born to freedom are naturally alert to repel invasion of their liberty by evil-minded rulers. The greatest dangers to liberty lurk in insidious encroachment by men of zeal, well-meaning but without understanding.

A. The Mandate of the Committee's Inquiry

On January 27, 1975, Senate Resolution 21 established a select committee "to conduct an investigation and study of governmental operations with respect to intelligence activities and of the extent, if any, to which illegal, improper, or unethical activities were engaged in by any agency of the

Federal Government." Senate Resolution 21 lists specific areas of inquiry and study:

(1) Whether the Central Intelligence Agency has conducted an illegal domestic intelligence operation in the United States.

(2) The conduct of domestic intelligence or counterintelligence operations against United States citizens by the Federal Bureau of Investigation or any other Federal agency.

(3) The origin and disposition of the so-called Huston Plan to apply United States intelligence agency capabilities against individuals or organizations within the United States.

(4) The extent to which the Federal Bureau of Investigation, the Central Intelligence Agency, and other Federal law enforcement or intelligence agencies coordinate their respective activities, any agreements which govern that coordination, and the extent to which a lack of coordination has contributed to activities or actions which are illegal, improper, inefficient, unethical, or contrary to the intent of Congress.

(5) The extent to which the operation of domestic intelligence or counterintelligence activities and the operation of any other activities within the United States by the Central Intelligence Agency conforms to the legislative charter of that Agency and the intent of the Congress.

(6) The past and present interpretation by the Director of Central Intelligence of the responsibility to protect intelligence sources and methods as it relates to that provision of the National Security Act of 1947 which provides "that the agency shall have no police, subpoena, law enforcement powers, or internal security functions."

(7) The nature and extent of executive branch oversight of all United States intelligence activities.

(8) The need for specific legislative authority to govern the operations of any intelligence agencies of the Federal Government now existing without that explicit statutory authority, including but not limited to agencies such as the Defense Intelligence Agency and the National Security Agency.

(9) The nature and extent to which Federal agencies cooperate and exchange intelligence information and the adequacy of any regulations or statutes which govern such cooperation and exchange of intelligence information.

(10) The extent to which United States intelligence agencies are governed by Executive Orders, rules, or regulations either published or secret and the extent to which those Executive Orders, rules, or regulations interpret, expand, or are in conflict with specific legislative authority.

(11) The violation or suspected violation of any State or Federal statute by any intelligence agency or by any person by or on behalf of any intelligence agency of the Federal Government including but not limited to surreptitious entries, surveillance, wiretaps, or eavesdropping, illegal opening of the United States mail, or the monitoring of the United States mail.

(12) The need for improved, strengthened, or consolidated oversight of United States intelligence activities by the Congress.

(13) Whether any of the existing laws of the United States are inadequate, either in their provisions or manner of enforcement, to safeguard the rights of American citizens, to improve executive and legislative control of intelligence and related activities, and to resolve uncertainties as to the authority of United States intelligence and related agencies.

(14) Whether there is unnecessary duplication of expenditure and effort in the collection and processing of intelligence information by United States agencies.

(15) The extent and necessity of overt and covert intelligence activities in the United States and abroad.

In addressing these mandated areas of inquiry, the Committee has focused on three broad questions:

1. Whether intelligence activities have functioned in accordance with the Constitution and the laws of the United States.
2. Whether the structure, programs, past history, and present policies of the American intelligence system have served the national interests in a manner consistent with declared national policies and purposes.
3. Whether the processes through which the intelligence agencies have been directed and controlled have been adequate to assure conformity with policy and the law.

Over the past year, the Committee and its staff have carefully examined the intelligence structure of the United States. Considerable time and effort have been devoted in order to understand what has been done by the United States Government in secrecy during the thirty-year period since the end of World War II. It is clear to the Committee that there are many necessary and proper governmental activities that must be conducted in secrecy. Some of these activities affect the security and the very existence of the nation.

It is also clear from the Committee's inquiry that intelligence activities conducted outside the framework of the Constitution and statutes can undermine the treasured values guaranteed in the Bill of Rights. Further, if the intelligence agencies act in ways inimical to declared national purposes, they damage the reputation; power, and influence of the United States abroad.

The Committee's investigation has documented that a number of actions committed in the name of "national security" were inconsistent with declared policy and the law. Hearings have been held and the Committee has issued reports on alleged assassination plots, covert action in Chile and the interception of domestic communications by the National Security Agency (NSA). Regrettably, some of these abuses cannot be regarded as aberrations.

B. The Purpose of the Committee's Findings and Recommendations

It is clear that a primary task for any successor oversight committee, and the Congress as a whole, will be to frame basic statutes necessary under the Constitution within which the intelligence agencies of the United States can function efficiently under clear guidelines. Charters delineating the missions, authorities, and limitations for some of the United States' most important intelligence agencies do not exist. For example, there is no statutory authority for the NSA's intelligence activities. Where statutes do exist, as with the CIA, they are vague and have failed to provide the necessary guidelines defining missions and limitations.

The Committee's investigation has demonstrated, moreover, that the lack of legislation has had the effect of limiting public debate upon some important national issues. The CIA's broad statutory charter, the 1947 National Security Act, makes no specific mention of covert action. The CIA's former

General Counsel, Lawrence Houston, who was deeply involved in drafting the 1947 Act, wrote in September 1947, "we do not believe that there was any thought in the minds of Congress that the CIA under [the authority of the National Security Act] would take positive action for subversion and sabotage." Yet, a few months after enactment of the 1947 legislation, the National Security Council authorized the CIA to engage in covert action programs; The provision of the Act often cited as authorizing CIA covert activities provides for the Agency:

> . . . to perform such other functions and duties related to intelligence affecting the national security as the National Security Council may from time to time direct.

Secret Executive Orders issued by the NSC to carry out covert action programs were not subject to congressional review. Indeed, until recent years, except for a few members, Congress was not fully aware of the existence of the so-called "secret charter for intelligence activities." Those members who did know had no institutional means for discussing their knowledge of secret intelligence activities with their colleagues. The problem of how the Congress can effectively use secret knowledge in its legislative processes remains to be resolved. It is the Committee's view that a strong and effective oversight committee is an essential first step that must be taken to resolve this fundamental issue.

C. The Focus and Scope of the Committee's Inquiry and Obstacles Encountered

The inquiry mandated in S. Res. 21 falls into two main categories. The first concerns allegations of wrong-doing. The nature of the Committee's inquiry into these matters tends, quite properly, to be akin to the investigations conducted by Senate and Congressional committees in the past. We decided from the outset, however, that this committee is neither a court, nor a law enforcement agency, and that while using many traditional congressional investigative techniques, our inquiry has served primarily to illustrate the problems before Congress and the country. The Justice Department and the courts in turn have their proper roles to play.

The second category of inquiry has been an examination of the intelligence agencies themselves. The Committee wished to learn enough about their past and present activities to make the legislative judgments required to assure the American people that whatever necessary secret intelligence activities were being undertaken were subject to constitutional processes and were being conducted in as effective, humane, and efficient a manner as possible.

The Committee focused on many issues affecting the intelligence agencies which had not been seriously addressed since our peacetime intelligence system was created in 1947. The most important questions relating to intelligence, such as its value to national security purposes and its cost and quality, have been carefully examined over the past year. Although some of the Committee's findings can be reported to the public only in outline, enough can be set forth to justify the recommendations. The Committee has necessarily been selective. A year was not enough time to investigate everything relevant to intelligence activities.

These considerations guided the Committee's choices:

1. A limited number of programs and incidents were examined in depth rather than reviewing hundreds superficially. The Committee's purpose was to understand the causes for the particular performance or behavior of an agency.
2. The specific cases examined were chosen because they reflected generic problems.
3. Where broad programs were closely reviewed (for example, the CIA's covert action programs), the Committee sought to examine successes as well as apparent failures.
4. Programs were examined from Franklin Roosevelt's administration to the present. This was done in order to present the historical context within which intelligence activities have developed and to assure that sensitive, fundamental issues would not be subject to possible partisan biases.

It is clear from the Committee's inquiry that problems arising from the use of the national intelligence system at home and abroad are to be found in every administration. Accordingly, the Committee chose to emphasize particular parts of the national intelligence system and to address particular cases in depth. The Committee has concentrated its energies on the six executive branch groups that make up what is called "National Intelligence."

1. The Central Intelligence Agency.
2. The counterintelligence activities of the Federal Bureau of Investigation.
3. The National Security Agency.
4. The national intelligence components of the Department of Defense other than NSA.
5. The National Security Council.
6. The intelligence activities of the Department of State.

The investigation of these national intelligence groupings included examining the degree of command and control exercised over them by the President and other key Government officials or institutions. The Committee also sought to evaluate the ability and effectiveness of Congress to assert its oversight right and responsibilities. The agencies the Committee has concentrated on have great powers and extensive activities which must be understood in order to judge fairly whether the United States intelligence system needs reform and change. The Committee believes that many of its general recommendations can and should be applied to the intelligence operations of all other government agencies.

Based on its investigation, the Committee concludes that solutions to the main problems can be developed by analyzing the broad patterns emerging from the examination of particular cases. At the same time, neither the dangers, nor the causes of abuses within the intelligence system, nor their possible solutions can be fairly understood without evaluating the historical context in which intelligence operations have been conducted.

Individual cases and programs of government surveillance which the Committee examined raise questions concerning the inherent conflict between the government's perceived need to conduct surveillance and the citizens' constitutionally protected rights of privacy and dissent. It has become clear that if some lose their liberties unjustly, all may lose their liberties. The protections and obligations of law must apply to all. Only by looking at the broad scope of questionable activity over a long period can we realistically assess the potential dangers of intrusive government. For example, only through an understanding of the totality of government efforts against dissenters over the past thirty years can one weigh the extent to which such an emphasis may "chill" legitimate free expression and assembly.

The Select Committee has conducted the only thorough investigation ever made of United States intelligence and its post–World War II emergence as a complex, sophisticated system of multiple agencies and extensive activities. The Committee staff of 100, including 60 professionals, has assisted the 11 members of the Committee in this in-depth inquiry which involved more than 800 interviews, over 250 executive hearings, and documentation in excess of 110,000 pages.

The advice of former and current intelligence officials, Cabinet members, State, Defense, and Justice Department experts, and citizens from the private sector who have served in national security areas has been sought throughout the Committee's inquiry. The Committee has made a conscious effort to seek the views of all principal officials who have served in the intelligence agencies since the end of World War II. We also solicited the opinions of constitutional experts and the wisdom of scientists knowledgeable about the technology used by intelligence agencies. It was essential to learn the views of these sources outside of the government to obtain as full and balanced an understanding of intelligence activities as possible.

The fact that government intelligence agencies resist any examination of their secret activities even by another part of the same government should not be minimized. The intelligence agencies are a sector of American government set apart. Employees' loyalties to their organizations have been conditioned by the closed, compartmented and secretive circumstances of their agencies' formation and operation. In some respects, the intelligence profession resembles monastic life with some of the disciplines and personal sacrifices reminiscent of medieval orders. Intelligence work is a life of service, but one in which the norms of American national life are sometimes distressingly distorted. Despite its legal Senate mandate, and the issuance of subpoenas, in no instance has the Committee been able to examine the agencies' files on its own. In all the agencies, whether CIA, FBI, NSA, INR, DIA, or the NSC, documents and evidence have been presented through the filter of the agency itself.

Although the Senate inquiry was congressionally ordered and although properly constituted committees under the Constitution have the right of full inquiry, the Central Intelligence Agency and other agencies of the executive branch have limited the Committee's access to the full record. Several reasons have been given for this limitation. In some instances, the so-called doctrine of executive privilege has been asserted. Despite these assertions of executive privilege, there are no classes of documents which the Committee has not obtained, whether from the NSC, the personal papers of former Presidents and their advisors, or, as in the case of the Committee's *Report on Alleged Assassination Plots Involving Foreign Leaders*, all classes of documents available in the executive branch. The exception, of course, involves the Nixon files which were not made available because of court order.

It should be noted that in some highly important areas of its investigation, the Committee has been refused access to files or documents. These involve, among others, the arrangements and agreements made between the intelligence agencies and their informers and sources, including other intelligence agencies and governments. The Committee has agreed that in general, the names of agents, and their methods of conducting certain intelligence activities should remain in the custody of a few within the executive branch. But there is a danger and an uncertainty which arises from accepting at face value the assertions of the agencies and departments which in the past have abused or exceeded their authority. If the occasion demands, a duly authorized congressional committee must have the right to go behind agency assertions, and review the full evidence on which agency responses to committee inquiries have been based. There must be a check: some means to ascertain whether the secrets being kept are, in fact, valid national secrets. The Committee believes that the burden of proof should be on those who ask that a secret program or policy be kept secret.

The Committee's report consists of a number of case studies which have been pursued to the best of the Committee's ability and which the Committee believes illuminate the purposes, character, and usefulness of the shielded world of intelligence activities. The inquiry conducted over the past 15 months will probably provide the only broad insight for some time into the now permanent role of the intelligence community in our national government. Because of this, and because of the need to assure that necessary secret activities remain under constitutional control, the recommendations set forth by the Committee are submitted with a sense of urgency and with the admonition that to ignore the dangers posed by secret government action is to invite the further weakening of our democracy.

{ . . . }

FINDINGS AND RECOMMENDATIONS

A. Introduction

{ . . . }

The Committee's investigation and the body of its report seek, within the limits of prudence, to perform the crucial task of informing the American people concerning the nature and scope of their Government's foreign intelligence activities. The fundamental issue faced by the Committee in its investigation was how the requirements of American democracy can be properly balanced in intelligence matters against the need for secrecy. Secrecy is essential for the success of many important intelligence activities. At the same time, secrecy contributed to many of the abuses, excesses and inefficiencies uncovered by the Committee. Secrecy also makes it difficult to establish a public consensus for the future conduct of certain intelligence operations.

Because of secrecy, the Committee initially had difficulty gaining access to executive branch information required to carry out the investigation. It was not until the Committee became responsible for investigating allegations of assassination plots that many of the obstacles were cleared away. The resulting access by the Committee was in some cases unprecedented. But the Committee's access to documents and records was hampered nonetheless in a number of other instances either because the materials did not exist or because the executive branch was unwilling to make them available.

Secrecy was also a major issue in preparing this report. In order to safeguard what are now agreed to be necessary intelligence activities, the Committee decided not to reveal publicly the full and complete picture of the intelligence operations of the United States Government. The recommendations as a whole have not been materially affected by the requirements of secrecy, but some important findings of the Committee must remain classified in accordance with the Committee's policy of protecting valid secrets. In this connection it should be noted that some information which in the Committee's opinion the American public should know remains classified and has been excluded from the report at the request of the intelligence community agencies. Only the Senate will receive the full version of the Committee's Final Report in accordance with the standing rules of the Senate.

In trying to reconcile the requirements of secrecy and open democratic processes, the Committee found itself with a difficult dilemma. As an investigating committee, it cannot take affirmative legislative action respecting some of the matters that came to its attention. On the other hand, because of necessary secrecy, the Committee cannot publicly present the full case as to why its recommendations are essential.

This experience underscores the need for an effective legislative oversight committee which has sufficient power to resolve such fundamental conflicts between secrecy and democracy. As stated previously, it is the Committee's view that effective congressional oversight requires the power to authorize the budgets of the national intelligence agencies. Without such authority, an oversight committee may find itself in possession of important secret information but unable to act effectively to protect the principles, integrity, and reputation of the United States.

The findings and recommendations which follow are organized principally by agency. There are, however, common themes in the recommendations which cut across agency lines. Some of these themes are: guarding against abuse of America's institutions and reputation; ensuring clear accountability for clandestine activities; establishing effective management of intelligence activities; and creating a framework of statutory law and congressional oversight for the agencies and activities of the United States intelligence community.

{. . .}

B. General Findings

The Committee finds that United States foreign and military intelligence agencies have made important contributions to the nation's security and generally have performed their missions with dedication and distinction. The Committee further finds that the individual men and women serving America in difficult and dangerous intelligence assignments deserve the respect and gratitude of the nation.

The Committee finds that there is a continuing need for an effective system of foreign and military intelligence. United States interests and responsibilities in the world will be challenged, for the foreseeable future, by strong and potentially hostile powers. This requires the maintenance of an effective American intelligence system. The Committee has found that the Soviet KGB and other hostile intelligence services maintain extensive foreign intelligence operations for both intelligence collection and covert operational purposes. These activities pose a threat to the intelligence activities and interests of the United States and its allies.

The Committee finds that Congress has failed to provide the necessary statutory guidelines to ensure that intelligence agencies carry out their missions in accord with constitutional processes. Mechanisms for, and the practice of, congressional oversight have not been adequate. Further, Congress has not devised appropriate means to effectively use the valuable information developed by the intelligence agencies. Intelligence information and analysis that exist within the executive branch clearly would contribute to sound judgments and more effective legislation in the areas of foreign policy and national security.

The Committee finds that covert action operations have not been an exceptional instrument used only in rare instances when the vital interests of the United States have been at stake. On the contrary, presidents and administrations have made excessive, and at times self-defeating, use of covert action. In addition, covert action has become a routine program with a bureaucratic momentum of its own. The long-term impact, at home and abroad, of repeated disclosure of U.S. covert action never appears to have been assessed. The cumulative effect of covert actions has been increasingly costly to America's interests and reputation. The Committee believes that covert action must be employed only in the most extraordinary circumstances.

Although there is a question concerning the extent to which the Constitution requires publication of intelligence expenditures information, the Committee finds that the Constitution at least requires public disclosure and public authorization of an annual aggregate figure for United States national intelligence activities. Congress' failure as a whole to monitor the intelligence agencies' expenditures has been a major element in the ineffective legislative oversight of the intelligence community. The permanent intelligence oversight committee(s) of Congress should give further consideration to the question of the extent to which further public disclosure of intelligence budget information is prudent and constitutionally necessary.

At the same time, the Committee finds that the operation of an extensive and necessarily secret intelligence system places severe strains on the nation's constitutional government. The Committee is convinced, however, that the competing demands of secrecy and the requirements of the democratic process—our Constitution and our laws—can be reconciled. The need to protect secrets must be balanced with the assurance that secrecy is not used as a means to hide the abuse of power or the failures and mistakes of policy. Means must and can be provided for lawful disclosure of unneeded or unlawful secrets.

The Committee finds that intelligence activities should not be regarded as ends in themselves. Rather, the nation's intelligence functions should be organized and directed to assure that they serve the needs of those in the executive and legislative branches who have responsibility for formulating or carrying out foreign and national security policy.

The Committee finds that Congress has failed to provide the necessary statutory guidelines to ensure that intelligence agencies carry out their necessary missions in accord with constitutional processes.

In order to provide firm direction for the intelligence agencies, the Committee finds that new statutory charters for these agencies must be written that take account of the experience of the past three and a half decades. Further, the Committee finds that the relationship among the various intelligence agencies and between them and the Director of Central Intelligence should be restructured in order to achieve better accountability, coordination, and more efficient use of resources.

These tasks are urgent. They should be undertaken by the Congress in consultation with the executive branch in the coming year. The recent proposals and executive actions by the President are most welcome. However, further action by Congress is necessary.

8.

Alleged Assassination Plots Involving Foreign Leaders

PROLOGUE

The events discussed in this Interim Report must be viewed in the context of United States policy and actions designed to counter the threat of spreading Communism. Following the end of World War II, many nations in Eastern Europe and elsewhere fell under Communist influence or control. The defeat of the Axis powers was accompanied by rapid disintegration of the Western colonial empires. The Second World War had no sooner ended than a new struggle began. The Communist threat, emanating from what came to be called the "Sino-Soviet bloc," led to a policy of containment intended to prevent further encroachment into the "Free World."

United States strategy for conducting the Cold War called for the establishment of interlocking treaty arrangements and military bases throughout the world. Concern over the expansion of an aggressive Communist monolith led the United States to fight two major wars in Asia. In addition, it was considered necessary to wage a relentless cold war against Communist expansion wherever it appeared in the "back alleys of the world." This called for a full range of covert activities in response to the operations of Communist clandestine services.

The fear of Communist expansion was particularly acute in the United States when Fidel Castro emerged as Cuba's leader in the late 1950s. His takeover was seen as the first significant penetration by the Communists into the Western Hemisphere. United States leaders, including most Members of Congress, called for vigorous action to stem the Communist infection in this hemisphere. These policies rested on widespread popular support and encouragement.

Throughout this period, the United States felt impelled to respond to threats which were, or seemed to be, skirmishes in a global Cold War against Communism. Castro's Cuba raised the spectre of a Soviet outpost at America's doorstep. Events in the Dominican Republic appeared to offer an additional opportunity for the Russians and their allies. The Congo, freed from Belgian rule, occupied the strategic center of the African continent, and the prospect of Communist penetration there was viewed as a threat to American interests in emerging African nations. There was great concern that a Communist takeover in Indochina would have a "domino effect" throughout Asia. Even the election in 1970 of a Marxist president in Chile was seen by some as a threat similar to that of Castro's takeover in Cuba.

The Committee regards the unfortunate events dealt with in this Interim Report as an aberration, explainable at least in part, but not justified, by the pressures of the time. The Committee believes that it is still in the national interest of the United States to help nations achieve self-determination and resist Communist domination. However, it is clear that this interest cannot justify resorting to the kind of abuses covered in this report. Indeed, the Committee has resolved that steps must be taken to prevent those abuses from happening again.

I. INTRODUCTION AND SUMMARY

This interim report covers allegations of United States involvement in assassination plots against foreign political leaders. The report also examines certain other instances in which foreign political leaders in fact were killed and the United States was in some manner involved in activity leading up to the killing, but in which it would be incorrect to say that the purpose of United States involvement had been to encourage assassination.

The evidence establishes that the United States was implicated in several assassination plots. The Committee believes that, short of war, assassination is incompatible with American principles, international order, and morality. It should be rejected as a tool of foreign policy.

Our inquiry also reveals serious problems with respect to United States involvement in coups directed against foreign governments. Some of these problems are addressed here on the basis of our investigation to date; others we raise as questions to be answered after our investigation into covert action has been completed.

We stress the interim nature of this report. In the course of the Committee's continuing work, other alleged assassination plots may surface, and new evidence concerning the cases covered herein may come to light. However, it is the Committee's view that these cases have been developed in sufficient detail to clarify the issues which are at the heart of the Committee's mandate to recommend legislative and other reforms.

{ . . . }

A. Committee's Mandate

Senate Resolution 21 instructs the Committee to investigate the full range of governmental intelligence activities and the extent, if any, to which such activities were "illegal, improper or unethical." In addition to that broad general mandate, the Committee is required to investigate, study and make recommendations concerning various specific matters, several of which relate to the assassination issue.

Although the Rockefeller Commission initiated an inquiry into reported assassination plots, the Commission declared it was unable, for a variety of reasons, to complete its inquiry. At the direction of the President, the Executive Branch turned over to the Select Committee the work the Commission had done, along with certain other documents relating to assassination.

B. Committee Decision to Make Report Public

This report raises important questions of national policy. We believe that the public is entitled to know what instrumentalities of their Government have done. Further, our recommendations can only be judged in light of the factual record. Therefore, this interim report should be made public.

The Committee believes the truth about the assassination allegations should be told because democracy depends upon a well-informed electorate. We reject any contention that the facts disclosed in this report should be kept secret because they are embarrassing to the United States. Despite the temporary injury to our national reputation, the Committee believes that foreign peoples will, upon sober reflection, respect the United States more for keeping faith with its democratic ideal than they will condemn us for the misconduct revealed. We doubt that any other country would have the courage to make such disclosures.

The fact that portions of the story have already been made public only accentuates the need for full disclosure. Innuendo and misleading partial disclosures are not fair to the individuals involved. Nor are they a responsible way to lay the groundwork for informed public policy judgments.

C. Scope of Committee's Investigation

Investigating the assassination issue has been an unpleasant duty, but one that the Committee had to meet. The Committee has compiled a massive record in the months that the inquiry has been underway. The record comprises over 8,000 pages of sworn testimony taken from over 75 witnesses during 60 hearing days and numerous staff interviews. The documents which the Committee has obtained include raw files from agencies and departments, the White House, and the Presidential libraries of the Administrations of former Presidents Dwight Eisenhower, John Kennedy and Lyndon Johnson.

We have obtained two types of evidence: *first,* evidence relating to the general setting in which the events occurred, the national policy of the time, and the normal operating procedures, including channels of command and control; and *second,* evidence relating to the specific events.

A Senate Committee is not a court. It looks to the past, not to determine guilt or innocence, but in order to make recommendations for the future. When we found the evidence to be ambiguous—as we did on some issues—we have set out both sides, in order that the evidence may speak for itself.

Despite the number of witnesses and documents examined by the Committee, the available evidence has certain shortcomings.

— Many of the events considered occurred as long as fifteen years ago. With one exception, they occurred during the administrations of Presidents now dead. Other high officials whose testimony might have shed additional light on the thorny issues of authorization and control are also dead. Moreover, with the passage of time, the memories of those still alive have dimmed.

—The Committee has often faced the difficult task of distinguishing refreshed recollection from speculation. In many instances, witnesses were unable to testify from independent recollection and had to rely on documents contemporaneous with the events to refresh their recollections. While informed speculation is of some assistance, it can only be assigned limited weight in judging specific events.

—Although assassination is not a subject on which one would expect many records or documents to be made or retained, there were, in fact, more relevant contemporaneous documents than expected. In addition, in 1967 the Central Intelligence Agency had made an internal study of the Castro, Trujillo and Diem assassination allegations. That study was quite useful, particularly in suggesting leads for uncovering the story of the actual assassination activity. Unfortunately, the working papers relating to that investigation were destroyed upon the completion of the Report, pursuant to instructions from CIA Director Richard Helms. These notes were destroyed because of their sensitivity and because the information they contained had already been incorporated into the Report. In fairness to Director Helms, it should be added, however, that he was responsible for requesting the preparation of the Inspector General's Report and for preserving the Report.

—Some ambiguities in the evidence result from the practice of concealing CIA covert operations from the world and performing them in such a way that if discovered, the role of the United States could be plausibly denied. An extension of the doctrine of "plausible deniability" had the result that communications between the Agency and high Administration officials were often convoluted and imprecise.

The evidence contains sharp conflicts, some of which relate to basic facts. But the most important conflicts relate not so much to basic facts as to differing perceptions and opinions based upon relatively undisputed facts. With respect to both kinds of conflicts, the Committee has attempted to set forth the evidence extensively so that it may speak for itself, and in our section on findings and conclusions, we suggest resolutions for some of the conflicts. However, because the Committee's main task is to find lessons for the future, resolving conflicts in the evidence may be less important than making certain that the system which produced the ambiguities is corrected.

D. Summary of Findings and Conclusions

1. The Questions Presented

The Committee sought to answer four broad questions:

Assassination plots.—Did United States officials instigate, attempt, aid and abet, or acquiesce in plots to assassinate foreign leaders?

Involvement in other killings.—Did United States officials assist foreign dissidents in a way which significantly contributed to the killing of foreign leaders?

Authorization.—Where there was involvement by United States officials in assassination plots or other killings, were such activities authorized and if so, at what levels of our Government?

Communication and control.—Even if not authorized in fact, were the assassination activities perceived by those involved to be within the scope of their lawful authority? If they were so perceived, was there inadequate control exercised by higher authorities over the agencies to prevent such misinterpretation?

2. Summary of Findings and Conclusions on the Plots

The Committee investigated alleged United States involvement in assassination plots in five foreign countries:

Country	*Individual involved*
Cuba	Fidel Castro
Congo (Zaire)	Patrice Lumumba
Dominican Republic	Rafael Trujillo
Chile	General Rene Schneider
South Vietnam	Ngo Dinh Diem

The evidence concerning each alleged assassination can be summarized as follows:

Patrice Lumumba (Congo/Zaire).—In the Fall of 1960, two CIA officials were asked by superiors to assassinate Lumumba. Poisons were sent to the Congo and some exploratory steps were taken toward gaining access to Lumumba. Subsequently, in early 1961, Lumumba was killed by Congolese rivals. It does not appear from the evidence that the United States was in any way involved in the killing.

Fidel Castro (Cuba).—United States Government personnel plotted to kill Castro from 1960 to 1965. American underworld figures and Cubans hostile to Castro were used in these plots, and were provided encouragement and material support by the United States.

Rafael Trujillo (Dominican Republic).—Trujillo was shot by Dominican dissidents on May 31, 1961. From early in 1960 and continuing to the time of the assassination, the United States Government generally supported these dissidents. Some Government personnel were aware that the dissidents intended to kill Trujillo. Three pistols and three carbines were furnished by American officials, although a request for machine guns was later refused. There is conflicting evidence concerning whether the weapons were knowingly supplied for use in the assassination and whether any of them were present at the scene.

Ngo Dinh Diem (South Vietnam).—Diem and his brother, Nhu, were killed on November 2, 1963, in the course of a South Vietnamese Generals' coup. Although the United States Government supported the coup, there is no evidence that American officials favored the assassination. Indeed, it appears that the assassination of Diem was not part of the Generals' pre-coup planning but was instead a spontaneous act which occurred during the coup and was carried out without United States involvement or support.

General Rene Schneider (Chile).—On October 25, 1970, General Schneider died of gunshot wounds inflicted three days earlier while resisting a kidnap attempt. Schneider, as Commander-in-Chief of the Army and a constitutionalist opposed to military coups, was considered an obstacle in efforts to prevent Salvador Allende from assuming the office of President of Chile. The United States Government supported, and sought to instigate a military coup to block Allende. U.S. officials supplied financial aid, machine guns and other equipment to various military figures who opposed Allende. Although the

CIA continued to support coup plotters up to Schneider's shooting, the record indicates that the CIA had withdrawn active support of the group which carried out the actual kidnap attempt on October 22, which resulted in Schneider's death. Further, it does not appear that any of the equipment supplied by the CIA to coup plotters in Chile was used in the kidnapping. There is no evidence of a plan to kill Schneider or that United States officials specifically anticipated that Schneider would be shot during the abduction.

Assassination capability (Executive action).—In addition to these five cases, the Committee has received evidence that ranking Government officials discussed, and may have authorized, the establishment within the CIA of a generalized assassination capability. During these discussions, the concept of assassination was not affirmatively disavowed.

Similarities and differences among the plots.—The assassination plots all involved Third World countries, most of which were relatively small and none of which possessed great political or military strength. Apart from that similarity, there were significant differences among the plots:

> (1) Whether United States officials initiated the plot, or were responding to requests of local dissidents for aid.
>
> (2) Whether the plot was specifically intended to kill a foreign leader, or whether the leader's death was a reasonably foreseeable consequence of an attempt to overthrow the government.

The Castro and Lumumba cases are examples of plots conceived by United States officials to kill foreign leaders.

In the Trujillo case, although the United States Government certainly opposed his regime, it did not initiate the plot. Rather, United States officials responded to requests for aid from local dissidents whose aim clearly was to assassinate Trujillo. By aiding them, this country was implicated in the assassination, regardless of whether the weapons actually supplied were meant to kill Trujillo or were only intended as symbols of support for the dissidents.

The Schneider case differs from the Castro and Trujillo cases. The United States Government, with full knowledge that Chilean dissidents considered General Schneider an obstacle to their plans, sought a coup and provided support to the dissidents. However, even though the support included weapons, it appears that the intention of both the dissidents and the United States officials was to abduct General Schneider, not to kill him. Similarly, in the Diem case, some United States officials wanted Diem removed and supported a coup to accomplish his removal, but there is no evidence that any of those officials sought the death of Diem himself.

3. Summary of Findings and Conclusions on the Issues of Authority and Control

To put the inquiry into assassination allegations in context, two points must be made clear. First, there is no doubt that the United States Government opposed the various leaders in question. Officials at the highest levels objected to the Castro and Trujillo regimes, believed the accession of Allende to power in Chile would be harmful to American interests, and thought of Lumumba as a dangerous force in the heart of Africa. Second, the evidence on assassinations has to be viewed in the context of other, more massive activities against the regimes in question. For example, the plots against Fidel Castro personally cannot be understood without considering the fully authorized, comprehensive assaults upon his regime, such as the Bay of Pigs invasion in 1961 and Operation MONGOOSE in 1962.

Once methods of coercion and violence are chosen, the probability of loss of life is always present. There is, however, a significant difference between a coldblooded, targeted, intentional killing of an individual foreign leader and other forms of intervening in the affairs of foreign nations. Therefore, the Committee has endeavored to explore as fully as possible the questions of how and why the plots happened, whether they were authorized, and if so, at what level.

The picture that emerges from the evidence is not a clear one. This may be due to the system of deniability and the consequent state of the evidence, which, even after our long investigation, remains conflicting and inconclusive. Or it may be that there were in fact serious shortcomings in the system of authorization so that an activity such as assassination could have been undertaken by an agency of the United States Government without express authority.

The Committee finds that the system of executive command and control was so ambiguous that it is difficult to be certain at what levels assassination activity was known and authorized. This situation creates the disturbing prospect that Government officials might have undertaken the assassination plots without it having been uncontrovertibly clear that there was explicit authorization from the Presidents. It is also possible that there might have been a successful "plausible denial" in which Presidential authorization was issued but is now obscured. Whether or not the respective Presidents knew of or authorized the plots, as chief executive officer of the United States, each must bear the ultimate responsibility for the activities of his subordinates.

The Committee makes four other major findings. The first relates to the Committee's inability to make a finding that the assassination plots were authorized by the Presidents or other persons above the governmental agency or agencies involved. The second explains why certain officials may have perceived that, according to their judgment and experience, assassination was an acceptable course of action. The third criticizes agency officials for failing on several occasions to disclose their plans and activities to superior authorities, or for failing to do so with sufficient detail and clarity. The fourth criticizes Administration officials for not ruling out assassination, particularly after certain Administration officials had become aware of prior assassination plans and the establishment of a general assassination capability.

There is admittedly a tension among the findings. This tension reflects a basic conflict in the evidence. While there are some conflicts over facts, it may be more important that there appeared to have been two differing perceptions of the same facts. This distinction may be the result of the differing backgrounds of those persons experienced in covert operations as distinguished from those who were not. Words of urgency which may have meant killing to the former, may have meant nothing of the sort to the latter.

While we are critical of certain individual actions, the Committee is also mindful of the inherent problems in a system which relies on secrecy, compartmentation, circumlocution, and the avoidance of clear responsibility. This system creates the risk of confusion and rashness in the very areas where clarity and sober judgment are most necessary. {. . .}

{. . .}

III. ASSASSINATION PLANNING AND THE PLOTS

A. Congo

1. Introduction

The Committee has received solid evidence of a plot to assassinate Patrice Lumumba. Strong hostility to Lumumba, voiced at the very highest levels of government, may have been intended to initiate an assassination operation; at the least it engendered such an operation. The evidence indicates that it is likely that President Eisenhower's expression of strong concern about Lumumba at a meeting of the National Security Council on August 18, 1960, was taken by Allen Dulles as authority to assassinate Lumumba. There is, however, testimony by Eisenhower Administration officials, and ambiguity and lack of clarity in the records of high-level policy meetings, which tends to contradict the evidence that the President intended an assassination effort against Lumumba.

The week after the August 18 NSC meeting, a presidential advisor reminded the Special Group of the "necessity for very straight-forward action" against Lumumba and prompted a decision not to rule out consideration of "any particular kind of activity which might contribute to getting rid of Lumumba." The following day, Dulles cabled a CIA Station Officer in Leopoldville, Republic of the Congo, that "in high quarters" the "removal" of Lumumba was "an urgent and prime objective." Shortly thereafter the CIA's clandestine service formulated a plot to assassinate Lumumba. The plot proceeded to the point that lethal substances and instruments specifically intended for use in an assassination were delivered by the CIA to the Congo Station. There is no evidence that these instruments of assassination were actually used against Lumumba.

A thread of historical background is necessary to weave these broad questions together with the documents and testimony received by the Committee.

In the summer of 1960, there was great concern at the highest levels in the United States government about the role of Patrice Lumumba in the Congo. Lumumba, who served briefly as Premier of the newly independent nation, was viewed with alarm by United States policymakers because of what they perceived as his magnetic public appeal and his leanings toward the Soviet Union.

Under the leadership of Lumumba and the new President, Joseph Kasavubu, the Congo declared its independence from Belgium on June 30, 1960. In the turbulent month that followed, Lumumba threatened to invite Soviet troops to hasten the withdrawal of Belgian armed forces. The United Nations Security Council requested Belgium's withdrawal and dispatched a neutral force to the Congo to preserve order. In late July, Lumumba visited Washington and received pledges of economic aid from Secretary of State Christian Herter. By the beginning of September, Soviet airplanes, trucks, and technicians were arriving in the province where Lumumba's support was strongest.

In mid-September, after losing a struggle for the leadership of the government to Kasavubu and Joseph Mobutu, Chief of Staff of the Congolese armed forces, Lumumba sought protection from the United Nations forces in Leopoldville. Early in December, Mobutu's troops captured Lumumba while he was traveling toward his stronghold at Stanleyville and imprisoned him. On January 17, 1961, the central government of the Congo transferred Lumumba to the custody of authorities in Katanga province, which was then asserting its own independence from the Congo. Several weeks later, Katanga authorities announced Lumumba's death.

Accounts of the circumstances and timing of Lumumba's death vary. The United Nations investigation concluded that Lumumba was killed on January 17, 1961.

2. Dulles Cable to Leopoldville: August 26, 1960

The Congo declared its independence from Belgium on June 30, 1960. Shortly thereafter, the CIA assigned a new officer to its Leopoldville Station. The "Station Officer" said that assassinating Lumumba was not discussed during his CIA briefings prior to departing for the Congo, nor during his brief return to Headquarters in connection with Lumumba's visit to Washington in late July.

During August, there was increasing concern about Lumumba's political strength in the Congo among the national security policymakers of the Eisenhower Administration. This concern was nurtured by intelligence reports such as that cabled to CIA Headquarters by the Station Officer:

> EMBASSY AND STATION BELIEVE CONGO EXPERIENCING CLASSIC COMMUNIST EFFORT TAKEOVER GOVERNMENT.

> MANY FORCES AT WORK HERE: SOVIETS *** COMMUNIST PARTY, ETC. ALTHOUGH DIFFICULT DETERMINE MAJOR INFLUENCING FACTOR TO PREDICT OUTCOME STRUGGLE FOR POWER, DECISIVE PERIOD NOT FAR OFF. WHETHER OR NOT LUMUMBA ACTUALLY COMMIE OR JUST PLAYING COMMIE GAME TO ASSIST HIS SOLIDIFYING POWER, ANTI-WEST FORCES RAPIDLY INCREASING POWER CONGO AND THERE MAY BE LITTLE TIME LEFT IN WHICH TAKE ACTION TO AVOID ANOTHER CUBA.

This cable stated the Station's operational "objective [of] replacing Lumumba with pro Western Group." Bronson Tweedy, who was Chief of the Africa Division of CIA's clandestine services, replied that he was seeking State Department approval for the proposed operation based upon "your and our belief Lumumba must be removed if possible." On August 19, DDP Richard Bissell, Director of CIA's covert operations branch, signed a follow-up cable to Leopoldville, saying: "You are authorized proceed with operation."

Several days later, the Station Officer reported:

> ANTI-LUMUMBA LEADERS APPROACHED KASAVUBU WITH PLAN ASSASSINATE LUMUMBA * * * KASAVUBU REFUSED AGREE SAYING HE RELUCTANT RESORT VIOLENCE AND NO OTHER LEADER SUFFICIENT STATURE REPLACE LUMUMBA.

On August 25, Director of Central Intelligence Allen Dulles attended a meeting of the Special Group—the National Security Council subcommittee responsible for the planning of covert operations. In response to the outline of some CIA plans for political actions against Lumumba, such as arranging a vote of no confidence by the Congolese Parliament, Gordon Gray, the Special Assistant to the President for National Security Affairs reported that the President "had expressed extremely strong feelings on the necessity for very straightforward action in this situation, and he wondered whether the plans as outlined were sufficient to accomplish this." The Special Group "finally agreed that planning for the Congo would not necessarily rule out 'consideration' of any particular kind of activity which might contribute to getting rid of Lumumba."

The next day, Allen Dulles signed a cable to the Leopoldville Station Officer stating:

> IN HIGH QUARTERS HERE IT IS THE CLEAR-CUT CONCLUSION THAT IF [LUMUMBA] CONTINUES TO HOLD HIGH OFFICE, THE INEVITABLE RESULT WILL AT BEST BE CHAOS AND AT WORST PAVE THE WAY TO COMMUNIST TAKEOVER OF THE CONGO WITH DISASTROUS CONSEQUENCES FOR THE PRESTIGE OF THE UN AND FOR THE INTERESTS OF THE FREE WORLD GENERALLY. CONSEQUENTLY WE CONCLUDE THAT HIS REMOVAL MUST BE AN URGENT AND PRIME OBJECTIVE AND THAT UNDER EXISTING CONDITIONS THIS SHOULD BE A HIGH PRIORITY OF OUR COVERT ACTION.

The cable said that the Station Officer was to be given "wider authority"—along the lines of the previously authorized operation to replace Lumumba with a pro-Western group—"including even more aggressive action if it can remain covert . . . we realize that targets of opportunity may present themselves to you." Dulles' cable also authorized the expenditure of up to $100,000 "to carry out any crash programs on which you do not have the opportunity to consult HQS," and assured the Station Officer that the message had been "seen and approved at competent level" in the State Department. The cable continued:

> TO THE EXTENT THAT AMBASSADOR MAY DESIRE TO BE CONSULTED, YOU SHOULD SEEK HIS CONCURRENCE. IF IN ANY PARTICULAR CASE, HE DOES NOT WISH TO BE CONSULTED YOU CAN ACT ON YOUR OWN AUTHORITY WHERE TIME DOES NOT PERMIT REFERRAL HERE.

This cable raises the question of whether the DCI was contemplating action against Lumumba for which the United States would want to be in a position to "plausibly deny" responsibility. On its face, the cable could have been read as authorizing only the "removal" of Lumumba from office. DDP Richard Bissell was "almost certain" that he was informed about the Dulles cable shortly after its transmission. He testified that it was his "belief" that the cable was a circumlocutious means of indicating that the President wanted Lumumba killed.

Bronson Tweedy testified that he may have seen Dulles' cable of August 26, before it was transmitted and that he "might even have drafted it." Tweedy called this cable the "most authoritative statement" on the "policy consensus in Washington about the need for the removal of Lumumba" by any means, including assassination. He said that he "never knew" specifically who was involved in formulating this policy. But he believed that the cable indicated that Dulles had received authorization at the "policy level" which "certainly * * * would have involved the National Security Council." Tweedy testified that the $100,000 was probably intended for "political operations against Lumumba * * * not assassination-type programs."

3. CIA Encouragement of Congolese Efforts to "Eliminate" Lumumba

On September 5, 1960, President Kasavubu dismissed Premier Lumumba from the government despite the strong support for Lumumba in the Congolese Parliament. After losing the ensuing power struggle with Kasavubu and Mobutu, who seized power by a military coup on September 14, Lumumba asked the United Nations peace-keeping force for protection.

The evidence indicates that the ouster of Lumumba did not alleviate the concern about him in the United States government. Rather CIA and high Administration officials continued to view him as a threat. During this period, CIA officers in the Congo advised and aided Congolese contacts known to have an intent to assassinate Lumumba. The officers also urged the "permanent disposal" of Lumumba by some of these Congolese contacts. Moreover, the CIA opposed reopening Parliament after the coup because of the likelihood that Parliament would return Lumumba to power.

The day after Kasavubu deposed Lumumba, two CIA officers met with a high-level Congolese politician who was in close contact with the Leopoldville Station. The Station reported to CIA Headquarters:

> TO [STATION OFFICER] COMMENT THAT LUMUMBA IN OPPOSITION IS ALMOST AS DANGEROUS AS IN OFFICE, [THE CONGOLESE, POLITICIAN] INDICATED UNDERSTOOD AND IMPLIED MIGHT PHYSICALLY ELIMINATE LUMUMBA.

The cable also stated that the Station Officer had offered to assist this politician "in preparation new government program" and assured him that the United States would supply technicians.

As the struggle for power raged, Bronson Tweedy summarized the prevalent apprehension of the United States about Lumumba's ability to influence events in the Congo by virtue of his personality, irrespective of his official position:

> LUMUMBA TALENTS AND DYNAMISM APPEAR OVERRIDING FACTOR IN REESTABLISHING HIS POSITION EACH TIME IT SEEMS HALF LOST. IN OTHER WORDS EACH TIME LUMUMBA HAS OPPORTUNITY HAVE LAST WORD HE CAN SWAY EVENTS TO HIS ADVANTAGE.

The day after Mobutu's coup, the Station Officer reported that he was serving as an advisor to a Congolese effort to "eliminate" Lumumba due to his "fear" that Lumumba might, in fact, have been strengthened by placing himself in U.N. custody, which afforded a safe base of operations. {Victor} Hedgman concluded: "Only solution is remove him from scene soonest."

{ . . . }

4. The Plot to Assassinate Lumumba

Summary

In the Summer of 1960, DDP Richard Bissell asked the Chief of the Africa Division, Bronson Tweedy, to explore the feasibility of assassinating Patrice Lumumba. Bissell also asked a CIA scientist, Joseph Scheider, to make preparations to assassinate or incapacitate an unspecified "African leader." According to Scheider, Bissell said that the assignment had the "highest authority." Scheider procured toxic biological materials in response to Bissell's request, and was then ordered by Tweedy to take these materials to the Station Officer in Leopoldville. According to Scheider, there was no explicit requirement that the Station check back with Headquarters for final approval before proceeding to assassinate Lumumba. Tweedy maintained, however, that whether or not he had explicitly levied such a requirement, the Station Officer was not authorized to move from exploring means of assassination to actually attempting to kill Lumumba without referring the matter to Headquarters for a policy decision.

In late September, Scheider delivered the lethal substances to the Station Officer in Leopoldville and instructed him to assassinate Patrice Lumumba. The Station Officer testified that after requesting and receiving confirmation from CIA Headquarters that he was to carry out Scheider's instructions, he proceeded to take "exploratory steps" in furtherance of the assassination plot. The Station Officer also testified that he was told by Scheider that President Eisenhower had ordered the assassination of Lumumba. Scheider's testimony generally substantiated this account, although he acknowledged that his meetings with Bissell and Tweedy were the only bases for his impression about Presidential authorization. Scheider's mission to the Congo was preceded and followed by cables from Headquarters urging the "elimination" of Lumumba transmitted through an extraordinarily restricted "Eyes Only" channel—including two messages bearing the personal signature of Allen Dulles.

The toxic substances were never used. But there is no evidence that the assassination operation was terminated before Lumumba's death. There is, however, no suggestion of a connection between the assassination plot and the events which actually led to Lumumba's death.

(a) Bissell/Tweedy meetings on feasibility of assassinating Lumumba

Bronson Tweedy testified that Richard Bissell initiated a discussion with him in the summer of 1960 about the feasibility of assassinating Patrice Lumumba, and that they discussed the subject "more than once" during the following fall. Tweedy said the first such conversation probably took place shortly before Dulles' cable of August 26, instructing the Station Officer that Lumumba's "removal" was a "high priority of our covert action." Whether his talk with Bissell was "shortly before or shortly after" the Dulles cable, it was clear to Tweedy that the two events "were totally in tandem."

Tweedy testified that he did not recall the exact exchange but the point of the conversation was clear:

> What Mr. Bissell was saying to me was that there was agreement, policy agreement, in Washington that Lumumba must be removed from the position of control and influence in the Congo * * * and that among the possibilities of that elimination was indeed assassination.

> * * * The purpose of his conversation with me was to initiate correspondence with the Station for them to explore with Headquarters the possibility of * * * assassination, or indeed any other means of removing Lumumba from power * * * to have the Station start reviewing possibilities, assets, and discussing them with Headquarters in detail in the same way we would with any operation.

Tweedy was "sure" that in his discussions with Bissell poisoning "must have" been mentioned as one means of assassination that was being considered and which the Station Officer should explore.

{ . . . }

(b) Bissell/Scheider meetings on preparations for assassinating "an African leader"

Joseph Scheider testified that he had "two or three conversations" with Richard Bissell in 1960 about the Agency's technical capability to assassinate foreign leaders. In the late spring or early summer, Bissell asked Scheider generally about technical means of assassination or incapacitation that could be developed or procured by the CIA. Scheider informed Bissell that the CIA had access to lethal or potentially lethal biological materials that could be used in this manner. Following their initial "general discussion," Scheider said he discussed assassination capabilities with Bissell in the context of "one or two meetings about Africa."

Scheider testified that in the late summer or early fall, Bissell asked him to make all preparations necessary for having biological materials ready on short notice for use in the assassination of an unspecified African leader, "in case the decision was to go ahead." Scheider testified that Bissell told him that "he had direction from the highest authority * * * for getting into that kind of operation." Scheider stated that the reference to "highest authority" by Bissell "signified to me that he meant the President."

Scheider said that he "must have" outlined to Bissell the steps he planned to take to execute Bissell's orders. After the meeting, Scheider reviewed a list of biological materials available at the Army Chemical Corps installation at Fort Detrick, Maryland, which would produce diseases that would "either kill the individual or incapacitate him so severely that he would be out of action." Scheider selected one material from the list which "was supposed to produce a disease that was * * * indigenous to that area of Africa and that could be fatal." Scheider testified that he obtained this material and made preparation for its use:

> We had to get it bottled and packaged in a way that it could pass for something else and I needed to have a second material that could absolutely inactivate it in case that is what I desired to do for some contingency.

Scheider also "prepared a packet of * * * accessory materials," such as hypodermic needles, rubber gloves, and gauze masks, "that would be used in the handling of this pretty dangerous material."

{ . . . }

(*d*) *Congo Station Officer told to expect Scheider: Dulles cables about "elimination" of Lumumba*

On September 19, 1960, several days after Lumumba placed himself in the protective custody of the United Nations peacekeeping force in Leopoldville, Richard Bissell and Bronson Tweedy sent a cryptic cable to Leopoldville to arrange a clandestine meeting between the Station Officer and "Joseph Braun," who was traveling to the Congo on an unspecified assignment. Joseph Scheider testified that "Joseph Braun" was his alias and was used because this was "an extremely sensitive operation." The cable informed the Station Officer:

> ["JOE"] SHOULD ARRIVE APPROX 27 SEPT * * * WILL ANNOUNCE HIMSELF AS "JOE FROM PARIS" * * * IT URGENT YOU SHOULD SEE ["JOE"] SOONEST POSSIBLE AFTER HE PHONES YOU. HE WILL FULLY IDENTIFY HIMSELF AND EXPLAIN HIS ASSIGNMENT TO YOU.

The cable bore the codeword "PROP," which indicated extraordinary sensitivity and restricted circulation at CIA headquarters to Dulles, Bissell, Tweedy, and Tweedy's Deputy. The PROP designator restricted circulation in the Congo to the Station Officer.

Tweedy testified that the PROP channel was established and used exclusively for the assassination operation. The Bissell/Tweedy cable informed the Station Officer that the PROP channel was to be used for:

> ALL [CABLE] TRAFFIC THIS OP, WHICH YOU INSTRUCTED HOLD ENTIRELY TO YOURSELF.

Tweedy testified that the fact that he and Bissell both signed the cable indicated that authorization for Scheider's trip to the Congo had come from Bissell. Tweedy stated that Bissell "signed off" on cables originated by a Division Chief "on matters of particular sensitivity or so important that the DDP wished to be constantly informed about correspondence." Tweedy said that Bissell read much of the cable traffic on this operation and was "generally briefed on the progress of the planning."

The Station Officer, Victor Hedgman, testified to a clear, independent recollection of receiving the Tweedy/Bissell cable. He stated that in September of 1960 he received a "most unusual" cable from CIA Headquarters which advised that:

> someone who I would have recognized would arrive with instructions for me * * * I believe the message was also marked for my eyes only * * * and contained instructions that I was not to discuss the message with anyone.

He said that the cable did not specify the kind of instructions he was to receive, and it "did not refer to Lumumba in any way."

Three days after the Bissell/Tweedy cable, Tweedy sent another cable through the PROP channel which stated that if it was decided that "support for prop objectives [was] essential" a third country national should be used as an agent in the assassination operation to completely conceal the American role. Tweedy testified that "PROP objectives" referred to an assassination attempt. Tweedy also indicated to the Station Officer and his "colleague" Scheider:

> YOU AND COLLEAGUE UNDERSTAND WE CANNOT READ OVER YOUR SHOULDER AS YOU PLAN AND ASSESS OPPORTUNITIES. OUR PRIMARY CONCERN MUST BE CONCEALMENT [AMERICAN] ROLE, UNLESS OUTSTANDING OPPORTUNITY EMERGES WHICH MAKES CALCULATED RISK FIRST CLASS BET. READY ENTERTAIN ANY SERIOUS PROPOSALS YOU MAKE BASED OUR HIGH REGARD BOTH YOUR PROFESSIONAL JUDGMENTS.

On September 24, the DCI personally sent a cable to Leopoldville stating:

> WE WISH GIVE EVERY POSSIBLE SUPPORT IN ELIMINATING LUMUMBA FROM ANY POSSIBILITY RESUMING GOVERNMENTAL POSITION OR IF HE FAILS IN LEOPOLDVILLE, SETTING HIMSELF IN STANLEYVILLE OR ELSEWHERE.

Dulles had expressed a similar view three days before in President Eisenhower's presence at an NSC meeting.

Scheider recalled that Tweedy and his Deputy had told him that the Station Officer would receive a communication assuring him that there was support at CIA Headquarters for the assignment Scheider was to give him.

(*e*) *Assassination instructions issued to Station Officer and lethal substances delivered: September 26,1960*

Station Officer Hedgman reported through the PROP channel that he had contacted Scheider on September 26.

According to Hedgman:

> HEDGMAN: It is my recollection that he advised me, or my instructions were, to eliminate Lumumba.
>
> Q: By eliminate, do you mean assassinate?
>
> HEDGMAN: Yes, I would say that was * * * my understanding of the primary means. I don't think it was probably limited to that, if there was some other way of * * * removing him from a position of political threat.

Hedgman said that he and Scheider also may have discussed non-lethal means of removing Lumumba as a "political threat," but he could not "recall with certainty on that."

Scheider testified:

> I explained to him [Station Officer] what Tweedy and his Deputy had told me, that Headquarters wanted him to see if he could use this [biological] capability I brought against Lumumba [and] to caution him that it had to be done * * * without attribution to the USA.

The Station Officer testified that he received "rubber gloves, a mask, and a syringe" along with lethal biological material from Scheider, who also instructed him in their use. Hedgman indicated that this paraphernalia was for administering the poison to Lumumba for the purpose of assassination. Scheider explained that the toxic material was to be injected into some substance that Lumumba would ingest: "it had to do with anything he could get to his mouth, whether it was food or a toothbrush, * * * [so] that some of the material could get to his mouth."

Hedgman said that the means of assassination was not restricted to use of the toxic material provided by Scheider.

He testified that he may have "suggested" shooting Lumumba to Scheider as an alternative to poisoning. Scheider said it was his "impression" that Tweedy and his Deputy empowered him to tell the Station Officer that he could pursue other means of assassination. Station Officer Hedgman testified that, although the selection of a mode of assassination was left to his judgment, there was a firm requirement that:

> [I]f I implemented these instructions * * * it had to be a way which could not be traced back * * * either to an American or the United States government.

Hedgman said Scheider assured him that the poisons were produced to "[leave] normal traces found in people that die of certain diseases."

Hedgman said that he had an "emotional reaction of great surprise" when it first became clear that Scheider had come to discuss an assassination plan. He told Scheider he "would explore this" and left Scheider with the impression "that I was going to look into it and try and figure if there was a way * * * I believe I stressed the difficulty of trying to carry out such an operation." Scheider said that the Station Officer was "sober [and] grim" but willing to proceed with the operation.

The Station Officer's report of his initial contact with Scheider was clearly an affirmative response to the assignment, and said that he and Scheider were "on same wavelength." Hedgman was "afraid" that the central government was "weakening under" foreign pressure to effect a reconciliation with Lumumba, and said:

> HENCE BELIEVE MOST RAPID ACTION CONSISTENT WITH SECURITY INDICATED.

{ . . . }

(g) *Steps in furtherance of the assassination operation*

(i) Hedgman's testimony about confirmation from Headquarters of the assassination Plan.

Hedgman's testimony, taken fifteen years after the events in question and without the benefit of reviewing the cables discussed above, was compatible with the picture presented by the cables of a fully authorized and tightly restricted assassination operation. The only variance is that the cables portray Hedgman as taking an affirmative, aggressive attitude toward the assignment, while he testified that his pursuit of the operation was less vigorous.

The Station Officer testified that soon after cabling his request for confirmation that he was to carry out the assassination assignment, he received a reply from Headquarters, which he characterized as follows:

> I believe I received a reply which I interpreted to mean yes, that he was the messenger and his instructions were * * * duly authorized.

Despite the cryptic nature of the cables, Hedgman said "I was convinced that yes, it was right," but he had no "desire to carry out these instructions." Hedgman stated:

> I think probably that I would have gone back and advised that I intended to carry out and sought final approval before carrying it out had I been going to do it, had there been a way to do it. I did not see it as * * * a matter which could be accomplished practically, certainly.

Hedgman said that his reason for seeking a final approval would have been to receive assurances about the practicality of the specific mode of assassination that he planned to use.

All CIA officers involved in the plot to kill Lumumba testified that, by virtue of the standard operating procedure of the clandestine services, there was an implicit requirement that a field officer check back with Headquarters for approval of any major operational plan. Moreover, Hedgman's cable communications with Headquarters indicate that he consistently informed

Tweedy of each significant step in the formulation of assassination plans, thus allowing Headquarters the opportunity to amend or disapprove the plans. The personal cable from Dulles to the Station Officer on August 26, made it clear, however, that if Lumumba appeared as a "target of opportunity" in a situation where time did not permit referral to headquarters, Hedgman was authorized to proceed with the assassination.

The Station Officer testified that for several months after receiving Scheider's instructions he took "exploratory steps in furtherance of the assassination plot." He sent several cables to CIA Headquarters which "probably reflected further steps I had taken," and stated that his cables to Headquarters were essentially "progress reports" on his attempts to find access to Lumumba.

The cable traffic conforms to the Station Officer's recollection. For two months after Scheider's arrival in the Congo, a regular stream of messages assessing prospects for the assassination operation flowed through the PROP channel between Headquarters and Leopoldville.

(II) "EXPLORATORY STEPS"

On the basis of his talks with Scheider, Station Officer Hedgman listed a number of "possibilities" for covert action against Lumumba. At the top of the list was the suggestion that a particular agent be used in the following manner:

> HAVE HIM TAKE REFUGE WITH BIG BROTHER. WOULD THUS ACT AS INSIDE MAN TO BRUSH UP DETAILS TO RAZOR EDGE.

Tweedy testified that "Big Brother" referred to Lumumba. Tweedy and Scheider both said that this cable indicated that Hedgman's top priority plan was to instruct his agent to infiltrate Lumumba's entourage to explore means of poisoning Lumumba. The Station Officer reported that he would begin to follow this course by recalling the agent to Leopoldville, and informed Headquarters:

> BELIEVE MOST RAPID ACTION CONSISTENT WITH SECURITY INDICATED *** PLAN PROCEED ON BASIS

PRIORITIES AS LISTED ABOVE, UNLESS INSTRUCTED TO CONTRARY.

Scheider testified that at this point the Station Officer was reporting to Headquarters that he was proceeding to "go ahead" to carry out Scheider's instructions as quickly as possible. Tweedy's Deputy stated that the form of the Station Officers request would have satisfied the standard requirement for confirmation of an operational plan:

> *** it is my professional opinion that, under normal operational procedure at that time, the Station Officer would have been expected to advise Headquarters that he was preparing to implement the plan unless advised to the contrary.

On September 30, the Station Officer specifically urged Headquarters to authorize "exploratory conversations" to launch his top priority plan:

> NO REALLY AIRTIGHT OP POSSIBLE WITH ASSETS NOW AVAILABLE. MUST CHOOSE BETWEEN CANCELLING OP OR ACCEPTING CALCULATED RISKS OF VARYING DEGREES.
>
> *** [IN] VIEW NECESSITY ACT IMMEDIATELY, IF AT ALL, URGE HQS AUTHORIZE EXPLORATORY CONVERSATIONS TO DETERMINE IF [AGENT] WILLING TAKE ROLE AS ACTIVE AGENT OR CUT-OUT THIS OP. (WOULD APPROACH ON HYPOTHETICAL BASIS AND NOT REVEAL PLANS.) IF HE APPEARS WILLING ACCEPT ROLE, WE BELIEVE IT NECESSARY REVEAL OBJECTIVE OP TO HIM.
>
> *** REQUEST HQS REPLY [IMMEDIATELY].

Headquarters replied:

> YOU ARE AUTHORIZED HAVE EXPLORATORY TALKS WITH [AGENT] TO ASSESS HIS ATTITUDE TOWARD POSSIBLE ACTIVE AGENT OR CUTOUT ROLE * * * IT DOES APPEAR FROM HERE THAT OF POSSIBILITIES AVAILABLE

[THIS AGENT] IS BEST * * * WE WILL WEIGH VERY CAREFULLY YOUR INITIAL ASSESSMENT HIS ATTITUDE AS WELL AS ANY SPECIFIC APPROACHES THAT MAY EMERGE * * * APPRECIATE MANNER YOUR APPROACH TO PROBLEM. "HOPE * * * FOR MODERATE HASTE."

Tweedy and his Deputy made it clear that the agent was being viewed as a potential assassin. Tweedy stated that it would have been proper for his Deputy to issue this cable authorizing the Station Officer to take the assassination operation "one step further" and it was "quite possible" that Richard Bissell was informed of this directive.

On October 7, the Station Officer reported to Headquarters on his meeting with the agent who was his best candidate for gaining access to Lumumba:

CONDUCTED EXPLORATORY CONVERSATION WITH [AGENT] * * * AFTER EXPLORING ALL POSSIBILITIES [AGENT] SUGGESTED SOLUTION RECOMMENDED BY HQS. ALTHOUGH DID NOT PICK UP BALL, BELIEVE HE PREPARED TAKE ANY ROLE NECESSARY WITHIN LIMITS SECURITY ACCOMPLISH OBJECTIVE.

The Station Officer testified that the subject "explored" was the agent's ability to find a means to inject the toxic material into Lumumba's food or toothpaste:

I believe that I queried the agent who had access to Lumumba, and his entourage, in detail about just what access he actually had, as opposed to speaking to people. In other words, did he have access to the bathroom, did he have access to the kitchen. Things of that sort.

I have a recollection of having queried him on that without specifying why I wanted to know this.

The Station Officer said that he was left with doubts about the wisdom or practicality of the assassination plot:

[C]ertainly I looked on it as a pretty wild scheme professionally. I did not think that it * * * was practical professionally, certainly, in a short

> time, if you were going to keep the U.S. out of it * * * I explored it, but I doubt that I ever really expected to carry it out.

(III) THE ASSASSINATION OPERATION MOVES FORWARD AFTER SCHEIDER'S RETURN TO HEADQUARTERS: OCTOBER 5–7, 1960

Despite the Station Officer's testimony about the dubious practicality of the assassination operation, the cables indicate that he planned to continue his efforts to implement the operation and sought the resources to do so successfully. For example, he urged Headquarters to send an alternate agent:

> IF HQS BELIEVE [AGENT'S CIRCUMSTANCES] BAR HIS PARTICIPATION, WISH STRESS NECESSITY PROVIDE STATION WITH QUALIFIED THIRD COUNTRY NATIONAL.

Tweedy cabled the Station Officer that he "had good discussion your colleague 7 Oct"—referring to a debriefing of Scheider upon his return to the United States. Tweedy indicated that he continued to support the assassination operation and advised:

> BE ASSURED DID NOT EXPECT PROP OBJECTIVES BE REACHED IN SHORT PERIOD * * * CONSIDERING DISPATCHING THIRD COUNTRY NATIONAL OPERATIVE WHO, WHEN HE ARRIVES, SHOULD BE ASSESSED BY YOU OVER PERIOD TO SEE WHETHER HE MIGHT PLAY ACTIVE OR CUTOUT ROLE ON FULL TIME BASIS. IF YOU CONCLUDE HE SUITABLE AND BEARING IN MIND HEAVY EXTRA LOAD THIS PLACES ON YOU, WOULD EXPECT DISPATCH [TEMPORARY DUTY] SENIOR CASE OFFICER RUN THIS OP * * * UNDER YOUR DIRECTION.

According to the report of the Station Officer, Joseph Scheider left the Congo to return to Headquarters on October 5 in view of the "expiration date his material"—a reference to the date beyond which the substances would no longer have lethal strength. The cable from the Station Officer further stated that:

> [JOE] LEFT CERTAIN ITEMS OF CONTINUING USEFULNESS. [STATION OFFICER] PLANS CONTINUE TRY IMPLEMENT OP.

Notwithstanding the influence of the Station Officer's October 7 cable that some toxic substances were left with Hedgman, Scheider specifically recalled that he had "destroyed the viability" of the biological material and disposed of it in the Congo River before he departed for the United States on October 5, 1960. In the only real conflict between his testimony and Scheider's, Hedgman testified that the toxic material was not disposed of until after Lumumba was imprisoned by the Congolese in early December.

The central point remains that the Station Officer planned to continue the assassination effort, by whatever means, even after Scheider's departure. Scheider was under the impression that the Station Officer was still authorized to move ahead with an assassination attempt against Lumumba at that point, although he would have continued to submit his plans to Headquarters.

(IV) Headquarters continues to place "highest priority" on the assassination operation

SUMMARY

The cable traffic during this period demonstrates that there was a clear intent at Headquarters to authorize and support rapid progress of the assassination operation. Even after Lumumba placed himself in the protective custody of the United Nations, CIA Headquarters continued to regard his assassination as the "highest priority" of covert action in the Congo. The cables also show an intent at Headquarters to severely restrict knowledge of the assassination operation among officers in CIA's Africa Division and among United States diplomatic personnel in the Congo, excluding even those who were aware of, and involved in, other covert activities.

The Station Officer, despite the burden of his other operational responsibilities, was actively exploring, evaluating, and reporting on the means and agents that might be used in an attempt to assassinate Lumumba. When his implementation of the assassination operation was thwarted by the failure of his prime candidate to gain access to Lumumba, Hedgman requested additional operational and supervisory personnel to help him carry out the assignment, which he apparently pursued until Lumumba was imprisoned by Congolese authorities.

On October 15, 1960, shortly after Tweedy offered additional manpower for the assassination operation, a significant pair of cables were sent from CIA Headquarters to Leopoldville.

One cable was issued by a desk officer in CIA's Africa Division, released under Bronson Tweedy's signature, and transmitted through standard CIA channels, thus permitting distribution of the message to appropriate personnel in the CIA Station and the United States Embassy. The cable discussed the possibility of covertly supplying certain Congolese leaders with funds and military aid and advised:

> ONLY DIRECT ACTION WE CAN NOW STAND BEHIND IS TO SUPPORT IMMOBILIZING OR ARRESTING [LUMUMBA], DESIRABLE AS MORE DEFINITIVE ACTION MIGHT BE. ANY ACTION TAKEN WOULD HAVE TO BE ENTIRELY CONGOLESE.

On the same day Tweedy dispatched a second cable, via the PROP channel for Hedgman's "Eyes Only," which prevented the message from being distributed to anyone else, including the Ambassador. Tweedy's Deputy stated that "the cable which carried the PROP indicator would have controlling authority as between the two cables." The second cable stated:

> YOU WILL NOTE FROM CABLE THROUGH NORMAL CHANNEL CURRENTLY BEING TRANSMITTED A PARA[GRAPH] ON PROP TYPE SUGGESTIONS. YOU WILL PROBABLY RECEIVE MORE ALONG THESE LINES AS STUMBLING BLOC [LUMUMBA] REPRESENTS INCREASINGLY APPARENT ALL STUDYING CONGO SITUATION CLOSELY AND HIS DISPOSITION SPONTANEOUSLY BECOMES NUMBER ONE CONSIDERATION.
>
> RAISE ABOVE SO YOU NOT CONFUSED BY ANY APPARENT DUPLICATION. THIS CHANNEL REMAINS FOR SPECIFIC PURPOSE YOU DISCUSSED WITH COLLEAGUE AND ALSO REMAINS HIGHEST PRIORITY.

Tweedy testified that the "specific purpose discussed with colleague" referred to the Station Officer's discussion of "assassination with Scheider." He stated that the premise of his message was that "there is no solution to the Congo as long as Lumumba stays in a position of power or influence there."

Tweedy went on to request the Station Officer's reaction to the prospect of sending a senior CIA case officer to the Congo on a "direct assignment * * * to concentrate entirely this aspect."

The cable also provided an insight into why the assassination operation had not progressed more rapidly under the Station Officer:

> SEEMS TO US YOUR OTHER COMMITMENTS TOO HEAVY GIVE NECESSARY CONCENTRATION PROP.

In contradiction of the limitations on anti-Lumumba activity outlined in the cable sent through normal channels, Tweedy's cable suggested:

> POSSIBILITY USE COMMANDO TYPE GROUP FOR ABDUCTION [LUMUMBA], EITHER VIA ASSAULT ON HOUSE UP CLIFF FROM RIVER OR, MORE PROBABLY, IF [LUMUMBA] ATTEMPTS ANOTHER BREAKOUT INTO TOWN * * * REQUEST YOUR VIEWS.

Two days later the Station Officer made a number of points in a reply to Tweedy. First, the agent he had picked for the assassination operation had difficulty infiltrating Lumumba's inner circle:

> HAS NOT BEEN ABLE PENETRATE ENTOURAGE. THUS HE HAS NOT BEEN ABLE PROVIDE OPS INTEL NEEDED THIS JOB. * * * ALTHOUGH MAINTAINING PRIORITY INTEREST THIS OP, ABLE DEVOTE ONLY LIMITED AMOUNT TIME, VIEW MULTIPLE OPS COMMITMENTS. * * * BELIEVE EARLY ASSIGNMENT SENIOR CASE OFFICER HANDLE PROP OPS EXCELLENT IDEA * * * IF CASE OFFICER AVAILABLE [STATION OFFICER] WOULD DEVOTE AS MUCH TIME AS POSSIBLE TO ASSISTING AND DIRECTING HIS EFFORTS.

The Station Officer concluded this cable with the following cryptic recommendation, reminiscent of his testimony that he may have "suggested" shooting Lumumba to Scheider as an alternative to poisoning:

> IF CASE OFFICER SENT, RECOMMEND HQS POUCH SOONEST HIGH POWERED FOREIGN MAKE RIFLE WITH TELESCOPIC SCOPE AND SILENCER. HUNTING GOOD HERE WHEN LIGHTS RIGHT. HOWEVER AS HUNTING RIFLES NOW FORBIDDEN, WOULD KEEP RIFLE IN OFFICE PENDING OPENING OF HUNTING SEASON.

Tweedy testified that the Station Officer's recommendation clearly referred to sending to the Congo via diplomatic pouch a weapon suited for assassinating Lumumba. Senior case officer Mulroney stated that he never heard discussion at Headquarters of sending a sniper-type weapon to the Congo, nor did he have any knowledge that such a weapon had been "pouched" to the Congo.

The oblique suggestion of shooting Lumumba at the "opening of hunting season" could be interpreted as a plan to assassinate Lumumba as soon as he was seen outside the residence where he remained in U.N. protective custody. Tweedy interpreted the cable to mean that "an operational plan involving a rifle" had not yet been formulated by the Station Officer and that the "opening of hunting season" would depend upon approval of such a plan by CIA headquarters.

A report sent the next month by the Station Officer through the PROP channel for Tweedy's "Eyes Alone" indicated that, whatever the intention about moving forward with a plan for assassination by rifle fire, Lumumba was being viewed as a "target" and his movements were under close surveillance. Hedgman's cable described the stalemate which prevailed from mid-September until Lumumba's departure for Stanleyville on November 27; Lumumba was virtually a prisoner in U.N. custody, and inaccessible to CIA agents, and the Congolese:

> TARGET HAS NOT LEFT BUILDING IN SEVERAL WEEKS. HOUSE GUARDED DAY AND NIGHT BY CONGOLESE AND UN TROOPS * * * CONGOLESE TROOPS ARE THERE TO PREVENT TARGET'S ESCAPE AND TO ARREST HIM IF HE

ATTEMPTS. UN TROOPS THERE TO PREVENT STORMING OF PALACE BY CONGOLESE. CONCENTRIC RINGS OF DEFENSE MAKE ESTABLISHMENT OF OBSERVATION POST IMPOSSIBLE. ATTEMPTING GET COVERAGE OF ANY MOVEMENT INTO OR OUT OF HOUSE BY CONGOLESE * * * . TARGET HAS DISMISSED MOST OF SERVANTS SO ENTRY THIS MEANS SEEMS REMOTE.

{ . . . }

5. The Question of a Connection Between the Assassination Plot and Other Actions of CIA Officers and Their Agents in the Congo

SUMMARY

Michael Mulroney, a senior CIA officer in the Directorate for Plans, testified that in October 1960 he had been asked by Richard Bissell to go to the Congo to carry out the assassination of Lumumba. Mulroney said that he refused to participate in an assassination operation, but proceeded to the Congo to attempt to draw Lumumba away from the protective custody of the U.N. guard and place him in the hands of Congolese authorities.

Shortly after Mulroney's arrival in the Congo, he was joined by Q J/WIN, a CIA agent with a criminal background. Late in 1960, WI/ROGUE, one of Hedgman's operatives approached Q J/WIN with a proposition to join an "execution squad."

It is unlikely that Mulroney was actually involved in implementing the assassination assignment. Whether there was any connection between the assassination plot and either of the two operatives—Q J/WIN and WI/ROGUE—is less clear.

{ . . . }

(IV) MULRONEY'S PLAN TO "NEUTRALIZE" LUMUMBA

After Mulroney arrived in the Congo, he formulated a plan for "neutralizing" Lumumba by drawing him away from the custody of the U.N. force which was guarding his residence:

MULRONEY: [W]hat I wanted to do was to get him out, to trick him out, if I could, and then turn him over * * * to the legal authorities and let him stand trial. Because he had atrocity attributed to him for which he could very well stand trial.

Q: And for which he could very well have received capital punishment?

MULRONEY: Yes. And I am not opposed to capital punishment.

To implement his plan, Mulroney made arrangements to rent "an observation post over the palace in which Lumumba was safely ensconced." He also made the acquaintance of a U.N. guard to recruit him for an attempt to lure Lumumba outside U.N. protective custody. Mulroney said that he cabled progress reports to CIA Headquarters, and kept the Station Officer informed about his activities.

Mulroney arranged for CIA agent QJ/WIN to come to the Congo to work with him:

> What I wanted to use him for was * * * counter-espionage. * * * I had to screen the U.S. participation in this * * * by using a foreign national whom we knew, trusted, and had worked with * * * the idea was for me to use him as an alter ego.

In mid-November two cables from Leopoldville urged CIA Headquarters to send QJ/WIN:

> LOCAL OPERATIONAL CIRCUMSTANCES REQUIRE IMMEDIATE EXPEDITION OF QJ/WIN TRAVEL TO LEOPOLDVILLE.

The cables did not explain the "operational circumstances."

(B) QJ/WIN'S MISSION IN THE CONGO: NOVEMBER–DECEMBER 1960

QJ/WIN was a foreign citizen with a criminal background, recruited in Europe. In November 1960, agent QJ/WIN was dispatched to the Congo to undertake a mission that "might involve a large element of personal risk."

A cable from Headquarters to Leopoldville stated:

> IN VIEW OF THE EXTREME SENSITIVITY OF THE OBJECTIVE FOR WHICH WE WANT [QJ/WIN] TO

> PERFORM HIS TASK, HE WAS NOT TOLD PRECISELY WHAT WE WANT HIM TO DO * * * INSTEAD, HE WAS TOLD * * * THAT WE WOULD LIKE TO HAVE HIM SPOT, ASSESS, AND RECOMMEND SOME DEPENDABLE, QUICK-WITTED PERSONS FOR OUR USE * * * IT WAS THOUGHT BEST TO WITHHOLD OUR TRUE, SPECIFIC REQUIREMENTS PENDING THE FINAL DECISION TO USE [HIM].

This message itself was deemed too sensitive to be retained at the station: "this dispatch should be reduced to cryptic necessary notes and destroyed after the first reading."

QJ/WIN arrived in Leopoldville on November 21, 1960, and returned to Europe in late December 1960.

Mulroney described QJ/WIN as follows:

> MULRONEY: * * * I would say that he would not be a man of many scruples.
>
> Q: So he was a man capable of doing anything?
>
> MULRONEY: I would think so, yes.
>
> Q: And that would include assassination?
>
> MULRONEY: I would think so.

But Mulroney had no knowledge that QJ/WIN was ever used for an assassination operation.

Mulroney said that, as far as he knew, he was the only CIA officer with supervisory responsibility for QJ/WIN, and QJ/WIN did not report independently to anyone else. When asked if it was possible that QJ/WIN had an assignment independent of his operations for Mulroney, he said:

> Yes, that is possible—or it could have been that somebody contacted him after he got down there, that they wanted him to do something along the lines of assassination. I don't know.

Mulroney discounted this possibility as "highly unlikely" because it would be a departure from standard CIA practice by placing an agent in a position of knowledge superior to that of his supervising officer.

Despite Mulroney's doubt that QJ/WIN had an independent line of responsibility to Station Officer Hedgman, Hedgman's November 29 cable to Tweedy reported that QJ/WIN had begun implementing a plan to "pierce both Congolese and U.N. guards" to enter Lumumba's residence and "provide escort out of residence." Mulroney said that he had directed QJ/WIN to make the acquaintance of the member of U.N. force. By this point, Lumumba had already left U.N. custody to travel toward his stronghold at Stanleyville. This did not deter QJ/WIN:

> VIEW CHANGE IN LOCATION TARGET, QJ/WIN ANXIOUS GO STANLEYVILLE AND EXPRESSED DESIRE EXECUTE PLAN BY HIMSELF WITHOUT USING ANY APPARAT.

It is unclear whether this latter "plan" contemplated assassination as well as abduction. Headquarters replied affirmatively the next day in language which could have been interpreted as an assassination order:

> CONCUR QJ/WIN GO STANLEYVILLE * * *. WE ARE PREPARED CONSIDER DIRECT ACTION BY QJ/WIN BUT WOULD LIKE YOUR READING ON SECURITY FACTORS. HOW. CLOSE WOULD THIS PLACE [UNITED STATES] TO THE ACTION?

Mulroney said that QJ/WIN's stay in the Congo was "coextensive with my own, allowing for the fact that he came after I did."

In a memorandum to arrange the accounting for QJ/WIN's activities in the Congo, William Harvey, Mulroney's immediate superior in the Directorate of Plans, noted: "QJ/WIN was sent on this trip for a specific, highly sensitive operational purpose which has been completed." Mulroney explained Harvey's reference by saying that once Lumumba was in the hands of the Congolese authorities "the reason for the mounting of the project * * * had become moot." When asked if he and QJ/WIN were responsible for Lumumba's departure from U.N. custody and subsequent capture, Mulroney replied: "Absolutely not."

Despite the suggestive language of the cables at the end of November about the prospect of "direct action" by QJ/WIN and an indication in the Inspector General's Report that QJ/WIN may have been recruited initially for an assassination mission there is no clear evidence that QJ/WIN was actually involved in any assassination plan or attempt. The Inspector General's Report may have accurately reported a plan for the use of

QJ/WIN which predated Mulroney's refusal to accept the assassination assignment from Bissell. But there is no evidence from which to conclude that QJ/WIN was actually used for such an operation.

Station Officer Hedgman had a "vague recollection" that QJ/WIN was in the Congo working for Mulroney. But Hedgman did not recall why QJ/WIN was in the Congo and said that QJ/WIN was not one of his major operatives. Bissell and Tweedy did not recall anything about QJ/WIN's activities in the Congo.

Harvey, whose division "loaned" QJ/WIN to the Congo Station, testified:

> I was kept informed of the arrangements for QJ/WIN's trip to the Congo and, subsequently, of his presence in the Congo. I do not know specifically what QJ/WIN did in the Congo. I do not think that I ever had such knowledge * * * . If QJ/WIN were to be used on an assassination mission, it would have been cleared with me. I was never informed that he was to be used for such a mission.

A 1962 CIA cable indicates the value the CIA accorded QJ/WIN and the inherent difficulty for an intelligence agency in employing criminals. The CIA had learned that QJ/WIN was about to go on trial in Europe on smuggling charges and Headquarters suggested:

> IF * * * INFOR[MATION] TRUE WE MAY WISH ATTEMPT QUASH CHARGES OR ARRANGE SOMEHOW SALVAGE QJ/WIN FOR OUR PURPOSES.

(c) WI/ROGUE asks QJ/WIN to join "execution squad": December 1960

The only suggestion that QJ/WIN had any connection with assassination was a report that WI/ROGUE, another asset of the Congo Station, once asked QJ/WIN to join an "execution squad."

WI/ROGUE was an "essentially stateless" soldier of fortune, "a forger and former bank robber." The CIA sent him to the Congo after providing him with plastic surgery and a toupee so that Europeans traveling in the Congo would not recognize him. The CIA characterized WI/ROGUE as a man who "learns quickly and carries out any assignment without regard for danger." CIA's Africa Division recommended WI/ROGUE as an agent in the following terms:

> He is indeed aware of the precepts of right and wrong, but if he is given an assignment which may be morally wrong in the eyes of the world, but necessary because his case officer ordered him to carry it out, then it is right, and he will dutifully undertake appropriate action for its execution without pangs of conscience. In a word, he can rationalize all actions.

Station Officer Hedgman described WI/ROGUE as "a man with a rather unsavory reputation, who would try anything once, at least." Hedgman used him as "a general utility agent" because "I felt we needed surveillance capability, developing new contacts, various things." Hedgman supervised WI/ROGUE directly and did not put him in touch with Mulroney.

A report on agent WI/ROGUE, prepared for the CIA Inspector General's Office in 1975, described the training he received:

> On 19 September 1960 two members of Africa Division met with him to discuss "an operational assignment in Africa Division." In connection with this assignment, WI/ROGUE was to be trained in demolitions, small arms, and medical immunization.

The report also outlined WI/ROGUE's assignment to the Congo and recorded no mention of the use to which WI/ROGUE's "medical immunization" training would be put:

> In October 1960 a cable to Leopoldville stated that * * * Headquarters [had] * * * intent to use him as utility agent in order to "(a) organize and conduct a surveillance team; (b) intercept packages; (c) blow up bridges; and (d) execute other assignments requiring positive action. His utilization is not to be restricted to Leopoldville."

WI/ROGUE made his initial contact with Hedgman in Leopoldville on December 2, 1960. Hedgman instructed him to "build cover during initial period"; and to "spot persons for [a] surveillance team" of intelligence agents in the province where Lumumba's support was strongest.

Soon thereafter Hedgman cabled Headquarters:

> Q J/WIN WHO RESIDES SAME HOTEL AS WI/ROGUE REPORTED * * * WI/ROGUE SMELLED AS THOUGH HE IN INTEL BUSINESS. STATION DENIED ANY INFO ON WI/ROGUE. 14 DEC Q J/WIN REPORTED WI/ROGUE HAD OFFERED HIM THREE HUNDRED DOLLARS PER MONTH TO PARTICIPATE IN INTEL NET AND BE MEMBER "EXECUTION SQUAD." WHEN Q J/WIN SAID HE NOT INTERESTED, WI/ROGUE ADDED THERE WOULD BE BONUSES FOR SPECIAL JOBS. UNDER Q J/WIN QUESTIONING, WI/ROGUE LATER SAID HE WORKING FOR [AMERICAN] SERVICE.
>
> * * * IN DISCUSSING LOCAL CONTACTS, WI/ROGUE MENTIONED Q J/WIN BUT DID NOT ADMIT TO HAVING TRIED RECRUIT HIM. WHEN [STATION OFFICER] TRIED LEARN WHETHER WI/ROGUE HAD MADE APPROACH LATTER CLAIMED HAD TAKEN NO STEPS. [STATION OFFICER] WAS UNABLE CONTRADICT, AS DID NOT WISH REVEAL Q J/WIN CONNECTION [WITH CIA].

The cable also expressed Hedgman's concern about WI/ROGUE's actions:

> * * * LEOP CONCERNED BY WI/ROGUE FREE WHEELING AND LACK SECURITY. STATION HAS ENOUGH HEADACHES WITHOUT WORRYING ABOUT AGENT WHO NOT ABLE HANDLE FINANCES AND WHO NOT WILLING FOLLOW INSTRUCTIONS. IF HQS DESIRES, WILLING KEEP HIM ON PROBATION, BUT IF CONTINUE HAVE DIFFICULTIES, BELIEVE WI/ROGUE RECALL BEST SOLUTION.

Hedgman explained WI/ROGUE's attempt to recruit Q J/WIN for an execution squad as an unauthorized unexpected contact. He testified that he had not instructed WI/ROGUE to make this kind of proposition to Q J/WIN or anyone else:

> I would like to stress that I don't know what WI/ROGUE was talking about as an "execution squad," and I am sure he was never asked to go out and execute anyone.

Hedgman suggested that WI/ROGUE had concocted the idea of an execution squad:

> His idea of what an intelligence operative should do, I think, had been gathered by reading a few novels or something of the sort.

Mulroney said he knew of no attempt by anyone connected with the CIA to recruit an execution squad and he did not remember WI/ROGUE. He stated that QJ/WIN was considered for use on "strong arm squad[s]," unrelated to assassinations:

> Surveillance teams where you have to go into crime areas * * * where you need a fellow that if he gets in a box can fight his way out of it.

Richard Bissell recalled nothing about WI/ROGUE's approach to QJ/WIN. Bronson Tweedy remembered that WI/ROGUE was "dispatched on a general purpose mission" to the Congo. But Tweedy testified that WI/ROGUE would "absolutely not" have been used on an assassination mission against Lumumba because "he was basically dispatched, assessed and dealt with by the balance of the Division" rather than by the two people in the Africa Division, Tweedy and his Deputy, who would have known that the assassination of Lumumba was being considered.

The Station Officer said that if WI/ROGUE had been involved in an actual assassination plan, he would have transmitted messages concerning WI/ROGUE in the PROP channel. Instead, he limited distribution of the cable about WI/ROGUE in a routine manner—as a CIA officer would "normally do * * * when you speak in a derogatory manner of an asset."

Hedgman maintained that WI/ROGUE's proposition to QJ/WIN to join an "execution squad" could be attributed to WI/ROGUE's "free-wheeling" nature:

> I had difficulty controlling him in that he was not a professional intelligence officer as such. He seemed to act on his own without seeking guidance or authority * * * I found he was rather an unguided missile * * * the kind of man that could get you in trouble before you knew you were in trouble.

But Hedgman did not disavow all responsibility for WI/ROGUE's actions:

> [I]f you give a man an order and he carries it out and causes a problem for the Station, then you accept responsibility.

In sum, the testimony of the CIA officers involved in the PROP operation and the concern about WI/ROGUE's "freewheeling" in Hedgman's cable suggests that agent WI/ROGUE's attempt to form an "execution squad" was an unauthorized, maverick action, unconnected to any CIA operation. However, the fact that WI/ROGUE was to be trained in "medical immunization" precludes a definitive conclusion to that effect.

6. The Question of Whether the CIA Was Involved in Bringing About Lumumba's Death in Katanga Province

The CIA officers most closely connected with the plot to poison Lumumba testified uniformly that they knew of no CIA involvement in Lumumba's death. The Congo Station had advance knowledge of the central government's plan to transport Lumumba into the hands of his bitterest enemies, where he was likely to be killed. But there is no evidentiary basis for concluding that the CIA conspired in this plan or was connected to the events in Katanga that resulted in Lumumba's death.

{ . . . }

The contemporaneous cable traffic shows that the CIA was kept informed of Lumumba's condition and movements in January of 1961 by the Congolese and that the CIA continued to consider Lumumba a serious political threat. Despite the fact that the Station Officer knew of a plan to deliver Lumumba into the hands of his enemies at a time when the CIA was convinced that "drastic steps" were necessary to prevent Lumumba's return to power, there is no evidence of CIA involvement in this plan or in bringing about the death of Lumumba in Katanga.

There is no doubt that the CIA and the Congolese government shared a concern in January 1961 that Lumumba might return to power, particularly since the Congolese army and police were threatening to mutiny if they were not given substantial pay raises. Station Officer Hedgman reported that a mutiny "almost certainly would * * * bring about [Lumumba] return power" and said he had advised the Congolese government of his opinion that the army garrison at Leopoldville:

> WILL MUTINY WITHIN TWO OR THREE DAYS UNLESS DRASTIC ACTION TAKEN SATISFY COMPLAINTS.

Hedgman urged Headquarters to consider an immediate reaction to the crisis. This cable, which was sent through the ordinary channel, made no reference, even indirectly, to assassination, and instead recommended a different course of action.

The next day, Hedgman called Headquarters:

> STATION AND EMBASSY BELIEVE PRESENT GOVERNMENT MAY FALL WITHIN FEW DAYS. RESULT WOULD ALMOST CERTAINLY BE CHAOS AND RETURN [LUMUMBA] TO POWER.

Hedgman advised that reopening the Congolese Parliament under United Nations supervision was unacceptable because:

> THE COMBINATION OF [LUMUMBA'S] POWERS AS DEMAGOGUE, HIS ABLE USE OF GOON SQUADS AND PROPAGANDA AND SPIRIT OF DEFEAT WITHIN [GOVERNMENT] COALITION WHICH WOULD INCREASE RAPIDLY UNDER SUCH CONDITIONS WOULD ALMOST CERTAINLY INSURE [LUMUMBA] VICTORY IN PARLIAMENT. * * * REFUSAL TAKE DRASTIC STEPS AT THIS TIME WILL LEAD TO DEFEAT OF [UNITED STATES] POLICY IN CONGO.

On January 14, Hedgman was advised by a Congolese government leader that Lumumba was to be transferred from the Thysville military camp, where he had been held since shortly after Mobutu's troops captured him, to a prison in Bakwanga, the capital of another Congolese province reported to be the "home territory of * * * Lumumba's sworn enemy."

On January 17, authorities in Leopoldville placed Lumumba and two of his leading supporters, Maurice Mpolo and Joseph Okito, aboard an airplane bound for Bakwanga. Apparently the aircraft was redirected in midflight to Elisabethville in Katanga Province "when it was learned that United Nations troops were at Bakwanga airport." On February 13, the government of Katanga reported that Lumumba and his two companions escaped the previous day and died at the hands of hostile villagers.

The United Nations Commission on Investigation was "not convinced by the version of the facts given by the provincial government of Katanga." The Commission concluded, instead, that Lumumba was killed on January 17, almost immediately after his arrival in Katanga, probably with the knowledge of the central government and at the behest of the Katanga authorities:

> The Commission wishes to put on record its view that President Kasavubu and his aides, on the one hand, and the provincial government of Katanga headed by Mr. {Moïse} Tshombe on the other, should not escape responsibility for the death of Mr. Lumumba, Mr. Okito, and Mr. Mpolo. For Mr. Kasavubu and his aides had handed over Mr. Lumumba and his colleagues to the Katanga authorities knowing full well, in doing so, that they were throwing them into the hands of their bitterest political enemies. The government of the province of Katanga in turn not only failed to safeguard the lives of the three prisoners but also had, by its action, contributed, directly or indirectly, to the murder of the prisoners.

Cables from the Station Officer demonstrated no CIA involvement in the plan to transport Lumumba to Bakwanga. But the Station Officer clearly had prior knowledge of the plan to transfer Lumumba to a state where it was probable that he would be killed. Other supporters of Lumumba who had been sent to Bakwanga earlier by Leopoldville authorities

> were killed there in horrible circumstances, and the place was known as the 'slaughterhouse.' It was therefore improbable that Mr. Lumumba and his companions would have met a different fate at Bakwanga if they had been taken there.

After learning that Lumumba was to be flown to Bakwanga, the Station Officer cabled:

> IT NOW MORE IMPORTANT THAN EVER SUPPORT THOSE SINGLE ELEMENTS WHICH CAN STRENGTHEN FABRIC

> OVERALL * * * OPPOSITION [LUMUMBA]. WISH ASSURE HQS WE TRYING SHORE UP * * * DEFENSES ONLY IN TERMS OUR OWN OBJECTIVES DENY CONGO GOVT CONTROL [LUMUMBA].

Despite his perception of an urgent need to prevent Lumumba's return to power at this time, the Station Officer testified that the CIA was not involved in bringing about Lumumba's death in Katanga and that he did not have any first-hand knowledge of the circumstances of Lumumba's death.

In late November, Hedgman attended a meeting of CIA officers from African Stations with Bissell and Tweedy. Hedgman testified that he briefed Bissell and Tweedy on developments in the Congo, including Lumumba's flight from Leopoldville, but he could not recall any discussion at the meeting of the possibility of assassinating Lumumba.

Two days after Lumumba was flown to Katanga, the CIA Base Chief in Elisabethville sent an unusual message to headquarters:

> THANKS FOR PATRICE. IF WE HAD KNOWN HE WAS COMING WE WOULD HAVE BAKED A SNAKE.

The cable also reported that the Base's sources had provided "no advance word whatsoever" of Lumumba's flight to Katanga and that the Congolese central government "does not plan to liquidate Lumumba."

This cable indicates that the CIA did not have knowledge of the central government's decision to transfer Lumumba from Thysville military camp to a place where he would be in the hands of his avowed enemies. This cable indicates that the CIA was not kept informed of Lumumba's treatment after he arrived in Katanga because, according to the report of the United Nations Commission, Lumumba had already been killed when the cable was sent.

On February 10, several weeks after Lumumba died, but before his death was announced by the Katanga government, the Elisabethville Base cabled Headquarters that "Lumumba fate is best kept secret in Katanga." The cable gave different versions from several sources about Lumumba's death. Hedgman testified that the cable conformed to his recollection that the CIA "did not have any hard information" as of that date about Lumumba's fate after arrival in Katanga.

Hedgman acknowledged that the CIA was in close contact with some

Congolese officials who "quite clearly knew" that Lumumba was to be shipped to Katanga "because they were involved." But Hedgman said that these Congolese contacts "were not acting under CIA instructions if and when they did this." Tweedy and Mulroney agreed with Hedgman's account that the CIA was not involved in the events that led to Lumumba's death.

{ . . . }

B. Cuba

{ . . . }

1. The Assassination Plots

We have found concrete evidence of at least eight plots involving the CIA to assassinate Fidel Castro from 1960 to 1965. Although some of the assassination plots did not advance beyond the stage of planning and preparation, one plot, involving the use of underworld figures, reportedly twice progressed to the point of sending poison pills to Cuba and dispatching teams to commit the deed. Another plot involved furnishing weapons and other assassination devices to a Cuban dissident. The proposed assassination devices ran the gamut from high-powered rifles to poison pills, poison pens, deadly bacterial powders, and other devices which strain the imagination.

The most ironic of these plots took place on November 22, 1963—the very day that President Kennedy was shot in Dallas—when a CIA official offered a poison pen to a Cuban for use against Castro while at the same time an emissary from President Kennedy was meeting with Castro to explore the possibility of improved relations.

The following narrative sets forth the facts of assassination plots against Castro as established before the Committee by witnesses and documentary evidence. { . . . }

(*a*) *Plots: Early 1960*

(I) PLOTS TO DESTROY CASTRO'S PUBLIC IMAGE

Efforts against Castro did not begin with assassination attempts. From March through August 1960, during the last year of the Eisenhower

Administration, the CIA considered plans to undermine Castro's charismatic appeal by sabotaging his speeches. According to the 1967 Report of the CIA's Inspector General, an official in the Technical Services Division (TSD) recalled discussing a scheme to spray Castro's broadcasting studio with a chemical which produced effects similar to LSD, but the scheme was rejected because the chemical was unreliable. During this period, TSD impregnated a box of cigars with a chemical which produced temporary disorientation, hoping to induce Castro to smoke one of the cigars before delivering a speech. The Inspector General also reported a plan to destroy Castro's image as "The Beard" by dusting his shoes with thallium salts, a strong depilatory that would cause his beard to fall out. The depilatory was to be administered during a trip outside Cuba, when it was anticipated Castro would leave his shoes outside the door of his hotel room to be shined. TSD procured the chemical and tested it on animals, but apparently abandoned the scheme because Castro cancelled his trip.

(ii) Accident plot

The first action against the life of a Cuban leader sponsored by the CIA of which the Committee is aware took place in 1960. A Cuban who had volunteered to assist the CIA in gathering intelligence informed his case officer in Havana that he would probably be in contact with Raul Castro. CIA Headquarters and field stations were requested to inform the Havana Station of any intelligence needs that the Cuban might fulfill. The case officer testified that he and the Cuban contemplated only acquiring intelligence information and that assassination was not proposed by them.

The cable from the Havana Station was received at Headquarters on the night of July 20. The duty officer, who was summoned to Headquarters from his home, contacted Tracy Barnes, Deputy to Richard Bissell, CIA's Deputy Director for Plans and the man in charge of CIA's covert action directorate. The duty officer also contacted J. C. King, Chief of the Western Hemisphere Division within the Directorate for Plans.

Following their instructions, he sent a cable to the Havana Station early in the morning of July 21, stating: "Possible removal top three leaders is receiving serious consideration at HQS." The cable inquired whether the Cuban was sufficiently motivated to risk "arranging an accident" involving Raul Castro and advised that the station could "at discretion contact subject to determine willingness to cooperate and his suggestions on details."

Ten thousand dollars was authorized as payment "after successful completion," but no advance payment was permitted because of the possibility that the Cuban was a double agent. According to the case officer, this cable represented "quite a departure from the conventional activities we'd been asked to handle."

The case officer contacted the Cuban and told him of the proposal. The case officer avoided the word "assassinate" but made it clear that the CIA contemplated an "accident to neutralize this leader's [Raul's] influence." After being assured that his sons would be given a college education in the event of his death, the Cuban agreed to take a "calculated risk," limited to possibilities that might pass as accidental.

Immediately after returning to the station the case officer was told that a cable had just arrived stating: "Do not pursue ref. Would like to drop matter." This cable was signed by Tracy Barnes.

It was, of course, too late to "drop the matter" since the Cuban had already left to contact Raul Castro. When the Cuban returned, he told the case officer that he had not had an opportunity to arrange an accident.

(iii) Poison cigars

A notation in the records of the Operations Division, CIA's Office of Medical Services, indicates that on August 16, 1960, an official was given a box of Castro's favorite cigars with instructions to treat them with lethal poison. The cigars were contaminated with a botulinum toxin so potent that a person would die after putting one in his mouth. The official reported that the cigars were ready on October 7, 1960; TSD notes indicate that they were delivered to an unidentified person on February 13, 1961. The record does not disclose whether an attempt was made to pass the cigars to Castro.

(b) Use of underworld figures: Phase I (pre-Bay of Pigs)

(i) The initial plan

In August 1960, the CIA took steps to enlist members of the criminal underworld with gambling syndicate contacts to aid in assassinating Castro. The origin of the plot is uncertain. According to the 1967 Inspector General's Report,

Bissell recalls that the idea originated with J.C. King, then Chief of W. H. Division, although King now recalls having only had limited knowledge of such a plan and at a much later date-about mid-1962.

Bissell testified that:

> I remember a conversation which I would have put in early autumn or late summer between myself and Colonel Edwards [Director of the Office of Security], and I have some dim recollection of some earlier conversation I had had with Colonel J. C. King, Chief of the Western Hemisphere Division, and the subject matter of both of those conversations was a capability to eliminate Castro if such action should be decided upon.

The earliest concrete evidence of the operation is a conversation between DDP Bissell and Colonel Sheffield Edwards, Director of the Office of Security. Edwards recalled that Bissell asked him to locate someone who could assassinate Castro. Bissell confirmed that he requested Edwards to find someone to assassinate Castro and believed that Edwards raised the idea of contacting members of a gambling syndicate operating in Cuba.

Edwards assigned the mission to the Chief of the Operational Support Division of the Office of Security. The Support Chief recalled that Edwards had said that he and Bissell were looking for someone to "eliminate" or "assassinate" Castro.

Edwards and the Support Chief decided to rely on Robert A. Maheu to recruit someone "tough enough" to handle the job. Maheu was an ex-FBI agent who had entered into a career as a private investigator in 1954. A former FBI associate of Maheu's was employed in the CIA's Office of Security and had arranged for the CIA to use Maheu in several sensitive covert operations in which "he didn't want to have an Agency person or a government person get caught." Maheu was initially paid a monthly retainer by the CIA of $500, but it was terminated after his detective agency became more lucrative. The Operational Support Chief had served as Maheu's case officer since the Agency first began using Maheu's services, and by 1960 they had become close personal friends.

Sometime in late August or early September 1960, the Support Chief approached Maheu about the proposed operation. As Maheu recalls the conversation, the Support Chief asked him to contact John Rosselli, an underworld figure with possible gambling contacts in Las Vegas, to determine if he would participate in a plan to "dispose" of Castro. The Support Chief testified, on the other hand, that it was Maheu who raised the idea of using Rosselli.

Maheu had known Rosselli since the late 1950s. Although Maheu claims not to have been aware of the extent of Rosselli's underworld connections and activities, he recalled that "it was certainly evident to me that he was able to accomplish things in Las Vegas when nobody else seemed to get the same kind of attention."

The Support Chief had previously met Rosselli at Maheu's home. The Support Chief and Maheu each claimed that the other had raised the idea of using Rosselli, and Maheu said the Chief was aware that Rosselli had contacts with the gambling syndicate.

At first Maheu was reluctant to become involved in the operation because it might interfere with his relationship with his new client, Howard Hughes. He finally agreed to participate because he felt that he owed the Agency a commitment. The Inspector General's Report states that:

> Edwards and Maheu agreed that Maheu would approach Rosselli as the representative of businessmen with interests in Cuba who saw the elimination of Castro as the first essential step to the recovery of their investments.

The Support Chief also recalled that Maheu was to use this cover story when he presented the plan to Rosselli, but Rosselli said that the story was developed after he had been contacted, and was used as a mutual "cover" by him, the Chief, and Maheu in dealing with Cubans who were subsequently recruited for the project. The Support Chief testified that Maheu was told to offer money, probably $150,000, for Castro's assassination.

(II) Contact with the syndicate

According to Rosselli, he and Maheu met at the Brown Derby Restaurant in Beverly Hills in early September 1960. Rosselli testified that Maheu told him that "high government officials" needed his cooperation in getting rid of Castro, and that he asked him to help recruit Cubans to do the job. Maheu's recollection of that meeting was that "I informed him that I had been asked by my Government to solicit his cooperation in this particular venture."

Maheu stated that Rosselli "was very hesitant about participating in the project, and he finally said that he felt that he had an obligation to his government, and he finally agreed to participate." Maheu and Rosselli both testified that Rosselli insisted on meeting with a representative of the Government.

A meeting was arranged for Maheu and Rosselli with the Support Chief at the Plaza Hotel in New York. The Inspector General's Report placed the meeting on September 14, 1960. Rosselli testified that he could not recall the precise date of the meeting, but that it had occurred during Castro's visit to the United Nations, which the *New York Times* Index places from September 18 through September 28, 1960.

The Support Chief testified that he was introduced to Rosselli as a business associate of Maheu. He said that Maheu told Rosselli that Maheu represented international business interests which were pooling money to pay for the assassination of Castro. Rosselli claimed that Maheu told him at that time that the Support Chief was with the CIA.

It was arranged that Rosselli would go to Florida and recruit Cubans for the operation. Edwards informed Bissell that contact had been made with the gambling syndicate.

During the week of September 24, 1960, the Support Chief, Maheu, and Rosselli met in Miami to work out the details of the operation. Rosselli used the cover name "John Rawlston" and represented himself to the Cuban contacts as an agent of "* * * some business interests of Wall Street that had * * * nickel interests and properties around in Cuba, and I was getting financial assistance from them."

Maheu handled the details of setting up the operation and keeping the Support Chief informed of developments. After Rosselli and Maheu had been in Miami for a short time, and certainly prior to October 18. Rosselli introduced Maheu to two individuals on whom Rosselli intended to rely: "Sam Gold," who would serve as a "back-up man," or "key" man, and "Joe," whom "Gold" said would serve as a courier to Cuba and make arrangements there. The Support Chief, who was using the name "Jim Olds," said he had met "Sam" and "Joe" once, and then only briefly.

The Support Chief testified that he learned the true identities of his associates one morning when Maheu called and asked him to examine the "Parade" supplement to the *Miami Times.* An article on the Attorney General's ten-most-wanted criminals list revealed that "Sam Gold" was Momo Salvatore Giancana, a Chicago-based gangster, and "Joe" was Santos Trafficante, the Cosa Nostra chieftain in Cuba. The Support Chief reported his discovery to Edwards but did not know whether Edwards reported this fact to his superiors. The Support Chief testified that this incident occurred after "we were up to our ears in it," a month or so after Giancana had been brought into the operation, but prior to giving the poison pills to Rosselli.

Maheu recalled that it was Giancana's job to locate someone in Castro's entourage who could accomplish the assassination and that he met almost daily with Giancana over a substantial period of time. Although Maheu described Giancana as playing a "key role," Rosselli claimed that none of the Cubans eventually used in the operation were acquired through Giancana's contacts.

(iii) Las Vegas wiretap

In late October 1960, Maheu arranged for a Florida investigator, Edward DuBois, to place an electronic "bug" in a room in Las Vegas. DuBois' employee, Arthur J. Balletti, flew to Las Vegas and installed a tap on the phone. The Support Chief characterized the ensuing events as a "Keystone Comedy act." On October 31, 1960, Balletti, believing that the apartment would be vacant for the afternoon, left the wiretap equipment unattended. A maid discovered the equipment and notified the local sheriff, who arrested Balletti and brought him to the jail. Balletti called Maheu in Miami, tying "Maheu into this thing up to his ear." Balletti's bail was paid by Rosselli.

(1) CIA Involvement in the Wiretap.—The Committee received conflicting evidence on whether the Agency was consulted prior to the installation of the tap. The Support Chief testified that he had called Edwards and cleared the placement of an electronic "bug" in the apartment prior to the installation of the tap. Maheu recalled that he had initially asked the Support Chief if the CIA would handle the job, and that the Chief had told him that:

> He would call Mr. Edwards and see if they would have the capability of accomplishing this * * * and that subsequently he informed me that

> Mr. Edwards had said that they would not do it, but approved paying for it if we hired an independent private detective to put it on.

On the other hand, Edwards, in a May 14, 1962 memorandum for the Attorney General { . . . } stated that "At the time of the incident neither the Agency nor the undersigned knew of the proposed technical installation."

The Inspector General's Report accepted Edwards' assertion that "the Agency was first unwitting and then a reluctant accessory after the fact," but offered no further evidence to support that contention.

The Committee also received conflicting evidence concerning whether the tap had been placed to keep Giancana in Miami or to check on security leaks. The Support Chief testified that during the early stages of negotiations with the gambling syndicate, Maheu informed him that a girlfriend of Giancana was having an affair with the target of the tap. Giancana wanted Maheu to bug that person's room; otherwise, Giancana threatened to fly to Las Vegas himself. Maheu was concerned that Giancana's departure would disrupt the negotiations, and secured the Chief's permission to arrange for a bug to insure Giancana's presence and cooperation. Maheu substantially confirmed this account.

There is some evidence, however, suggesting that the CIA itself may have instituted the tap to determine whether Giancana was leaking information about his involvement in an assassination attempt against Castro. An October 18, 1960 memorandum from J. Edgar Hoover to Bissell, stated that "a source whose reliability has not been tested" reported:

> [D]uring recent conversations with several friends, Giancana stated that Fidel Castro was to be done away with very shortly. When doubt was expressed regarding this statement, Giancana reportedly assured those present that Castro's assassination would occur in November. Moreover, he allegedly indicated that he had already met with the assassin-to-be on three occasions. * * * Giancana claimed that everything has been perfected for the killing of Castro, and that the "assassin" had arranged with a girl, not further described, to drop a "pill" in some drink or food of Castro's.

Rosselli testified that Maheu had given him two explanations for the tap on different occasions: First, that Giancana was concerned that his girlfriend was having an affair; and, second, that he had arranged the tap to determine whether Giancana had told his girlfriend about the assassination plot, and whether she was spreading the story. Maheu gave the second explanation to the FBI when he was questioned about his involvement in the tap, and Edwards wrote in the memorandum to the Attorney General:

> Maheu stated that Sam Giancana thought that [Giancana's girlfriend] might know of the proposed operation and might pass on the information to * * * a friend of [Giancana's girlfriend].

(2) Consequences of the Wiretap.—Edwards told Maheu that if he was "approached by the FBI, he could refer them to me to be briefed that he was engaged in an intelligence operation directed at Cuba." FBI records indicate that on April 18, 1961, Maheu informed the FBI that the tap involved the CIA, and suggested that Edwards be contacted. Edwards subsequently informed the Bureau that the CIA would object to Maheu's prosecution because it might reveal sensitive information relating to the abortive Bay of Pigs invasion.

In a memo dated April 24, 1962, Herbert J. Miller, Assistant Attorney General, Criminal Division, advised the Attorney General that the "national interest" would preclude any prosecutions based upon the tap. Following a briefing of the Attorney General by the CIA, a decision was made not to prosecute.

(IV) POISON IS PREPARED AND DELIVERED TO CUBA

The Inspector General's Report described conversations among Bissell, Edwards, and the Chief of the Technical Services Division (TSD) concerning the most effective method of poisoning Castro. There is some evidence that Giancana or Rosselli originated the idea of depositing a poison pill in Castro's drink to give the "asset" a chance to escape. The Support Chief recalled Rosselli's request for something "nice and clean, without getting into any kind of out and out ambushing," preferably a poison that would disappear without a trace. The Inspector General's Report cited the Support Chief as stating that the Agency had first considered a "gangland-style killng" in which Castro would be gunned down. Giancana reportedly opposed the idea because it would be difficult to recruit someone for such a dangerous operation, and suggested instead the use of poison.

Edwards rejected the first batch of pills prepared by TSD because they would not dissolve in water. A second batch, containing botulinum toxin, "did the job expected of them" when tested on monkeys. The Support Chief received the pills from TSD, probably in February 1961, with assurances that they were lethal, and then gave them to Rosselli.

The record clearly establishes that the pills were given to a Cuban for delivery to the island some time prior to the Bay of Pigs invasion in mid-April 1961. There are discrepancies in the record, however, concerning whether one or two attempts were made during that period, and the precise date on which the passage(s) occurred. The Inspector General's Report states that in late February or March 1961, Rosselli reported to the Support Chief that the pills had been delivered to an official close to Castro who may have received kickbacks from the gambling interests. The Report states that the official returned the pills after a few weeks, perhaps because he had lost his position in the Cuban Government, and thus access to Castro, before he received the pills. The Report concludes that yet another attempt was made in April 1961, with the aid of a leading figure in the Cuban exile movement.

Rosselli and the Support Chief testified that the Cuban official described by the Inspector General as having made the first attempt was indeed involved in the assassination plot, and they ascribed his failure to a case of "cold feet." Rosselli was certain, however, that only one attempt to assassinate Castro had been made prior to the Bay of Pigs, and the Support Chief and Maheu did not clarify the matter. It is possible, then, that only one pre-Bay of Pigs attempt was made and that the Cuban exile leader was the contact in the United States who arranged for the Cuban described in the Inspector General's Report to administer the poison.

In any event, Rosselli told the Support Chief that Trafficante believed a certain leading figure in the Cuban exile movement might be able to accomplish the assassination. The Inspector General's Report suggests that this Cuban may have been receiving funds from Trafficante and other racketeers interested in securing "gambling, prostitution, and dope monopolies" in Cuba after the overthrow of Castro. The Report speculated that the Cuban was interested in the assassination scheme as a means of financing the purchase of arms and communications equipment.

The Cuban claimed to have a contact inside a restaurant frequented by Castro. As a prerequisite to the deal, he demanded cash and $1,000 worth of communications equipment. The Support Chief recalled that Colonel J. C. King, head of the Western Hemisphere Division, gave him $50,000 in

Bissell's office to pay the Cuban if he successfully assassinated Castro. The Support Chief stated that Bissell also authorized him to give the Cuban the requested electronics equipment.

Bissell testified that he did not doubt that some cash was given to the Support Chief, and that he was aware that the poison pills had been prepared. Bissell did not recall the meeting described above, and considered it unlikely that the Support Chief would have been given the money in his office. The Inspector General's Report, relying on an Office of Security memorandum to the DDCI dated June 24, 1966, as well as on an interview with the person who signed the voucher for the funds, placed the amount passed at $10,000. If the Inspector General's conclusions were correct, the funds which Bissell allegedly authorized were probably the advance payment to the Cuban, and not the $150,000 that was to be paid to him after Castro's death.

The record does clearly reflect, however, that communications equipment was delivered to the Cuban and that he was paid advance money to cover his expenses, probably in the amount of $10,000. The money and pills were delivered at a meeting between Maheu, Rosselli, Trafficante, and the Cuban at the Fontainebleau Hotel in Miami. As Rosselli recalled, Maheu

> * * * opened his briefcase and dumped a whole lot of money on his lap * * * and also came up with the capsules and he explained how they were going to be used. As far as I remember, they couldn't be used in boiling soups and things like that, but they could be used in water or otherwise, but they couldn't last forever. * * * It had to be done as quickly as possible.

A different version of the delivery of the pills to the Cuban was given to the Committee by Joseph Shimon, a friend of Rosselli and Giancana who testified that he was present when the passage occurred. Shimon testified that he had accompanied Maheu to Miami to see the third Patterson-Johansson World Heavyweight Championship fight, which took place on March 12, 1961. According to Shimon, he, Giancana, Rosselli, and Maheu shared a suite in the Fontainebleau Hotel. During a conversation, Maheu stated that he had a "contract" to assassinate Castro, and had been provided with a "liquid" by the CIA to accomplish the task. Shimon testified that Maheu had said the liquid was to be put in Castro's food, that Castro would become ill and die after two or three days, and that an autopsy would not reveal what had killed him.

Shimon testified that the Cuban was contacted outside the Boom Boom Room of the Fontainebleau Hotel. Shimon said that Rosselli left with the Cuban, and that Maheu said, "Johnny's going to handle everything, this is Johnny's contract." Shimon testified that Giancana subsequently told him "I am not in it, and they are asking me for the names of some guys who used to work in casinos. * * * Maheu's conning the hell out of the CIA."

Shimon testified that a few days later, he received a phone call from Maheu, who said: "* * * did you see the paper? Castro's ill. He's going to be sick two or three days. Wow, we got him."

Rosselli testified that he did not recall Shimon's having been present when the pills were delivered to the Cuban. Maheu recalled having seen the fight with Rosselli and Giancana, but did not recall whether Shimon had been present, and denied that the poison had been delivered in the lobby of the Fontainebleau.

The attempt met with failure. According to the Inspector General's Report, Edwards believed the scheme failed because Castro stopped visiting the restaurant where the "asset" was employed. Maheu suggested an alternative reason. He recalled being informed that after the pills had been delivered to Cuba, "the go signal still had to be received before in fact they were administered." He testified that he was informed by the Support Chief sometime after the operation that the Cubans had an opportunity to administer the pills to Fidel Castro and either Che Guevarra or Raul Castro, but that the "go signal" never came. Maheu did not know who was responsible for giving the signal. The Cuban subsequently returned the cash and the pills.

The date of the Cuban operation is unclear. The Inspector General's Report places it in March–April 1961, prior to the Bay of Pigs. Shimon's testimony puts it around March 12, 1961. Bissell testified that the effort against Castro was called off after the Bay of Pigs, and Maheu testified that he had no involvement in the operation after the Bay of Pigs. The Support Chief however, was certain that it occurred during early 1962.

(*c*) *Use of underworld figures: Phase II (Post–Bay of Pigs)*

(I) CHANGE IN LEADERSHIP

The Inspector General's Report divides the gambling syndicate operation into Phase I, terminating with the Bay of Pigs, and Phase II, continuing with the transfer of the operation to William Harvey in late 1961. The distinction between a clearly demarcated Phase I and Phase II may be an artificial one, as there is considerable evidence that the operation was continuous, perhaps lying dormant for the period immediately following the Bay of Pigs.

In early 1961, Harvey was assigned the responsibility for establishing a general capability within the CIA for disabling foreign leaders, including assassination as a "last resort." The capability was called Executive Action and was later included under the cryptonym ZR/RIFLE. Executive Action and the evidence relating to its connection to the "White House" and to whether or not it involved action as well as "capability" is discussed extensively [in subsequent sections of the Interim Report].

Harvey's notes reflect that Bissell asked him to take over the gambling syndicate operation from Edwards and that they discussed the "application of ZR/RIFLE program to Cuba" on November 16, 1961. Bissell confirmed that the conversation took place and accepted the November date as accurate. He also testified that the operation "was not reactivated, in other words, no instructions went out to Rosselli or to others * * * to renew the attempt, until after I had left the Agency in February 1962." Harvey agreed that his conversation with Bissell was limited to exploring the feasibility of using the gambling syndicate against Castro.

Richard Helms replaced Bissell as DDP in February 1962. As such, he was Harvey's superior. The degree to which Helms knew about and participated in the assassination plot is discussed in the section of this Report dealing with the level to which the plots were authorized within the Agency.

(II) The operation is reactivated

In early April 1962, Harvey, who testified that he was acting on "explicit orders" from Helms, requested Edwards to put him in touch with Rosselli. The Support Chief first introduced Harvey to Rosselli in Miami, where Harvey told Rosselli to maintain his Cuban contacts, but not to deal with Maheu or Giancana, whom he had decided were "untrustworthy" and "surplus." The Support Chief recalled that initially Rosselli did not trust Harvey although they subsequently developed a close friendship.

Harvey, the Support Chief and Rosselli met for a second time in New

York on April 8–9, 1962. A notation made during this time in the files of the Technical Services Division indicates that four poison pills were given to the Support Chief on April 18, 1962. The pills were passed to Harvey, who arrived in Miami on April 21, and found Rosselli already in touch with the same Cuban who had been involved in the pre-Bay of Pigs pill passage. He gave the pills to Rosselli, explaining that "these would work anywhere and at any time with anything." Rosselli testified that he told Harvey that the Cubans intended to use the pills to assassinate Che Guevara as well as Fidel and Raul Castro. According to Rosselli's testimony, Harvey approved of the targets, stating "everything is all right, what they want to do."

The Cuban requested arms and equipment as a *quid pro quo* for carrying out the assassination operation. With the help of the CIA's Miami station which ran covert operations against Cuba (JM/WAVE), Harvey procured explosives, detonators, rifles, handguns, radios, and boat radar costing about $5,000. Harvey and the chief of the JM/WAVE station rented a U-Haul truck under an assumed name and delivered the equipment to a parking lot. The keys were given to Rosselli, who watched the delivery with the Support Chief from across the street. The truckload of equipment was finally picked up by either the Cuban or Rosselli's agent. Harvey testified that the arms "could" have been for use in the assassination attempt, but that they were not given to the Cuban solely for that purpose.

Rosselli kept Harvey informed of the operation's progress. Sometime in May 1962, he reported that the pills and guns had arrived in Cuba. On June 21, he told Harvey that the Cuban had dispatched a three-man team to Cuba. The Inspector General's report described the team's mission as "vague" and conjectured that the team would kill Castro or recruit others to do the job, using the poison pills if the opportunity arose.

Harvey met Rosselli in Miami on September 7 and 11, 1962. The Cuban was reported to be preparing to send in another three-man team to penetrate Castro's bodyguard. Harvey was told that the pills, referred to as "the medicine," were still "safe" in Cuba.

Harvey testified that by this time he had grave doubts about whether the operation would ever take place, and told Rosselli that "there's not much likelihood that this is going anyplace, or that it should be continued." The second team never left for Cuba, claiming that "conditions" in Cuba were not right. During early January 1963, Harvey paid Rosselli $2,700 to defray the Cuban's expenses. Harvey terminated the operation in mid-February

1963. At a meeting with Rosselli in Los Angeles, it was agreed that Rosselli would taper off his communications with the Cubans. Rosselli testified that he simply broke off contact with the Cubans. However, he never informed them that the offer of $150,000 for Castro's assassination had been withdrawn.

The agency personnel who dealt with Rosselli attributed his motivation to patriotism and testified that he was not paid for his services. According to the Support Chief, Rosselli "paid his way, he paid his own hotel fees, he paid his own travel. * * * And he never took a nickel, he said, no, as long as it is for the Government of the United States, this is the least I can do, because I owe it a lot."

Edwards agreed that Rosselli was "never paid a cent," and Maheu testified that "Giancana was paid nothing at all, not even for expenses, and that Mr. Rosselli was given a pittance that did not even begin to cover his expenses." It is clear, however, that the CIA did pay Rosselli's hotel bill during his stay in Miami in October 1960. The CIA's involvement with Rosselli caused the Agency some difficulty during Rosselli's subsequent prosecutions for fraudulent gambling activities and living in the country under an assumed name.

(*d*) *Plans in early 1963*

Two plans to assassinate Castro were explored by Task Force W, the CIA section then concerned with covert Cuban operations, in early 1963. Desmond Fitzgerald (now deceased), Chief of the Task Force, asked his assistant to determine whether an exotic seashell, rigged to explode, could be deposited in an area where Castro commonly went skin diving. The idea was explored by the Technical Services Division and discarded as impractical.

A second plan involved having James Donovan (who was negotiating with Castro for the release of prisoners taken during the Bay of Pigs operation) present Castro with a contaminated diving suit.

The Inspector General's Report dates this operation in January 1963, when Fitzgerald replaced Harvey as Chief of Task Force W, although it is unclear whether Harvey or Fitzgerald conceived the plan. It is likely that the activity took place earlier, since Donovan had completed his negotiations by the middle of January 1963. Helms characterized the plan as "cockeyed."

The Technical Services Division bought a diving suit, dusted the inside with a fungus that would produce a chronic skin disease (Madura foot), and contaminated the breathing apparatus with a tubercule bacillus. The Inspector General's Report states that the plan was abandoned because Donovan gave Castro a different diving suit on his own initiative. Helms testified that the diving suit never left the laboratory.

(e) *AM/LASH*

(I) Origin of the project

In early 1961, a CIA official met with a highly-placed Cuban official to determine if the Cuban would cooperate in efforts against the Castro regime. The Cuban was referred to by the cryptonym AM/LASH. The meeting was inconclusive, but led to subsequent meetings at which AM/LASH agreed to cooperate with the CIA.

The CIA regarded AM/LASH as an important "asset" inside Cuba. As a high-ranking leader who enjoyed the confidence of Fidel Castro, AM/LASH could keep the CIA informed of the internal workings of the regime. It was also believed that he might play a part in fomenting a coup within Cuba.

From the first contact with AM/LASH until the latter part of 1963, it was uncertain whether he would defect or remain in Cuba. His initial requests to the CIA and FBI for aid in defecting were rebuffed. When Case Officer 1 joined the operation in June 1962, his assignment was to ensure that AM/LASH would "stay in place and report to us." At a meeting in the fall of 1963, AM/LASH stated that he would remain in Cuba if he "could do something really significant for the creation of a new Cuba" and expressed a desire to plan the "execution" of Fidel Castro. The subject of assassinating Castro was again discussed by AM/LASH and the case officer at another meeting a few days later. The case officer's contact report states that assassination was raised in discussing AM/LASH's role in Cuba, and that AM/LASH was visibly upset. "It was not the act that he objected to, but merely the choice of the word used to describe it. 'Eliminate' was acceptable."

Each case officer testified that he did not ask AM/LASH to assassinate Castro. The record clearly reveals, however, that both officers were aware of his desire to take such action. A cable to Headquarters reporting on a 1963 meeting with AM/LASH stated:

> Have no intention give AM/LASH physical elimination mission as requirement but recognize this something he could or might try to carry out on his own initiative.

At a meeting late in the fall of 1963, AM/LASH again raised the possibility of defecting, but indicated that he would be willing to continue working against the Castro Regime if he received firm assurances of American support. According to Case Officer 2, AM/LASH requested military supplies, a device with which to protect himself if his plots against Castro were discovered, and a meeting with Attorney General Robert Kennedy.

Desmond Fitzgerald, Chief of the Special Affairs Staff, agreed to meet AM/LASH and give him the assurances he sought. The Inspector General's Report states that Fitzgerald consulted with the DDP, Helms, who agreed that Fitzgerald should hold himself out as a personal representative of Attorney General Kennedy.

Helms testified that he did not recall the conversation with Fitzgerald. He also said that he had not consulted the Attorney General and speculated that his reason for not having done so might have been because "this was so central to the whole theme of what we had been trying to do * * * (find someone inside Cuba who might head a government and have a group to replace Castro). This is obviously what we had been pushing, what everybody had been pushing for us to try to do, and it is in that context that I would have made some remark like this."

Helms recalled that he told Fitzgerald to "go ahead and say that from the standpoint of political support, the United States government will be behind you if you are successful. This had nothing to do with killings. This had only to do with the political action part of it."

Fitzgerald met AM/LASH in late fall 1963 and promised him that the United States would support a coup against Castro. When later interviewed for the Inspector General's Report, Fitzgerald recalled that AM/LASH repeatedly requested an assassination weapon, particularly a "high-powered rifle with telescopic sights that could be used to kill Castro from a distance." Fitzgerald stated that he told AM/LASH that the United States would have "no part of an attempt on Castro's life." Case Officer 2 recalled that AM/LASH raised the prospect of assassinating Castro, but did not propose an explicit plan. AM/LASH was, however, "convinced that Castro had to be removed from power before a coup could be undertaken in Cuba."

AM/LASH also requested high-powered rifles and grenades. A memorandum by Case Officer 2 states:

> C/SAS [Fitzgerald] approved telling AM/LASH he would be given a cache inside Cuba. Cache could, if he requested it, include * * *high-powered rifles with scopes * * *.

AM/LASH was told on November 22, 1963 that the cache would be dropped in Cuba.

(II) THE POISON PEN DEVICE

Another device offered to AM/LASH was a ball-point pen rigged with a hypodermic needle. The needle was designed to be so fine that the victim would not notice its insertion.

According to the Inspector General's Report, when Case Officer 2 was interviewed in 1967, he stated that AM/LASH had requested the Agency to "devise some technical means of doing the job that would not automatically cause him to lose his own life in the try."

The Report concluded that "although none of the participants so stated, it may be inferred that they were seeking a means of assassination of a sort that AM/LASH might reasonably have been expected to have devised himself."

Fitzgerald's assistant told the Committee that the pen was intended to show "bona fides" and "the orders were to do something to get rid of Castro * * * and we thought this other method might work whereas a rifle wouldn't."

Helms confirmed that the pen was manufactured "to take care of a request from him that he have some device for getting rid of Castro, for killing him, murdering him, whatever the case may be." "* * * [t]his was a temporizing gesture."

On November 22, 1963, Fitzgerald and the case officer met with AM/LASH and offered him the poison pen, recommending that he use Blackleaf-40, a deadly poison which is commercially available. The Inspector General's Report noted that "it is likely that at the very moment President Kennedy was shot a CIA officer was meeting with a Cuban agent * * * and giving him an assassination device for use against Castro."

The case officer later recalled that AM/LASH did not "think much of the device," and complained that CIA could surely "come up with something more sophisticated than that."

The case officer recalled offering the pen to AM/LASH, but could not remember whether AM/LASH threw it away then or took it with him. He did recall that AM/LASH said he would not take the pen back to Cuba, but did not know what AM/LASH in fact did with the pen.

An entry in the CIA AM/LASH files written in 1965 states:

> Although Fitzgerald and the case officer assured AM/LASH on November 22, 1963 that CIA would give him everything he needed (telescopic sight, silencer, all the money he wanted) the situation changed when the case officer and Fitzgerald left the meeting to discover that President Kennedy had been assassinated. Because of this fact, plans with AM/LASH changed and it was decided that we could have no part in the assassination of a government leader (including Castro) and would not aid AM/LASH in this attempt * * * AM/LASH was not informed of (this decision) until he was seen by the case officer in November, 1964.

In fact, however, assassination efforts involving AM/LASH continued into 1965.

(III) Providing AM/LASH with arms

CIA cables indicate that one cache of arms for AM/LASH was delivered in Cuba in March 1964 and another in June. An entry in the AM/LASH file for May 5, 1964 states that the case officer requested the Technical Services Division to produce, on a "crash basis," a silencer which would fit an FAL rifle. The contact report of a meeting between the case officer and a confidante of AM/LASH states that AM/LASH was subsequently informed that it was not feasible to make a silencer for an FAL rifle.

Toward the latter part of 1964, AM/LASH became more insistent that the assassination of the Cuban leadership was a necessary initial step in a successful coup. A memorandum written in the fall of 1964 stated:

> AM/LASH was told and fully understands that the United States Government cannot become involved to any degree in the "first step" of his plan. If he needs support, he realizes he will have to get

> it elsewhere. FYI: This is where B-1 could fit in nicely in giving any support he would request.

Documents in the AM/LASH file establish that in early 1965, the CIA put AM/LASH in contact with B-1, the leader of an anti-Castro group. As the Case Officer explained to the Inspector General:

> * * * What had happened was that SAS had contrived to put B-1 and AM/LASH together in such a way that neither of them knew that the contact had been engineered by CIA. The thought was that B-1 needed a man inside and AM/LASH wanted a silenced weapon, which CIA was unwilling to furnish to him directly. By putting the two together, B-1 might get its man inside Cuba and AM/LASH might get his silenced weapon-from B-1.

A report of a meeting between a case officer and B-1 states that B-1, in his initial contacts with AM/LASH, discussed plans for assassinating Castro. AM/LASH suggested that guerrilla raids against Cuba should be stepped up one month before the "attempt on Fidel Castro" to "prepare the public and raise the morale and resistance spirit of the people." B-1 reported that:

> AM/LASH believed that the only solution to the problems in Cuba would be to get rid of Fidel Castro. He is able either to shoot him with a silencer or place a bomb in some place where Fidel will be. He might use, for example, a small bomb, that he can carry and place, or with his group attack the residence where Fidel lives * * * B-1 is going to provide AM/LASH with escape routes and places where B-1 is able to pick him up. He will memorize these points and escape routes * * * Next, B-1 is to provide AM/LASH either a silencer for a FAL or a rifle with a silencer.

A CIA document dated January 3, 1965 states that B-1, in a lengthy interview with a case officer, said that he and AM/LASH had reached firm agreement on the following points:

> 1. B-1 is to provide AM/LASH with a silencer for the FAL; if this is impossible, B-1 is to cache in a designated location a rifle with a scope

and silencer plus several bombs, concealed either in a suitcase, a lamp or some other concealment device which he would be able to carry, and place next to Fidel Castro.

2. B-1 is to provide AM/LASH with escape routes controlled by B-1 and not by the Americans. The lack of confidence built up by the Bay of Pigs looms large.

3. B-1 is to prepare one of the western provinces, either Pinar del Rio or Havana, with arms caches and a clandestine underground mechanism. This would be a fall back position and a safe area where men and weapons are available to the group.

4. B-1 is to be in Cuba one week before the elimination of Fidel, but no one, including AM/LASH, will know B-l's location.

5. B-1 is to arrange for recognition by at least five Latin American countries as soon as Fidel is neutralized and a junta is formed. This junta will be established even though Raul Castro and Che Guevara may still be alive and may still be in control of part of the country. This is the reason AM/LASH requested that B-1 be able to establish some control over one of the provinces so that the junta can be formed in that location.

6. One month to the day before the neutralization of Fidel, B-1 will increase the number of commando attacks to a maximum in order to raise the spirit and morale of the people inside Cuba. In all communiques, in all radio messages, in all propaganda put out by B-1 he must relate that the raid was possible thanks to the information received from clandestine sources inside Cuba and from the clandestine underground apparatus directed by "P." This will be AM/LASH's war name.

A CIA cable dated in early 1965 stated that B-1 had given AM/LASH a silencer and that AM/LASH had "small, highly concentrated explosives." Shortly afterwards, a CIA station cabled that AM/LASH would soon receive "one pistol with silencer and one FAL rifle with a silencer from B-l's secretary." A subsequent cable reported that "B-1 had three packages of special items made up by his technical people and delivered to AM/LASH." In June 1965, CIA terminated all contact with AM/LASH and his associates for reasons related to security.

{...}

D. Trujillo

1. Summary

Rafael Trujillo was assassinated by a group of Dominican dissidents on May 30, 1961.

Trujillo was a brutal dictator, and both the Eisenhower and Kennedy Administrations encouraged the overthrow of his regime by Dominican dissidents. Toward that end the highest policy levels of both Administrations approved or condoned supplying arms to the dissidents. Although there is no evidence that the United States instigated any assassination activity, certain evidence tends to link United States officials to the assassination plans.

Material support, consisting of three pistols and three carbines, was supplied to various dissidents. While United States' officials knew that the dissidents intended to overthrow Trujillo, probably by assassination, there is no direct evidence that the weapons which were passed were used in the assassination. The evidence is inconclusive as to how high in the two Administrations information about the dissidents' assassination plots had been passed prior to the spring of 1961.

Beginning in March of 1961, the dissidents began asking United States officials for machine guns. By the time four M-3 machine guns were shipped to the CIA Station in the Dominican capital in April, it was well known that the dissidents wanted them for use in connection with the assassination. Thereafter, however, permission to deliver the machine guns to the dissidents was denied, and the guns were never passed. The day before the assassination a cable, personally authorized by President Kennedy, was sent to the United States' Consul General in the Dominican Republic stating that the United States Government, as a matter of general policy, could not condone political assassination, but at the same time indicating the United States continued to support the dissidents and stood ready to recognize them in the event they were successful in their endeavor to overthrow Trujillo.

2. Background

Rafael Trujillo came to power in the Dominican Republic in 1930. For most of his tenure, the United States Government supported him and he was regarded throughout much of the Caribbean and Latin America as a protege of the United States. Trujillo's rule, always harsh and dictatorial, became more arbitrary during the 1950s. As a result, the United States' image was increasingly tarnished in the eyes of many Latin Americans.

Increasing American awareness of Trujillo's brutality and fear that it would lead to a Castro-type revolution caused United States' officials to consider various plans to hasten his abdication or downfall.

As early as February 1960, the Eisenhower Administration gave high level consideration to a program of covert aid to Dominican dissidents. In April 1960 President Eisenhower approved a contingency plan for the Dominican Republic which provided, in part, that if the situation deteriorated still further:

> * * * the United States would immediately take political action to remove Trujillo from the Dominican Republic as soon as a suitable successor regime can be induced to take over with the assurance of U.S. political, economic, and—if necessary—military support.

Simultaneously, the United States was trying to organize hemispheric opposition to the Castro regime in Cuba. Latin American leaders, such as President Betancourt of Venezuela, pressed the United States to take affirmative action against Trujillo to dispel criticism that the U.S. opposed dictatorships of the left only. A belief that Castro's road to power was paved by the excesses of Batista led to concern that the Dominican Republic might also eventually fall victim to a Castro-style Communist regime.

3. Initial Contact with Dissidents and Request for Arms

During the spring of 1960, the U.S. Ambassador to the Dominican Republic, Joseph Farland, made initial contact with dissidents who sought to free their country from Trujillo's grasp. They asked for sniper rifles. Although documentary evidence indicates that a recommendation to provide these rifles was approved both within the State Department and the CIA, the rifles were never provided.

(*a*) *Dissident contacts*

Ambassador Farland established contact with a group of dissidents regarded as moderate, pro-United States and desirous of establishing a democratic form of government. Prior to his final departure from the

Dominican Republic in May 1960, the Ambassador introduced his Deputy Chief-of-Mission, Henry Dearborn, to the dissident leaders, indicating that Dearborn could be trusted. Then on June 16, 1960, CIA Headquarters cabled a request that Dearborn become the "communications link" between the dissidents and CIA. The cable stated that Dearborn's role had the "*unofficial* approval of [Assistant Secretary of State for Inter-American Affairs, Roy R.] Rubottom." (Emphasis in original.)

Dearborn agreed. He requested, however, that the CIA confirm the arrangement with the dissidents as being that the United States would "clandestinely" assist the opposition to "develop effective force to accomplish Trujillo overthrow," but would not "undertake any overt action itself against Trujillo government while it is in full control of Dominican Republic." CIA Headquarters confirmed Dearborn's understanding of the arrangement.

(*b*) *The request for sniper rifles*

During the course of a cocktail party in the Dominican Republic, a leading dissident made a specific request to Ambassador Farland for a limited number of rifles with telescopic sights. The Ambassador promised to pass on the request. He apparently did so after returning to Washington in May 1960.

Documents indicate that consideration was given within the CIA to airdropping rifles into the Dominican Republic. At a June 21, 1960, meeting with an officer of the CIA's Western Hemisphere Division, Ambassador Farland reportedly suggested possible sites for the drops.

Documents also indicate that a meeting was held around the end of June 1960 between Assistant Secretary of State for Inter-American Affairs Roy R. Rubottom and Col. J. C. King, Chief of CIA's Western Hemisphere Division. Apparently King sought to learn the Assistant Secretary's view regarding "[to] what extent will the U.S. government participate in the overthrow of Trujillo." A number of questions were raised by King, among them:

> Would it provide a small number of sniper rifles or other devices for the removal of key Trujillo people from the scene?

King's handwritten notes indicate that Rubottom's response to that question was "yes."

On July 1, 1960, a memorandum directed to General {Charles P.} Cabell, the Acting Director of Central Intelligence, was prepared for Colonel King's signature and, in his absence, signed by his principal deputy. The memorandum stated that a principal leader of the anti-Trujillo opposition had asked Ambassador Farland for a limited number of arms to precipitate Trujillo's overthrow, and recognized that such arms presumably "would be used against key members of the Trujillo regime." The memorandum recommended that the arms be provided, since the fall of the Trujillo regime appeared inevitable, and therefore United States relations with the opposition should be as close as possible. "Providing the arms as requested would contribute significantly toward this end."

Specifically, the recommendation was to deliver to dissidents in the Dominican Republic 12 sterile rifles with telescopic sights, together with 500 rounds of ammunition.

Paragraph 4 of the memorandum stated:

> Approval for delivery of these arms has been given by Assistant Secretary of State Roy Rubottom, who requests that the arms be placed in hands of the opposition at the earliest possible moment.

The Acting Chief of the Western Hemisphere Division's recommendation was concurred in by Richard Helms, as Acting DDP, and approved by General Cabell.

The kind of arms approved, sterile rifles with telescopic sights, together with the statement that they presumably would be used against key members of the Trujillo regime clearly indicated the "targeted use" for which the weapons were intended.

On July 1, 1960, a cable was sent to Dearborn by CIA Headquarters informing him of the plan to airdrop 12 telescopically-sighted rifles into the Dominican Republic. The cable inquired whether the dissidents had the capability to realign the sights if thrown off by the drop. On July 14, 1960, Dearborn replied that the dissident leaders were against any further action in the Dominican Republic until after resolution by the OAS of a Venezuelan complaint then pending against Trujillo. The dissidents reportedly believed that sufficiently strong action by the OAS could bring Trujillo's downfall without further effort on their part. The 12 sniper rifles were never furnished to the dissidents.

On August 26, 1960, Dearborn cabled Deputy Assistant Secretary of

State Lester Mallory reporting on a meeting between a dissident leader and a Consulate political officer. The dissident leader was reported to have lost enthusiasm for an assassination attempt and was then speaking of an invasion from Venezuela. However, by September 1, 1960, dissidents were again speaking about the possible provision to them of arms. This time the request was for 200 rifles. For the next several months, consideration centered on providing 200 to 300 guns.

4. *Summer and Fall of 1960*

In August 1960, the United States interrupted diplomatic relations with the Dominican Republic and recalled most of its personnel. Dearborn was left as Consul General and *de facto* CIA Chief of Station. Consideration was given both to providing arms and explosive devices and to the use of high-level emissaries to persuade Trujillo to abdicate. By the end of the year, a broad plan of general support to anti-Trujillo forces, both within and without the country, was approved.

(*a*) *Diplomatic development–withdrawal of United States personnel*

Events occurring during the Summer of 1960 further intensified hemispheric opposition to the Trujillo regime. In June, agents of Trujillo tried to assassinate Venezuelan President Betancourt. As a result, the OAS censured the Trujillo government. At the same time, in August 1960, the United States interrupted diplomatic relations with the Dominican Republic and imposed economic sanctions.

With the interruption of diplomatic relations, the United States closed its Embassy. Most American personnel, including the CIA Chief of Station, left the Dominican Republic. With the departure of the CIA Chief of Station, Dearborn became *de facto* CIA Chief of Station and was recognized as such by both CIA and the State Department. Although in January 1961, a new CIA Chief of Station came to the Dominican Republic, Dearborn continued to serve as a link to the dissidents.

(*b*) *Dearborn reports assassination may be only way to overthrow Trujillo regime*

Dearborn came to believe that no effort to overthrow the Trujillo government could be successful unless it involved Trujillo's assassination.

He communicated this opinion to both the State Department and the CIA. In July 1960, he advised Assistant Secretary Rubottom that the dissidents were

> * * * in no way ready to carry on any type of revolutionary activity in the foreseeable future except the assassination of their principal enemy.

It is uncertain what portion of the information provided by Dearborn to State was passed above the Assistant Secretary level. Through August of 1960, only Assistant Secretary Rubottom, his Deputy, Lester Mallory, and his Staff Assistant, were, within the Latin American Division of the Department, aware of Dearborn's "current projects."

By September 1960, Thomas Mann had replaced Roy Rubottom as Assistant Secretary for Inter-American Affairs, and the Staff Assistant had become a Special Assistant to Mr. Mann. While serving as Special Assistant to the Assistant Secretary, the Special Assistant reportedly spent ninety percent of his time coordinating State Department-CIA activities in Latin America. It was in this capacity that the Special Assistant maintained almost daily communication with officials of the CIA's Western Hemisphere Division.

Mann solicited Dearborn's comments concerning plans under discussion for forcing Trujillo from power. Dearborn replied in a detailed letter which concluded:

> One further point which I should probably not even make. From a purely practical standpoint, it will be best for us, for the OAS, and for the Dominican Republic if the Dominicans put an end to Trujillo before he leaves this island. If he has his millions and is a free agent, he will devote his life from exile to preventing stable government in the D.R., to overturning democratic governments and establishing dictatorships in the Caribbean, and to assassinating his enemies. If I were a Dominican, which thank heaven I am not, I would favor destroying Trujillo as being the first necessary step in the salvation of my country and I would regard this, in fact, as my Christian duty. If you recall Dracula, you will remember it was necessary to drive a stake through his heart to prevent a continuation of his crimes. I believe sudden death would be more humane than the solution of the Nuncio who

once told me he thought he should pray that Trujillo would have a long and lingering illness.

(c) *Efforts to convince Trujillo to abdicate*

Throughout the fall of 1960, efforts were made on both the diplomatic and economic fronts aimed at pressuring Trujillo into relinquishing control, and ideally, leaving the Dominican Republic. The use of high-level emissaries, both from within and without the ranks of government, was considered. None of the efforts proved successful, and at the end of 1960, Trujillo was still in absolute control.

(d) *CIA plans of October 1960*

A CIA internal memorandum dated October 3, 1960 entitled "Plans of the Dominican Internal Opposition and Dominican Desk for Overthrow of the Trujillo Government" set forth plans which "have been developed on a tentative basis which appear feasible and which might be carried out * * * covertly by CIA with a minimal risk of exposure." These plans provided, in part, for the following:

> a. Delivery of approximately 300 rifles and pistols, together with ammunition and a supply of grenades, to secure cache on the South shore of the island, about 14 miles East of Ciudad Trujillo.
>
> b. Delivery to the same cache described above, of an electronic detonating device with remote control features, which could be planted by the dissidents in such manner as to *eliminate certain key Trujillo henchmen.* This might necessitate training and introducing into the country by illegal entry, a trained technician to set the bomb and detonator. (Emphasis added.)

(e) *December 1960 Special Group plan of covert actions*

On December 29, 1960, the Special Group considered and approved a broad plan of covert support to anti-Trujillo forces. The plan, presented by Bissell, envisioned support to both Dominican exile groups and internal dissidents. The exile groups were to be furnished money to organize and undertake anti-Trujillo propaganda efforts and to refurbish a yacht for use in paramilitary activities. Bissell emphasized to the Special Group that "the proposed actions would not, of themselves, bring about the desired result in the near future, lacking some decisive stroke against Trujillo himself."

5. January 12, 1961 Special Group Approval of "Limited Supplies of Small Arms and Other Material"

On January 12, 1961, with all members present, the Special Group met and, according to its Minutes, took the following action with respect to the Dominican Republic:

> Mr. {Livingston} Merchant explained the feeling of the Department of State that limited supplies of small arms and other material should be made available for dissidents inside the Dominican Republic. Mr. {Thomas} Parrott said that we believe this can be managed securely by CIA, and that the plan would call for final transportation into the country being provided by the dissidents themselves. The Group approved the project.

(a) Memorandum underlying the Special Group action

On January 12, 1961, Thomas Mann sent a memorandum to Under Secretary Livingston Merchant. The memorandum, sent through Joseph Scott, Merchant's Special Assistant, reported the disillusionment of Dominican dissidents with the United States for its failure to furnish them with any tangible or concrete assistance. Further, it reported:

> Opposition elements have consistently asked us to supply them with "hardware" of various types. This has included quantities of conventional arms and also, rather persistently, they have asked for some of the more exotic items and devices which they associate with revolutionary effort.

Mann suggested for Merchant's consideration and, if he approved, for discussion by the Special Group, the provision of token quantities of selected items desired by the dissidents. Mann specifically mentioned small explosive devices which would place some "sabotage potential" in the hands of dissident elements, but stated that there "would be no thought of toppling the GODR [Government of Dominican Republic] by any such minor measure." This memorandum was drafted on January 11 by Mann's Special Assistant for CIA liaison.

A covering memorandum from Scott to Merchant, forwarding Mann's memo, was apparently taken by Merchant to the Special Group meeting. Merchant's handwritten notations indicate that the Special Group "agreed in terms of Tom Mann's memo" and that the Secretary of State was informed of that decision by late afternoon on January 12, 1961.

There is no evidence that any member of the Special Group, other than Allen Dulles, knew that the dissidents had clearly and repeatedly expressed a desire for arms and explosives to be used by them in assassination efforts. While it is, of course, possible that such information was passed orally to some or all of the members of the Special Group, and perhaps even discussed by them on January 12, 1961, there is no documentary evidence of which the Committee is aware which would establish this to be the case.

On January 19, 1961, the last day of the Eisenhower Administration, Consul General Dearborn was advised that approval had been given for supplying arms and other material to the Dominican dissidents. Shortly thereafter, Dearborn informed the Special Assistant that the dissidents were "delighted" about the decision to deliver "exotic equipment."

6. January 20, 1961–April 17, 1961 (the Kennedy Administration Through the Bay of Pigs)

On January 20, 1961, the Kennedy Administration took office. Three of the four members of the Special Group (all except Allen Dulles) retired.

Prior to the failure of the Bay of Pigs invasion on April 17, 1961, a number of significant events occurred. These events included meetings with Dominican dissidents in which specific assassination plans were discussed, requests by dissidents for explosive devices, the passage by United States officials of pistols and carbines to dissidents inside the Dominican Republic and the pouching to the Dominican Republic of machine guns which had been requested by the dissidents for use in connection with an assassination attempt. { . . . }

{ . . . } As used herein, "senior American officials" means individuals in the White House or serving as members of the Special Group.

(a) *Specific events indirectly linking United States to dissidents' assassination plans*

(I) Assassination discussions and requests for explosives

At meetings held with dissident leaders in New York City on February 10 and 15, 1961, CIA officials were told repeatedly by dissident leaders that "the key to the success of the plot [to overthrow the Trujillo regime] would be the assassination of Trujillo." Among the requests made of the CIA by dissident leaders were the following:

> (a) Ex-FBI agents who would plan and execute the death of Trujillo.
>
> (b) Cameras and other items that could be used to fire projectiles.
>
> (c) A slow-working chemical that could be rubbed on the palm of one's hand and transferred to Trujillo in a handshake, causing delayed lethal results.
>
> (d) Silencers for rifles that could kill from a distance of several miles.

Other methods of assassinating Trujillo proposed by dissidents at the February 10 or February 15 meetings included poisoning Trujillo's food or medicines, ambushing his automobile, and attacking him with firearms and grenades.

The dissidents' "latest plot," as described in the February CIA memoranda, was said to involve the planting of a powerful bomb, which could be detonated from a nearby electric device, along the route of Trujillo's evening walk.

On March 13, 1961, a dissident in the Dominican Republic asked for fragmentation grenades "for use during the next week or so." This request was communicated to CIA Headquarters on March 14, 1961, and was followed the next day by an additional request for 50 fragmentation grenades, 5 rapid-fire weapons, and 10 64-mm. anti-tank rockets. This further request was also passed on to CIA Headquarters. There is no evidence that any of these arms were supplied to the dissidents.

The documentary record makes clear that the Special Assistant at the State Department was also advised of related developments in a March 16, 1961, "picnic" letter from Dearborn who complained that his spirits were in the doldrums because:

> * * * the members of our club are now prepared in their minds to have a picnic but do not have the ingredients for the salad. Lately they have developed a plan for the picnic, which just might work if they could find the proper food. They have asked us for a few sandwiches, hardly more, and we are not prepared to make them available. Last week we were asked to furnish three or four pineapples for a party in the near future, but I could remember nothing in my instructions that would have allowed me to contribute this ingredient. Don't think I wasn't tempted. I have rather specific guidelines to the effect that salad ingredients will be delivered outside the picnic grounds and will be brought to the area by another club.

After reviewing his "picnic" letter, together with the requests in the March 14 and 15 cables discussed above, Dearborn concluded during his testimony before the Committee that the "pineapples" were probably the requested fragmentation grenades and the restriction on delivering salad ingredients outside of the picnic grounds was, almost certainly, meant to refer to the requirement of the January 12 Special Group decision that arms be delivered outside the Dominican Republic.

(II) THE PASSAGE OF PISTOLS

(1) Pouching to the Dominican Republic.—In a March 15, 1961 cable, a Station officer reported that Dearborn had asked for three .38 caliber pistols for issue to several dissidents. In reply, Headquarters cabled: "Regret no authorization exists to suspend pouch regulations against shipment of arms," and indicated that their reply had been coordinated with State. The Station officer then asked Headquarters to seek the necessary authorization and noted that at his last two posts he had received pistols via the pouch for "worthy purposes" and, therefore, he knew it could be done. Two days later, Headquarters cabled that the pistols and ammunition were being pouched. However, the Station was instructed *not* to advise Dearborn.

(2) Reason for the CIA instruction not to tell Dearborn.—A Station officer testified that he believed the "don't tell Dearborn the pistol is being pouched" language simply meant that the sending of firearms through the diplomatic pouch was not something to be unnecessarily discussed. Dearborn said he

never doubted the pouch was used, since he knew the Station had no other means of receiving weapons.

(3) Were the pistols related to assassination?—Dearborn testified that he had asked for a single pistol for purposes completely unrelated to any assassination activity. He said he had been approached by a Dominican contact who lived in a remote area and who was concerned for the safety of his family in the event of political reprisals. Dearborn testified that he had believed the man's fears were well-founded and had promised to seek a pistol.

Although there is no direct evidence linking any of these pistols to the assassination of Trujillo, a June 7, 1961, CIA memorandum, unsigned and with no attribution as to source, states that two of the three pistols were passed by a Station officer to a United States citizen who was in direct contact with the action element of the dissident group. It should also be noted that the assassination was apparently conducted with almost complete reliance upon hand weapons. Whether one or more of these .38 caliber Smith & Wesson pistols eventually came into the hands of the assassins and, if so, whether they were used in connection with the assassination, remain open questions.

Both Dearborn and the Station officer testified that they regarded the pistols as weapons for self-defense purposes and that they never considered them to be connected, in any way, with the then-current assassination plans. However, none of the Headquarters cables inquired as to the purpose for which the handguns were sought and the Station's cable stated only that Dearborn wanted them for passage to dissidents. Indeed, the March 24, 1961, cable advising that the pistols were being pouched was sent in response to a request by the dissidents for machine guns to be used in an assassination effort. As with the carbines discussed below, it appears that little, if any, concern was expressed within the Agency over passing these weapons to would-be assassins.

(III) PASSING OF THE CARBINES

(1) Request by the Station and by Dearborn and approval by CIA—In a March 26, 1961, cable to CIA Headquarters, the Station asked for permission to pass to the dissidents three 30 caliber Ml carbines. The guns had been left behind in the Consulate by Navy personnel after the United States interrupted formal diplomatic relations in August 1960. Dearborn testified that he knew of

and concurred in the proposal to supply the carbines to the dissidents. On March 31, 1961, CIA Headquarters cabled approval of the request to pass the carbines.

(2) Were the carbines related to assassination?—The carbines were passed to the action group contact on April 7, 1961. Eventually, they found their way into the hands of one of the assassins, Antonio de la Maza. Both Dearborn and a Station officer testified that the carbines were at all times viewed as strictly a token show of support, indicating United States support of the dissidents' efforts to overthrow Trujillo.

(3) Failure to Disclose to State Department Officials in Washington—There is no indication that the request or the passage of the carbines was disclosed to State Department officials in Washington until several weeks after the passage. In fact, on April 5, Headquarters requested its Station to ask Dearborn not to comment in correspondence with State that the carbines and ammunition were being passed to the dissidents. This cable was sent while a Station officer was in Washington, and it indicated that upon his return to the Dominican Republic, he would explain the request. The Station replied that Dearborn had not commented on the carbines and ammunition in his correspondence with State and he realized the necessity not to do so.

Dearborn testified, however, that he believed, at the time of his April 6 cable, that someone in the State Department had been consulted in advance and had approved the passage of the carbines.

(IV) Requests for and Pouching of the Machine Guns

(1) Requests for Machine Guns—The Station suggested that Headquarters consider pouching an M3 machine gun on February 10, 1961. The request was raised again in March but no action was taken. On March 20, 1961, the Station cabled a dissident request for five M3 or comparable machine guns specifying their wish that the arms be sent via the diplomatic pouch or similar means. The dissidents were said to feel that delivery by air drop or transfer at sea would overly tax their resources.

The machine guns sought by the dissidents were clearly identified, in the Station cable, as being sought for use in connection with an attempt to assassinate Trujillo. This plan was to kill Trujillo in the apartment of his mistress and, according to the Station cable:

> To do they need five M3 or comparable machine guns, and 1500 rounds ammo, for personal defense in event fire fight. Will use quiet weapons for basic job.

In essence, CIA's response was that the timing for an assassination was wrong. The Station was told that precipitous or uncoordinated action could lead to the emergence of a leftist, Castro-type regime and the "mere disposal of Trujillo may create more problems than solutions." It was Headquarters' position that:

> * * * we should attempt to avoid precipitous action by the internal dissidents until opposition group and HQS are better prepared to support [assassination] effect a change in the regime, and cope with the aftermath.

The cable also stated that Headquarters was prepared to deliver machine guns and ammunition to the dissidents when they developed a capability to receive them, but that security considerations precluded use of United States facilities as a carrier. Soon thereafter, on April 6, 1961, while a station officer was in Washington for consultation with Headquarters, he reported on events in the Dominican Republic and:

> * * * especially on the insistence of the EMOTH [dissident] leaders that they be provided with a limited number of small arms for their own protection (specifically, five M3 .45 SMG's).

(2) Pouching of Machine Guns Approved by Bissell—On April 7, 1961 a Pouch Restriction Waiver Request and Certification was submitted seeking permission to pouch "four M3 machine guns and 240 rounds of ammunition on a priority basis for issuance to a small action group to be used for self protection."

The request submitted on behalf of the Chief, Westem Hemisphere Division, further provided:

> A determination has been made that the issuance of this equipment to the action group is desirable if for no other reason than to assure this important group's continued cooperation with and confidence in this Agency's determination to live up to its earlier commitments to

> the group. These commitments took the form of advising the group in January 1961 that we would provide limited arms and assistance to them provided they develop the capability to receive it. Operational circumstances have prevented this group from developing the assets capable of receiving the above equipment through normal clandestine channels such as air drops or sea infiltration.

The Waiver Request was approved by Richard Bissell, as DDP, on April 10, 1961.

Walter Elder, Assistant to the Director, issued a memorandum, also on April 10, which stated:

> Mr. Dulles wants no action on drops of leaflets or arms in the Dominican Republic taken without his approval.

The Elder memorandum suggests that Dulles did not then know that an air drop of arms was regarded as unfeasible and that consequently pouching of the arms had been approved.

The machine guns were pouched to the Dominican Republic and were received by the Station on April 19, 1961.

{ . . . }

7. April 17, 1961–May 31, 1961 (Bay of Pigs Through Trujillo Assassination)

Following the failure of the Bay of Pigs invasion, attempts were made by State and CIA representatives in the Dominican Republic to dissuade the dissidents from a precipitous assassination attempt. These efforts to halt the assassination of Trujillo were the result of instructions from CIA Headquarters and were prompted by concern over filling the power vacuum which would result from Trujillo's death.

The machine guns arrived in the Dominican Republic but permission to pass them to the dissidents was never given and the guns never left the Consulate.

Dearborn returned to Washington for consultation and a contingency plan for the Dominican Republic was drafted.

The day before Trujillo's assassination, Dearborn received a cable of instructions and guidance from President Kennedy. The cable advised that the United States must not run the risk of association with political assassination, since the United States, as a matter of general policy, could not condone assassination. The cable further advised Dearborn to continue to hold open offers of material assistance to the dissidents and to advise them of United States support for them if they were successful in overthrowing the Trujillo government. The cable also reconfirmed the decision not to pass the machine guns.

(a) Decision not to pass the machine guns and unsuccessful United States attempt to stop assassination effort

By April 17, 1961, the Bay of Pigs invasion had failed. As a result, there developed a general realization that precipitous action should be avoided in the Dominican Republic until Washington was able to give further consideration to the consequences of a Trujillo overthrow and the power vacuum which would be created. A cable from Headquarters to the Station, on April 17, 1961, advised that it was most important that the machine guns not be passed without additional Headquarters approval.

The machine guns arrived in the Dominican Republic on April 19, 1961, and Headquarters was so advised. The earlier admonition that the machine guns should be held in Station custody until further notice was repeated in a second cable from Headquarters, sent April 20, 1961. This decision was said to have been "based on judgment that filling a vacuum created by assassination now bigger question than ever view unsettled conditions in Caribbean area."

The dissidents continued to press for the release of the machine guns and their requests were passed on to Headquarters in cables from Dearborn and from the Station. On April 25, 1961, the Station advised Headquarters that an American living in the Dominican Republic and acting as a cut-out to the dissidents had informed the Station that Antonio de la Maza was going to attempt the assassination between April 29 and May 2. The Station also reported that this attempt would use the three carbines passed from the American Consulate, together with whatever else was available.

In response to the April 25 cable, Headquarters restated that there was no approval to pass any additional arms to the dissidents and requested the Station to advise the dissidents that the United States was simply not prepared at that time to cope with the aftermath of the assassination. The following day, April 27, 1961, the Station replied that, based upon further discussions with the dissidents, "We doubt statement U.S. government not now prepared to cope with aftermath will dissuade them from attempt."

Dearborn recalls receiving instructions that an effort be made to turn off the assassination attempt and testified that efforts to carry out the instructions were unsuccessful. In effect, the dissidents informed him that this was their affair and it could not be turned off to suit the convenience of the United States government.

On April 30, 1961, Dearborn advised Headquarters that the dissidents had reported to him the assassination attempt was going to take place during the first week of May. The action group was reported to have in its possession three carbines, four to six 12-gauge shotguns and other small arms. Although they reportedly still wanted the machine guns, Dearborn advised Headquarters that the group was going to go ahead with what they had, whether the United States wanted them to or not.

Dearborn's cable set forth the argument of the action group that, since the United States had already assisted the group to some extent and was therefore implicated, the additional assistance of releasing the machine guns would not change the basic relationship. The cable concluded:

> Owing to far-reaching political implications involved in release or non-release of requested items, Headquarters may wish discuss foregoing with State Department.

Beginning with Dearborn's April 30 cable, there was a fairly constant stream of cables and reports predicting Trujillo's imminent assassination. Certain of these reports predicted the specific date or dates on which the assassination would be attempted, while others spoke of the attempt being made at the first propitious opportunity. In addition to cables sent directly to CIA Headquarters, the substance of these assassination forecasts was circulated throughout the intelligence community and the higher echelons of the government in the form of intelligence bulletins. These bulletins did not, however, contain references to any United States involvement in the assassination planning.

As a result of these reports, Robert Kennedy had a discussion with Allen Dulles, apparently sometime in the early part of May, and thereafter "looked into the matter." Robert Kennedy reportedly called the President and it was "decided at that time that we'd put a task force on the problem and try to work out some kind of alternative course of action in case this event did occur." Robert Kennedy's notes state that at the time he called the President, "He [the President] had known nothing about it [the reports of Trujillo's imminent assassination]."

There is no record as to the specificity with which Allen Dulles discussed the matter of Trujillo's predicted assassination with Robert Kennedy. Dulles was, of course, fully informed at this time both as to the relationship between State Department and CIA representatives in the Dominican Republic and the dissidents planning Trujillo's removal, and, also, of the weapons which had been furnished to the dissidents and those which they were then requesting for use in connection with the assassination effort.

(*b*) *Further consideration of passing machine guns*

In response to Dearborn's cable, a cable was drafted at CIA Headquarters authorizing passage of the machine guns. The cable which was sent to Allen Dulles, with Bissell's recommendation for its dispatch, provided:

> Since it appears that opposition group has committed itself to action with or without additional support, coupled with fact ref. C items [the carbines] already made available to them for personal defense; station authorized pass ref. A items [the machine guns] to opposition member for their additional protection on their proposed endeavor.

The cable was never sent.

In his testimony before the Committee, Bissell characterized his reasoning for recommending release of the machine guns as

> * * * having made already a considerable investment in this dissident group and its plans that we might as well make the additional investment.

The following day, May 3, 1961, the Deputy Chief of the Western Hemisphere Division of CIA, who frequently acted as liaison with the State Department in matters concerning covert operations in the Dominican Republic, met with Adolph Berle, Chairman of the Interagency Task Force on Latin America.

A Berle memorandum of the meeting states that the CIA officer informed Berle that a local group in the Dominican Republic wished to overthrow Trujillo and sought arms for that purpose. The memorandum continued:

> On cross examination it developed that the real plan was to assassinate Trujillo and they wanted guns for that purpose. [The CIA officer] wanted to know what the Policy should be.
>
> I told him I could not care less for Trujillo and that this was the general sentiment. But we did not wish to have anything to do with any assassination plots anywhere, any time. [The CIA officer] said he felt the same way.

Copies of Berle's memorandum were sent to Wymberly Coerr, the Acting Assistant Secretary for Inter-American Affairs, and to the Special Assistant.

Both the CIA officer and the Special Assistant, who had been in almost daily contact with each other since August of 1960, had been advised of the assassination plans of the dissident group. In fact, the CIA officer, along with Bissell, had signed off on the proposed cable of May 2, releasing the machine guns for passage.

{ . . . }

(*d*) *Final requests by dissidents for machine guns*

On May 16, 1961, Dearborn cabled the State Department (attention Acting Assistant Secretary Coerr) with an urgent request from the dissidents for the machine guns. The cable advised that the assassination attempt was scheduled for the night of May 16 and that, while the chances of success were 80 percent, provision of the machine guns would reduce the possibility of failure. The dissidents reportedly stressed to Dearborn that if the effort failed, due to United States refusal to supply the machine guns, the United States would be held responsible and would never be forgiven. Dearborn reported that he had informed the dissidents that, based on his recent conversations in Washington, he was reasonably certain that authorization could not be obtained for handing over machine guns.

A return cable from the State Department to Dearborn, sent the same day, confirmed Dearborn's judgment. It instructed him to continue to take the same line until he received contrary instructions which clearly indicated they had been cleared in advance by the State Department itself. This cable from State was approved by Under Secretary {Chester B.} Bowles.

An officer in the CIA's Western Hemisphere Division referred to Dearborn's May 16 request in a memorandum be sent to the Special Assistant on the same date and asked to be advised as to the Department's policy concerning passage of the machine guns. The CIA officer noted that when this request was last taken to the Department, Berle made the decision that the weapons not be passed.

Devine responded to the CIA officer's memorandum on the same day, advising him that the Department's policy continued to be negative on the matter of passing the machine guns. The CIA officer's attention was directed to the January 12, 1961 Special Group limitation concerning the passage of arms outside of the Dominican Republic. A copy of the Special Assistant's memorandum to the CIA officer was forwarded to the Office of the Under Secretary of State, to the attention of his personal assistant, Joseph Scott.

{. . .}

(*f*) *Cable of May 29, 1961*

A copy of Dearborn's cable of May 16, 1961, requesting urgent State Department guidance, was forwarded to Richard Goodwin. At the specific request of Goodwin, the State Department replied to Dearborn on May 17, and advised him to keep in mind the President's view, as expressed at the May 5 National Security Council Meeting, that the United States should not initiate the overthrow of Trujillo before knowing what government would succeed him.

Dearborn responded on May 21, 1961, pointing out that for over a year State Department representatives in the Dominican Republic had been nurturing the effort to overthrow Trujillo and had assisted the dissidents in numerous ways, all of which were known to the Department. It was, Dearborn stated, "too late to consider whether United States will initiate overthrow of Trujillo." Dearborn invited further guidance from State.

In response to Dearborn's request for guidance, the State Department drafted a reply on May 24. The draft discussed a conflict between two objectives:

> (1) To be so associated with removal Trujillo regime as to derive credit among DR dissidents and liberal elements throughout Latin America;
>
> (2) To disassociate US from any obvious intervention in Dominican Republic and even more so from any political assassination which might occur.

It was said to be the Department's considered opinion that "former objective cannot, repeat not, easily override latter."

This State Department draft was forwarded to Under Secretary Bowles with the comment that Goodwin considered it "too negative" and that he would try his hand on a draft "for Bundy to present tomorrow morning."

A May 26, 1961, memorandum from Bowles to Bundy begins:

> Following up on our discussion of the Dominican Republic at yesterday's meeting of the Special Group, I am forwarding you a draft telegram which we would like to send to Henry Dearborn, our Consul General in Ciudad Trujillo, supplementing the guidance he will be receiving on the recently approved contingency plans.

The minutes of the Special Group meeting on May 25, 1961, do not, however, reflect any discussion of the Dominican Republic. If, as Bowles' memorandum suggests, a discussion concerning the Dominican Republic did occur at the May 25 meeting, it is not known what the discussion involved or what decisions, if any, were made.

Richard Goodwin personally prepared alternate drafts to the proposed State Department cable to Dearborn. Goodwin testified that it was his intent in revising the cable to communicate to Dearborn, President Kennedy's personal belief that the United States "* * * didn't want to do anything that would involve us further, the United States further, in any effort to assassinate Trujillo."

At the same time, Goodwin's draft raised the issue of further covert action and transfer of arms to the dissidents and advised Dearborn to hold out the arms as being available to the dissidents pending their ability to receive them.

It was the twofold intent of the cable as revised by Goodwin, (1) to express the desire to remain in the good graces of the dissidents who, it was believed, would constitute the new government following Trujillo's assassination, and (2) to avoid any action which might further involve the United States in the anticipated assassination. This dual purpose is clearly evident in the cable which advised:

> * * * we must not run risk of U.S. association with political assassination, since U.S. *as matter of general policy cannot condone assassination.* This last principle is overriding and must prevail in doubtful situation. (Emphasis added)
>
> . . . .
>
> Continue to inform dissident elements of U.S. support for their position.

According to Goodwin, the italicized material was inserted in the cable at the specific direction of President Kennedy.

With respect to the four machine guns which were in the Consulate and which had been repeatedly requested by the dissidents, the cable advised Dearborn that the United States was unable to transfer these arms to the dissidents. Dearborn was instructed:

> Tell them that this is because of our suspicion that method of transfer may be unsafe. In actual fact, we feel that the transfer of arms would serve very little purpose and expose the United States to great danger of association with assassination attempt.

The cable, as revised by Goodwin and approved by President Kennedy, was sent to Dearborn on May 29, 1961.

8. May 30, 1961 and Immediately Thereafter

(*a*) *Trujillo assassinated*

Late in the evening of May 30, 1961, Trujillo was ambushed and assassinated near San Cristobal, Dominican Republic. The assassination closely paralleled the plan disclosed by the action group to American representatives in the Dominican Republic and passed on to officials in Washington at both the CIA and the State Department. The assassination was conducted by members of the action group, to whom the American carbines had been passed, and such sketchy information as is available indicates that one or more of the carbines was in the possession of the assassination group when Trujillo was killed. This evidence indicates, however, that the actual assassination was accomplished by handguns and shotguns.

(b) Cables to Washington

After receiving the May 29 cable from Washington, both Consul General Dearborn and the CIA Station sent replies. According to Dearborn's testimony, he did not regard the May 29 cable as a change in U.S. policy concerning support for assassinations. He interpreted the May 29 cable as saying:

> * * * we don't care if the Dominicans assassinate Trujillo, that is all right. But we don't want anything to pin this on us, because we aren't doing it, it is the Dominicans who are doing it.

Dearborn testified that this accorded with what he said had always been his personal belief: that the U.S. should not be involved in an assassination and that if an assassination occurred it would be strictly a Dominican affair.

In contrast, the CIA Station officer did regard the cable as manifesting a change in U.S. policy, particularly on the question of supplying arms. He believed the May 29 cable was the final word in United States policy on this matter and consequently felt that the government had retreated from its prior position, of offering material support to the dissidents, and had adopted a new position of withholding such support. His responsive cable to Headquarters stated:

> HQ AWARE EXTENT TO WHICH U.S. GOVERNMENT ALREADY ASSOCIATED WITH ASSASSINATION. IF WE ARE TO AT LEAST COVER UP TRACKS, CIA PERSONNEL DIRECTLY INVOLVED IN ASSASSINATION PREPARATION MUST BE WITHDRAWN.

Immediately following the assassination, all CIA personnel in the Dominican Republic were removed from the country and within a few days

Consul General Dearborn was back in Washington. The State Department cabled the CIA station in the Dominican Republic to destroy all records concerning contacts with dissidents and any related matters, except not to destroy the contingency plans or the May 29, 1961 cable to Dearborn.

(c) *Immediate post-assassination period*

The United States Consulate in the Dominican Republic was quick to dispatch its early reports that Trujillo had been assassinated, and the United States communications network transmitted the report to President Kennedy in Paris. The President's Press Secretary, Pierre Salinger, made the first public announcement of the assassination, preceding by several hours release of the news in the Dominican Republic. Secretary of State {Dean} Rusk testified that when he learned of Salinger's announcement he was most concerned. Rusk said that Trujillo's son Ramfis was also in Paris and he was afraid that Ramfis, upon first learning of his father's death from the press secretary to the President of the United States, might reason that the United States had been in some way involved and he might therefore try to retaliate against President Kennedy.

Following the assassination, there were several high-level meetings in Washington attended by President Kennedy, Vice President Johnson, Secretary of State Rusk, Secretary of Defense McNamara, Attorney General Kennedy, and many lower-level officials who had been involved in the Dominican Republic operation. The meetings considered the crisis in the Dominican Republic, caused by Trujillo's assassination, and attempted to ascertain the facts concerning the degree of United States involvement in the assassination. The passage of carbines to the dissidents was discussed at one such meeting.

On June 1, 1961, Robert Kennedy dictated four pages of personal notes reflecting his contemporaneous thoughts on the situation in the Dominican Republic. A review of these notes evidences considerable concern regarding the lack of information available in Washington as to events in the Dominican Republic. The notes end with the following statement:

> The great problem now is that we don't know what to do because we don't (sic) what the situation is and this shouldn't be true, particularly when we have known that this situation was pending for some period of time.

There is no indication or suggestion contained in the record of those post-assassination meetings, or in the Robert Kennedy notes, of concern as to the propriety of the known United States involvement in the assassination. Nor is there any record that anyone took steps following Trujillo's assassination to reprimand or censure any of the American officials involved either on the scene or in Washington, or to otherwise make known any objections or displeasure as to the degree of United States involvement in the events which had transpired. Whether this was due to the press of other matters, including concern over Trujillo's successor and the future government of the Dominican Republic, or whether it represented a condonation or ratification of the known United States involvement, is uncertain.

In any event, when, some years later, the project covering American involvement in changing the government of the Dominican Republic was terminated by the Agency, the project was described in Agency documents as a "success" in that it assisted in moving the Dominican Republic from a totalitarian dictatorship to a Western-style democracy.

{ . . . }

9.

Testing and Use of Chemical and Biological Agents by the Intelligence Community

Under its mandate the Select Committee has studied the testing and use of chemical and biological agents by intelligence agencies. { . . . }

Fears that countries hostile to the United States would use chemical and biological agents against Americans or America's allies led to the development of a defensive program designed to discover techniques for American intelligence agencies to detect and counteract chemical and biological agents. The defensive orientation soon became secondary as the possible use of these agents to obtain information from, or gain control over, enemy agents became apparent.

Research and development programs to find materials which could be used to alter human behavior were initiated in the late 1940s and early 1950s. These experimental programs originally included testing of drugs involving witting human subjects, and culminated in tests using unwitting, nonvolunteer human subjects. These tests were designed to determine the potential effects of chemical or biological agents when used operationally against individuals unaware that they had received a drug.

The testing programs were considered highly sensitive by the intelligence agencies administering them. Few people, even within the agencies, knew of the programs and there is no evidence that either the executive branch or Congress were ever informed of them. The highly compartmented nature of these programs may be explained in part by an observation made by the CIA Inspector General that, "the knowledge that the Agency is engaging in unethical and illicit activities would have serious repercussions in political and diplomatic circles and would be detrimental to the accomplishment of its missions."

The research and development program, and particularly the covert testing programs, resulted in massive abridgments of the rights of American citizens, sometimes with tragic consequences. The deaths of two Americans can be attributed to these programs; other participants in the testing programs may still suffer from the residual effects. While some controlled testing of these substances might be defended, the nature of the tests, their scale, and the fact that they were continued for years after the danger of surreptitious administration of LSD to unwitting individuals was known, demonstrate a fundamental disregard for the value of human life.

The Select Committee's investigation of the testing and use of chemical and biological agents also raises serious questions about the adequacy of command and control procedures within the Central Intelligence Agency and military intelligence, and about the relationships among the intelligence agencies, other governmental agencies, and private institutions and individuals. The CIA's normal administrative controls were waived for programs involving chemical and biological agents to protect their security. According to the head of the Audit Branch of the CIA, these waivers produced "gross administrative failures." They prevented the CIA's internal review mechanisms (the Office of General Counsel, the Inspector General, and the Audit Staff) from adequately supervising the programs. In general, the waivers had the paradoxical effect of providing less restrictive administrative controls and less effective internal review for controversial and highly sensitive projects than those governing normal Agency activities.

The security of the programs was protected not only by waivers of normal administrative controls, but also by a high degree of compartmentation within the CIA. This compartmentation excluded the CIA's Medical Staff from the principal research and testing program employing chemical and biological agents.

It also may have led to agency policymakers receiving differing and inconsistent responses when they posed questions to the CIA component involved.

Jurisdictional uncertainty within the CIA was matched by jurisdictional conflict among the various intelligence agencies. A spirit of cooperation and reciprocal exchanges of information which initially characterized the programs disappeared. Military testers withheld information from the CIA, ignoring suggestions for coordination from their superiors. The CIA similarly failed to provide information to the military on the CIA's testing program. This failure to cooperate was conspicuously manifested in an attempt by the Army to conceal their overseas testing program, which included surreptitious administration of LSD, from the CIA. Learning of the Army's program, the Agency surreptitiously attempted to obtain details of it.

The decision to institute one of the Army's LSD field testing projects had been based, at least in part, on the finding that no long-term residual effects had ever resulted from the drug's administration. The CIA's failure to inform the Army of a death which resulted from the surreptitious administration of LSD to unwitting Americans may well have resulted in the institution of an unnecessary and potentially lethal program.

The development, testing, and use of chemical and biological agents by intelligence agencies raises serious questions about the relationship between the intelligence community and foreign governments, other agencies of the Federal Government, and other institutions and individuals. The questions raised range from the legitimacy of American complicity in actions abroad which violate American and foreign laws to the possible compromise of the integrity of public and private institutions used as cover by intelligence agencies.

A. The Programs Investigated

1. Project CHATTER

Project CHATTER was a Navy program that began in the fall of 1947. Responding to reports of "amazing results" achieved by the Soviets in using "truth drugs," the program focused on the identification and testing of such drugs for use in interrogations and in the recruitment of agents. The research included laboratory experiments on animals and human subjects involving *Anabasis aphylla*, scopolamine, and mescaline in order to determine their speech-inducing qualities. Overseas experiments were conducted as part of the project.

The project expanded substantially during the Korean War, and ended shortly after the war, in 1953.

2. Project BLUEBIRD/ARTICHOKE

The earliest of the CIA's major programs involving the use of chemical and biological agents, Project BLUEBIRD, was approved by the Director in 1950. Its objectives were:

> (a) discovering means of conditioning personnel to prevent unauthorized extraction of information from them by known means,
>
> (b) investigating the possibility of control of an individual by application of special interrogation techniques,
>
> (c) memory enhancement,
>
> (d) establishing defensive means for preventing hostile control of Agency personnel.

As a result of interrogations conducted overseas during the project, another goal was added—the evaluation of offensive uses of unconventional interrogation techniques, including hypnosis and drugs. In August 1951, the project was renamed ARTICHOKE. Project ARTICHOKE included in-house experiments on interrogation techniques, conducted "under medical and security controls which would ensure that no damage was done to individuals who volunteer for the experiments." Overseas interrogations utilizing a combination of sodium pentothal and hypnosis after physical and psychiatric examinations of the subjects were also part of ARTICHOKE.

The Office of Scientific Intelligence (OSI), which studied scientific advances by hostile powers, initially led BLUEBIRD/ARTICHOKE efforts. In 1952, overall responsibility for ARTICHOKE was transferred from OSI to the Inspection and Security Office (I&SO), predecessor to the present Office of Security. The CIA's Technical Services and Medical Staffs were to be called upon as needed; OSI would retain liaison function with other government agencies. The change in leadership from an intelligence unit to an operating unit apparently reflected a change in emphasis; from the study of actions by hostile powers to the use, both for offensive and defensive purposes, of special interrogation techniques—primarily hypnosis and truth serums.

Representatives from each Agency unit involved in ARTICHOKE met almost monthly to discuss their progress. These discussions included the planning of overseas interrogations as well as further experimentation in the U.S.

Information about project ARTICHOKE after the fall of 1953 is scarce. The CIA maintains that the project ended in 1956, but evidence suggests that Office of Security and Office of Medical Services use of "special interrogation" techniques continued for several years thereafter.

3. MKNAOMI

MKNAOMI was another major CIA program in this area. In 1967, the CIA summarized the purposes of MKNAOMI:

> (a) To provide for a covert support base to meet clandestine operational requirements.
>
> (b) To stockpile severely incapacitating and lethal materials for the specific use of TSD [Technical Services Division].
>
> (c) To maintain in operational readiness special and unique items for the dissemination of biological and chemical materials.
>
> (d) To provide for the required surveillance, testing, upgrading, and evaluation of materials and items in order to assure absence of defects and complete predictability of results to be expected under operational conditions.

Under an agreement reached with the Army in 1952, the Special Operations Division (SOD) at Fort Detrick was to assist CIA in developing, testing, and maintaining biological agents and delivery systems. By this agreement, CIA acquired the knowledge, skill, and facilities of the Army to develop biological weapons suited for CIA use.

SOD developed darts coated with biological agents and pills containing several different biological agents which could remain potent for weeks or months. SOD also developed a special gun for firing darts coated with a chemical which could allow CIA agents to incapacitate a guard dog, enter an installation secretly, and return the dog to consciousness when leaving. SOD scientists were unable to develop a similar incapacitant for humans. SOD also physically transferred to CIA personnel biological agents in "bulk" form, and delivery devices, including some containing biological agents.

In addition to the CIA's interest in biological weapons for use against humans, it also asked SOD to study the use of biological agents against crops and animals. In its 1967 memorandum, the CIA stated:

> Three methods and systems for carrying out a covert attack against crops and causing severe crop loss have been developed and evaluated under field conditions. This was accomplished in anticipation of a requirement which was later developed but was subsequently scrubbed just prior to putting into action.

MKNAOMI was terminated in 1970. On November 25, 1969, President Nixon renounced the use of any form of biological weapons that kill or incapacitate and ordered the disposal of existing stocks of bacteriological weapons. On February 14, 1970, the President clarified the extent of his earlier order and indicated that toxins—chemicals that are not living organisms but are produced by living organisms—were considered biological weapons subject to his previous directive and were to be destroyed. Although instructed to relinquish control of material held for the CIA by SOD, a CIA scientist acquired approximately 11 grams of shellfish toxin from SOD personnel at Fort Detrick which were stored in a little-used CIA laboratory where it went undetected for five years.

4. MKULTRA

MKULTRA was the principal CIA program involving the research and development of chemical and biological agents. It was "concerned with the research and development of chemical, biological, and radiological materials capable of employment in clandestine operations to control human behavior."

In January 1973, MKULTRA records were destroyed by Technical Services Division personnel acting on the verbal orders of Dr. Sidney Gottlieb, Chief of TSD. Dr. Gottlieb has testified, and former Director Helms has confirmed, that in ordering the records destroyed, Dr. Gottlieb was carrying out the verbal order of then DCI Helms.

MKULTRA began with a proposal from the Assistant Deputy Director for Plans, Richard Helms, to the DCI, outlining a special funding mechanism for highly sensitive CIA research and development projects that studied the use of biological and chemical materials in altering human behavior. The projects involved:

> Research to develop a capability in the covert use of biological and chemical materials. This area involves the production of various

> physiological conditions which could support present or future clandestine operations. Aside from the offensive potential, the development of a comprehensive capability in this field of covert chemical and biological warfare gives us a thorough knowledge of the enemy's theoretical potential, thus enabling us to defend ourselves against a foe who might not be as restrained in the use of these techniques as we are.

MKULTRA was approved by the DCI on April 13, 1953 along the lines proposed by ADDP Helms.

Part of the rationale for the establishment of this special funding mechanism was its extreme sensitivity. The Inspector General's survey of MKULTRA in 1963 noted the following reasons for this sensitivity:

> a. Research in the manipulation of human behavior is considered by many authorities in medicine and related fields to be professionally unethical, therefore the reputation of professional participants in the MKULTRA program are on occasion in jeopardy.
>
> b. Some MKULTRA activities raise questions of legality implicit in the original charter.
>
> c. A final phase of the testing of MKULTRA products places the rights and interests of U.S. citizens in jeopardy.
>
> d. Public disclosure of some aspects of MKULTRA activity could induce serious adverse reaction in U.S. public opinion, as well as stimulate offensive and defensive action in this field on the part of foreign intelligence services.

Over the ten-year life of the program, many "additional avenues to the control of human behavior" were designated as appropriate for investigation under the MKULTRA charter. These include "radiation, electroshock, various fields of psychology, psychiatry, sociology, and anthropology, graphology, harassment substances, and paramilitary devices and materials."

The research and development of materials to be used for altering human behavior consisted of three phases: first, the search for materials suitable for study; second, laboratory testing on voluntary human subjects in various types of institutions; third, the application of MKULTRA materials in normal life settings.

The search for suitable materials was conducted through standing arrangements with specialists in universities, pharmaceutical houses, hospitals, state and federal institutions, and private research organizations. The annual grants of funds to these specialists were made under ostensible research foundation auspices, thereby concealing the CIA's interest from the specialist's institution.

The next phase of the MKULTRA program involved physicians, toxicologists, and other specialists in mental, narcotics, and general hospitals, and in prisons. Utilizing the products and findings of the basic research phase, they conducted intensive tests on human subjects. One of the first studies was conducted by the National Institute of Mental Health. This study was intended to test various drugs, including hallucinogenics, at the NIMH Addiction Research Center in Lexington, Kentucky. The "Lexington Rehabilitation Center," as it was then called, was a prison for drug addicts serving sentences for drug violations.

The test subjects were volunteer prisoners who, after taking a brief physical examination and signing a general consent form, were administered hallucinogenic drugs. As a reward for participation in the program, the addicts were provided with the drug of their addiction. LSD was one of the materials tested in the MKULTRA program. The final phase of LSD testing involved surreptitious administration to unwitting nonvolunteer subjects in normal life settings by undercover officers of the Bureau of Narcotics acting for the CIA.

The rationale for such testing was "that testing of materials under accepted scientific procedures fails to disclose the full pattern of reactions and attributions that may occur in operational situations."

According to the CIA, the advantage of the relationship with the Bureau was that

> test subjects could be sought and cultivated within the setting of narcotics control. Some subjects have been informers or members of suspect criminal elements from whom the [Bureau of Narcotics] has obtained results of operational value through the tests. *On the other hand, the effectiveness of the substances on individuals at all social levels, high and low, native American and foreign, is of great significance and testing has been performed on a variety of individuals within these categories.* [Emphasis added.]

A special procedure, designated MKDELTA, was established to govern the use of MKULTRA materials abroad. Such materials were used on a number of occasions. Because MKULTRA records were destroyed it is impossible to reconstruct the operational use of MKULTRA materials by the CIA overseas; it has been determined that the use of these materials abroad began in 1953, and possibly as early as 1950.

Drugs were used primarily as an aid to interrogations, but MKULTRA/MKDELTA materials were also used for harassment, discrediting, or disabling purposes. According to an Inspector General Survey of the Technical Services Division of the CIA in 1957—an inspection which did not discover the MKULTRA project involving the surreptitious administration of LSD to unwitting, nonvolunteer subjects—the CIA had developed six drugs for operational use and they had been used in six different operations on a total of thirty-three subjects. By 1963 the number of operations and subjects had increased substantially.

In the spring of 1963, during a wide-ranging Inspector General survey of the Technical Services Division, a member of the Inspector General's staff, John Vance, learned about MKULTRA and about the project involving the surreptitious administration of LSD to unwitting, nonvoluntary human subjects. As a result of the discovery and the Inspector General's subsequent report, this testing was halted and much tighter administrative controls were imposed on the program. According to the CIA, the project was decreased significantly each budget year until its complete termination in the late 1960s.

5. The Testing of LSD by the Army

There were three major phases in the Army's testing of LSD. In the first, LSD was administered to more than 1,000 American soldiers who volunteered to be subjects in chemical warfare experiments. In the second phase, Material Testing Program EA 1729, 95 volunteers received LSD in clinical experiments designed to evaluate potential intelligence uses of the drug. In the third phase, Projects THIRD CHANCE and DERBY HAT, 16 unwitting nonvolunteer subjects were interrogated after receiving LSD as part of operational field tests.

B. CIA Drug Testing Programs

1. The Rationale for the Testing Programs

The late 1940s and early 1950s were marked by concern over the threat posed by the activities of the Soviet Union, the People's Republic of China, and other Communist bloc countries. United States concern over the use of chemical and biological agents by these powers was acute. The belief that hostile powers had used chemical and biological agents in interrogations, brainwashing, and in attacks designed to harass, disable, or kill Allied personnel created considerable pressure for a "defensive" program to investigate chemical and biological agents so that the intelligence community could understand the mechanisms by which these substances worked and how their effects could be defeated.

Of particular concern was the drug LSD. The CIA had received reports that the Soviet Union was engaged in intensive efforts to produce LSD, and that the Soviet Union had attempted to purchase the world's supply of the chemical. As one CIA officer who was deeply involved in work with this drug described the climate of the times: "[It] is awfully hard in this day and age to reproduce how frightening all of this was to us at the time, particularly after the drug scene has become as widespread and as knowledgeable in this country as it did. But we were literally terrified, because this was the one material that we had ever been able to locate that really had potential fantastic possibilities if used wrongly."

But the defensive orientation soon became secondary. Chemical and biological agents were to be studied in order "to perfect techniques . . . for the abstraction of information from individuals whether willing or not" and in order to "develop means for the control of the activities and mental capacities of individuals whether willing or not." One Agency official noted that drugs would be useful in order to "gain control of bodies whether they were willing or not" in the process of removing personnel from Europe in the event of a Soviet attack. In other programs, the CIA began to develop, produce, stockpile, and maintain in operational readiness materials which could be used to harass, disable, or kill specific targets.

Reports of research and development in the Soviet Union, the People's Republic of China, and the Communist Bloc countries provided the basis for the transmutation of American programs from a defensive to an offensive orientation. As the Chief of the Medical Staff of the Central Intelligence Agency wrote in 1952:

> There is ample evidence in the reports of innumerable interrogations that the Communists were utilizing drugs, physical duress, electric shock, and possibly hypnosis against their enemies. With such evidence it is difficult not to keep from becoming rabid about our apparent laxity. We are forced by this mounting evidence to assume a more aggressive role in the development of these techniques, but must be cautious to maintain strict inviolable control because of the havoc that could be wrought by such techniques in unscrupulous hands.

In order to meet the perceived threat to the national security, substantial programs for the testing and use of chemical and biological agents—including projects involving the surreptitious administration of LSD to unwitting nonvolunteer subjects "at all social levels, high and low, native American and foreign"—were conceived, and implemented. These programs resulted in substantial violations of the rights of individuals within the United States.

Although the CIA recognized these effects of LSD to unwitting individuals within the United States, the project continued. As the Deputy Director for Plans, Richard Helms, wrote the Deputy Director of Central Intelligence during discussions which led to the cessation of unwitting testing:

> While I share your uneasiness and distaste for any program which tends to intrude upon an individual's private and legal prerogatives, I believe it is necessary that the Agency maintain a central role in this activity, keep current on enemy capabilities the manipulation of human behavior, and maintain an offensive capability.

There were no attempts to secure approval for the most controversial aspects of these programs from the executive branch or Congress. The nature and extent of the programs were closely held secrets; even DCI {John A.} McCone was not briefed on all the details of the program involving the surreptitious administration of LSD until 1963. It was deemed imperative that these programs be concealed from the American people. As the CIA's Inspector General wrote in 1957:

Precautions must be taken not only to protect operations from exposure to enemy forces but also to conceal these activities from the American public in general. The knowledge that the Agency is engaging in unethical and illicit activities would have serious repercussions in political and diplomatic circles and would be detrimental to the accomplishment of its mission.

2. The Death of Dr. Frank Olson

The most tragic result of the testing of LSD by the CIA was the death of Dr. Frank Olson, a civilian employee of the Army, who died on November 27, 1953. His death followed his participation in a CIA experiment with LSD. As part of this experiment, Olson unwittingly received approximately 70 micrograms of LSD in a glass of Cointreau he drank on November 19, 1953. The drug had been placed in the bottle by a CIA officer, Dr. Robert Lashbrook, as part of an experiment he and Dr. Sidney Gottlieb performed at a meeting of Army and CIA scientists.

Shortly after this experiment, Olson exhibited symptoms of paranoia and schizophrenia. Accompanied by Dr. Lashbrook, Olson sought psychiatric assistance in New York City from a physician, Dr. Harold Abramson, whose research on LSD had been funded indirectly by the CIA. While in New York for treatment, Olson fell to his death from a tenth story window in the Statler Hotel.

a. Background.—Olson, an expert in aerobiology who was assigned to the Special Operations Division (SOD) of the U.S. Army Biological Center at Camp Detrick, Maryland. This Division had three primary functions:

(1) assessing the vulnerability of American installations to biological attack;

(2) developing techniques for offensive use of biological weapons; and

(3) biological research for the CIA.

Professionally, Olson was well respected by his colleagues in both the Army and the CIA. Colonel Vincent Ruwet, Olson's immediate superior at the time of his death, was in almost daily contact with Olson. According to Colonel Ruwet: "As a professional man . . . his ability . . . was outstanding." Colonel Ruwet stated that "during the period prior to the experiment . . . I noticed nothing which would lead me to believe that he was of unsound mind." Dr. Lashbrook, who had monthly contacts with Olson from early 1952 until the time of his death, stated publicly that before Olson received LSD, "as far as I know, he was perfectly normal." This assessment is in direct contradiction to certain statements evaluating Olson's emotional stability made in CIA internal memoranda written after Olson's death.

b. The Experiment.— On November 18, 1953, a group of ten scientists from the CIA and Camp Detrick attended a semi-annual review and analysis conference at a cabin located at Deep Creek Lake, Maryland. Three of the participants were from the CIA's Technical Services Staff. The Detrick representatives were all from the Special Operations Division.

According to one CIA official, the Special Operations Division participants "agreed that an unwitting experiment would be desirable." This account directly contradicts Vincent Ruwet's recollection. Ruwet recalls no such discussion, and has asserted that he would remember any such discussion because the SOD participants would have strenuously objected to testing on unwitting subjects.

In May, 1953, Richard Helms, Assistant DDP, held a staff meeting which the Chief of Technical Services Staff attended. At this meeting Helms "indicated that the drug [LSD] was dynamite and that he should be advised at all times when it was intended to use it." In addition, the then DDP, Frank Wisner, sent a memorandum to TSS stating the requirement that the DDP personally approve the use of LSD. Gottlieb went ahead with the experiment, securing the approval of his immediate supervisor. Neither the Chief of TSS nor the DDP specifically authorized the experiment in which Dr. Olson participated.

According to Gottlieb, a "very small dose" of LSD was placed in a bottle of Cointreau which was served after dinner on Thursday, November 19. The drug was placed in the liqueur by Robert Lashbrook. All but two of the SOD participants received LSD. One did not drink; the other had a heart condition. About twenty minutes after they finished their Cointreau, Gottlieb informed the other participants that they had received LSD.

Dr. Gottlieb stated that "up to the time of the experiment," he observed nothing unusual in Olson's behavior. Once the experiment was underway,

Gottlieb recalled that "the drug had a definite effect on the group to the point that they were boisterous and laughing and they could not continue the meeting or engage in sensible conversation." The meeting continued until about 1:00 a.m., when the participants retired for the evening. Gottlieb recalled that Olson, among others, complained of "wakefulness" during the night. According to Gottlieb on Friday morning "aside from some evidence of fatigue, I observed nothing unusual in [Olson's] actions, conversation, or general behavior." Ruwet recalls that Olson "appeared to be agitated" at breakfast, but that he "did not consider this to be abnormal under the circumstances."

c. The Treatment.—The following Monday, November 23, Olson was waiting for Ruwet when he came in to work at 7:30 a.m. For the next two days Olson's friends and family attempted to reassure him and help him "snap out" of what appeared to be a serious depression. On Tuesday, Olson again came to Ruwet and, after an hour-long conversation, it was decided that medical assistance for Dr. Olson was desirable.

Ruwet then called Lashbrook and informed him that "Dr. Olson was in serious trouble and needed immediate professional attention." Lashbrook agreed to make appropriate arrangements and told Ruwet to bring Olson to Washington, D.C. Ruwet and Olson proceeded to Washington to meet with Lashbrook, and the three left for New York at about 2:30 p.m. to meet with Dr. Harold Abramson.

At that time Dr. Abramson was an allergist and immunologist practicing medicine in New York City. He held no degree in psychiatry, but was associated with research projects supported indirectly by the CIA. Gottlieb and Dr. Lashbrook both followed his work closely in the early 1950s. Since Olson needed medical help, they turned to Dr. Abramson as the doctor closest to Washington who was experienced with LSD and cleared by the CIA.

Ruwet, Lashbrook, and Olson remained in New York for two days of consultations with Abramson. On Thursday, November 26, 1953, the three flew back to Washington so that Olson could spend Thanksgiving with his family. En route from the airport Olson told Ruwet that he was afraid to face his family. After a lengthy discussion, it was decided that Olson and Lashbrook would return to New York, and that Ruwet would go to Frederick to explain these events to Mrs. Olson.

Lashbrook and Olson flew back to New York the same day, again for consultations with Abramson. They spent Thursday night in a Long Island hotel and the next morning returned to the city with Abramson. In further discussions with Abramson, it was agreed that Olson should be placed under regular psychiatric care at an institution closer to his home.

d. The Death.—Because they could not obtain air transportation for a return trip on Friday night, Lashbrook and Olson made reservations for Saturday morning and checked into the Statler Hotel. Between the time they checked in and 10:00 p.m., they watched television, visited the cocktail lounge, where each had two martinis, and dinner. According to Lashbrook, Olson "was cheerful and appeared to enjoy the entertainment." He "appeared no longer particularly depressed, and almost the Dr. Olson I knew prior to the experiment."

After dinner Lashbrook and Olson watched television for about an hour, and at 11:00, Olson suggested that they go to bed, saying that "he felt more relaxed and contented than he had since [they] came to New York." Olson then left a call with the hotel operator to wake them in the morning. At approximately 2:30 a.m. Saturday, November 28, Lashbrook was awakened by a loud "crash of glass." In his report on the incident, he stated only that Olson "had crashed through the closed window blind and the closed window and he fell to his death from the window of our room on the 10th floor."

Immediately after finding that Olson had leapt to his death, Lashbrook telephoned Gottlieb at his home and informed him of the incident. Gottlieb called Ruwet and informed him of Olson's death at approximately 2:45 a.m. Lashbrook then called the hotel desk and reported the incident to the operator there. Lashbrook called Abramson and informed him of the occurrence. Abramson told Lashbrook he "wanted to be kept out of the thing completely," but later changed his mind and agreed to assist Lashbrook.

Shortly thereafter, uniformed police officers and some hotel employees came to Lashbrook's room. Lashbrook told the police he didn't know why Olson had committed suicide, but he did know that Olson "suffered from ulcers."

e. The Aftermath.—Following Dr. Olson's death, the CIA made a substantial effort to ensure that his family received death benefits, but did not notify the Olsons of the circumstances surrounding his demise. The Agency also made considerable efforts to prevent the death being connected with the CIA, and supplied complete cover for Lashbrook so that his association with the CIA would remain a secret.

After Dr. Olson's death the CIA conducted an internal investigation of the incident. As part of his responsibilities in this investigation, the General Counsel wrote the Inspector General, stating:

> I'm not happy with what seems to be a very casual attitude on the part of TSS representatives to the way this experiment was conducted and the remarks that this is just one of the risks running with scientific experimentation. I do not eliminate the need for taking risks, but I do believe, especially when human health or life is at stake, that at least the prudent, reasonable measures which can be taken to minimize the risk must be taken and failure to do so was culpable negligence. The actions of the various individuals concerned after effects of the experiment on Dr. Olson became manifest also revealed the failure to observe normal and reasonable precautions.

As a result of the investigation DCI Allen Dulles sent a personal letter to the Chief of Technical Operations of the Technical Services Staff who had approved the experiment criticizing him for "poor judgment . . . in authorizing the use of this drug on such an unwitting basis and without proximate medical safeguards." Dulles also sent a letter to Dr. Gottlieb, Chief of the Chemical Division of the Technical Services Staff, criticizing him for recommending the "unwitting application of the drug" in that the proposal "did not give sufficient emphasis for medical collaboration and for the proper consideration of the rights of the individual to whom it was being administered."

The letters were hand carried to the individuals to be read and returned. Although the letters were critical, a note from the Deputy Director of Central Intelligence to Mr. Helms instructed him to inform the individuals that: "These are not reprimands and no personnel file notation are being made."

Thus, although the Rockefeller Commission has characterized them as such, these notes were explicitly not reprimands. Nor did participation in the events which led to Dr. Olson's death have any apparent effect on the advancement within the CIA of the individuals involved.

3. The Surreptitious Administration of LSD to Unwitting Non-Volunteer Human Subjects by the CIA After the Death of Dr. Olson

The death of Dr. Olson could be viewed, as some argued at the time, as a tragic accident, one of the risks inherent in the testing of new substances. It might be argued that LSD was thought to be benign. After the death of Dr. Olson the dangers of the surreptitious administration of LSD were clear, yet the CIA continued or initiated a project involving the surreptitious administration of LSD to non-volunteer human subjects. This program exposed numerous individuals in the United States to the risk of death or serious injury without their informed consent, without medical supervision, and without necessary follow-up to determine any long-term effects.

Prior to the Olson experiment, the Director of Central Intelligence had approved MKULTRA, a research program designed to develop a "capability in the covert use of biological and chemical agent materials." In the proposal describing MKULTRA Mr. Helms, then ADDP, wrote the Director that:

> we intend to investigate the development of a chemical material which causes a reversible non-toxic aberrant mental state, the specific nature of which can be reasonably well predicted for each individual. This material could potentially aid in discrediting individuals, eliciting information, and implanting suggestions and other forms of mental control.

On February 12, 1954, the Director of the Central Intelligence Agency wrote TSS officials criticizing them for "poor judgment" in administering LSD on "an unwitting basis and without proximate medical safeguards" to Dr. Olson and for the lack of "proper consideration of the rights of the individual to whom it was being administered." On the same day, the Inspector General reviewed a report on Subproject Number 3 of MKULTRA, in which the same TSS officers who had just received letters from the Director were quoted as stating that one of the purposes of Subproject Number 3 was to "observe the behavior of unwitting persons being questioned after having been given a drug." There is no evidence that Subproject Number 3 was terminated even though these officers were unequivocally aware of the dangers of the surreptitious administration of LSD and the necessity of obtaining informed consent and providing medical safeguards. Subproject Number 3, in fact, used methods which showed even less concern than did the Olson experiment for the safety and security of the participants. Yet the evidence indicates the project continued until 1963.

In the project, the individual conducting the test might make initial contact with a prospective subject selected at random in a bar. He would then invite the person to a "safehouse" where the test drug was administered to the subject through drink or in food. CIA personnel might debrief the individual conducting the test, or observe the test by using a one-way mirror and tape recorder in an adjoining room.

Prior consent was obviously not obtained from any of the subjects. There was also, obviously, no medical prescreening. In addition, the tests were conducted by individuals who were not qualified scientific observers. There were no medical personnel on hand either to administer the drugs or to observe their effects, and no follow-up was conducted on the test subjects.

As the Inspector General noted in 1963:

> A significant limitation on the effectiveness of such testing is the infeasibility of performing scientific observation of results. The [individuals conducting the test] are not qualified scientific observers. Their subjects are seldom accessible beyond the first hours of the test. The testing may be useful in perfecting delivery techniques, and in identifying surface characteristics of onset, reaction, attribution, and side-effect.

This was particularly troublesome as in a

> number of instances . . . the test subject has become ill for hours or days, including hospitalization in at least one case, and the agent could only follow up by guarded inquiry after the test subject's return to normal life. Possible sickness and attendant economic loss are inherent contingent effects of the testing.

Paradoxically, greater care seems to have been taken for the safety of foreign nationals against whom LSD was used abroad. In several cases medical examinations were performed prior to the use of LSD. Moreover, the administration abroad was marked by constant observation made possible because the material was being used against prisoners of foreign intelligence or security organizations. Finally, during certain of the LSD interrogations abroad, local physicians were on call, though these physicians had had no experience with LSD and would not be told that hallucinogens had been administered.

The CIA's project involving the surreptitious administration of LSD to unwitting human subjects in the United States was finally halted in 1963, as a result of its discovery during the course of an Inspector General survey of the Technical Services Division. When the Inspector General learned of the project, he spoke to the Deputy Director for Plans, who agreed that the Director should be briefed. The DDP made it clear that the DCI and his Deputy were generally familiar with MKULTRA. He indicated, however, that he was not sure it was necessary to brief the DDCI at that point.

On May 24, 1963, the DDP advised the Inspector General that he had briefed the Director on the MKULTRA program and in particular had covered the question of the surreptitious administration of LSD to unwitting human subjects. According to the Inspector General, the DDP said that "the Director indicated no disagreement and therefore the 'testing' will continue."

One copy of an "Eyes Only" draft report on MKULTRA was prepared by the Inspector General who recommended the termination of the surreptitious administration project. The project was suspended following the Inspector General's report.

On December 17, 1963, Deputy Director for Plans Helms wrote a memo to the DDCI, who with the Inspector General and the Executive Director-Comptroller had opposed the covert testing. He noted two aspects of the problem: (1) "for over a decade the Clandestine Services has had the mission of maintaining a capability for influencing human behavior"; and (2) "testing arrangements in furtherance of this mission should be as operationally realistic and yet as controllable as possible." Helms argued that the individuals must be "unwitting" as this was "the only realistic method of maintaining the capability, considering the intended operational use of materials to influence human behavior as the operational targets will certainly be unwitting." Should the subjects of the testing not be unwitting, the program would only be "pro forma" resulting in a "false sense of accomplishment and readiness." Helms continued:

> If one grants the validity of the mission of maintaining this unusual capability and the necessity for unwitting testing, there is only then the question of how best to do it. Obviously, the testing should be

> conducted in such a manner as to permit the opportunity to observe the results of the administration on the target. It also goes without saying that whatever testing arrangement we adopt must afford maximum safeguards for the protection of the Agency's role in this activity, as well as minimizing the possibility of physical or emotional damage to the individual tested.

In another memo to the Director of Central Intelligence in June 1964, Helms again raised the issue of unwitting testing. At that time General {Marshall S.} Carter, then acting DCI, approved several changes in the MKULTRA program proposed by Mr. Helms as a result of negotiations between the Inspector General and the DDP. In a handwritten note, however, Director Carter added that "unwitting testing will be subject to a separate decision."

No specific decision was made then or soon after. The testing had been halted and, according to Walter Elder, Executive Assistant to DCI McCone, the DCI was not inclined to take the positive step of authorizing a resumption of the testing. At least through the summer, the DDP did not press the issue. On November 9, 1964, the DDP raised the issue again in a memo to the DCI, calling the Director's attention to what he described as "several other indications during the past year of an apparent Soviet aggressiveness in the field of covertly administered chemicals which are, to say the least, inexplicable and disturbing."

Helms noted that because of the suspension of covert testing, the Agency's "positive operational capability to use drugs is diminishing, owing to a lack of realistic testing. With increasing knowledge of the state of the art, we are less capable of staying up with Soviet advances in this field. This in turn results in a waning capability on our part to restrain others in the intelligence community (such as the Department of Defense) from pursuing operations in this area."

Helms attributed the cessation of the unwitting testing to the high risk of embarrassment to the Agency as well as the "moral problem." He noted that no better covert situation had been devised than that which had been used, and that "we have no answer to the moral issue."

Helms asked for either resumption of the testing project or its definitive cancellation. He argued that the status quo of a research and development program without a realistic testing program was causing the Agency to live "with the illusion of a capability which is becoming minimal and furthermore is expensive." Once again no formal action was taken in response to the Helms request.

From its beginning in the early 1950s until its termination in 1963, the program of surreptitious administration of LSD to unwitting non-volunteer human subjects demonstrates a failure of the CIA's leadership to pay adequate attention to the rights of individuals and to provide effective guidance to CIA employees. Though it was known that the testing was dangerous, the lives of subjects were placed in jeopardy and their rights were ignored during the ten years of testing which followed Dr. Olson's death. Although it was clear that the laws of the United States were being violated, the testing continued. While the individuals involved in the Olson experiment were admonished by the Director, at the same time they were also told that they were not being reprimanded and that their "bad judgment" would not be made part of their personnel records. When the covert testing project was terminated in 1963, none of the individuals involved were subject to any disciplinary action.

{. . .}

4. Monitoring and Control of the Testing and Use of Chemical and Biological Agents by the CIA

The Select Committee found numerous failures in the monitoring and control of the testing and use of chemical and biological agents within the CIA.

{. . .}

The internal controls within any agency rest on: (1) clear and coherent regulations; (2) clear lines of authority; and (3) clear rewards for those who conduct themselves in accord with agency regulations and understandable and immediate sanctions against those who do not. In the case of the testing and use of chemical and biological agents, normal CIA administrative controls were waived. The destruction of the documents on the largest CIA program in this area constituted a prominent example of the waiver of normal Agency procedures by the Director.

These documents were destroyed in early 1973 at the order of then DCI Richard Helms. According to Helms, Dr. Sidney Gottlieb, then Director of TSD

> . . . came to me and said that he was retiring and that I was retiring and he thought it would be a good idea if these files were destroyed. And I also believe part of the reason for our thinking this was advisable was there had been relationships with outsiders in government agencies and other organizations and that these would be sensitive in this kind of a thing but that since the program was over and finished and done with, we thought we would just get rid of the files as well, so that anybody who assisted us in the past would not be subject to follow-up or questions, embarrassment, if you will.

The destruction was based on a waiver of an internal CIA regulation, CSI 70–10, which regulated the "retirement of inactive records." As Thomas Karamessines, then Deputy Director of Plans, wrote in regulation CSI 70–10: "Retirement is not a matter of convenience or of storage but of conscious judgment in the application of the rules modified by knowledge of individual component needs. The heart of this judgment is to ensure that the complete story can be reconstructed in later years and by people who may be unfamiliar with the events."

The destruction of the MKULTRA documents made it impossible for the Select Committee to determine the full range and extent of the largest CIA research program involving chemical and biological agents. The destruction also prevented the CIA from locating and providing medical assistance to the individuals who were subjects in the program. Finally, it prevented the Committee from determining the full extent of the operations which made use of materials developed in the MKULTRA program.

{ . . . }

C. Covert Testing on Human Subjects by Military Intelligence Groups: Material Testing Program EA 1729, Project THIRD CHANGE, and Project DERBY HAT

EA 1729 is the designator used in the Army drug testing program for lysergic acid diethylamide (LSD). Interest in LSD was originally aroused at the Army's Chemical Warfare Laboratories by open literature on the unusual effects of the compound. The positive intelligence and counterintelligence potential envisioned for compounds like LSD, and suspected Soviet interest in such materials, supported the development of an American military capability and resulted in experiments conducted jointly by the U.S. Army Intelligence Board and the Chemical Warfare Laboratories.

These experiments, designed to evaluate potential intelligence uses of LSD, were known collectively as "Material Testing Program EA 1729." Two projects of particular interest conducted as part of these experiments, "THIRD CHANCE" and "DERBY HAT," involved the administration of LSD to unwitting subjects in Europe and the Far East.

In many respects, the Army's testing programs duplicated research which had already been conducted by the CIA. They certainly involved the risks inherent in the early phases of drug testing. In the Army's tests, as with those of the CIA, individual rights were also subordinated to national security considerations; informed consent and follow-up examinations of subjects were neglected in efforts to maintain the secrecy of the tests. Finally, the command and control problems which were apparent in the CIA's programs are paralleled by a lack of clear authorization and supervision in the Army's programs.

1. Scope of Testing

Between 1955 and 1958 research was initiated by the Army Chemical Corps to evaluate the potential for LSD as a chemical warfare incapacitating agent. In the course of this research, LSD was administered to more than 1,000 American volunteers who then participated in a series of tests designed to ascertain the effects of the drug on their ability to function as soldiers. With the exception of one set of tests at Fort Bragg, these and subsequent laboratory experiments to evaluate chemical warfare potential were conducted at the Army Chemical Warfare Laboratories, Edgewood, Maryland.

In 1958 a new series of laboratory tests were initiated at Edgewood. These experiments were conducted as the initial phase of Material Testing Program EA 1729 to evaluate the intelligence potential of LSD, and included LSD tests on 95 volunteers. As part of these tests, three structured experiments were conducted:

> 1. LSD was administered surreptitiously at a simulated social reception to volunteer subjects who were unaware of the purpose or nature of the tests in which they were participating;

2. LSD was administered to volunteers who were subsequently polygraphed; and

3. LSD was administered to volunteers who were then confined to "isolation chambers."

These structured experiments were designed to evaluate the validity of the traditional security training all subjects had undergone in the face of unconventional, drug enhanced interrogations.

At the conclusion of the laboratory test phase of Material Testing Program EA 1729 in 1960, the Army Assistant Chief of Staff for Intelligence (ACSI) authorized operational field testing of LSD. The first field tests were conducted in Europe by an Army Special Purpose Team (SPT) during the period from May to August of 1961. These tests were known as Project THIRD CHANCE and involved eleven separate interrogations of ten subjects. None of the subjects were volunteers and none were aware that they were to receive LSD. All but one subject, a U.S. soldier implicated in the theft of classified documents, were alleged to be foreign intelligence sources or agents. While interrogations of these individuals were only moderately successful, at least one subject (the U.S. soldier) exhibited symptoms of severe paranoia while under the influence of the drug.

The second series of field tests, Project DERBY HAT, were conducted by an Army SPT in the Far East during the period from August to November of 1962. Seven subjects were interrogated under DERBY HAT, all of whom were foreign nationals either suspected of dealing in narcotics or implicated in foreign intelligence operations. The purpose of this second set of experiments was to collect additional data on the utility of LSD in field interrogations, and to evaluate any different effects the drug might have on "Orientals."

2. Inadequate Coordination Among Intelligence Agencies

On October 15, 1959, the U.S. Army Intelligence Center prepared a lengthy staff study on Material Testing Program EA 1729. The stated purpose of the staff study was "to determine the desirability of EA 1729 on non-US subjects in selected actual operations under controlled conditions." It was on the basis of this study that operational field tests were later conducted.

After noting that the Chemical Warfare Laboratories began experiments with LSD on humans in 1955 and had administered the drug to over 1,000 volunteers, the "background" section of the study concluded:

> There has not been a single case of residual ill effect. Study of the prolific scientific literature on LSD-25 and personal communication between US Army Chemical Corps personnel and other researchers in this field have failed to disclose an authenticated instance of irreversible change being produced in normal humans by the drug.

This conclusion was reached despite an awareness that there were inherent medical dangers in such experimentation. In the body of this same study it is noted that:

> The view has been expressed that EA 1729 is a potentially dangerous drug, whose pharmaceutical actions are not fully understood and there has been cited the possibility of the continuance of a chemically induced psychosis in chronic form, particularly if a latent schizophrenic were a subject, with consequent claim or representation against the U.S. Government.

An attempt was made to minimize potential medical hazards by careful selection of subjects prior to field tests. Rejecting evidence that the drug might be hazardous, the study continued:

> The claim of possible permanent damage caused by EA 1729 is an unproven hypothesis based on the characteristic effect of the material. While the added stress of a real situation may increase the probability of permanent adverse effect, *the resulting risk is deemed to be slight by the medical research personnel of the Chemical Warfare Laboratories.* To prevent even such a slight risk, the proposed plan for field experimentation calls for overt, if possible, or contrived-through-ruse, if necessary, physical and mental examination of any real situation subject prior to employment of the subject.

This conclusion was drawn six years after one death had occurred which could be attributed, at least in part, to the effects of the very drug the Army was proposing to field test. The USAINTC staff, however, was apparently unaware of the circumstances surrounding Dr. Olson's death. This lack of knowledge is indicative of the general lack of interagency communication on drug related research. As the October 1959 study noted, "there has been no coordination with other intelligence agencies up to the present."

On December 7, 1959, the Army Assistant Chief of Staff for Intelligence (ACSI, apparently a General {John M.} Willems) was briefed on the proposed operational use of LSD by USAINTC Project Officer {William} Jacobson, in preparation for Project THIRD CHANCE. General Willems expressed concern that the project had not been coordinated with the FBI and the CIA. He is quoted as saying "that if this project is going to be worth anything it [LSD] should be used on higher types of non-F.S. subjects"—in other words "staffers." He indicated this could be accomplished if the CIA were brought in. The summary of the briefing prepared by a Major Mehovsky continues: "Of particular note is that ACSI did not direct coordination with CIA and the FBI but only mentioned it for consideration by the planners."

After the briefing, four colonels, two lieutenant colonels and Major Mehovsky met to discuss interagency cooperation with CIA and FBI. The group consensus was to postpone efforts toward coordination:

> Lt. Col. Jacobson commented that before we coordinate with CIA we should have more factual findings from field experimentation with counterintelligence cases that will strengthen our position and proposal for cooperation. This approach was agreed to by the conferees.

Had such coordination been achieved, the safety of these experiments might have been viewed differently and the tests themselves might have been seen as unnecessary.

3. Subordination of Individual Rights to National Security Considerations

Just as many of these experiments may have been unnecessary, the nature of the operational tests (polygraph-assisted interrogations of drugged suspects) reflects a basic disregard for the fundamental human rights of the subjects. The interrogation of an American soldier as part of the THIRD CHANCE 1961 tests is an example of this disregard.

The "trip report" for Project THIRD CHANCE, dated September 6,

1961, recounts the circumstances surrounding and the results of the tests as follows:

> [The subject] was a U.S. soldier who had confessed to theft of classified documents. Conventional methods had failed to ascertain whether espionage intent was involved. A significant new admission by subject that he told a fellow soldier of the theft while he still had the documents in his possession was obtained during the EA 1729 interrogation along with other variations of Subject's previous account. The interrogation results were deemed by the local operational authority satisfactory evidence of Subject's claim of innocence in regard to espionage intent.

The subject apparently reacted very strongly to the drug, and the interrogation, while productive, was difficult. The trip report concluded:

> (1) This case demonstrated the ability to interrogate a subject profitably throughout a highly sustained and almost incapacitating reaction to EA 1729.
>
> (2) The apparent value of bringing a subject into the EA 1729 situation in a highly stressed state was indicated.
>
> (3) The usefulness of employing as a duress factor the device of inviting the subject's attention to his EA 1729-influenced state and threatening to extend this state indefinitely even to a permanent condition of insanity, or to bring it to an end at the discretion of the interrogators was shown to be effective.
>
> (4) The need for preplanned precautions against extreme paranoiac reaction to EA 1729 was indicated.
>
> (5) It was brought to attention by this case that where subject has undergone extended intensive interrogation prior to the EA 1729 episode and has persisted in a version repeatedly during conventional interrogation, adherence to the same version while under EA 1729 influence, however extreme the reaction, may not necessarily be evidence of truth but merely the ability to adhere to a well-rehearsed story.

This strong reaction to the drug and the accompanying discomfort this individual suffered were exploited by the use of traditional interrogation techniques. While there is no evidence that physical violence or torture were employed in connection with this interrogation, physical and psychological techniques were used in the THIRD CHANCE experiments to exploit the subjects' altered mental state, and to maximize the stress situation. Jacobson described these methods in his trip report:

> Stressing techniques employed included silent treatment before or after EA 1729 administration, sustained conventional interrogation prior to EA 1729 interrogation, deprivation of food, drink, sleep or bodily evacuation, sustained isolation prior to EA 1729 administration, hot-cold switches in approach, duress "pitches," verbal degradation and bodily discomfort, or dramatized threats to subject's life or mental health.

Another gross violation of an individual's fundamental rights occurred in September 1962 as part of the Army's DERBY HAT tests in the Far East. A suspected Asian espionage agent was given 6 micrograms of LSD per kilogram of bodyweight. The administration of the drug was completed at 1035 that morning:

> At 1120, sweating became evident, his pulse became thready. He was placed in a supine position. He began groaning with expiration and became semicomatose.

For the next 28 minutes, the subject remained semicomatose.

> At 1148, responses to painful stimuli were slightly improved. At 1155, he was helped to a sitting position.
>
> At 1200, he became shocky again and was returned to supine position.
>
> At 1212, he was more alert and able to sit up with help. At 1220, Subject was assisted to the interrogation table.
>
> At 1230, he began moaning he wanted to die and usually ignored questions. Rarely he stated "he didn't know."
>
> At 1250, his phasic alertness persisted. He frequently refocused his eyes with eyelid assistance. He frequently threw his head back with eyes closed.
>
> At 1330, he was slightly more alert. He was forced-walked for 5 minutes. He physically could cooperate until he became shocky again (sweating, thready pulse, pale).

For the next three hours the subject remained in about the same condition. Continued attempts at interrogation yielded no relevant answers. Six hours after receiving the drug, the subject began giving relevant answers to questions. Eight and one-half hours after the initial dosage, the subject was polygraphed. The interrogation continued for seventeen and one-half hours after the drug was administered.

There was some psychological and medical screening of the individuals tested within the United States, in Europe, and in Asia. The proposal for the field experimentation in fact called for such examinations. The fact of prescreening did not eliminate the risk of injury; the availability of medical staff did, however, limit injury and may well have prevented the death of one or more of the subjects. As the medical corps member of the team which surreptitiously administered the LSD noted, "one subject . . . did collapse after the interrogation and the presence of the medical officer was not only of value to the subject but to the interrogation team who were thus assured that an unnecessary untoward result would not occur."

In the October 15, 1959, USAINTC staff study, moral and legal ramifications of covert administration of LSD in field conditions were considered.

> It was always a tenet of Army Intelligence that the basic American principle of the dignity and welfare of the individual will not be violated. . . . A more meticulous regard for the prohibition against violence or duress is taken in practice when the suspect is a US citizen or ally as against an actual or potential enemy, in peace as against war, and in respect to the nature of the crime. . . . In intelligence, the stakes involved and the interests of national security may permit a more tolerant interpretation of moral-ethical values, but not legal limits, through necessity. . . . Any claim against the US Government for alleged injury due to EA 1729 must be legally shown to have been due to the material. Proper security and appropriate operational techniques can protect the fact of employment of EA 1729.

On the basis of this evaluation, the study concluded that in view of "the stakes involved and the interests of national security," the proposed plan for field testing should be approved.

The surreptitious administration of drugs to unwitting subjects by the Army raises serious constitutional and legal issues. The consideration given these issues by the Army was wholly insufficient. The character of the Army's volunteer testing program and the possibility that drugs were simply substituted for other forms of violence or duress in field interrogations raises serious doubts as to whether national security imperatives were properly interpreted. The "consent" forms which each American volunteer signed prior to the administration of LSD are a case in point. These forms contained no mention of the medical and psychological risks inherent in such testing, nor do they mention the nature of the psychotropic drug to be administered:

> The general nature of the experiments in which I have volunteered have been explained to me from the standpoint of possible hazards to my health. *It is my understanding* that the experiments are so designed, based on the results of animals and previous human experimentation, *that the anticipated results will justify the performance of the experiment.* I understand further that experiments will be so conducted as to avoid all unnecessary physical and medical suffering and injury, and that *I will be at liberty to request that the experiments be terminated at any time* if in my opinion I have reached the physical or mental state where continuation of the experiments becomes undesirable.
>
> *I recognize that* in the pursuit of certain experiments *transitory discomfort may occur.* I recognize, also, that under these circumstances, *I must rely upon the skill and wisdom of the physician supervising the experiment* to institute whatever medical or surgical measures are indicated. [Emphasis added.]

The exclusion of any specific discussion of the nature of LSD in these forms raises serious doubts as to their validity. An "understanding . . . that the anticipated results will justify the performance of the experiment" without full knowledge of the nature of the experiment is an incomplete "understanding." Similarly, the nature of the experiment limited the ability of both the subject to request its termination and the experimenter to implement such a request. Finally, the euphemistic characterization of "transitory discomfort" and the agreement to "rely on the skill and wisdom of the physician" combine to conceal inherent risks in the experimentation and may be viewed as dissolving the experimenter of personal responsibility for damaging aftereffects. In summary, a "volunteer" program in which subjects are not fully informed of potential hazards to their persons is "volunteer" in name only.

This problem was compounded by the security statements signed by each volunteer before he participated in the testing. As part of this statement, potential subjects agreed that they would:

> . . . not divulge or make available any information related to U.S. Army Intelligence Center interest or participation in the Department of the Army Medical Research Volunteer Program to any individual, nation, organization, business, association, or other group or entity, not officially authorized to receive such information.
>
> I understand that any action contrary to the provisions of this statement will render me liable to punishment under the provisions of the Uniform Code of Military Justice.

Under these provisions, a volunteer experiencing aftereffects of the test might have been unable to seek immediate medical assistance.

This disregard for the well-being of subjects of drug testing is inexcusable. Further, the absence of any comprehensive long-term medical assistance for the subjects of these experiments is not only unscientific; it is also unprofessional.

4. Lack of Normal Authorization and Supervision

It is apparent from documents supplied to the Committee that the Army's testing program often operated under informal and nonroutine authorization. Potentially dangerous operations such as these testing programs are the very projects which ought to be subject to the closest internal scrutiny at the highest levels of the military command structure. There are numerous examples of inadequate review, partial consideration, and incomplete approval in the administration of these programs.

When the first Army program to use LSD on American soldiers in "field stations" was authorized in May 1955, the Army violated its own procedures in obtaining approval. Under Army Chief of Staff Memorandum 385, such proposals were to be personally approved by the Secretary of the Army. Although the plan was submitted to him on April 26, 1956, the Secretary issued no written authorization for the project, and there is no evidence that he either reviewed or approved the plan. Less than a month later, the Army Chief of Staff issued a memorandum authorizing the tests.

Subsequent testing of LSD under Material Testing Program EA 1729 operated generally under this authorization. When the plans for this testing were originally discussed in early 1958 by officials of the Army Intelligence Center at Fort Holabird and representatives of the Chemical Warfare Center at Edgewood Arsenal, an informal proposal was formulated. This proposal was submitted to the Medical Research Directorate at Edgewood by the President of the Army Intelligence Board on June 3, 1958. There is no evidence that the plan was approved at any level higher than the President of the Intelligence Board or the Commanding General of Edgewood. The approval at Edgewood appears to have been issued by the Commander's Adjutant. The Medical Research Laboratories did not submit the plan to the Surgeon General for approval (a standard procedure) because the new program was ostensibly covered by the authorizations granted in May 1956.

The two projects involving the operational use of LSD (THIRD CHANCE and DERBY HAT) were apparently approved by the Army Assistant Chief of Staff for Intelligence (General Willems) on December 7, 1960. This verbal approval came in the course of a briefing on previous drug programs and on the planned field experimentation. There is no record of written approval being issued by the ACSI to authorize these specific projects until January 1961, and there is no record of any specific knowledge or approval by the Secretary of the Army.

On February 4, 1963, Major General C{harles} F. Leonard, Army ACSI, forwarded a copy of the THIRD CHANCE Trip Report to Army Chief of Staff, General Earl Wheeler. Wheeler had apparently requested a copy on February 2. The report was routed through a General Hamlett. While this report included background on the origins of the LSD tests, it appears that General Wheeler may only have read the conclusion and recommendations. The office memorandum accompanying the Trip Report bears Wheeler's initials.

5. Termination of Testing

On April 10, 1963, a briefing was held in the ACSI's office on the results of Projects THIRD CHANCE and DERBY HAT. Both SPTs concluded that more field testing was required before LSD could be utilized as an integral aid to counterintelligence interrogations. During the presentation of the DERBY HAT results, General Leonard (Deputy ACSI) directed that no further field testing be undertaken. After this meeting the ACSI sent a letter to the Commanding General of the Army Combat Developments

Command (CDC) requesting that he review THIRD CHANCE and DERBY HAT and "make a net evaluation concerning the adoption of EA 1729 for future use as an effective and profitable aid in counterintelligence interrogations." On the same day the ACSI requested that the CDC Commander revise regulation FM 30–17 to read in part:

> . . . in no instance will drugs be used as an aid to interrogations in counterintelligence or security operations without prior permission of the Department of the Army. Requests to use drugs as an investigative aid will be forwarded through intelligence channels to the OACSI, DA, for approval. . . .
>
> Medical research has established that information obtained through the use of these drugs is unreliable and invalid. . . .
>
> It is considered that DA [Army] approval must be a prerequisite for use of such drugs because of the moral, legal, medical and political problems inherent in their use for intelligence purposes.

The subsequent adoption of this regulation marked the effective termination of field testing of LSD by the Army.

The official termination date of these testing programs is rather unclear, but a later ACSI memo indicates that it may have occurred in September of 1963. On the 19th of that month a meeting was held between Dr. Van Sim (Edgewood Arsenal), Major {Ernest R.} Clovis (Chemical Research Laboratory), and ACSI representatives (General {Charles} Denholm and Colonel {G. E.} Schmidt). "As a result of this conference a determination was made to suspend the program and any further activity pending a more profitable and suitable use."

D. Cooperation and Competition Among the Intelligence Community Agencies and Between These Agencies and Other Individuals and Institutions

1. Relationships Among Agencies Within the Intelligence Community

Relationships among intelligence community agencies in this area varied considerably over time, ranging from full cooperation to intense and wasteful competition. The early period was marked by a high degree of cooperation among the agencies of the intelligence community. Although the military dominated research involving chemical and biological agents, the information developed was shared with the FBI and the CIA. But the spirit of cooperation did not continue. The failure by the military to share information apparently breached the spirit, if not the letter, of commands from above.

As noted above, the Army Assistant Chief of Staff for Intelligence was briefed on the proposed operational testing of LSD under Project THIRD CHANCE, and expressed concern that the project had not been coordinated with FBI and CIA. Despite this request, no coordination was achieved between the Army and either of these agencies. Had such cooperation been forthcoming, this project may have been evaluated in a different light.

The competition between the agencies in this area reached bizarre levels. A military officer told a CIA representative in confidence about the military's field testing of LSD in Europe under Project THIRD CHANCE, and the CIA promptly attempted to learn surreptitiously the nature and extent of the program. At roughly the same time Mr. Helms argued to the DDCI that the unwitting testing program should be continued, as it contributed to the CIA's capability in the area and thus allowed the CIA "to restrain others in the intelligence community (such as the Department of Defense) from pursuing operations."

The MKNAOMI program was also marked by a failure to share information. The Army Special Forces (the principal customer of the Special Operations Division at Fort Detrick) and the CIA rather than attempting to coordinate their efforts promulgated different requirements which varied only slightly. This apparently resulted in some duplication of effort. In order to insure the security of CIA operations, the Agency would request materials from SOD for operational use without fully or accurately describing the operational requirements. This resulted in limitations on SOD's ability to assist the CIA.

2. Relationships Between the Intelligence Community Agencies and Foreign Liaison Services

The subjects of the CIA's operational testing of chemical and biological agents abroad were generally being held for interrogation by foreign intelligence or security organizations. Although information about the use of drugs was generally withheld from these organizations, cooperation with them necessarily jeopardized the security of CIA interest in these materials. Cooperation also placed the American Government in a position of complicity in actions which violated the rights of the subjects, and which may have violated the laws of the country in which the experiments took place.

Cooperation between the intelligence agencies and organizations in foreign countries was not limited to relationships with the intelligence or internal security organizations. Some MKULTRA research was conducted abroad. While this is, in itself, not a questionable practice, it is important that such research abroad not be undertaken to evade American laws. That this was a possibility is suggested by an ARTICHOKE memorandum in which it is noted that working with the scientists of a foreign country "might be very advantageous" since that government "permitted certain activities which were not permitted by the United States government (i.e., experiments on anthrax, etc.)."

{ . . . }

4. Relationships Between the Intelligence Community Agencies and Other Institutions and Individuals, Public and Private

The Inspector General's 1963 Survey of MKULTRA noted that "the research and development" phase was conducted through standing arrangements with "specialists in universities, pharmaceutical houses, hospitals, state and federal institutions, and private research organizations" in a manner which concealed "from the institution the interests of the CIA." Only a few "key individuals" in each institution were "made witting of Agency sponsorship." The research and development phase was succeeded by a phase involving "physicians, toxicologists, and other specialists in mental, narcotics, and general hospitals and prisons, who are provided the products and findings of the basic research projects and proceed with intensive testing on human subjects."

According to the Inspector General, the MKULTRA testing programs were "conducted under accepted scientific procedures . . . where health permits, test subjects are voluntary participants in the programs." This was clearly not true in the project involving the surreptitious administration of LSD, which was marked by a complete lack of screening, medical supervision, opportunity to observe, or medical or psychological follow-up.

The intelligence agencies allowed individual researchers to design their project. Experiments sponsored by these researchers (which included one where narcotics addicts were sent to Lexington, Kentucky, who were rewarded with the drug of their addiction in return for participation in experiments with LSD) call into question the decision by the agencies not to fix guidelines for the experiments.

The MKULTRA research and development program raises other questions, as well. It is not clear whether individuals in prisons, mental, narcotics and general hospitals can provide "informed consent" to participation in experiments such as these. There is doubt as to whether institutions should be unwitting of the ultimate sponsor of research being done in their facilities. The nature of the arrangements also made it impossible for the individuals who were not aware of the sponsor of the research to exercise any choice about their participation based on the sponsoring organization.

Although greater precautions are now being taken in research conducted on behalf of the intelligence community agencies, the dilemma of classification remains. These agencies obviously wished to conceal their interest in certain forms of research in order to avoid stimulating interest in the same areas by hostile governments. In some cases today contractors or researchers wish to conceal their connection with these agencies. Yet the fact of classification prevents open discussion and debate upon which scholarly work depends.

10.

National Security Agency Surveillance Affecting Americans

I. INTRODUCTION AND SUMMARY

This report describes the Committee's investigation into certain questionable activities of the National Security Agency (NSA). The Committee's primary focus in this phase of its investigation was on NSA's electronic surveillance practices and capabilities, especially those involving American citizens, groups, and organizations.

NSA has intercepted and disseminated international communications of American citizens whose privacy ought to be protected under our Constitution. For example, from August 1945 to May 1975, NSA obtained copies of many international telegrams sent to, from, or through the United States from three telegraph companies. In addition, from the early 1960s until 1973, NSA targeted the international communications of certain American citizens by placing their names on a "watch list." Intercepted messages were disseminated to the FBI, CIA, Secret Service, Bureau of Narcotics and Dangerous Drugs (BNDD), and the Department of Defense. In neither program were warrants obtained.

With one exception, NSA contends that its interceptions of Americans' private messages were part of monitoring programs already being conducted against various international communications channels for "foreign intelligence" purposes. This contention is borne out by the record. Yet to those Americans who have had their communications—sent with the expectation that they were private—intentionally intercepted and disseminated by their Government, the knowledge that NSA did not monitor specific communications channels solely to acquire their messages is of little comfort.

In general, NSA's surveillance of Americans was in response to requests from other Government agencies. Internal NSA directives now forbid the targeting of American citizens' communications. Nonetheless, NSA may still acquire communications of American citizens as part of its foreign intelligence mission, and information derived from these intercepted messages may be used to satisfy foreign intelligence requirements.

NSA's current surveillance capabilities and past surveillance practices were both examined in our investigation. The Committee recognizes that NSA's vast technological capability is a sensitive national asset which ought to be zealously protected for its value to our common defense. If not properly controlled, however, this same technological capability could be turned against the American people, at great cost to liberty. This concern is compounded by the knowledge that the proportion of telephone calls and telegrams being sent through the air is still increasing. { . . . }

A. NSA's Origins and Official Responsibilities

NSA does not have a statutory charter; its operational responsibilities are set forth exclusively in executive directives first issued in the 1950s. One of the questions which the Senate asked the Committee to consider was the "need for specific legislative authority to govern the operations of . . . the National Security Agency."

According to NSA's General Counsel, no existing statutes control, limit, or define the signals intelligence activities of NSA. Further, the General Counsel asserts that the Fourth Amendment does not apply to NSA's interception of Americans' international communications for foreign intelligence purposes.

1. Origins

NSA was established in 1952 by a Top Secret directive issued by President Truman. Under this directive, NSA assumed the responsibilities of the Armed Forces Security Agency, which had been created after World War II to integrate American cryptologic efforts. These efforts had expanded rapidly after World War II as a result of the demonstrated wartime value of breaking enemy codes, particularly those of the Japanese.

2. Responsibilities

(a) Subject Matter Responsibilities.—The executive branch expects NSA to collect political, economic, and military information as part of its "foreign intelligence" mission. "Foreign intelligence" is an ambiguous term. Its meaning changes, depending upon the prevailing needs and views of policymakers, and the current world situation. The internal politics of a nation also play a role in setting requirements for foreign intelligence; the domestic economic situation, an upcoming political campaign, and internal unrest can all affect the kind of foreign intelligence that a political leader desires. Thus, the definition constantly expands and contracts to satisfy the changing needs of American policymakers for information. This flexibility was illustrated in the late 1960s, when NSA and other intelligence agencies were asked to produce "foreign intelligence" on domestic activists in the wake of major civil disturbances and increasing antiwar activities.

NSA's authority to collect foreign intelligence is derived from a Top Secret National Security Council directive which is implemented by directives issued by the Director of Central Intelligence. These directives give NSA the responsibility for "Signals Intelligence" (SIGINT) and "Communications Security" (COMSEC). SIGINT is subdivided into "Communications Intelligence" (COMINT) and "Electronics Intelligence" (ELINT). COMINT entails the interception of foreign communications and ELINT involves the interception of electronic signals from radars, missiles, and the like. The COMSEC mission includes the protection of United States Government communications by providing the means for enciphering messages and by establishing procedures for maintaining the security of equipment used to transmit them.

NSA's interception of communications—the area on which the Committee focused—arises under the COMINT program. The controlling NSCID defines COMINT in broad terms as "technical and intelligence information derived from foreign communications by other than the intended recipients." The same NSC directive also states that COMINT "shall not include (a) any intercept and processing of unencrypted written communications, press and propaganda broadcasts, or censorship."

The specific exclusion of unencrypted *written* communications from NSA's mandate would appear to prohibit NSA's interception of telegrams. NSA contends that this exclusion is and always has been limited to mail and communications other than those sent electronically.

The same NSCID which discusses foreign communications also states that NSA is to produce intelligence "in accordance with objectives, requirements, and priorities established by the Director of Central Intelligence with the advice of the United States Intelligence Board." USIB was composed of representatives from the FBI, CIA, Treasury Department, Energy Research and Development Administration, State Department, and Defense Department. Since 1966, NSA annually received general requirements from USIB for the collection of foreign intelligence. These requirements ordinarily identified broad areas of interest, such as combating international terrorism, and were supplemented by more specific "amplifying requirements" periodically submitted to NSA by other USIB members.

(b) Geographic Responsibilities.—Although none of the applicable executive directives explicitly prohibit NSA from intercepting communications which occur wholly within the United States, internal NSA policy has always prohibited such interceptions. In practice, NSA limits itself to communications where at least one of the terminals is in a foreign country. This means that when Americans use a telephone or other communications link between this country and overseas, their words may be intercepted by NSA.

(c) Jurisdiction with Respect to Nationality.—Although the controlling NSCID contains no limitation relating to the citizenship of persons whose "foreign communications" may be intercepted, the relevant DCID does exclude messages "exchanged among private organizations and nationals, acting in a private capacity, of the U.S." This restriction is designed to prevent NSA from processing communications between two Americans, regardless of their location.

In the late 1960s and early 1970s, however, NSA did intercept and disseminate some messages exchanged between two Americans where one of the terminals was foreign. NSA does not now knowingly process or disseminate messages where both the sender and recipient are American citizens, groups, or organizations.

B. Summary of Interception Programs

The Committee's hearings disclosed three NSA interception programs: the "watch lists" containing names of American citizens; "Operation SHAMROCK," whereby NSA received copies of millions of telegrams leaving or transiting the United States; and the monitoring of certain telephone links between the United States and South America at the request of the Bureau of Narcotics and Dangerous Drugs. In addition, the Committee's investigation revealed that although NSA no longer includes the names of specific citizens in its selection criteria, it still intercepts international communications of Americans as part of its foreign intelligence collection activity. Information derived from such communications is disseminated by NSA to other intelligence agencies to satisfy foreign intelligence requirements.

1. Watch Lists Containing Names of Americans

From the early 1960s until 1973, NSA intercepted and disseminated international communications of selected American citizens and groups on the basis of lists of names supplied by other Government agencies. In 1967, as part of a general concern within the intelligence community over civil disturbances and peace demonstrations, NSA responded to Defense Department requests by expanding its watch list program. Watch lists came to include the names of individuals, groups, and organizations involved in domestic antiwar and civil rights activities in an attempt to discover if there was "foreign influence" on them.

In 1969, NSA formalized the watch list program under the codename MINARET. The program applied not only to alleged foreign influence on domestic dissent, but also to American groups and individuals whose activities "may result in civil disturbances or otherwise subvert the national security of the U.S." At the same time, NSA instructed its personnel to "restrict the knowledge" that NSA was collecting such information and to keep its name off the disseminated "product." Prior to 1973, NSA generally relied on the agencies requesting information to determine the propriety and legality of their actions in submitting names to NSA. NSA's new director, General Lew Allen, Jr., indicated some concern about Project MINARET in August 1973, and suspended the dissemination of messages under the program. In September 1973, Allen wrote the agencies involved in the watch lists, requesting a recertification of their requirements, particularly as to the appropriateness of their requests.

In October 1973, Assistant Attorney General Henry Petersen and Attorney General Elliot Richardson concluded that the watch lists were of "questionable legality" and so advised NSA. In response, NSA took the position that although specific names had been targeted, the communications of particular Americans included on the watch lists had been collected "as an incidental and unintended act in the conduct of the interception of foreign communications." Allen concluded:

> [NSA's] current practice conforms with your guidance that relevant information acquired [by NSA] in the routine pursuit of the collection of foreign intelligence information may continue to be furnished to appropriate government agencies.

2. Obtaining Copies of Messages from International Telegraph Companies: Operation SHAMROCK

From August 1945 until May 1975, NSA received copies of millions of international telegrams sent to, from, or transiting the United States. Codenamed Operation SHAMROCK, this was the largest governmental interception program affecting Americans, dwarfing CIA's mail opening program by comparison. Of the messages provided to NSA by the three major international telegraph companies, it is estimated that in later years approximately 150,000 per month were reviewed by NSA analysts.

NSA states that the original purpose of the program was to obtain the enciphered telegrams of certain foreign targets. Nevertheless, NSA had access to virtually all the international telegrams of Americans carried by RCA Global and ITT World Communications. Once obtained, these telegrams were available for analysis and dissemination according to NSA's selection criteria, which included the watch lists.

The SHAMROCK program began in August 1945, when representatives of the Army Signals Security Agency approached the commercial telegraph companies to seek post-war access to foreign governmental traffic passing over the facilities of the companies. Despite advice from their attorneys that the contemplated intercept operation would be illegal in peacetime, the companies agreed to participate, provided they received the personal assurance of the Attorney General of the United States that he would protect them from suit, and that efforts be immediately undertaken to legalize the intercept operation. Apparently these assurances were forthcoming, because the intercept program began shortly thereafter.

In 1947, representatives of the companies met with Secretary of Defense {James V.} Forrestal to discuss their continued participation in

SHAMROCK. Forrestal told them that the program was "in the highest interests of national security" and urged them to continue. The companies were told that President Truman and Attorney General Tom C. Clark approved and that they would not suffer criminal liability, at least while the current Administration was in office. Those assurances were renewed in 1949, when it was again emphasized that future administrations could not be bound. There is no evidence that the companies ever sought such assurances again.

Throughout the operation NSA never informed the companies that it was analyzing and disseminating telegrams of Americans. Yet the companies, who had feared in 1945 that their conduct might be illegal, apparently never sought assurances that NSA was limiting its use to the messages of the foreign targets once the intercept program had begun.

3. Monitoring of South American Links for Drug Traffic Control Purposes

From 1970 to 1973, at the request of the Bureau of Narcotics and Dangerous Drugs, NSA monitored selected telephone circuits between the United States and certain countries in South America to obtain information relating to drug trafficking.

The BNDD was initially concerned about drug deals that were being arranged in calls to a South American city from public telephone booths in New York City. The Bureau determined that it could not legally tap the public telephones and enlisted NSA's help to monitor international communications links that carried these telephone calls. Thus, instead of intercepting calls from a few telephone booths, as the BNDD would have done with a wiretap, NSA had access to international calls placed from, or received in, cities all over the United States that were switched through New York.

In addition, BNDD submitted the names of 450 Americans to NSA for a "drug" watch list. This list resulted in the dissemination of about 1,900 reports on drug traffickers to BNDD and CIA.

The CIA began to assist NSA's monitoring effort in late 1972, but later determined that the program served a law enforcement function and terminated its participation in February 1973. NSA was affected by the CIA decision, as it had come to view this program as possibly serving a law enforcement function and thus beyond the scope of its proper mission. NSA terminated this activity in June 1973, but continued to monitor some of the *same* United States–South American links for foreign intelligence purposes until July 1975.

4. "Incidental" Intercepts of Americans' Communications

Although NSA does not *now* target communications of American citizens, groups, or organizations for interception by placing their names on watch lists, other selection criteria are used which result in NSA's reviewing many communications to, from, or about an American. The initial interception of a stream of communications is analogous to a vacuum cleaner: NSA picks up all communications carried over a specific link that it is monitoring. The combination of this technology and the use of words to select communications of interest results in NSA analysts reviewing the international messages of American citizens, groups, and organizations for foreign intelligence.

The interception and subsequent processing of communications are conducted in a manner that minimizes the number of unwanted messages. Only after an analyst determines that the content of a message meets a legitimate requirement will it be disseminated to the interested intelligence agencies. In practically all cases, the name of an American citizen, group, or organization is deleted by NSA before a message is disseminated.

Internal NSA guidelines ensure that the decision to disseminate an intercepted communication is now made on the basis of the importance of the foreign intelligence it contains, not because a United States citizen, group, or organization is involved. This procedure is, of course, subject to change by internal NSA directives.

In short, NSA's pursuit of international communications does result in the incidental interception and dissemination of communications which the American sender or receiver expected to be kept private. This issue of the latitude NSA should be given in disseminating incidental intercepts must be dealt with if we are to resolve the dilemma between the need for effective foreign intelligence and the need to protect the rights of American citizens.

C. Issues and Questions

Pursuant to its mandate, the Committee has studied whether NSA's jurisdiction and operations should be governed and controlled by a legislative charter. The facts discovered by the Committee with respect to NSA's programs and capabilities suggest that the following questions should be posed for legislative resolution:

1. Should NSA, which like the CIA has vast powers intended for "foreign" purposes, be barred from using those powers domestically?
2. Should NSA, like the CIA, be prohibited from exercising "law enforcement powers" or "internal security functions"?
3. Should NSA be permitted specifically to target the international communications of Americans? If so, for what purposes and should a warrant be required?
4. Should NSA be permitted to disseminate information derived from the "incidental" interception of Americans' messages obtained by monitoring an international communications link for foreign intelligence purposes? If so, to whom, for what use, and under what controls?

II. NSA'S MONITORING OF INTERNATIONAL COMMUNICATIONS

A. Summary of the Watch List Activity

Lists of words and phrases, including the names of individuals and groups, have long been used by the National Security Agency to select information of intelligence value from intercepted communications. These lists are referred to as "watch lists" by NSA and the agencies requesting intelligence information from them, such as the Federal Bureau of Investigation, Central Intelligence Agency, Bureau of Narcotics and Dangerous Drugs, Secret Service, and Department of Defense. The great majority of names on watch lists have always been foreign citizens and organizations.

The Committee examined two types of watch lists which included Americans. One focused on domestic civil disturbances, the other on drug trafficking. Messages selected on the basis of these watch lists were analyzed and forwarded to other Federal agencies, including the FBI, CIA, BNDD, and DOD. The Secret Service also received information from NSA regarding potential threats to persons under its protection.

Between 1967 and 1973, NSA received watch lists from these agencies which included the names of Americans as well as foreign citizens and organizations. These lists were used to select messages from intercepted traffic and to discover whether there was foreign influence on, or support of, domestic antiwar and civil rights activities. From 1970 until 1973, similar lists were used to gather intelligence on international drug traffic.

NSA itself added names to the watch lists to enhance the selection criteria used to support the requirements levied by other agencies. NSA's Office of Security also added names to the lists for counterintelligence and counterespionage purposes.

Between 1969 and 1973, NSA disseminated approximately 2,000 reports (e.g., the text or summaries of intercepted messages) to the various requesting agencies as a result of the inclusion of American names on the watch lists. No evidence was found, however, of any significant foreign support or control of domestic dissidents.

Information generated by the watch list activity was the product of collection conducted against channels of international communications ("links") with at least one terminal in a foreign country. Nevertheless, the messages NSA intercepted and disseminated were sometimes between two American citizens, one in the United States and one abroad. With one exception, NSA intercepted messages only from "links" it was already monitoring as part of its foreign intelligence mission.

This exception occurred in 1970, when the Bureau of Narcotics and Dangerous Drugs asked NSA to provide intelligence on international drug trafficking. NSA began to monitor certain international communications links between the United States and South America to acquire intelligence on drugs entering the United States. The BNDD also supplied NSA with the names of Americans suspected of drug trafficking for inclusion on a watch list. Reports on drug-related activities of American citizens were disseminated to both the BNDD and CIA.

Both the drug and "nondrug" watch lists of United States citizens were discontinued in 1973 as a result of questions concerning their legality and propriety, raised by the Justice Department and by NSA itself.

B. History

1. Early Period: 1960–1967

The exact details of the origin of the watch list activity are unclear. Testimony from NSA employees indicates that the early 1960s marked the beginning of watch lists and the inclusion of names of American citizens. According to a senior NSA official, "the term watch list had to do with a list of names of people, places or events that a customer would ask us to have our analysts keep in mind as they scan large volumes of material."

Originally these lists were used for two purposes: (1) monitoring travel to Cuba and other communist countries; and (2) protecting the President and other high Government officials. According to NSA, neither of these tasks involved a regular program for including American names on the lists: requests from other agencies were infrequent and generally *ad hoc.* Prior to 1962, NSA did not have an office specifically in charge of interagency dealings, which also limited the number of requests for information from other agencies.

In the early 1960s requesting agencies, usually the FBI, submitted names of United States citizens and business firms having dealings with Cuba to NSA. In turn, NSA provided the FBI with intelligence on American commercial and personal communications with Cuba. A May 18, 1962, internal FBI memorandum from Raymond Wannall, Chief of the Nationalities Intelligence Section of the Domestic Intelligence Division, to Assistant Director William Sullivan reported on a meeting with NSA officials concerning Cuba. The purpose of the meeting was to devise a way for the FBI to make better use of NSA intercepts relating to "commercial and personal communications between persons in Cuba and in the United States." The memorandum stated:

> . . . of the raw traffic now available, the material which would be most helpful to us would consist of periodic listing of firms in the U.S. which are doing business with individuals in Cuba and the Cuban government. . . . [W]ith regard to personal messages, we feel that those relating to individuals travelling between Cuba and the U.S. would be the most significant. . . . *We will furnish NSA a list of persons in whom we have an investigative or an intelligence interest.* [Emphasis added.]

The second area of concern in the early 1960s was protection of the President. According to NSA, the Secret Service submitted the names of the Presidents and others under its protection, possibly as early as 1962. This activity, however, was not instituted for the purpose of acquiring the communications of the protectees, but to determine possible threats to their well-being. After President Kennedy was assassinated in November 1963, interest in presidential protection naturally intensified, and NSA's joint efforts with the Secret Service were expanded.

This early activity was not directed against American citizens; no intelligence program called for the systematic inclusion of American citizens on a watch list. The evidence indicates, however, that NSA did intentionally monitor certain international activities of some American citizens as early as 1962. These objectives, which began as legitimate concerns for the life of the President, expanded when the watch list activity intensified in 1967.

2. Systematic Inclusion of American Names: 1967

The major watch list effort against American citizens began in the fall of 1967. In response to pressures from the White House, FBI, and the Attorney General, the Department of the Army established a civil disturbance unit. An area of special interest was possible foreign involvement in American civil rights and antiwar groups. General William Yarborough, the Army Assistant Chief of Staff for Intelligence (ACSI), directed the operations of this unit.

On October 20, 1967, Yarborough sent a message to the Director of NSA, General Marshall Carter, requesting that NSA provide any available information concerning possible foreign influence on civil disturbances in the United States. Yarborough specifically asked for "any information on a continuing basis" concerning:

> A. Indications that foreign governments or individuals or organizations acting as agents of foreign governments are controlling or attempting to control or influence the activities of U.S. "peace" groups and "Black Power" organizations.
>
> B. Identities of foreign agencies exerting control or influence on U.S. organizations.
>
> C. Identities of individuals and organizations in U.S. in contact with agents of foreign governments.
>
> D. Instructions or advice being given to U.S. groups by agents of foreign governments.

A senior NSA official knowledgeable in this area testified that such a request for information on civil disturbances or political activities was "unprecedented. . . . It is kind of a landmark in my memory; it stands out as a first." The initial request was also vague; it did not discuss the targeting of American citizens, or what specific organizations or groups were of interest.

The Army was "interested in determining whether or not there is evidence of any foreign action to develop or control these anti-Vietnam and other domestic demonstrations."

The following day, Carter sent a cable to Yarborough, Director of Central Intelligence Richard Helms, and each member of the United States Intelligence Board, informing them that NSA was "concentrating additional and continuing effort to obtain SIGINT" in support of the Army request. Although USIB members were notified of this new requirement, there is no record of discussion at USIB meetings of the watch list, nor did USIB ever validate a requirement for monitoring in support of the civil disturbance unit.

Watch list names were submitted directly to NSA by the FBI, Secret Service, Defense Intelligence Agency, the military services, and the CIA. These same agencies received reports of intercepted communications pertaining to their areas of interest. The State Department also received some reports on international terrorism and drug activities, but it is unclear whether they submitted any American names.

Between 1967 and 1973, a cumulative total of about 1,200 American names appeared on the civil disturbance watch list. The FBI submitted the largest proportion, approximately 950. The Secret Service's list included about 180 American individuals and groups active in civil rights and antiwar activities. The DIA submitted the names of 20 American citizens who traveled to North Vietnam, and the CIA submitted approximately 30 names of alleged American radicals. The Air Force Office of Special Investigations, the Naval Investigative Service, and the Army Assistant Chief of Staff for Intelligence all submitted a small number of names to NSA. In addition, NSA contributed about 50–75 names to support the watch list activity.

At its height in early 1973, there were 600 American names and 6,000 foreign names on the watch lists. According to NSA, these lists produced about 2,000 reports that were disseminated to other agencies between 1967 and 1973. NSA estimates 10 percent of these reports were derived from communications between two American citizens.

3. Increasing Security and Concealment of Programs Involving American Citizens

The watch list activity was always a highly sensitive, compartmented operation. The secrecy was not due to the nature of the communications intercepted (most were personal and innocuous) but to the fact that American citizens were involved. NSA requested that some of the agencies receiving watch list product either destroy the material or return it within two weeks. This procedure was not followed with even the most sensitive of NSA's legitimate foreign intelligence product.

When NSA intercepts, analyzes, and disseminates a foreign communication, the regular procedure is for the communication to be classified, given a serial number, and filed. From 1967–1969, much of the watch list material was treated in this manner, and given the same classification as the most sensitive NSA intercepts. As a senior NSA official testified:

> During the 1967–1969 period, communications that had a U.S. citizen on one end and a foreigner on the other were given [a high-level security classification] . . . and went out as serialized product, through a limited by name only distribution.

Other material was even more highly classified. Whenever communications between *two* Americans were intercepted, they were classified Top Secret, prepared with no mention of NSA as the source, and disseminated "For Background Use Only." No serial number was assigned to them, and they were not filed with regular communications intelligence intercepts. This effectively limited access to the material and prevented its use in any official study or report. As Benson Buffham, Deputy Director of NSA, testified:

> first it is true that we maintain permanent type records of all of our product. However, it is my understanding that this material was dealt with separately. It was not serialized and put out in regular distribution lists. These items were produced as display items, show-to items and thus the normal procedures that would be followed for our serialized product were not followed. So as best as I know, there would not be any record of this material held in other places within the Agency in the permanent files.

The project's sensitivity was due to a number of factors. The requirements—protection of the President, terrorism, civil disturbances, drug activities—involved sensitive subjects. NSA also wanted to ensure protection of the SIGINT source and of other intercept operations, which could be jeopardized by unauthorized release of the watch list material.

Finally, American citizens, firms, and groups were involved, and this was "different from the normal mission of the National Security Agency."

The fact that NSA did not serialize and file the intercepted communications between Americans indicates they did not view this activity as part of their "normal" mission. Buffham stated that he believed the interception and dissemination of communications between American citizens to be outside NSA's mission, as defined in applicable executive directives.

4. Project MINARET: Further Expansion and Increased Secrecy

The civil disturbance watch list program became even more compartmented in July 1969, when NSA issued a charter to establish Project MINARET.

MINARET established more stringent controls over the information collected on American citizens and groups involved in civil disturbances. To enhance security, MINARET effectively classified all of this information as Top Secret, "For Background Use Only," and stipulated that the material was *not* to be serialized or identified with the National Security Agency. Prior to 1969, only communications *between two Americans* were classified in this manner; with the adoption of MINARET, communications to, from, or mentioning United States citizens were so classified.

The MINARET charter established tighter security procedures for intercepted messages which contained:

> a. information on foreign governments, organizations, or individuals who are attempting to influence, coordinate or control U.S. organizations or individuals who may foment civil disturbance or otherwise undermine the national security of the U.S.;
>
> b. information on U.S. organizations or individuals who are engaged in activities which may result in civil disturbances or otherwise subvert the national security of the U.S. *An equally important aspect of MINARET will be to restrict the knowledge that such information is being collected and processed by the National Security Agency.* [Emphasis added.]

This charter was prepared within NSA and issued by an NSA Assistant Director. According to testimony given the Committee, the charter was discussed with NSA Deputy Director Louis Tordella and probably with the Director, but other agencies involved in the watch list activity were not informed of the new procedures until the charter had been adopted.

In addition to regulating the distribution and format of watch list product, MINARET also initiated a more formal procedure for submission of names. No longer were names accepted over the telephone or by word of mouth. According to NSA, the watch list "was handled less systematically prior to 1969. . . . some watch lists entered NSA during that time via direct channels, including secure telephone." NSA maintains, however, that the regular procedure was for agencies submitting names by secure telephone or in person to confirm them with written requests. A senior NSA official testified: "From 1969 on [the watch list] was handled in a very careful, reviewed and systematic way."

The MINARET charter was an effort both to restrict knowledge of the watch list program and to disguise NSA's participation in it. NSA maintains that its concern for the security of SIGINT sources, i.e., NSA's intercept operations, was the primary reason for initiating these measures. NSA further maintains that it was concerned with the privacy of U.S. communications and, by imposing the MINARET restrictions, sought to ensure that dissemination was made exclusively to those outside NSA who had a legitimate need for the information. It is apparent that the MINARET restrictions also protected NSA's role from exposure. Dissemination of foreign communications to domestic agencies was obviously a sensitive matter. It involved considerable risk of exposure which would increase if the number of people within the intelligence community who were aware of the activity grew. Therefore, NSA placed more restrictive security controls on MINARET material than it placed on other highly classified foreign intercepts in order to conceal its involvement in activities which were beyond its regular mission.

C. Types of Names on Watch Lists

The names of Americans submitted to NSA for the watch lists ranged from members of radical political groups, to celebrities, to ordinary citizens involved in protests against their Government. Names of organizations were also included; some were communist-front groups, others were nonviolent and peaceful in nature.

The use of names, particularly those of groups and organizations, to select international communications results in NSA unnecessarily reviewing many messages. There is a multiplier effect: if an organization is targeted, all its members' communications may be intercepted; if an individual is on the watch list, all communications to, from, or mentioning that individual may be intercepted. These communications may also contain the names of other "innocent" parties. For example, a communication mentioning the wife of a U.S. Senator was intercepted by SA, as were communications discussing a peace concert, a correspondent's report from Southeast Asia to his magazine in New York, and a pro-Vietnam war activist's invitations to speakers for a rally. According to testimony before the Committee, the material that resulted from the watch lists was not very valuable; most communications were of a private and personal nature, or involved rallies and demonstrations that were public knowledge.

D. Overlapping Nature of Intelligence Community Requests

As noted above, the primary purpose of the watch lists on Americans from 1967–1973 was to collect intelligence on civil disturbances. NSA also responded to a requirement from BNDD to monitor for illegal drug trafficking from 1970–1973. In addition, NSA supplied information to Federal agencies (FBI, CIA, Secret Service, and Department of Defense) on possible terrorist activity, and disseminated reports to the Secret Service which related to the protection of the President. The demarcations between these categories, however, were not always clear.

Secret Service officials, for example, have told the Committee that presidential and executive protection includes "providing a secure environment" for the White House for foreign embassies within the United States and in areas where high Government officials travel. According to the Secret Service, this requires "information regarding civil disturbances and anti-American or anti-U.S. Government demonstrations in the U.S. or overseas, as these demonstrations may affect the Secret Service's mission of protecting U.S. and foreign officials." After the October 20, 1967, Yarborough cable, the Secret Service began submitting names of individuals and organizations active in the antiwar and civil rights movements to NSA. Although these individuals and groups were not considered a direct threat to protectees, it was believed they might participate in demonstrations against United States policy which would endanger the physical well-being of Government officials. Intercepted communications to, from, or mentioning these individuals and groups were always disseminated by NSA to the Secret Service and the CIA, and often to the FBI.

There was considerable overlap among various agencies in submissions for watch list coverage and requests for material. For example, the CIA was interested in:

> *The activities of U.S. individuals involved in either civil disorders, radical student or youth activities, racial militant activities, radical antiwar activities, draft evasion/deserter support activities, or in radical related media activities, where such individuals have some foreign connection* by virtue of: foreign residence, foreign travel, attendance at international conferences or meetings and/or involvement or contact with foreign governments, organizations, political parties or individuals; or with Communist front organizations. [Emphasis added.]

The FBI was interested in similar kinds of information, as illustrated by excerpts of two memoranda from J. Edgar Hoover to the Director, NSA:

> This is to advise you that this Bureau has a continuing interest in receiving intelligence information obtained under MINARET regarding the targets previously furnished you. . . . Information derived from this coverage has been helpful in determining the extent of international cooperation among New Leftists and has been used for lead purposes.
>
> The purpose of this communication is to advise of general areas of interest to this Bureau in connection with racial extremist matters and to request your assistance in such matters.
>
> *There are both white and black racial extremists in the United States advocating and participating in illegal and violent activities for the purpose of destroying our present form of government. Because of this goal, such racial extremists are natural allies of foreign enemies of the United States.* Both material and propaganda support is being given to United States racial extremists by foreign elements. The Bureau is most interested in all information showing ties between United States racial extremists and such foreign elements. [Emphasis added.]

These requests reflect an underlying similarity of interests among agencies, despite the differing needs which are expressed in their requirements.

To some extent the DIA, FBI, CIA, and the Secret Service received information on Black activists and groups, and on the antiwar movement. All were concerned with how civil disturbances and antiwar demonstrations were affecting the internal security of the United States. Although their general area of concern was the same, each agency used the information for its own particular purposes. The DIA was interested in travel to North Vietnam; the CIA kept files on alleged antiwar radicals for its Project CHAOS; the FBI used the information to develop "leads" on new left activists, at the same time it was conducting COINTELPRO efforts against alleged radicals; and the Secret Service was concerned with protecting the President. Despite slight variations in focus, the different agencies' requests reflected the overriding fear that the nation was being undermined internally and externally. It was this perception which produced the watch list program directed against Americans.

E. Drug Watch Lists: United States–South American Intercepts

1. Initial Monitoring: 1970

An unofficial requirement to collect and disseminate international communications concerning drug trafficking was levied on NSA by the Bureau of Narcotics and Dangerous Drugs on April 10, 1970. BNDD Director John Ingersoll sent a memorandum to NSA Director Noel Gayler requesting "any and all COMINT information which reflects illicit traffic in narcotics and dangerous drugs." NSA initiated its monitoring in June 1970, but a general requirement to obtain foreign intelligence on drug trafficking was not validated by the United States Intelligence Board until August 1971.

The Ingersoll memorandum specified that BNDD was interested in individuals and organizations involved in illegal drug activities, information on production centers, and all violations of United States laws pertaining to narcotics and dangerous drugs. In order to assist NSA in fulfilling the requirement, BNDD stated that they would provide NSA lists of individuals and organizations which had a history of involvement with illegal drug activities. According to the Ingersoll memorandum, "this watch list will be updated on a monthly basis and additions/deletions will be forwarded to NSA."

NSA implemented this request by monitoring international communications traffic. The first intercepts began in June 1970. Telephone traffic carried on circuits between the United States and certain South American cities was first monitored in September 1970. Unlike other watch list monitoring, the United States–South American effort required NSA to devote additional resources to intercepting communications over this specifically targeted link.

This link included the telephone circuits between New York City and a South American city. BNDD was initially concerned about drug deals that were being arranged in calls from public telephone booths in New York City to South America. According to a senior NSA official:

> BNDD had some information that led them to believe that arrangements were being made by telephone from New York City, a Grand Central Station telephone booth, to some individuals in [a South American city].

BNDD felt that it could not legally tap the public telephones and thus enlisted NSA's help to cover the international link that carried these telephone calls. At BNDD's request, NSA began to intercept telephone conversations carried over this link in September 1970. Additional United States–South American links were soon added. BNDD also supplied NSA with code names for drugs and names of individuals, including American citizens.

The telephone monitoring was conducted from one NSA site until December 1970, when that intercept station was closed. An NSA East Coast facility, operated by the military, began monitoring United States–South American links in March 1971. According to NSA, 19 United States–South American links were monitored for voice traffic at the two sites between 1970 and 1973. Six South American cities were of primary interest, in addition to New York and Miami.

During this period, BNDD submitted 450 American names to NSA for inclusion on the drug watch list. At the high point, in early 1973, 250 Americans were on the active list.

Of the calls intercepted at the East Coast site, less than 10 percent were sent to NSA headquarters, and less than 10 percent of these were disseminated. Yet it is clear that many personal and business calls of Americans were reviewed during this operation. This results from the lack of an effective method for avoiding the incidental interception of calls involving

American citizens when a link with one terminal in the United States is monitored.

2. CIA/NSA Drug Activity

In October 1972, NSA requested CIA assistance in monitoring United States–South American communication links to collect intelligence on illicit drug traffic. According to Buffham, NSA made this request

> because we felt that this was a sensitive matter, and that *greater security would be achieved by utilizing the career intercept operators of the CIA to perform the activity,* and, in addition, they could be more selective in providing items because *we would be able to give the CIA operators the specific names on the watch list, and we did not feel that we could or should provide those names to the* [East Coast military station]. [Emphasis added.]

NSA's concern about the security of American names being provided to the East Coast station stemmed from the fact that the operators were young military personnel on short tours of duty. They were not professional intelligence officers, and NSA felt that monitoring American citizens was too sensitive a task for them. The use of CIA career operators satisfied NSA that targeting of American citizens would not be disclosed.

The Rockefeller Commission also investigated this activity, but found no evidence that the CIA directly targeted American citizens. The Rockefeller Commission report stated:

> For a period of approximately six months, commencing in the fall of 1973 [sic], the Directorate monitored telephone conversations between the United States and Latin America in an effort to identify foreign drug traffickers. . . .
>
> A CIA intercept crew stationed at an East Coast site monitored calls to and from certain Latin American telephone numbers contained on a "watch list" provided by NSA. While the intercept was focused on foreign nationals, it is clear that American citizens were parties to many of the monitored calls. . . .
>
> *The Commission's investigation disclosed that, from the outset* of *the Agency's involvement in the narcotics control program, the Director and other CIA officials*

> *instructed involved personnel to collect only foreign intelligence and to make no attempt—either within the United States or abroad—to gather information on American citizens allegedly trafficking in narcotics.* [Emphasis added.]

The evidence examined by the Select Committee directly contradicts this finding. An internal CIA memorandum of November 17, 1972, to the Director of Communications from the Chief, Special Programs Division, reveals that the CIA *was* receiving the names of U.S. citizens.

> NSA had tasked [the East Coast site] with this requirement [to monitor for drug traffic] but were *unwilling to provide the site with the specific names and U.S. telephone numbers of interest on security/sensitivity grounds.* . . . To get around the problems mentioned above NSA requested the Agency undertake intercept of the long lines circuits of interest. *They have provided us with all information available (including the "sensitive") and the [CIA] facility is working on the requirement.* [Emphasis added.]

This memorandum and subsequent testimony by NSA officials revealed that the CIA was monitoring these circuits to intercept the calls of American citizens suspected of illegal drug trafficking. During this period, NSA continued to monitor the same circuits at its East Coast site, but that site did not have the specific BNDD "sensitive" watch lists of American names which were supplied to the CIA. Thus, the conclusion reached by the Rockefeller Commission—that CIA intercepts were not undertaken for the purpose of gathering intelligence on American citizens—is not supported by the evidence.

3. Termination of Drug Activity

Three months after the CIA monitoring was initiated, CIA General Counsel Lawrence Houston issued an opinion which stated that the intercepts may violate Section 605 of the Communications Act of 1934. This law, as amended in 1968, prohibits the unauthorized disclosure of any private communication of an American citizen to another party, unless undertaken pursuant to the President's constitutional authority to collect foreign intelligence which is crucial to the security of the United States. Since intercepted messages were provided to BNDD, Houston concluded that the activity was for law enforcement purposes, which is also outside the CIA's charter. As a result of this memorandum, the CIA suspended its collection. NSA, which has no charter, continued to monitor these links for drug information.

NSA officials have testified that they were told in early 1973 that the CIA was terminating collection because it was concerned about operating an intercept station *within* the United States. This concern is completely different from the one expressed in Houston's memorandum. NSA officials have told the Committee that questions concerning the legality of the activity were either not mentioned by the CIA, or else mentioned secondarily.

NSA Deputy Director Buffham testified that after the CIA decided to stop the United States–South American drug monitoring, NSA began to review the legality and appropriateness of its efforts in support of BNDD. Although NSA is not prohibited by statute or executive directive from disseminating information that may pertain to law enforcement, it has always viewed its sole mission as the collection and dissemination of foreign intelligence. A senior NSA official testified: "We do not understand our mission to be one of supporting an agency with a law enforcement responsibility."

Although BNDD clearly was a law enforcement agency, NSA initially held that the intelligence it was supplying BNDD was a part of a legitimate USIB-approved effort to prevent drugs from entering the United States. This international aspect of the requirement was interpreted by NSA as sufficient justification for classifying the activity as part of its "foreign intelligence" mission.

After discussions with the General Counsel's office at NSA and within the Office of the Secretary of Defense, the Director of NSA terminated the activity in June 1973. All of NSA's drug materials—product, internal memoranda, and administrative documents—were destroyed in late August or early September 1973. Ordinarily, NSA keeps material for five years or more. According to a senior NSA official: "it wasn't thought we would get back into the narcotics effort anytime soon. There didn't seem to be any point in keeping them."

4. Continuation of NSA's United States–South American Monitoring

In June 1975 the Committee received information that NSA continued to monitor United States–South American telephone calls after the June

1973 termination of the drug watch list activity. NSA officials confirmed that the same links targeted for the purpose of curbing illegal drug traffic were monitored by NSA for foreign intelligence after June 1973. Certain of these links were monitored until July 9, 1975.

According to NSA, this activity was terminated when "it did not prove productive." While this effort was underway, NSA states that it did not collect or disseminate any information on narcotics traffic from the United States–South American links. A senior NSA official stated: "Nothing ever came. No by-product. The problem was dead."

5. Current Internal Policy Concerning Telephone Monitoring

No statute or executive directive prohibits NSA's monitoring a telephone circuit with one terminal in the United States. An internal NSA instruction was issued on August 7, 1975, that requires the personal approval of the chief of a major element within the Agency before monitoring of voice communications with a terminal in the United States is initiated. According to Deputy Director Buffham, "It is obvious that no such collection will be undertaken unless it is extremely important and is properly reviewed within the Agency."

F. Termination of the Civil Disturbance Watch List Activity

The watch list activity involving civil disturbances was officially terminated in the fall of 1973. This was due to a combination of factors: growing concern within NSA regarding the program's vulnerability and propriety; the fact that courts were beginning to require the Government to reveal electronic surveillance conducted against particular criminal defendants; and the questions, raised by the drug watch list activity, about NSA's authority to engage in monitoring for law enforcement purposes. { . . . }

{ . . . }

It is important to note that the decision to terminate the watch list was ultimately the administrative decision of an executive agency. There is no statute which expressly forbids such activity, and no court case where it has been squarely at issue. Without legislative controls, NSA could resume the watch list activity at any time upon order of the Executive.

G. Authorization

Authorization of the watch list activity must be viewed in the context of how NSA operates. It is a service agency which provides foreign intelligence information at the request of consumer agencies. Specific requirements are levied on NSA, although the Agency also engages in collection activities that are not responsive to specific tasking. For example, many USIB requirements—such as those aimed at terrorist activities, gathering economic intelligence, or discovering foreign links to civil disturbances—were so broad that NSA was given wide discretion for selecting not only the communications channels to be monitored, but also what information was disseminated. While this is often appropriate because only NSA has the knowledge and expertise to make these decisions, it also allows NSA considerable flexibility in carrying out its mission.

NSA also responds to specific requests from other Federal agencies. Indeed, it is no exaggeration to state that NSA's operations are undertaken almost entirely to satisfy the intelligence needs of other agencies. The watch list activity was no exception.

1. Knowledge and Authorization Outside NSA

In the case of the 1967–1973 watch list activity, NSA clearly received instructions from the Army in 1967 to look for possible foreign influence on, or control of, American peace and Black power activists. NSA subsequently received the names of American and foreign citizens and groups from other intelligence agencies.

This activity was not formally approved by USIB. Although NSA notified USIB members that it was responding to the Army's request, the inclusion of American names on an NSA watch list was never discussed at subsequent USIB meetings. Although there were official USIB requirements for information concerning international drug activity, presidential protection, and terrorism, there was no approval or discussion of targeting American citizens. NSA officials contend that the submission of American names by USIB members constituted approval.

The desire for tight security over the watch list program resulted in limiting participation to those "with a need to know." Therefore, it was not in NSA's best interests to have formal USIB approval of a requirement since knowledge would have been more widely spread.

According to documents supplied to the Committee and testimony of NSA officials, Defense Secretaries Melvin Laird and James Schlesinger, as well as Attorneys General John Mitchell and Richard Kleindienst, were informed that NSA was monitoring Americans. Former NSA Director, Admiral Noel Gayler sent a Top Secret "Eyes Only" memorandum to Laird and Mitchell on January 26, 1971, which outlined ground rules for "NSA's Contribution to Domestic Intelligence." In this memorandum, Gayler refers to a discussion he had earlier that day with both men on how NSA could assist them with "intelligence bearing on domestic problems." The memorandum mentioned the monitoring for drug trafficking and foreign support of subversive activities, but did not discuss "watch lists" specifically.

NSA Deputy Director Buffham supplied the Committee with a Memorandum for Record which indicated that he had personally shown the Gayler memorandum to Mitchell and had been told by the Military Assistant to Secretary of Defense Laird that the Secretary had read and agreed to the memorandum. In a handwritten note made available to the Committee, Gayler recalls that he personally showed the January 26, 1971, memorandum to Kleindienst on July 1, 1972.

Finally, former NSA Deputy Director Tordella testified that he accompanied General Samuel C. Phillips, Gayler's successor as Director of NSA, to brief Secretary of Defense Schlesinger on the watch list in the summer of 1973.

In summary, a number of Federal agencies were aware of NSA's watch lists and used them. It is clear that the United States Intelligence Board, which ordinarily set the intelligence requirements to which NSA responded, never gave its formal approval for the watch list activity. It also appears that at least two Attorneys General and two Secretaries of Defense were generally aware that NSA was monitoring the international communications of American citizens, but none took measures to halt the practice.

2. Knowledge and Approval Within NSA

There is a discrepancy in the testimony of knowledgeable NSA staff members and a former NSA Director with regard to his knowledge of the watch list activity. When asked whether NSA had included the names of American citizens or organizations on its watch lists, Admiral Noel Gayler (who was Director of NSA during the height of the activity) responded:

> I don't know that I even knew that in that specific way. I knew that communications of one foreign terminal sometimes concerned doings of interest of people, including American citizens, yes. And when I became aware of that, I can't tell you, I guess it was a year or so after I got there.

Gayler became NSA Director in August 1969. He maintains that he first became aware of the watch list activity about the time of the June 1970 Huston plan for domestic surveillance, ten months after his arrival and eleven months after the MINARET Charter was issued.

Gayler was one of the original participants in the Huston plan deliberations and in the Intelligence Evaluation Committee (early 1971). Both of these efforts were designed to use the resources of NSA and other intelligence agencies to gather information on internal security matters. In fact, part of the Huston plan called for the expansion of the watch list activity. Buffham told the Committee that if the plan had been implemented he assumed "other intelligence agencies would then increase the numbers of names on their lists" and NSA would possibly target specific communications channels to obtain the international traffic of American citizens. NSA was particularly concerned that the executive branch directives would have had to be changed to permit such an expansion. The alternatives outlined in the Huston plan included the recommendation that the controlling NSCID and the relevant DCID be changed to allow NSA to target international communications links carrying the messages of American citizens.

NSA was already engaged in watch list activity, which although it did not involve targeting of specific communications links, did involve targeting Americans by name. The Huston Plan states:

> NSA is currently doing so on a restricted basis, and the information it has provided has been *most* helpful. Much of this information is particularly useful to the White House. . . .

As discussed earlier, the July 1, 1969, MINARET charter was designed to restrict knowledge of the watch list activity. It was released about a month before Gayler arrived at NSA and, according to a senior NSA official, Gayler "knew everything that was in it, what was going on, and endorsed it." Gayler recalls that his first knowledge of the watch list came during the Huston Plan deliberations, almost a year later. Another senior NSA official testified that Gayler *"review every piece of MINARET product"* and maintained that "the Director kept a close eye on this activity and reviewed the requirements." [Emphasis added.] This employee also testified that Gayler was shown the product of the watch list activity and was kept fully informed.

H. Conclusions

NSA's monitoring of international communications comprises only a portion of its total mission, but the examination of this capability to intrude on the telephone calls and telegrams of Americans represents a major part of the Committee's work on NSA. The watch list activities and the sophisticated technological capabilities that they highlight present some of the most crucial privacy issues facing this nation. Space age technology has outpaced the law. The secrecy that has surrounded much of NSA's activities and the lack of Congressional oversight have prevented, in the past, bringing statutes in line with NSA's capabilities. Neither the courts nor Congress have dealt with the interception of communications using NSA's highly sensitive and complex technology.

The analysis presented here of the deliberate targeting of American citizens and the associated incidental interception of their communications demonstrates the need for a legislative charter that will define, limit, and control the signals intelligence activities of the National Security Agency. This should be accomplished both to preserve and protect the Government's legitimate foreign intelligence operations, and to ensure that the constitutional rights of Americans are safeguarded.

The next section describes a recently terminated NSA collection program which also involved United States citizens—Operation SHAMROCK. This program did not require any special technology; international telegrams were simply turned over to NSA at the offices of three cable companies.

III. A SPECIAL NSA COLLECTION PROGRAM: SHAMROCK

SHAMROCK is the codename for a special program in which NSA received copies of most international telegrams leaving the United States between August 1945 and May 1975. Two of the participating international telegraph companies—RCA Global and ITT World Communications—

provided virtually all their international message traffic to NSA. The third, Western Union International, only provided copies of certain foreign traffic from 1945 until 1972. SHAMROCK was probably the largest governmental interception program affecting Americans ever undertaken. Although the total number of telegrams read during its course is not available, NSA estimates that in the last two or three years of SHAMROCK's existence, about 150,000 telegrams per month were reviewed by NSA analysts.

Initially, NSA received copies of international telegrams in the form of microfilm or paper tapes. These were sorted manually to obtain foreign messages. When RCA Global and ITT World Communications switched to magnetic tapes in the 1960s, NSA made copies of these tapes and subjected them to an electronic sorting process. This means that the international telegrams of American citizens on the "watch lists" could be selected out and disseminated.

A. Legal Restrictions

1. The Fourth Amendment to the Constitution of the United States

Obtaining the international telegrams of American citizens by NSA at the offices of the telegraph companies appears to violate the privacy of these citizens, as protected by the Fourth Amendment. That Amendment guarantees to the people the right to be "secure . . . in their papers . . . against unreasonable searches and seizures." It also provides that "no Warrants shall issue, but upon probable cause." In no case did NSA obtain a search warrant prior to obtaining a telegram.

2. Section 605 of the Communications Act of 1934 (47 U.S.C. 605)

As enacted in 1934, eleven years before SHAMROCK began, section 605 of the Communications Act provided:

> No person receiving, assisting in receiving, transmitting, or assisting in transmitting, any interstate or foreign communication by wire or radio shall divulge or publish the existence, contents, substance; purport, effect, or meaning thereof. . . .

Section 605 was amended in 1968 by the addition of the phrase: "Except as authorized by chapter 119, Title 18, no person. . . . " The import of this 1968 addition, however, is not clear, and the Supreme Court has yet to rule on the point.

The relevant provision in chapter 119, section 2511(3), provides that "nothing contained in this chapter or in section 605 of the Communications Act of 1934 . . . shall limit the constitutional power of the President . . . to obtain foreign intelligence information deemed essential to the security of the United States. . . . " Yet the Supreme Court, in the *Keith* decision (1972), held that this section "confers no power" and "merely provides that the Act shall not be interpreted to limit or disturb such power as the President may have under the Constitution."

It is thus uncertain what the phrase in the 1968 amendment to section 605—"except as *authorized* by chapter 119, title 18" [Emphasis added]—means. The Supreme Court has held that the relevant section of chapter 119 does not *authorize* any activity. The applicability of section 605 to the interception of international telegrams for foreign intelligence purposes is therefore unclear. It would appear that where such telegrams are intercepted for other than foreign intelligence purposes (e.g., the watch list activity), section 605 would be violated.

3. The Controlling National Security Council Intelligence Directive

Since 1958, this executive directive has authorized NSA to conduct communications intelligence activities. These have been defined as *excluding* "the intercept and processing of unencrypted written communications." It would appear that if copies of international telegrams are "written communications," NSA has exceeded its authority under the executive's own internal directives.

B. The Committee's Investigation

The SHAMROCK operation was alluded to in documents furnished to the Committee by the Rockefeller Commission in May 1975. They indicated that CIA had provided "cover" for an NSA operation in New York where international telegrams had been copied.

In early June 1975, an oral inquiry regarding the operation was made to

NSA officials, but no confirmation of the project was forthcoming. In July, the Committee sent written interrogatories to NSA, and was told that this subject was so sensitive that it would be disclosed only to Senators Church and Tower. No such briefing was immediately arranged, however.

In July and August, news stories were published which appeared to reveal small parts of the SHAMROCK operation.

The Committee continued to press the matter with NSA, and in early September the agency gave the Committee its first detailed information. This briefing was followed by interviews with present and former NSA employees who had been responsible for the program and by examinations of documents at NSA and the Department of Defense. NSA assured the Committee at the time that it had examined all NSA documents which pertained to SHAMROCK. On September 23, the full Committee was briefed by an NSA official in executive session. Following this briefing, the Committee interviewed officials in the telegraph companies which had participated in the SHAMROCK program.

On the basis of this investigation, the Committee prepared a report which it submitted to NSA for review. NSA had no specific comments regarding the accuracy of the report, but expressed its general objection to public disclosure of the operation on the grounds that the report was based on classified information.

On November 6, 1975, in a public session of the Committee, Chairman Frank Church read the report on SHAMROCK into the record. Due to the refusal of the executive branch to provide witnesses in public session, no other public record was made.

At this point, the Committee's active investigation ceased. The Committee presumed that it had exhausted all sources of information about SHAMROCK.

On March 25, 1976, as the Committee was about to send this report to press, it was informed by the Department of Defense that NSA had "discovered" a file containing various documents and memoranda about SHAMROCK. An NSA official explained that the file had been held by a lower-level employee at NSA until around March 1, 1976, when he brought it to the attention of his superiors. Since this occurred several months after the Committee's public report, and, in the opinion of NSA, did not substantially alter the Committee's findings, it was not immediately reported to the Committee.

After examining the documents, the Committee decided that the final NSA report should incorporate this new information. Although it does not alter the basic findings reported in November 1975, it does change some of the details.

C. The Origins of SHAMROCK

During World War II, under the wartime censorship laws, all international message traffic was made available to military censors. Copies of pertinent foreign traffic were turned over to military intelligence. With the cessation of the War in 1945, this practice was to end. In August 1945, the Army sought to continue that part of the wartime arrangement which had allowed military intelligence access to certain foreign traffic. At that time, most of this traffic was still conveyed via the facilities of three carriers.

On August 18, 1945, two representatives of the Army Signal Security Agency were sent to New York

> to make the necessary contacts with the heads of the Commercial Communications Companies in New York, secure their approval of the interception of all Governmental traffic entering the United States, leaving the United States, or transiting the United States, and make the necessary arrangements for this photographic intercept work.

They first approached an official at ITT, who "very definitely and finally refused" to agree to any of the Army proposals. The Army representatives then approached a vice president of Western Union Telegraph Company, who agreed to cooperate unless the Attorney General of the United States ruled that such intercepts were illegal.

Having succeeded with Western Union, the Army representatives returned to ITT on August 21, 1945, and suggested to an ITT vice president that "his company would not desire to be the only non-cooperative company on this project." The vice president decided to reconsider and broached the matter the same day with the president of the company. The ITT president agreed to cooperate with the Army, provided that the Attorney General decided that the program was not illegal.

These Army representatives also met with the president of RCA on August 21, 1945. The RCA president indicated his willingness to cooperate, but withheld final approval until he, too, had heard from the Attorney General.

After their trip, the Army representatives reported to their superiors that the companies were worried about the illegality of their participation in the program:

> Two very evident fears existed in the minds of the heads of each of these communications companies. One was the fear of the illegality of the procedure according to present FCC regulations. In spite of the fact that favorable opinions have been received from the Judge Advocate General of the Navy and the Judge Advocate General of the Army, it was feared that these opinions would not hold in civil court and, as a consequence, the companies would not be protected. If a favorable opinion is handed down by the Attorney General, this fear will be completely allayed, and cooperation may be expected for the complete intercept coverage of this material. The second fear uppermost in the minds of these executives is the fear of the ACA which is the communications union. This union has reported on many occasions minor infractions of FCC regulations and it is feared that a major infraction, such as the proposed intercept coverage, if disclosed by the Union, might cause severe repercussions.

Later memoranda by another Army representative who was present indicate that the companies had consulted their corporate attorneys during these three days of discussions, and that their attorneys uniformly advised against participation in the proposed intercept program. The company executives were apparently willing to ignore this advice if they received assurances from the Attorney General that he would protect them from any consequences.

The new documentary evidence made available to the Committee did not reveal that the Attorney General at that time, Tom C. Clark, actually made the assurances that the companies desired. It is clear, however, that the program began shortly after the August meetings: ITT and Western Union began their participation by September 1, and RCA by October 9, 1945.

In a letter from the Army Signals Security Agency to the Army Chief of Staff on March 19, 1946, the writer indicates that SHAMROCK was well underway, but that concerns about its legality had not vanished:

> It can be stated that both [Western Union and RCA] have placed themselves in precarious positions since the legality of such operations has not been established and has necessitated the utmost secrecy on their part in making these arrangements. Through their efforts, only two or three individuals in the respective companies are aware of the operation.

{On} April 26, 1976, while this report was being printed, DOD informed the Committee that nine additional documents relating to SHAMROCK had been found in the National Archives. The documents revealed that the Office of Secretary of Defense James Forrestal attempted unsuccessfully in June 1948 to have Congress pass an amendment to relax the disclosure restrictions of Section 605 of the Federal Communications Act of 1934. Agencies designated by the President would have been allowed to obtain the radio and wire communications of foreign governments. If the amendment had passed, the SHAMROCK program, as it was originally conceived, would have been authorized by law.

The proposed amendment sought to allay concerns of the companies on the legality of their participation in SHAMROCK. The companies were demanding assurances in 1947 not only from the Secretary of Defense and the Attorney General, but also from the President that their participation was essential to the national interest and that they would not be subject to prosecution in the Federal Courts. Secretary Forrestal, who stated he was speaking for the President, gave ITT and RCA representatives these assurances at a December 16, 1947, meeting in Washington, D.C. Forrestal warned, however, that the assurances he was making could not bind his successors in office.

Representatives of Western Union were not present at this meeting. Documents made available to the Committee indicate that the President and Operating Vice President of Western Union were briefed in January 1948 on the earlier meeting with RCA and ITT.

In early June 1948, the Chairmen of the Senate and House Judiciary Committees were informed of the Government's need for a relaxation of Section 605 and of its position with the telegraph companies. The delicacy of the problem and the top-secret nature of the information were made clear to these two Chairmen. The amendment was considered in an executive session of the Senate Judiciary Committee on June 16, 1948, and approved. Since support for the bill was not unanimous, however, the Committee voted to leave it to the Chairman's discretion whether or not to release the bill to the Senate floor. The representative of the Secretary of Defense then told the Senate Judiciary Chairman that "we did not desire an airing of the whole matter on the Floor of the Senate at this late date in the session." The bill apparently was not reported out.

A Defense Department official expressed the view that they thought a great deal had already been accomplished and that the administration had sufficient ammunition to be able to effect a continuation of the present practices with the companies. Apparently no other statutory attempts were made to authorize the companies' participation in SHAMROCK.

The companies sought renewed assurances from Forrestal's successor, Louis Johnson, in 1949. Johnson told them that the President and Attorney General had been consulted and had given their approval. To the knowledge of those interviewed by the Committee, this was the last instance in which the companies {received} such assurances from the Department of Defense.

Dr. Louis Tordella, who was NSA Deputy Director from 1958 until 1974 and the NSA official with chief administrative responsibility for SHAMROCK, testified that to the best of his knowledge, no President since Truman knew of the program. He "was not sure" whether any Attorney General since Tom Clark had been informed of it, or if succeeding Secretaries of Defense were aware of it. Tordella stated he briefed former Secretary of Defense Schlesinger about the SHAMROCK operation in the summer of 1973.

The Army Signals Security Agency controlled the collection program until 1949, when the Armed Forces Security Agency was formed. Responsibility for the program passed from AFSA to the National Security Agency when it was created in 1952.

D. The Participation of the Companies

None of the telegraph companies could find any record of an agreement with NSA or its predecessors wherein the companies would provide copies of telegrams to the Government, or which reflected anything about arrangements with NSA. No one interviewed by the Committee had any recollection or knowledge that the Government had given the companies specific assurances to ensure their cooperation in 1945, 1947, 1949, or at any time thereafter.

Apparently only a few people in each company—apart from those who physically turned over the materials—had any knowledge of the NSA arrangement. These were primarily mid-level executives charged with the operational aspects of the companies' business. All assumed that the arrangement was valid when it was made and thus continued it. No witness from the telegraph companies recalled that there had ever been a review of the arrangements at the executive levels of their respective companies.

Furthermore, none of the participating companies was apparently aware that information other than foreign traffic was extracted from the messages they were providing. Yet no official at any of the three companies could recall his company asking NSA what it was doing with the information it was furnished and, specifically, whether NSA was reading the telegrams of the companies' American customers.

Finally, both the telegraph companies and NSA deny that the companies ever received anything for their cooperation in SHAMROCK, whether in the form of compensation or favoritism from the Government. All claim they were motivated by purely patriotic considerations.

If there were similarities as to their involvement in SHAMROCK, the participation of each company varied in practice.

1. RCA Global

According to a memorandum prepared by Army representatives, RCA (the parent company of RCA Global) agreed in August 1945 to allow Army personnel, who were to be dressed in civilian clothes, to photograph foreign traffic passing over its facilities in New York, Washington, and San Francisco. The memorandum further provided that "only the desired traffic will be filmed."

The company official at RCA Global who was charged with implementing the SHAMROCK program testified that several alternatives were discussed with Army representatives. He stated that the Army had first proposed tapping into the company's overseas lines, but the official rejected this idea as unfeasible. The Army representatives then proposed that company employees sort out pertinent traffic and turn it over to them; the official rejected this because he did not want company employees involved. The RCA official finally agreed to provide paper tapes of all international message traffic. It was understood that these messages would be sorted manually by persons from the Army Signals Security Agency on the company's premises, and that only certain foreign traffic would be selected. There was never a written agreement to this effect, however, according to the former official.

In New York, Army representatives were given office space in the area where the paper tapes of RCA Global's international message traffic were sorted manually for foreign traffic. Messages of interest were transmitted over teletype machines located in that office space. In Washington and San Francisco, Army agents were permitted to pick up copies of foreign messages, which they took to another office for microfilming. By 1950, a Recordak (microfilm) machine was placed in the New York office and was used to film messages of intelligence interest.

This arrangement continued without substantial disruption until 1963, when RCA Global began to store its message traffic on magnetic tapes. NSA made arrangements to obtain copies of these tapes from the RCA Global facilities in New York—they were taken "on loan," copied, and returned, the same day if possible. Gradually, magnetic tapes began to supersede paper tapes and microfilm as a means of storing messages. By 1966, the New York office was turning over only magnetic tapes to NSA. The offices in Washington and San Francisco, however, continued to furnish copies of international message traffic for microfilming by NSA. RCA Global employees in Washington, D.C., were under the impression they were providing information only to the FBI.

2. ITT World Communications

In August 1945, ITT agreed to allow the Army access to all incoming, outgoing, and transiting messages passing over the facilities of its subsidiaries involved in international communications. It was agreed that "all traffic will be recorded on microfilm, that all Governmental traffic will be recorded on a second microfilm in addition to the original one, that these films will be developed by the SSA [Signals Security Agency], and the complete traffic will be returned to ITT."

It is not clear whether these arrangements, agreed to at the outset, were actually implemented in the manner described. The ITT official with the earliest recollections of the program could recall only that by the early 1950s, ITT World Communications was providing NSA representatives with copies of the company's international message traffic, which NSA then sorted and microfilmed.

When ITT World Communications began to use paper tapes to transmit its messages, these were turned over to NSA as well. It is not clear whether these tapes were transmitted from the premises of ITT World Communications to another location (as with RCA Global) or whether they were simply transported to NSA for sorting.

When ITT World Communications began to use magnetic tapes to store its incoming and outgoing messages—the best recollection of this change places it around 1965—the magnetic tapes were turned over to NSA for duplication. They were returned to the company on the same day. By 1968, ITT World Communications was turning over only its magnetic tapes to NSA.

The Washington and San Francisco offices of ITT World Communications participated in a similar fashion. In Washington, however, company officials believed that they were providing the telegrams to the FBI, rather than NSA. It is clear from the information made available to the Committee that the Washington messages were sent to NSA.

3. Western Union International

At the August 1945 meeting between Army representatives and the Western Union Telegraph Company (the parent company of Western Union International), the company stated that it

> desired that Western Union personnel operate the [microfilm] camera and do all the actual handling of the messages. It was agreed that [the Army Signal Security Agency] would furnish the necessary cameras and film for the complete intercept coverage of Western Union traffic outlets. The film, after exposure, will be delivered [to the office of a company vice-president], at which place an officer from the Signal Security Agency, in civilian clothes, will pick it up.

The company agreed to implement this arrangement at its New York, San Francisco, Washington, and San Antonio facilities.

This arrangement was apparently implemented as originally agreed. In New York, at least, company employees segregated such messages and processed them through a microfilm machine on the transmission room floor. At approximately 4:00 each morning, an NSA courier would come to the floor to pick up the microfilm cartridge. In San Antonio, an Army signal officer from Ft. Sam Houston was tasked with picking up the microfilm each day.

It appears that Western Union turned over to NSA only its telegraph traffic to one foreign country. Approached in 1959 by persons who identified themselves as being from Ft. Holabird, Maryland (Army intelligence), Western Union agreed to allow them to duplicate the traffic going to a particular country. In 1970, the company also began to provide copies of messages going to a particular city within that country which were not being duplicated as part of the previous arrangement. These messages were apparently sorted by NSA personnel in space provided by Western Union at its New York offices.

Western Union International (which was formed in 1963) continued to microfilm certain foreign traffic for NSA until about 1965, when a company executive discovered the existence of the microfilm machine on the transmission room floor. After ascertaining its purpose, he demanded that NSA renew its request to have this information in writing. He recalled that instead of submitting such a request, NSA simply had the machine removed. This recollection, however, was not borne out by documents furnished by NSA. The documents showed that on February 2, 1968, a company vice president (not the one referred to above) had discovered the existence of NSA's Recordak (microfilm) machine in the Western Union transmission room. The machine was reported to the company president, who directed his employees to find out to whom the machine belonged and what the basis for the arrangement was. The NSA courier, when asked these questions by a Western Union International official on February 9, 1968, replied that he was from the Department of Defense and did not know what the basis for the arrangement was or what was being done with the microfilm being furnished. Yet the documents do not reflect whether the Recordak machine was removed, either in 1965 or in 1968.

It is clear that NSA continued to receive duplicates of all messages to the foreign country referred to above until 1972, when again as a result of "discovery" by company officials, this procedure was halted. Although the original request for this intercept procedure had been made by "Holabird people" (Army intelligence), when the company attempted to contact someone regarding its termination, it was ultimately referred to NSA.

Finally, Western Union International, unlike its competitors, never utilized magnetic tapes to store its message traffic. Accordingly, none was ever provided NSA.

In effect, Western Union International's participation in SHAMROCK ended by 1972.

E. NSA's Participation

1. Origins and Early Development

From 1952 (when NSA first inherited the SHAMROCK sources) until 1963, microfilm and paper tapes originating with the sources were brought to NSA's headquarters at Ft. Meade, Maryland several times a week. As noted above, some of these had undergone initial screening, either by NSA operatives or company employees. Even with this preliminary screening, however, the volume of messages which reached NSA daily was apparently quite large.

Several witnesses have told the Committee that during this period the sheer volume of traffic would have likely prohibited the selection of messages on the basis of content. Messages which were selected out were passed on to NSA analysts, who screened them further.

2. The Switch to Magnetic Tape

The character of the SHAMROCK operation changed markedly with the use of magnetic tape. RCA Global was the first company to begin using such tape in the early 1960s. NSA was notified of the changeover in early 1963 and, by 1964, was able to sort electronically the information provided by RCA Global against its selection criteria. This is significant because it meant that the telegrams of citizens whose names were on NSA's "watch list" could be selected for processing by NSA analysts.

From 1964 until 1966, magnetic tapes from RCA Global were brought to Ft. Meade daily and returned to New York the same day. By 1965, ITT World Communications had also begun its changeover to magnetic tapes and was beginning to provide traffic in this form to NSA messengers.

3. CIA Cover Support

To alleviate the administrative burden entailed by these daily round-trips, NSA in 1966 sought to find a place in New York City where the tapes could be duplicated. NSA Deputy Director Tordella requested that the CIA provide "safe" space where this operation could be conducted. The CIA agreed to rent office space in lower Manhattan, under the guise of a television tape processing company, where the tape duplication process could be carried out. CIA designated this project "LPMEDLEY."

The cover support began in November 1966 and lasted until August 1973, when CIA terminated its part of the program. Tordella was told that the CIA General Counsel was "concerned about any kind of operation in which the CIA was engaged in the continental United States. Regardless of whether CIA was doing anything so small as renting an office, he said 'get out of it.'" NSA subsequently moved its duplicating operation to new office space in Manhattan, where it remained until SHAMROCK was terminated in 1975.

4. Control of the Program

Numerous NSA employees were aware of SHAMROCK, but responsibility for its conduct rested only with the Director, Deputy Director, and one lower-level managerial employee. Throughout the program's existence, only two individuals occupied this lower-level managerial position: the first between 1952–1970; the other from 1970–1975.

The manager was instructed to report directly to the Deputy Director of NSA regarding any problems with the companies. As a routine matter, this individual was in charge of the NSA couriers who traveled between New York and Ft. Meade; he usually received information regarding the SHAMROCK operation from these couriers rather than from the companies. The individual who held this position between 1952–1970 told the Committee that he met with company officials on only two occasions during this time, and both meetings were perfunctory.

Both of the NSA employees who acted as liaison with the companies confirmed to the Committee that the companies had never asked what NSA was extracting from the materials provided, and that NSA had never volunteered this information. Neither of the lower-level employees knew what NSA did with the materials; they stated that the messengers who worked under them also had no knowledge of what was sorted from the telegrams. It seems clear, therefore, that the companies never learned that NSA sorted anything except foreign traffic from the telegrams that the companies provided NSA.

Since none of the companies (treating them as separate from their parent corporations) engage in domestic communications, they could not have provided NSA with domestic traffic. The Committee has no evidence to show that NSA has ever received domestic telegrams from any source.

5. Consideration of SHAMROCK in Connection with the Huston Plan

Former NSA Deputy Director Tordella told the Committee that in 1970, in connection with the Huston plan, the principals involved in this project—Helms of CIA, Sullivan of the FBI, {Donald V.} Bennett of DIA, and Gayler of NSA—discussed the feasibility of the FBI's taking over the SHAMROCK program in order to obtain more information on internal unrest. The FBI did not want the responsibility, according to Tordella, and NSA did not want to jeopardize its own working relationship with the companies. The idea was therefore dropped.

F. Termination of SHAMROCK

Operation SHAMROCK terminated on May 15, 1975, by order of Secretary of Defense James Schlesinger. NSA claims that the program was terminated because (1) it was no longer a valuable source of foreign intelligence, and (2) the risk of its exposure had increased.

{ . . . }

PART III

RECOMMENDATIONS

EDITORS' NOTE: *The Church Committee made ninety-six recommendations to curb the abuses of power it documented. Some of these recommendations led to landmark reforms, such as the formation of the Senate Select Committee on Intelligence and the passage of the Foreign Intelligence Surveillance Act (1978). Other recommendations were never enacted. Derived from Book II of the original Church Committee report, this section provides a look at the tangible outcomes of the investigation, as well as some important roads not taken in the history of intelligence.*

11.

Committee Recommendations

Pursuant to the requirement of Senate Resolution 21, these recommendations set forth the new congressional legislation {the Committee} deems necessary to "safeguard the rights of American citizens." We believe these recommendations are the appropriate conclusion to a traumatic year of disclosures of abuses. We hope they will prevent such abuses in the future.

i. Intelligence Agencies Are Subject to the Rule of Law

{ . . . }

Recommendation 1.—There is no inherent constitutional authority for the President or any intelligence agency to violate the law.

Recommendation 2.—It is the intent of the Committee that statutes implementing these recommendations provide the exclusive legal authority for federal domestic security activities.

(*a*) No intelligence agency may engage in such activities unless authorized by statute, nor may it permit its employees, informants, or other covert human sources to engage in such activities on its behalf.

(*b*) No executive directive or order may be issued which would conflict with such statutes.

Recommendation 3.—In authorizing intelligence agencies to engage in certain activities, it is not intended that such authority empower agencies, their informants, or covert human sources to violate any prohibition enacted pursuant to these Recommendations or contained in the Constitution or in any other law.

ii. United States Foreign and Military Agencies Should Be Precluded from Domestic Security Activities

{ . . . }

Recommendation 4.—To supplement the prohibitions in the 1947 National Security Act against the CIA exercising "police, subpoena, law enforcement powers or internal security functions," the CIA should be prohibited from conducting domestic security activities within the United States, except as specifically permitted by these recommendations.

Recommendation 5.—The Director of Central Intelligence should be made responsible for "coordinating" the protection of sources and methods of the intelligence community. As head of the CIA, the Director should also be responsible in the first instance for the security of CIA facilities, personnel, operations, and information. Neither function, however, authorizes the Director of Central Intelligence to violate any federal or state law, or to take any action which is otherwise inconsistent with statutes implementing these recommendations.

{ . . . }

Recommendation 6.—The CIA should not conduct electronic surveillance, unauthorized entry, or mail opening within the United States for any purpose.

Recommendation 7.—The CIA should not employ physical surveillance, infiltration of groups or any other covert techniques against Americans within the United States except:

(*a*) Physical surveillance of persons on the grounds of CIA installations;

(*b*) Physical surveillance during a preliminary investigation of allegations an employee is a security risk for a limited period outside of CIA installations. Such surveillance should be conducted only upon written authorization of the Director of Central Intelligence and should be limited to the subject of the investigation and, only to the extent necessary to identify them, to persons with whom the subject has contact;

(*c*) Confidential inquiries, during a preliminary investigation of allegations an employee is a security risk, of outside sources concerning medical or financial information about the subject which is relevant to those allegations;

(*d*) The use of identification which does not reveal CIA or government affiliation, in background and other security investigations permitted the CIA by these recommendations, and the conduct of checks, which do not reveal CIA or government affiliation for the purpose of judging the effectiveness of cover operations, upon the written authorization of the Director of Central Intelligence;

(*e*) In exceptional cases, the placement or recruitment of agents within an unwitting domestic group solely for the purpose of preparing them for assignments abroad and only for as long as is necessary to accomplish that purpose. This should take place only if the Director of Central Intelligence makes a written finding that it is essential for foreign intelligence collection of vital importance to the United States, and the Attorney General makes a written finding that the operation will be conducted under procedures designed to prevent misuse of the undisclosed participation or of any information obtained therefrom. In the case of any such action, no information received by CIA from the agent as a result of his position in the group should be disseminated outside the CIA unless it indicates felonious criminal conduct or threat of death or serious bodily harm, in which case dissemination should be permitted to an appropriate official agency if approved by the Attorney General.

Recommendation 8.—The CIA should not collect information within the United States concerning Americans except:

(*a*) Information concerning CIA employees, CIA contractors and their employees, or applicants for such employment or contracting;

(*b*) Information concerning individuals or organizations providing, or offering to provide, assistance to the CIA;

(*c*) Information concerning individuals or organizations being considered by the CIA as potential sources of information or assistance;

(*d*) Visitors to CIA facilities;

(*e*) Persons otherwise in the immediate vicinity of sensitive CIA sites; or (*f*) Persons who give their informed written consent to such collection.

In (a), (b) and (c) above, information should be collected only if necessary for the purpose of determining the person's fitness for employment, contracting or assistance. If, in the course of such collection, information is obtained which indicates criminal activity, it should be transmitted to the FBI or other appropriate agency. When an American's relationship with the CIA is prospective, information should only be collected if there is a bona fide expectation the person might be used by the CIA.

{ . . . }

Recommendation 9.—The CIA should not collect information abroad concerning Americans except:

(*a*) Information concerning Americans which it is permitted to collect within the United States;

(*b*) At the request of the Justice Department as part of criminal investigations or an investigation of an American for suspected terrorist, or hostile foreign intelligence activities or security leak or security risk investigations which the FBI has opened pursuant to Part iv of those recommendations and which is conducted consistently with recommendations contained in Part iv.

Recommendation 10.—The CIA should be able to transmit to the FBI or other appropriate agencies information concerning Americans acquired as the incidental byproduct of otherwise permissible foreign intelligence and counterintelligence operations, whenever such information indicates any activity in violation of American law.

Recommendation 11.—The CIA may employ covert techniques abroad against Americans:

(*a*) Under circumstances in which the CIA could use such covert techniques against Americans within the United States; or

(*b*) When collecting information as part of Justice Department investigation, in which case the CIA may use a particular covert technique under the standards and procedures and approvals applicable to its use against Americans within the United States by the FBI (See Part iv); or

(*c*) To the extent necessary to identify persons known or suspected to be Americans who come in contact with foreigners the CIA is investigating.

{ . . . }

Recommendation 12.—The CIA should not use in experimentation on human subjects, any drug, device or procedure which is designed or intended to harm, or is reasonably likely to harm, the physical or mental health of the human subject, except with the informed written consent, witnessed by a disinterested third party, of each human subject, and in accordance with the guidelines issued by the National Commission for the Protection of Human Subjects for Biomedical and Behavioral Research. The jurisdiction of the Commission should be amended to include the Central Intelligence Agency and other intelligence agencies of the United States Government.

{ . . . }

Recommendation 13.—Any CIA activity engaged in pursuant to Recommendations 7, 8, 9, 10, or 11 should be subject to periodic review and certification of compliance with the Constitution, applicable statutes, agency regulations and executive orders by:

(*a*) The Inspector General of the CIA;

(*b*) The General Counsel of the CIA in coordination with the Director of Central Intelligence;

(*c*) The Attorney General; and

(*d*) The oversight committee recommended in Part xii.

All such certifications should be available for review by congressional oversight committees.

{ . . . }

Recommendation 14.—NSA should not engage in domestic security activities. Its functions should be limited in a precisely drawn legislative charter to the collection of foreign intelligence from foreign communications.

Recommendation 15.—NSA should take all practicable measures consistent with its foreign intelligence mission to eliminate or minimize the interception, selection, and monitoring of communications of Americans from the foreign communications.

Recommendation 16.—NSA should not be permitted to select for monitoring any communication to, from, or about an American without his consent, except for the purpose of obtaining information about hostile foreign intelligence or terrorist activities, and then only if a warrant approving such monitoring is obtained in accordance with procedures similar to those contained in Title III of the Omnibus Crime Control and Safe Streets Act of 1968.

(This recommendation would eliminate the possibility that NSA would re-establish its "watch lists" of the late 1960s and early 1970s. In that case, the names of Americans were submitted to NSA by other federal agencies and were used as a basis for selecting and monitoring, without a warrant, the international communications of those Americans.)

Recommendation 17.—Any personally identifiable information about an American which NSA incidentally acquires, other than pursuant to a warrant, should not be disseminated without the consent of the American, but should be destroyed as promptly as possible, unless it indicates:

(*a*) Hostile foreign intelligence or terrorist activities; or

(*b*) Felonious criminal conduct for which a warrant might be obtained pursuant to Title III of the Omnibus Crime Control and Safe Streets Act of 1968; or

(*c*) A threat of death or serious bodily harm.

If dissemination is permitted, by (a), (b) and (c) above, it must only be made to an appropriate official and after approval by the Attorney General.

(This recommendation is consistent with NSA's policy prior to the Executive Order. NSA's practice prior to the Executive Order was not to disseminate material containing personally identifiable information about Americans.)

Recommendation 18.—NSA should not request from any commercial carrier any communication which it could not otherwise obtain pursuant to these recommendations.

(This recommendation is to ensure that NSA will not resume an operation such as SHAMROCK, disclosed during the Committee's hearings, whereby NSA received for almost 30 years copies of most international telegrams transmitted by certain international telegraph companies in the United States.)

Recommendation 19.—The Office of Security at NSA should be permitted to collect background information on present or prospective employees or contractors of NSA solely for the purpose of determining their fitness for employment. With respect to security risks or the security of its installations, NSA should be permitted to conduct physical surveillances, consistent with such surveillances as the CIA is permitted to conduct, in similar circumstances, by these recommendations.

{. . .}

Recommendation 20.—Except as specifically provided herein, the Department of Defense should not engage in domestic security activities. Its functions, as they relate to the activities of the foreign intelligence community, should be limited in a precisely drawn legislative charter to the conduct of foreign intelligence and foreign counterintelligence activities and tactical military intelligence activities abroad, and production, analysis, and dissemination of departmental intelligence.

Recommendation 21.—In addition to its foreign intelligence responsibility, the Department of Defense has a responsibility to investigate its personnel in order to protect the security of its installations and property, to ensure order and discipline within its ranks, and to conduct other limited investigations once dispatched by the President to suppress a civil disorder. A legislative charter should define precisely—in a manner which is not inconsistent with these recommendations—the authorized scope and purpose of any investigations undertaken by the Department of Defense to satisfy these responsibilities.

Recommendation 22.—No agency of the Department of Defense should conduct investigations of violations of criminal law or otherwise perform any law enforcement or domestic security functions within the United States, except on military bases or concerning military personnel, to enforce the Uniform Code of Military Justice.

{. . .}

Recommendation 23.—The Department of Defense should not be permitted to conduct investigations of Americans on the theory that the information derived therefrom might be useful in potential civil disorders. The Army should be permitted to gather information about geography, logistical matters, or the identity of local officials which is necessary to the positioning, support, and use of troops in an area where troops are likely to be deployed by the President in connection with a civil disturbance. The Army should be permitted to investigate Americans involved in such disturbances after troops have been deployed to the site of a civil disorder, (i) to the extent necessary to fulfill the military mission, and (ii) to the extent the information cannot be obtained from the FBI. (The FBI's responsibility in connection with civil disorders and its assistance to the Army is described in Part iv.)

Recommendation 24.—Appropriate agencies of the Department of Defense should be permitted to collect background information on their present or prospective employees or contractors. With respect to security risks or the security of its installations, the Department of Defense should be permitted to conduct physical surveillance consistent with such surveillances as the CIA is permitted to conduct, in similar circumstances, by these recommendations.

{ . . . }

Recommendation 25.—Except as provided in 27 below, the Department of Defense should not direct any covert technique (e.g., electronic surveillance, informants, etc.) at American civilians.

{ . . . }

Recommendation 26.—The Department of Defense should be permitted to conduct abroad preventive intelligence investigations of unaffiliated Americans, as described in Part iv below, provided such investigations are first approved by the FBI. Such investigations by the Department of Defense, including the use of covert techniques, should ordinarily be conducted in a manner consistent with the recommendations pertaining to the FBI, contained in Part iv; however, in overseas locations, where U.S. military forces constitute the governing power, or where U.S. military forces are engaged in hostilities, circumstances may require greater latitude to conduct such investigations.

iii. Non-Intelligence Agencies Should Be Barred from Domestic Security Activity

{ . . . }

Recommendation 27.—The IRS should not, on behalf of any intelligence agency or for its own use, collect any information about the activities of Americans except for the purposes of enforcing the tax laws.

Recommendation 28.—IRS should not select any person or group for tax investigation on the basis of political activity or for any other reason not relevant to enforcement of the tax laws.

Recommendation 29.—Any program of intelligence investigation relating to domestic security in which targets are selected by both tax and non-tax criteria should only be initiated:

(*a*) Upon the written request of the Attorney General or the Secretary of the Treasury, specifying the nature of the requested program and the need therefore; and

(*b*) After the written certification by the Commissioner of the IRS that procedures have been developed which are sufficient to prevent the infringement of the constitutional rights of Americans; and

(*c*) With congressional oversight committees being kept continually advised of the nature and extent of such programs.

{ . . . }

Recommendation 30.—No intelligence agency should request from the Internal Revenue Service tax returns or tax-related information except under the statutes and regulations controlling such disclosures. In addition, the existing procedures under which tax returns and tax-related information are released by the IRS should be strengthened, as suggested in the following five recommendations.

Recommendation 31.—All requests from an intelligence agency to the IRS for tax returns and tax-related information should be in writing, and signed by the head of the intelligence agency making the request, or his designee. Copies of such requests should be filed with the Attorney General. Each request should include a clear statement of:

(*a*) The purpose for which disclosure is sought;

(*b*) Facts sufficient to establish that the requested information is needed by the requesting agency for the performance of an authorized and lawful function;

(*c*) The uses which the requesting agency intends to make of the information;

(*d*) The extent of the disclosures sought;

(*e*) Agreement by the requesting agency not to use the documents or information for any purpose other than that stated in the request; and (*f*) Agreement by the requesting agency that the information will not be disclosed to any other agency or person except in accordance with the law.

Recommendation 32.—IRS should not release tax returns or tax-related information to any intelligence agency unless it has received a request satisfying the requirements of Recommendation 31, and the Commissioner of Internal Revenue has approved the request in writing.

Recommendation 33.—IRS should maintain a record of all such requests and responses thereto for a period of twenty years.

Recommendation 34.—No intelligence agency should use the information supplied to it by the IRS pursuant to a request of the agency except as stated in a proper request for disclosure.

Recommendation 35.—All requests for information sought by the FBI should be filed by the Department of Justice. Such requests should be signed by the Attorney General or his designee, following a determination by the Department that the request is proper under the applicable statutes and regulations.

{ . . . }

Recommendation 36.—The Post Office should not permit the FBI or any intelligence agency to inspect markings or addresses on first class mail, nor should the Post Office itself inspect markings or addresses on behalf of the FBI or any intelligence agency, on first class mail, except upon the written approval of the Attorney General or his designee. Where one of the correspondents is an American, the Attorney General or his designee should only approve such inspection for domestic security purposes upon a written finding that it is necessary to a criminal investigation or a preventive intelligence investigation of terrorist activity or hostile foreign intelligence activity.

Upon such a request, the Post Office may temporarily remove from circulation such correspondence for the purpose of such inspection of its exterior as is related to the investigation.

Recommendation 37.—The Post Office should not transfer the custody of any first class mail to any agency except the Department of Justice. Such mail should not be transferred or opened except upon a judicial search warrant.

(*a*) In the case of mail where one of the correspondents is an American, the judge must find that there is probable cause to believe that the mail contains evidence of a crime.

(*b*) In the case of mail where both parties are foreigners:

(1) The judge must find that there is probable cause to believe that both parties to such correspondence are foreigners, and one of the correspondents is an officer, employee or conscious agent of a foreign power; and

(2) The Attorney General must certify that the mail opening is likely to reveal information necessary either (i) to the protection of the nation against actual or potential attack or other hostile acts of force of a foreign power; (ii) to obtain foreign intelligence information deemed essential to the security of the United States; or (iii) to protect national security information against hostile foreign intelligence activity.

iv. Federal Domestic Security Activities Should Be Limited and Controlled to Prevent Abuses Without Hampering Criminal Investigations or Investigations of Foreign Espionage

{. . .}

Recommendation 38.—All domestic security investigative activity, including the use of covert techniques, should be centralized within the Federal Bureau of Investigation, except those investigations by the Secret Service designed to protect the life of the President or other Secret Service protectees. Such investigations and the use of covert techniques in those investigations should be centralized within the Secret Service.

Recommendation 39.—All domestic security activities of the federal government and all other intelligence agency activities covered by the Domestic Intelligence Recommendations should be subject to Justice Department oversight to assure compliance with the Constitution and laws of the United States.

{. . .}

Recommendation 40.—The FBI should be prohibited from engaging on its own or through informants or others, in any of the following activities directed at Americans:

(*a*) Disseminating any information to the White House, any other federal official, the news media, or any other person for a political or other improper purpose, such as discrediting an opponent of the administration or a critic of an intelligence or investigative agency.

(*b*) Interfering with lawful speech, publication, assembly, organizational activity, or association of Americans.

(*c*) Harassing individuals through unnecessary overt investigative techniques such as interviews or obvious physical surveillance for the purpose of intimidation.

Recommendation 41.—The Bureau should be prohibited from maintaining information on the political beliefs, political associations, or private lives of Americans except that which is clearly necessary for domestic security investigations as described in Part c.

{. . .}

Recommendation 42.—The FBI should be permitted to investigate a committed act which may violate a federal criminal statute pertaining to the domestic security to determine the identity of the perpetrator or to determine whether the act violates such a statute.

Recommendation 43.—The FBI should be permitted to investigate an American or foreigner to obtain evidence of criminal activity where there is "reasonable suspicion" that the American or foreigner has committed, is committing, or is about to commit a specific act which violates a federal statute pertaining to the domestic security.

{. . .}

Recommendation 44.—The FBI should be permitted to conduct a preliminary preventive intelligence investigation of an American or foreigner where it has a specific allegation or specific or substantiated information that the American or foreigner will soon engage in terrorist activity or hostile foreign intelligence activity. Such a preliminary investigation should not continue longer than thirty days from receipt of the information unless the Attorney General or his designee finds that the information and any corroboration which has been obtained warrants investigation for an additional period which may not exceed sixty days. If, at the outset or at any time during the course of a preliminary investigation the Bureau establishes "reasonable suspicion" that an American or foreigner will soon engage in terrorist activity or hostile foreign intelligence activity, it may conduct a full preventive intelligence investigation. Such full investigation should not continue longer than one year except upon a finding of compelling circumstances by the Attorney General or his designee.

In no event should the FBI open a preliminary or full preventive intelligence investigation based upon information that an American is advocating political ideas or engaging in lawful political activities or is associating with others for the purpose of petitioning the government for redress of grievances or other such constitutionally protected purpose.

{ . . . }

Recommendation 45.—The FBI should be permitted to collect information to assist federal, state, and local officials in connection with a civil disorder either

(i) After the Attorney General finds in writing that there is a clear and immediate threat of domestic violence or rioting which is likely to require implementation of 10 U.S.C. 332 or 333 (the use of federal troops for the enforcement of federal law or federal court orders), or likely to result in a request by the governor or legislature of a state pursuant to 10 U.S.C. 331 for the use of federal militia or other federal armed forces as a countermeasure; or

(ii) After such troops have been introduced.

Recommendation 46.—FBI assistance to federal, state, and local officials in connection with a civil disorder should be limited to collecting information necessary for

(1) the President in making decisions concerning the introduction of federal troops;

(2) military officials in positioning and supporting such troops; and

(3) state and local officials in coordinating their activities with such military officials.

{ . . . }

Recommendation 47.—The FBI should be permitted to participate in the federal government's program of background investigations of federal employees or employees of federal contractors. The authority to conduct such investigations should not, however, be used as the basis for conducting investigations of other persons. In addition, Congress should examine the standards of Executive Order 10450, which serves as the current authority for FBI background investigations, to determine whether additional legislation is necessary to:

(*a*) modify criteria based on political beliefs and associations unrelated to suitability for employment; such modification should make those criteria consistent with judicial decisions regarding privacy of political association; and

(*b*) restrict the dissemination of information from name checks of information related to suitability for employment.

{ . . . }

Recommendation 48.—Under regulations to be formulated by the Attorney General, the FBI should be permitted to investigate a specific allegation that an individual within the Executive branch with access to classified information is a security risk as described in Executive Order 10450. Such investigation should not continue longer than thirty days except upon written approval of the Attorney General or his designee.

{ . . . }

Recommendation 49.—Under regulations to be formulated by the Attorney General, the FBI should be permitted to investigate a specific allegation of the improper disclosure of classified information by employees or contractors of the Executive branch. Such investigation should not continue longer than thirty days except upon written approval of the Attorney General or his designee.

{ . . . }

Recommendation 50.—Overt techniques and name checks should be permitted in all of the authorized domestic security investigations described above, including preliminary and full preventive intelligence investigations.

{ . . . }

Recommendation 51.—All non-consensual electronic surveillance, mail-opening, and unauthorized entries should be conducted only upon authority of a judicial warrant.

Recommendation 52.—All non-consensual electronic surveillance should be conducted pursuant to judicial warrants issued under authority of Title III of the Omnibus Crime Control and Safe Streets Act of 1968.

The Act should be amended to provide, with respect to electronic surveillance of foreigners in the United States, that a warrant may issue if

(*a*) There is probable cause that the target is an officer, employee, or conscious agent of a foreign power.

(*b*) The Attorney General has certified that the surveillance is likely to reveal information necessary to the protection of the nation against actual or potential attack or other hostile acts of force of a foreign power; to obtain foreign intelligence information deemed essential to the security of the United States; or to protect national security information against hostile foreign intelligence activity.

(*c*) With respect to any such electronic surveillance, the judge should adopt procedures to minimize the acquisition and retention of non-foreign intelligence information about Americans.

(*d*) Such electronic surveillance should be exempt from the disclosure requirements of Title III of the 1968 Act as to foreigners generally and as to Americans if they are involved in hostile foreign intelligence activity.

As noted earlier, the Committee believes that the espionage laws should be amended to include industrial espionage and other modern forms of espionage not presently covered and Title III should incorporate any such amendment. The Committee's recommendation is that both that change and the amendment of Title III to require warrants for all electronic surveillance be promptly made.

Recommendation 53.—Mail opening should be conducted only pursuant to a judicial warrant issued upon probable cause of criminal activity as described in Recommendation 37.

Recommendation 54.—Unauthorized entry should be conducted only upon judicial warrant issued on probable cause to believe that the place to be searched contains evidence of a crime, except unauthorized entry, including surreptitious entry, against foreigners who are officers, employees, or conscious agents of a foreign power should be permitted upon judicial warrant under the standards which apply to electronic surveillance described in Recommendation 52.

{ . . . }

Recommendation 55.—Covert human sources may not be directed at an American except:

(1) In the course of a criminal investigation if necessary to the investigation provided that covert human sources should not be directed at an American as a part of an investigation of a committed act unless there is reasonable suspicion to believe that the American is responsible for the act and then only for the purpose of identifying the perpetrators of the act.

(2) If the American is the target of a full preventive intelligence investigation and the Attorney General or his designee makes a written finding that (i) he has considered and rejected less intrusive techniques; and (ii) he believes that covert human sources are necessary to obtain information for the investigation.

Recommendation 56.—Covert human sources which have been directed at an American in a full preventive intelligence investigation should not be used to collect information on the activities of the American for more than 90 days after the source is in place and capable of reporting, unless the Attorney General or his designee finds in writing either that there are "compelling circumstances" in which case they may be used for an additional 60 days, or that there is probable cause that the American will soon engage in terrorist activities or hostile foreign intelligence activities.

Recommendation 57.—All covert human sources used by the FBI should be reviewed by the Attorney General or his designee as soon as practicable, and should be terminated unless the covert human source could be directed against an American in a criminal investigation or a full preventive intelligence investigation under these recommendations.

Recommendation 58.—Mail surveillance and the review of tax returns and tax-related information should be conducted consistently with the recommendations contained in Part iii. In addition to restrictions contained in Part iii, the review of tax returns and tax-related information, as well as review of medical or social history records, confidential records of private institutions and confidential records of Federal, state, and local government agencies other than intelligence or law enforcement agencies may not be used against an American except:

(1) In the course of a criminal investigation if necessary to the investigation;

(2) If the American is the target of a full preventive intelligence investigation and the Attorney General or his designee makes a written finding that (i) he has considered and rejected less intrusive techniques; and (ii) he believes that the covert technique requested by the bureau is necessary to obtain information necessary to the investigation.

Recommendation 59.—The use of physical surveillance and review of credit and telephone records and any records of governmental or private institutions other than those covered in Recommendation 58 should be permitted to be used against an American, if necessary, in the course of either a criminal investigation or a preliminary or full preventive intelligence investigation.

Recommendation 60.—Covert techniques should be permitted at the scene of a potential civil disorder in the course of preventive criminal intelligence and criminal investigations as described above. Non-warrant covert techniques may also be directed at an American during a civil disorder in which extensive acts of violence are occurring and Federal troops have been introduced. This additional authority to direct such covert techniques at Americans during a civil disorder should be limited to circumstances where Federal troops are actually in use and the technique is used only for the purpose of preventing further violence.

Recommendation 61.—Covert techniques should not be directed at an American in the course of a background investigation without the informed written consent of the American.

Recommendation 62.—If Congress enacts a statute attaching criminal sanctions to security leaks, covert techniques should be directed at Americans in the course of security leak investigations only if such techniques are consistent with Recommendation 55(1), 58(1) or 59. With respect to security risks, Congress might consider authorizing covert techniques, other than those requiring a judicial warrant, to be directed at Americans in the course of security risk investigations, but only upon a written finding of the Attorney General that (i) there is reasonable suspicion to believe that the individual is a security risk, (ii) he has considered and rejected less intrusive techniques, and (iii) he believes the technique requested is necessary to the investigation.

{ . . . }

Recommendation 63.—Except as limited elsewhere in these recommendations or in Title III of the Omnibus Crime Control and Safe Streets Act of 1968, information obtained incidentally through an authorized covert technique about an American or a foreigner who is not the target of the covert technique can be used as the basis for any authorized domestic security investigation.

{ . . . }

Recommendation 64.—Information should not be maintained except where relevant to the purpose of an investigation.

{ . . . }

Recommendation 65.—Personally identifiable information on Americans obtained in the following kinds of investigations should be sealed or purged as follows (unless it appears on its face to be necessary for another authorized investigation):

(*a*) Preventive intelligence investigations of terrorist or hostile foreign intelligence activities—as soon as the investigation is terminated by the Attorney General or his designee pursuant to Recommendation 45 or 69.

(*b*) Civil disorder assistance—as soon as the assistance is terminated by the Attorney General or his designee pursuant to Recommendation 69, provided that where troops have been introduced such information need be sealed or purged only within a reasonable period after their withdrawal.

Recommendation 66.—Information previously gained by the FBI or any other intelligence agency through illegal techniques should be sealed or purged as soon as practicable.

{ . . . }

Recommendation 67.—Personally identifiable information on Americans from domestic security investigations may be disseminated outside the Department of Justice as follows:

(*a*) Preventive intelligence investigations of terrorist activities—personally identifiable information on Americans from preventive criminal intelligence investigations of terrorist activities may be disseminated only to:

(1) A foreign or domestic law enforcement agency which has jurisdiction over the criminal activity to which the information relates; or
(2) To a foreign intelligence or military agency of the United States, if necessary for an activity permitted by these recommendations; or
(3) To an appropriate federal official with authority to make personnel decisions about the subject of the information; or
(4) To a foreign intelligence or military agency of a cooperating foreign power if necessary for an activity permitted by these recommendations to similar agencies of the United States; or
(5) Where necessary to warn state or local officials of terrorist activity likely to occur within their jurisdiction; or
(6) Where necessary to warn any person of a threat to life or property from terrorist activity.

(*b*) Preventive intelligence investigations of hostile foreign intelligence activities—personally identifiable information on Americans from preventive criminal intelligence investigations of hostile intelligence activities may be disseminated only:

(1) To an appropriate federal official with authority to make personnel decisions about the subject of the information; or
(2) To the National Security Council or the Department of State upon request or where appropriate to their administration of U.S. foreign policy; or
(3) To a foreign intelligence or military agency of the United States, if relevant to an activity permitted by these recommendations; or
(4) To a foreign intelligence or military agency of a cooperating foreign power if relevant to an activity permitted by these recommendations to similar agencies of the United States.

(*c*) Civil disorders assistance–personally identifiable information on Americans involved in an actual or potential disorder, collected in the course of civil disorders assistance should not be disseminated outside the

Department of Justice except to military officials and appropriate state and local officials at the scene of a civil disorder where federal troops are present.

(*d*) Background investigations—to the maximum extent feasible, the results of background investigations should be segregated within the FBI and only disseminated to officials outside the Department of Justice authorized to make personnel decisions with respect to the subject.

(*e*) All other authorized domestic security investigations—to governmental officials who are authorized to take action consistent with the purpose of an investigation or who have statutory duties which require the information.

{ . . . }

Recommendation 68.—Officers of the Executive branch, who are made responsible by these recommendations for overseeing intelligence activities, and appropriate congressional committees should have access to all information necessary for their functions. The committees should adopt procedures to protect the privacy of subjects of files maintained by the FBI and other agencies affected by the domestic intelligence recommendations.

{ . . . }

Recommendation 69.—The Attorney General should:

(*a*) Establish a program of routine and periodic review of FBI domestic security investigations to ensure that the FBI is complying with all of the foregoing recommendations; and

(*b*) Assure, with respect to the following investigations of Americans, that:

(1) Preventive intelligence investigations of terrorist activity or hostile foreign intelligence activity are terminated within one year, except that the Attorney General or his designee may grant extensions upon a written finding of "compelling circumstances";

(2) Covert techniques are used in preventive intelligence investigations of terrorist activity or hostile foreign intelligence activity only so long as necessary and not beyond time limits established by the Attorney General except that the Attorney General or his designee may grant extensions upon a written finding of "compelling circumstances";

(3) Civil disorders assistance is terminated upon withdrawal of federal troops or, if troops were not introduced, within a reasonable time

after the finding by the Attorney General that troops are likely to be requested, except that the Attorney General or his designee may grant extensions upon a written finding of "compelling circumstances."

v. The Responsibility and Authority of the Attorney General for Oversight of Federal Domestic Security Activities Must Be Clarified and General Counsels and Inspectors General of Intelligence Agencies Strengthened

{ . . . }

Recommendation 70.—The Attorney General should review the internal regulations of the FBI and other intelligence agencies engaging in domestic security activities to ensure that such internal regulations are proper and adequate to protect the constitutional rights of Americans.

Recommendation 71.—The Attorney General or his designee (such as the Office of Legal Counsel of the Department of Justice) should advise the General Counsels of intelligence agencies on interpretations of statutes and regulations adopted pursuant to these recommendations and on such other legal questions as are described in b. below.

Recommendation 72.—The Attorney General should have ultimate responsibility for the investigation of alleged violations of law relating to the Domestic Intelligence Recommendations.

Recommendation 73.—The Attorney General should be notified of possible alleged violations of law through the Office of Professional Responsibility (described in c. below) by agency heads, General Counsel, or Inspectors General of intelligence agencies as provided in b. below.

Recommendation 74.—The heads of all intelligence agencies affected by these recommendations are responsible for the prevention and detection of alleged violations of the law by, or on behalf of, their respective agencies and for the reporting to the Attorney General of all such alleged violations. Each such agency head should also assure his agency's cooperation with the Attorney General in investigations of alleged violations.

{ . . . }

Recommendation 75.—To assist the Attorney General and the agency heads in the functions described in a. above, the FBI and each other intelligence agency should have a General Counsel, nominated by the President and confirmed by the Senate, and an Inspector General appointed by the agency head.

Recommendation 76.—Any individual having information on past, current, or proposed activities which appear to be illegal, improper, or in violation of agency policy should be required to report the matter immediately to the Agency head, General Counsel, or Inspector General. If the matter is not initially reported to the General Counsel, he should be notified by the Agency head or Inspector General. Each agency should regularly remind employees of their obligation to report such information.

Recommendation 77.—As provided in Recommendation 74, the heads of the FBI and of other intelligence agencies are responsible for reporting to the Attorney General alleged violations of law. When such reports are made, the appropriate congressional committees should be notified.

Recommendation 78.—The General Counsel and Inspector General of the FBI and of each other intelligence agency should have unrestricted access to all information in the possession of the agency and should have the authority to review all of the agency's activities. The Attorney General, or the Office of Professional Responsibility on his behalf should have access to all information in the possession of an agency which in the opinion of the Attorney General, is necessary for an investigation of illegal activity.

Recommendation 79.—The General Counsel of the FBI and of each other intelligence agency should review all significant proposed agency activities to determine their legality and constitutionality.

Recommendation 80.—The Director of the FBI and the heads of each other intelligence agency should be required to report, at least annually, to the appropriate committee of the Congress, on the activities of the General Counsel and the Office of the Inspector General.

Recommendation 81.—The Director of the FBI and the heads of each other intelligence agency should be required to report, at least annually, to the Attorney General on all reports of activities which appear illegal, improper, outside the legislative charter, or in violation of agency regulations. Such reports should include the General Counsel's findings concerning these activities, a summary of the Inspector General's investigations of these activities, and the practices and procedures developed to discover activities that raise questions of legality or propriety.

{ . . . }

Recommendation 82.—The Office of Professional Responsibility created by Attorney General Levi should be recognized in statute. The director of the office, appointed by the Attorney General, should report directly to the Attorney General or the Deputy Attorney General. The functions of the office should include:

(*a*) Serving as a central repository of reports and notifications provided the Attorney General; and

(*b*) Investigation, if requested by the Attorney General of alleged violations by intelligence agencies of statutes enacted or regulations promulgated pursuant to these recommendations.

{ . . . }

Recommendation 83.—The Attorney General is responsible for all of the activities of the FBI, and the Director of the FBI is responsible to, and should be under the supervision and control of, the Attorney General.

Recommendation 84.—The Director of the FBI should be nominated by the President and confirmed by the Senate to serve at the pleasure of the President for a single term of not more than eight years.

Recommendation 85.—The Attorney General should consider exercising his power to appoint Assistant Directors of the FBI. A maximum term of years should be imposed on the tenure of the Assistant Director for the Intelligence Division.

vi. Administrative Rulemaking and Increased Disclosure Should Be Required

{ . . . }

Recommendation 86.—The Attorney General should approve all administrative regulations required to implement statutes created pursuant to these recommendations.

Recommendation 87.—Such regulations, except for regulations concerning investigations of hostile foreign intelligence activity or other matters which are properly classified, should be issued pursuant to the Administrative Procedures Act and should be subject to the approval of the Attorney General.

Recommendation 88.—The effective date of regulations pertaining to the following matters should be delayed ninety days, during which time Congress would have the opportunity to review such regulations:

(*a*) Any CIA activities against Americans, as permitted in ii.a. above;

(*b*) Military activities at the time of a civil disorder;

(*c*) The authorized scope of domestic security investigations, authorized investigative techniques, maintenance and dissemination of information by the FBI; and,

(*d*) The termination of investigations and covert techniques as described in Part iv.

{ . . . }

Recommendation 89.—Each year the FBI and other intelligence agencies affected by these recommendations should be required to seek annual statutory authorization for their programs.

Recommendation 90.—The Freedom of Information Act (5 U.S.C. 552(b)) and the Federal Privacy Act (5 U.S.C. 552(a)) provide important mechanisms by which individuals can gain access to information on intelligence activity directed against them. The Domestic Intelligence Recommendations assume that these statutes will continue to be vigorously enforced. In addition, the Department of Justice should notify all readily identifiable targets of past illegal surveillance techniques, and all COINTELPRO victims, and third parties who had received anonymous COINTELPRO communications, of the nature of the activities directed against them, or the source of the anonymous communication to them.

vii. Civil Remedies Should Be Expanded

{...}

Recommendation 91.—Congress should enact a comprehensive civil remedies statute which would accomplish the following:

(*a*) Any American with a substantial and specific claim to an actual or threatened injury by a violation of the Constitution by federal intelligence officers or agents acting under color of law should have a federal cause of action against the government and the individual federal intelligence officer or agent responsible for the violation, without regard to the monetary amount in controversy. If actual injury is proven in court, the Committee believes that the injured person should be entitled to equitable relief, actual, general, and punitive damages, and recovery of the costs of litigation. If threatened injury is proven in court, the Committee believes that equitable relief and recovery of the costs of litigation should be available.

(*b*) Any American with a substantial and specific claim to actual or threatened injury by violation of the statutory charter for intelligence activity (as proposed by these Domestic Intelligence Recommendations) should have a cause of action for relief as in (a) above.

(*c*) Because of the secrecy that surrounds intelligence programs, the Committee believes that a plaintiff should have two years from the date upon which he discovers, or reasonably should have discovered, the facts which give rise to a cause of action for relief from a constitutional or statutory violation.

(*d*) Whatever statutory provision may be made to permit an individual defendant to raise an affirmative defense that he acted within the scope of his official duties, in good faith, and with a reasonable belief that the action he took was lawful, the Committee believes that to ensure relief to persons injured by governmental intelligence activity, this defense should be available solely to individual defendants and should not extend to the government. Moreover, the defense should not be available to bar injunctions against individual defendants.

viii. Criminal Penalties Should Be Enacted

Recommendation 92.—The Committee believes that criminal penalties should apply, where appropriate, to willful and knowing violations of statutes enacted pursuant to the Domestic Intelligence Recommendations.

ix. The Smith Act and the Voorhis Act Should Either Be Repealed or Amended

Recommendation 93.—Congress should either repeal the Smith Act (18 U.S.C. 2385) and the Voorhis Act (18 U.S.C. 2386), which on their face appear to authorize investigation of "mere advocacy" of a political ideology, or amend those statutes so that domestic security investigations are only directed at conduct which might serve as the basis for a constitutional criminal prosecution, under Supreme Court decisions interpreting these and related statutes.

x. The Espionage Statute Should Be Modernized

{ . . . }

Recommendation 94.—The appropriate committees of the Congress should review the Espionage Act of 1917 to determine whether it should be amended to cover modern forms of foreign espionage, including industrial, technological or economic espionage.

xi. Broader Access to Intelligence Agency Files Should be Provided to GAO, as an Investigative Arm of the Congress

Recommendation 95.—The appropriate congressional oversight committees of the Congress should, from time to time, request the Comptroller General of the United States to conduct audits and reviews of the intelligence activities of any department or agency of the United States affected by the Domestic Intelligence Recommendations. For such purpose, the Comptroller General, or any of his duly authorized representatives, should have access to, and the right to examine, all necessary materials of any such department or agency.

xii. Congressional Oversight Should Be Intensified

Recommendation 96.—The Committee reendorses the concept of vigorous Senate oversight to review the conduct of domestic security activities through a new permanent intelligence oversight committee.

ACKNOWLEDGMENTS

We would like to express our gratitude, first and foremost, for the institutional support provided by Emory University, Georgetown University, and the Library of Congress. We are also thankful for the Electronic Frontier Foundation, for its steadfast defense of civil liberties in the digital world. MuckRock, a Freedom of Information Act requesting tool and outlet, has provided inspiration and documentation that fueled our ongoing interest in government secrecy.

Helen Walker offered invaluable research assistance and editorial support throughout the most arduous phases of the writing process—we couldn't have done any of this without her help. Members of the Georgetown Americas Faculty Seminar commented on an early draft of the introduction to this volume: Kate Chandler, Jenny Guardado, Ben Harbert, Mike Kazin, Jane Komori, Erick Langer, Doug Reed, Milena Santoro, and John Tutino. At the eleventh hour, Nick Donofrio, Maggie Gram, and Jack Hamilton offered key insights and sentence-level clarity.

We owe a massive debt to the Church Committee experts—witnesses, participants, and historians—who took the time to speak to us about this project: Loch Johnson, Matthew Jones, Sam Lebovic, and James and Thomas Risen. Beverly Gage provided advice and inspiration, as well as a model for diligent and committed public scholarship.

Alane Mason at W. W. Norton & Co. saw the timeliness of the Church Committee investigation and envisioned an effective way to transmit its findings to a new generation of activists, policymakers, and scholars. We appreciate her wisdom much more than we can say.

Finally, we'd like to thank our families for their patience and encouragement.

FURTHER READING

Ashby, LeRoy, and Rod Gramer. *Fighting the Odds: The Life of Senator Frank Church.* Pullman: Washington State University Press, 1994.

Bamford, James. *The Puzzle Palace: Inside the National Security Agency, America's Most Secret Intelligence Organization.* New York: Penguin, 1983.

Gage, Beverly. *G-Man: J. Edgar Hoover and the Making of the American Century.* New York: Viking, 2023.

Garrow, David. *The FBI and Martin Luther King, Jr.: From "Solo" to Memphis.* New York: W. W. Norton, 1981.

Hochman, Brian. *The Listeners: A History of Wiretapping in the United States.* Cambridge: Harvard University Press, 2022.

Johnson, Loch K. *A Season of Inquiry: The Senate Intelligence Investigation.* Lexington: The University Press of Kentucky, 1985.

Kinzer, Stephen. *Poisoner in Chief: Sidney Gottlieb and the CIA Search for Mind Control.* New York: Henry Holt, 2019.

Olmsted, Kathryn S. *Challenging the Secret Government: The Post-Watergate Investigations of the CIA and FBI.* Chapel Hill: University of North Carolina Press, 1996.

Reid, Stuart A. *The Lumumba Plot: The Secret History of the CIA and a Cold War Assassination.* New York: Alfred A. Knopf, 2023.

Risen, James. *The Last Honest Man: The CIA, the FBI, the Mafia, and the Kennedys—and One Senator's Fight to Save Democracy.* New York and Boston: Little, Brown, 2023.

Scott, Katherine A. *Reining in the State: Civil Society and Congress in the Vietnam and Watergate Eras.* Lawrence: University Press of Kansas, 2013.

Scott, Katherine A. *Select Committee to Study Governmental Operations with Respect to Intelligence Activities (Church Committee) Members and Staff: Oral History Interviews.* Washington, DC: U.S. Senate Historical Office, 2015.

Smist, Frank J. *Congress Oversees the United States Intelligence Community, 1947–1994.* Knoxville: University of Tennessee Press, 1994.

Theoharis, Athan. *Spying on Americans: Political Surveillance from Hoover to the Huston Plan.* Philadelphia: Temple University Press, 1978.

Trenta, Luca. *The President's Kill List: Assassination and US Foreign Policy Since 1945.* Edinburgh: Edinburgh University Press, 2024.

Weiner, Tim. *Enemies: A History of the FBI.* New York: Random House, 2012.

Weiner, Tim. *Legacy of Ashes: The History of the CIA.* New York: Anchor, 2006.

Wilford, Hugh. *The CIA: An Imperial History.* New York: Basic Books, 2024.

INDEX